# MEANING, INTENTIONS, AND ARGUMENTATION

CSLI Lecture Notes No. 186

# MEANING, INTENTIONS, AND ARGUMENTATION

*edited by*
**Kepa Korta &**
**Joana Garmendia**

CSLI
PUBLICATIONS
Center for the Study of
Language and Information
Stanford, California

Center for the Study of Language and Information
Leland Stanford Junior University
Printed in the United States
12 11 10 09 08 1 2 3 4 5

*Library of Congress Cataloging-in-Publication Data*

Meaning, intentions, and argumentation /
edited by Kepa Korta and Joana Garmendia.

p. cm. – (CSLI lecture notes ; no. 186)

Includes bibliographical references and index.
ISBN-13: 978-1-57586-542-3 (pbk. : alk. paper)
ISBN-10: 1-57586-542-4 (pbk. : alk. paper)
ISBN-13: 978-1-57586-541-6 (cloth : alk. paper)
ISBN-10: 1-57586-541-6 (cloth : alk. paper)
1. Semantics (Philosophy) I. Korta, Kepa. II. Garmendia, Joana, 1978–

B840.M4575 2008
121′.68–dc22 2008009733
CIP

The cover of the paperback edition was designed by Juanba Berasategi.

∞ The acid-free paper used in this book meets the minimum requirements of the American National Standard for Information Sciences—Permanence of Paper for Printed Library Materials, ANSI Z39.48-1984.

CSLI was founded in 1983 by researchers from Stanford University, SRI International, and Xerox PARC to further the research and development of integrated theories of language, information, and computation. CSLI headquarters and CSLI Publications are located on the campus of Stanford University.

CSLI Publications reports new developments in the study of language, information, and computation. Please visit our web site at
http://cslipublications.stanford.edu/
for comments on this and other titles, as well as for changes and corrections by the authors, editors, and publisher.

To the memory of Isabel Gómez Txurruka

(1962-2006)

# Contents

# Contributors


NICHOLAS ASHER: The University of Texas. Austin.
nasher@bertie.la.utexas.edu

SALVATORE ATTARDO: Youngstown State University. Youngstown.
sattardo@gmail.com

EROS CORAZZA: Carleton University. Ottawa.
eros_corazza@carleton.ca

MARC DOMINICY: Université Libre de Bruxelles. Bruxelles.
mdomini@ulb.ac.be

FRANS H. VAN EEMEREN: University of Amsterdam. Amsterdam.
F.H.vanEemeren@uva.nl

TIM FERNANDO: Trinity College. Dublin.
Tim.Fernando@cs.tcd.ie

JOANA GARMENDIA: The University of the Basque Country. Donostia.
jgarmendia012@ikasle.ehu.es

PETER HOUTLOSSER: University of Amsterdam. Amsterdam.
P.Houtlosser@uva.nl

MANFRED KIENPOINTNER: University of Innsbruck. Innsbruck.
Manfred.Kienpointner@uibk.ac.at

KEPA KORTA: The University of the Basque Country. Donostia.
kepa.korta@ehu.es

ERIC MCCREADY: Osaka University. Osaka.

PHILIPPE MULLER: Université Paul Sabatier. Toulouse.
muller@irit.fr

JOHN PERRY: Stanford University. Stanford.
john@csli.stanford.edu

LAURENT PRÉVOT: Academia Sinica. Taipei.
prevot@gate.sinica.edu.tw

LUIS M. VALDÉS–VILLANUEVA: Universidad de Oviedo. Oviedo.
lmvaldes@uniovi.es

# The Roads to Meaning

Kepa Korta and Joana Garmendia

There is still a tendency to associate the term 'linguistics' with grammar or syntax, that is, with the study of the rules that govern the construction of complex expressions—sentences—out of simple ones—words—in a language. The study of meaning is left out of linguistics and restricted to the description of the meaning of particular words; something like the job of making good dictionaries. We are not going to dispute here this narrow view of linguistics. For one thing, almost no one holds it seriously any more. And, secondly, because we see no much interest in the defense of any monolithic view of linguistics or language sciences, or even the study of meaning. The aim of this volume is to offer a small but representative sample of the variety of approaches, issues and topics discussed in the four main roads discernible within the reflection about meaning at the beginning of the twenty-first century: the philosophy of language, rhetoric, semantics and pragmatics.

Ancient Greek philosophers possibly interpreted that an important way to comply with the saying carved at Delphi, "Know thyself," was to study one of the most characteristically human features: language. Plato's *Cratylus* is considered as the first text in the Western history of the philosophy of language; it's the first time that the issue of the relation between words and things is taken as a topic of investigation in its own right. This dialogue anticipated many of the crucial topics treated, and the perspectives taken by modern philosophy of language: meaning as a relation between words and things or ideas; meaning as the use established by human convention; the possibility of expressing truths (and falsities) by our utterances.

Another approach to the study of language had flourished in Greece before Plato's philosophy of language. Sophists saw language mainly as a useful tool for achieving one's goals —as a means for persuasion. They initiated the study of rhetoric. Despite Plato's overall negative attitude towards it (mitigated, we should say, at his *Phaedrus*), Isocrates and Aristotle, first, and Cicero and Quintilian, later in Rome, elevated rhetoric to one of the three most important disciplines for the study of language during subsequent centuries: together with logic —or 'dialectic'— and grammar it would constitute the

*Meaning, Intentions, and Argumentation.*
Kepa Korta and Joana Garmendia (eds.).

*trivium* of medieval education. From the Middle Ages to the twentieth century, rhetoric was often reduced to the study of ornamental or stylistic aspects of language, but the second half of the last century saw a revival of Aristotelian rhetoric.

The two other main roads to the study of meaning, semantics and pragmatics, did not begin until much later. The term 'semantics' was first introduced by Bréal in 1883, linked to the study of the historic change of words. Frege, the founder of modern logic, is also acknowledged as the founder of semantics as the study of the meaning of sentences in terms of their truth-conditions. De Saussure and Peirce, from different perspectives, also contributed to the study of word meaning, but the negative attitude towards semantics by linguists so influential as Bloomfield or Chomsky added quite a bit to the delay in the convergence of the roads of meaning with the main roads of linguistics.

Pragmatics was the last road to meaning to be opened. Wittgenstein, Austin and Grice are usually credited as the founders of this discipline, which is centered in how language is used *to do things*: first of all *to communicate* with others, but, often, to try to persuade and convince others. The way back from pragmatics to rhetoric didn't go unnoticed, and it is explored in Chapters 10 and 11.

This volume starts with four incursions into the philosophy of language. In Chapter 1, entitled 'Intention, Reference and Semantic Value,' John Perry addresses the role of the speaker's intention in determining the semantic value of referential expressions, i.e., indexicals, demonstratives and proper names. As we saw earlier, the nature of reference was one of the main topics of the *Cratylus*. It was probably the main issue, too, in the agenda of the philosophy of language as settled by Frege. As this essay shows, it is still alive at the beginning of the twenty-first century, under the new lights of semantics and pragmatics.

Something similar can be said about the problem of propositional-attitude reports. It does not seem to have been anticipated by the ancient wise Greeks, but it was clearly framed by Frege. Now, with the development of semantics and pragmatics, it goes under thorough scrutiny again. Eros Corazza's 'Singular Propositions, Quasi-singular Propositions, and Reports' (Chapter 2) discusses how to conciliate the direct reference of indexicals and proper names with substitution of co-referential terms in attitude reports.

In Chapter 3, Luis M. Valdés-Villanueva addresses another fundamental concept in the philosophy of language: the truth-conditions of an utterance. In *Reference and Reflexivity* (2001), Perry argues for what we could call a *pluripropositionalist* view of utterance content. A family of contents, from utterance-bound or reflexive contents to incremental ones, is associated with any utterance. 'On Perry's Relative Truth-conditions' is a thorough critique of that proposal.

Chapter 4 is concerned with a topic that, due perhaps to Plato's dismissal, has not been traditionally much discussed in the philosophy of language: fiction, in general, and literature, in particular. Salvatore Attardo's 'Fiction and Deception: How Cooperative is Literature?' tackles Plato's view about truth and deception in literature, considering insights from contemporary pragmatics and studying a great variety of examples from fictional and non-fictional literature.

Chapter 5 is a good example of one of the leitmotifs in the philosophy of language:

the ontological commitments made through our use of language. Does, for instance, the use of a proper name commit us to some kind of existence of an object designated by that name? Achille C. Varzi deals not with proper names but with descriptions of events that didn't happen, like in utterances such as 'John often doesn't go jogging' or 'Mary saw John not leave.' 'Failures, Omissions, and Negative Descriptions' shows again the ontological impact that a (semantic and pragmatic) theory of natural language can have.

'The Case for Core Meaning' (Chapter 6) takes on another fundamental issue in contemporary semantics and pragmatics: Is there still a place for the concept of 'core meaning' of words? Manfred Kienpointner considers recent debates about the context-dependency of words —their literal versus non-literal use, the coded versus the inferred meaning, and so on—, contrasting it with the concept of core-meaning that comes from European structural linguists like Jakobson or Coseriu and generative linguists like Jackendoff and Katz, and he develops in great detail. It is a representative piece boundary-crossing among different disciplines, among different schools within disciplines, and among different languages.

Chapter 7 leads us to another principal road within semantics: the use of logical tools for the analysis of natural language meaning. 'Situations from Events to Proofs' by Tim Fernando reveals how formal analysis provides us with new insights about meaning in natural language, and allow us to compare them in a very precise way; and, also, the other way around —how the study of natural language semantics stimulates the development of formal tools. Richard Montague's path goes on, as it is shown by the next two chapters, too.

Hans Kamp built upon Montague's work to develop *Discourse Representation Theory* (DRT), but he also broke a number of frontiers: the limits of the sentence as the unit of analysis, and the limits between semantics and pragmatics, among others. Nicholas Asher took this view further and developed *Segmented Discourse Representation Theory* (SDRT). In 'A Compositional Account of Counterfactuals' (Chapter 8), Nicholas Asher and Eric McCready give us the SDRT treatment for another classic issue that has concerned philosophers of language and semanticists: the meaning of conditionals and, in particular, of counterfactual conditionals. They study the interaction between counterfactuals and modal operators, arguing for their alternative to previous accounts on the matter.

SDRT also constitutes the framework for the analysis of questions and answers by Philippe Muller and Laurent Prévot in their 'The rhetorical attachment of questions and answers' (Chapter 9). The semantics and pragmatics of questions is a relatively new issue, that has been proved difficult to deal with by traditional theories. Muller and Prévot make a new proposal for treating question and answer dialogues within SDRT. As the title of their essay suggests, they point to the connection between their new semantico-pragmatic theory and rhetoric, through their notion of 'rhetorical relation.'

The explicit revision of Aristotelian rhetoric in terms of the Austinian (and Searlean) theory of speech acts is put forward by Marc Dominicy in his 'Epideictic Rhetoric and the Representation of Human Decision and Choice' (Chapter 10). The essay is focused on the analysis of rhetorical acts of praise and blame (epideictic), studying, in particular, whether their satisfaction requires some kind of mental act by the hearer. It clearly demonstrates how contemporary pragmatics can shed new lights on ancient rhetoric and, at the same time, it benefits from the insights of the study of the means for rational persuasion.

A similar project of integrating the wisdom in old disciplines like rhetoric and dialectic with new insights from semantics and pragmatics is pursued by the approach called 'pragma-dialectics,' led, among others, by Frans H. van Eemeren and Peter Houtlosser. Their 'Within the bounds of reason: Strategic Maneuvering in Argumentative Discourse' (Chapter 11) is a nice piece of pragma-dialectics applied to the analysis of arguments in real-life examples of advertising or propaganda. It is a proof that besides its intrinsic interest, the study of meaning, intention, and argumentation has clear implications in understanding the world we live in and, thus, in the knowledge of ourselves.

## Acknowledgments

The work of the first editor has been partially supported by the Spanish Ministry of Education and Culture (MEC, HUM2006-11663/FISO).

We would like to thank the contributors for their diligence and kind help in putting this volume together. We are also indebted with Dikran Karagueuzian and Lauri Kanerva from CSLI Publications. Without their help and encouragement this book would not have been possible.

We want to dedicate this volume to the memory of Isabel Gómez Txurruka.

1

# Intention, Reference and Semantic Value

JOHN PERRY

## 1.1 Introduction

The issue I wish to consider is the role that the intentions of the speaker play in determining the reference, or semantic value, of uses of indexicals, demonstratives, and names. In the course of the investigation it will prove necessary to refine and to a certain extent amend the way these questions are put, but I think they are clear enough to get started.

There is general agreement that the speaker's intentions play an important role in determining which speech acts the speaker performs, and which implicatures she makes. These issues are usually considered to be *pragmatic*.

There are also a number honorable roles for intentions to play in determining what is said, by almost everyone's lights:

- The speaker's intentions, constrained by the sounds the speaker makes or the letters he writes or types, and the phonological and orthographic conventions of the language she uses, determine which words she speaks or writes. It is up to the speaker whether he uses the word "red" or "read" when he pronounces the phone |red| for example.
- The speaker's intentions, constrained by the conventional meanings of the words he uses, determine, when there is ambiguity, with which meanings those words are used. It is up to the speaker who uses the word "vice", for example, whether a moral failing or a tool for holding objects is meant.
- The speaker's intentions determine which of various syntactic constructions, compatible with the word order employed, are being used. It is up to the speaker, for example, whether his utterance of "Flying planes can be dangerous" begins with "flying" used as a noun or an adjective.

But there is considerable disagreement on the role that intentions should be recognized as having in determining what is said, or the proposition expressed, once their role in determining which words, which syntactic structures, and which meanings are involved is taken into account. It is basically this issue that generates the range of

*Meaning, Intentions, and Argumentation.*
Kepa Korta and Joana Garmendia (eds.).

positions, from the minimalists to the contextualists, considered by François Recanati in *Literal Meaning* (Recanati (2004)). The minimalists eschew intentions in semantics, while the radical contextualists find them essential and ubiquitous.

I will argue that the phenomena I consider concerning indexicals, demonstratives and names support the position that Kepa Korta and I hold. We maintain the following:

- The semantics of a language consists of the study of the meaning conventions of expressions and modes of combination of that language.
- The semantics of the uttered sentence $S$ determines a condition the utterance $u$ must satisfy to be true (or attain some other appropriate kind of success); this is the *semantic contribution.* The proposition that $u$ satisfies this condition is the "utterance-bound" or "reflexive" content of $u$. This "utterance-bound" proposition should not be confused with "what is said" or "the proposition expressed."
- What is said, or the proposition expressed, is normally the *incremental* content of the utterance, given the values of the parameters called for by the semantic contribution.
- The values of these parameters are sometimes determined by, and often constrained by, the objective facts of the utterance: the speaker, time, locations and broader facts about the context. In virtually all cases of singular reference, and in many other cases, however, the intentions of the speaker are critical.
- Broadly Gricean reasoning can be employed to figure out the speaker's intentions, not only with respect to traditional pragmatic issues, such as speech acts performed and implicatures, but also with respect to the words used, the meanings and syntactic constructions exploited, and also with respect to intentions relevant to reference and other semantic values.

Three important concepts will be explained in the course of this discussion: *reference plans*, *channels of information* and *cognitive burden.*

## 1.2 The Gricean Circle

Stephen Levinson has noted an apparent problem with using Gricean reasoning to uncover intentions when we have not yet figured out what has been said (Levinson (2000, pp. 172-74)), Gricean reasoning involves figuring out which intentions would make sense of a speaker saying *that S*, given then overall purpose of the conversation and the assumption that the speaker is being helpful. But this sort of reasoning requires that we have identified which proposition *that S* is, that is, that we have discovered what is said. Hence we cannot use it to discover intentions, such as intentions about the words used, or the meanings exploited, or the syntactic form, or the parameters relevant to determining what is said, the determination of which is prior to the determination of what is said.

However, as Korta and I argue in "Three Demonstrations and a Funeral" (2006),[1] Gricean reasoning does not require that one identify what is said or the proposition expressed in a way adequate to *express* that proposition. It can proceed on the basis of an "utterance-bound" description of the proposition expressed. Suppose, for example, A says to B something that B hears as "I hope my book is |red|." He can't tell from

[1] See also Korta and Perry (2006b, 2007a,b).

what he hears whether the speaker intends to be using the noun "red" or the participle "read," which sound the same in many dialects of English. He can give an utterance bound description of the proposition expressed, however, such as:

> The proposition that is true if A hopes that A's book meets condition P, where condition P is the property of being red if he is using the word "red," and the property of being read if he is using the word "read."

Given this way of identifying the proposition, B may reason that, since the conversation has been about the fact that you can't change anyone's mind or make any money by publishing a book unless it is read, everything points in the direction of A's having used the word "read" rather than "red."

Or suppose that A is talking to B and C. A says, "You are probably wrong about that." To whom did A intend to refer with "you"? B, C, or both of them? B and C will grasp that what A said is true iff X is probably wrong about Y, where X is the addressee A intends to refer to with "you" and Y is the issue A intends to refer to with "that." It may be perfectly obvious, on grounds of relevance, that Y is the issue of the winner of the next election, on which C has just expressed an opinion, and so X is C.

These utterance-bound descriptions of the proposition expressed are based on Critical Referentialism or the "reflexive-referential" theory I developed in my book *Reference and Reflexivity* (2001).

There are various theories about what sort of reasoning is going on not only in these sorts of cases but in the cases of implicatures Grice originally considered. Grice's own theory relied on a general principle of conversational helpfulness plus a system of maxims. Relevance theorists such as Wilson, Sperber and Carston think that considerations of relevance are all that is needed in the context of a "processing model" (see, for instance, Sperber and Wilson (1986-1995) or Carston (2002)). One might suppose that simple reasoning to the best explanation, or ampliative reasoning, or Bayesian reasoning, would suffice. These issues won't matter for this essay.

The crucial point is simply that however one thinks of the "broadly Gricean" reasoning involved, it does not rely on the previous identification of the proposition the speaker expresses in a form that would allow the inferer to express it; utterance bound descriptions suffice. Hence we need not worry about the Gricean circle.

## 1.3 Humpty-Dumpty

Humpty-Dumpty famously claimed to be able to say "glorious" and mean thereby "that's a knockdown argument."[2] It seems scarcely possible that he could intend to say that, and even less possible that he should succeed in saying it. Intuitively we can fail to say what we intend to say, and can fail to refer to whomever or whatever we intend to refer to. A theory that denies that won't be plausible. But then how can we suppose that one's intentions play a major role in determining to whom or to what we refer?

Let's start with an example in which they don't seem to play much of a role. Let's suppose that I have succumbed to my fantasy life, and come to believe that I am John Searle. Entering the Philosophy Lounge at Stanford, I hear graduate students debating

[2] Lewis Carroll, *Through the Looking Glass*, Chapter VI.

about Searle's philosophy of mind. One claims that he is a closet dualist. "I'm certainly not a dualist, closet or otherwise!" I claim passionately. In using the word "I," I intend to refer to John Searle, about whom I intend to be saying something. But in spite of my intention, I don't refer to Searle, I refer to John Perry. Perhaps I nevertheless manage to say something true, but I don't manage to say the true thing I intended to say. No matter how hard I try, I can't refer to anyone but myself with the word "I."

In this case I don't refer to the person I intend to refer to, in one clear sense. I intended to refer to John Searle, and I failed. But in another clear sense, I do. I use the word "I" in English, exploiting its meaning or character, namely, that a use of it refers to the speaker using it. I intend to use it with its normal English meaning, and thereby refer to myself, the person who is using it. Crazy as I might be, I realize that I am the person whose speech I control, who is forming and pronouncing the word "I" in accord with my intentions, whose feet I can see by looking down and the tip of whose nose I can see by closing one eye. This is the person I intend to refer to, and I succeed.

My problem is that I have a false belief about this person, that he is John Searle. So, I think that *by* referring to myself, I can refer to John Searle. Our intentions to refer to things and to say things, like all of our intentions, are parts of complex intentions and plans, whereby one does one thing *by* doing another. I type these words *by* moving my fingers; I refer to John Perry *by* referring to myself.

In analyzing any act, we take some actions to be more or less basic, to be such that the agent can perform them at will without worrying about the circumstances, at least across a wide range of more or less normal circumstances. Other actions, the ones that one performs by executing such basic actions, depend on circumstances that one needs to take into account in one's plans. If I move my fingers in a certain way over a keyboard, I type certain words. If my fingers were poised above my cat's belly, I might tickle him, or perhaps expose some fleas. If I'm giving a lecture, with my elbows resting on the podium, and move my fingers in that way, I'll succeed in doing little more than looking stupid.

For current purposes, we can count the production of sounds of certain sorts as phones and morphemes of a language one knows as basic actions, which we can execute at will in the circumstances of interest. Simplifying somewhat, the conventions of English allow us to use certain sounds to utter certain simple expressions, and to utter complex expressions by uttering strings of simple ones. The conventions are *permissive*; by making the phone |red| I can say "red" or "read;" by uttering the expressions "Flying," "planes," "can," "be" and "dangerous" in that order I can produce a sentence whose head is "flying" or one whose head is "planes." So we have the basic actions, and by performing them we articulate English expressions, our intentions playing a very major role in determining which expressions and phrases English permits us to say with those sounds we do say. Usually, there will be various meanings available for the expressions we use, and here again our intentions play the major role in determining which of the available meanings is in play.

In the case of "I," my plan was to make a certain sound, and thereby say the English word "I," with its ordinary meaning, and thereby refer to the person who was speaking, and thereby refer to John Searle. The first three intentions were successfully carried out, but not the last. Thus a theory that gives intentions a major role need not amount to a Humpty-Dumpty theory. The words I can say by making certain sounds, and the meanings I can associate with various words, are constrained by the conventions of English. Once I am finished with English, other facts take over, such as the fact that a certain utterance was made by John Perry and not John Searle. I can fail in numerous way to say what I intend, and I can also say things, such as that John Perry is not a dualist, that I did not intend to say.

Most indexicals are not quite so "automatic" as "I" appears to be (and one suspects, on general principles, that it is also not quite as automatic as it appears to be, although I have not yet seen an utterly convincing example). Consider "here." I say, "It's not raining here." My remark is true if it's not raining in a certain region, and I am in that region. But how large a region? The room I am in? Perhaps. If you ask "Is it raining," and I, standing inside, say "Not here" meaning to include in the region referred to with "here" only the room or building in which I stand: a joke, or an attempt at one. Usually I would mean something larger, including the area into which you were likely to venture if you were to go outside. If it's not raining in the neighborhood, even if it's raining elsewhere in Palo Alto, I speak the truth. But I might intend a larger region, if, say, the question at issue was whether the drought in Northern California had lifted.

On these issues, "today" might seem to share the status that "I" has, or seems to have: speakers' intentions, beyond the intention to speak English, play no role in determining reference. But suppose I am on the phone to someone in Japan, to whom I have promised to email a paper, as soon as I complete it. It is six in the morning Pacific Coast Time, but already ten at night, the same day, in Tokyo. "I'll send it to you today," I say. Have I given myself eighteen or two hours to complete it? It seems to depend on whether I intend to refer to the twenty-four hour stretch that count as a day in Palo Alto or the one that counts as a day in Tokyo.

With "today" and "here," then, our reference to days and places seems a matter of the character of the indexical, plus a speaker's intention about the stretch of space, or twenty-four hour period, to be included. The listener can use Gricean reasoning to figure out what the speaker has in mind. If all goes according to plan my interlocutor in Japan will first simply assume he will get the paper in two hours, and the phone call will end amicably. But as time passes, he will figure out what I had in mind, and resign himself to getting the paper the next day.

The possibility of error in reference is present with both "here" and "today," just as it is with "I," but with much less drastic mistakes on the speaker's part being required; I needn't be crazy, simply confused. I may think that your birthday is March 3rd, and mistakenly think today is March 3rd, and so falsely say, "Today is your birthday." I refer, as I intended, to the day on which my utterance is made, but unintentionally to March 4th, if, as usual, I am a day late (and a dollar short).

## 1.4 Why we use indexicals and demonstratives

There is a phenomenon we might call "the unhelpful indexical," using "indexical" broadly to include pronouns used demonstratively. I am sitting quietly reading in the living room. But my mind wanders to current affairs, and I suddenly blurt out, "He is not only a fool but a tyrant." The thought boiling within me demanded to be expressed, and I expressed it. I wasn't trying to communicate anything to you. I put no thought into whether you would be able to identify to whom I referred with "he." Still, I referred to someone, and said something true or false of that person. I referred to the person I was thinking about, and intended to refer to with "he." But it was a pretty unhelpful indexical.

Now this much you could figure out: that I had someone in mind to whom I was referring with "he." That opens what I'll call a "channel" of information about this person. By this I mean that the person I referred to now has a relation to you, which you can (possibly) exploit to find out more about him or her. You have already learned, about this person, whomever it is, that he is a fool and a tyrant, or at least that I believe that he is. By asking me more questions, you can find out more information about him, if we construe "information" broadly enough so that what I think of him counts as information.

Compare this unhelpful indexical with some more helpful ones. All of a sudden I blurt out, "I am an idiot." Even if am merely expressing a current thought, with no communicative intention beyond self-criticism, I open *two* channels of information for you. The first is basically the same on as in the last example: the person the speaker is thinking about and intends to refer to with the pronoun he uses. This channel is open whether I say "he," unhelpfully, or "I," or "you" or "that woman." But the particular pronoun I used, "I," puts a further constraint on the person I am talking about, a certain relation he has to the utterance I produce, that he is the speaker of it. In the circumstance, this opens up an important new channel of information, for you can see me across the room; you know that I am the speaker of the utterance you hear; you can visually inspect me. You may see that I have just dumped the contents of my drink on my book, and form a hypothesis about why I think I am an idiot.

We use pronouns to refer to persons or things we are thinking about; other things being equal we refer to whichever of those person or thing we intend to. If we stick with unhelpful indexicals, rather than choosing a referring device that puts further constraints upon them, we cannot go wrong. But lots of pronouns do impose further constraints: being male, being female, being the speaker, being a member of the audience, and so forth. Why take the risk of getting things wrong? Because when we are communicating we want to be helpful, and this means using the pronoun not only to provide our listeners with the information that we are thinking about and referring to some person or thing, but to supply them with an additional channel of information about the person or thing. In general, we want to open up a channel that is not utterance-bound or even speaker-bound. When I simply said "He is not only an idiot, he is a tyrant" your only channel is bound to the speaker; you could ask me more about whom I had in mind. When I said "I am an idiot," you had a channel that allowed you to pick up all sorts of information about the subject of my remarks just by looking at me; you weren't limited to asking me questions.

At least when we are trying to communicate helpfully, then, our "reference plans" are more complicated than simply to refer to an object. We want to do so in a way that will open a useful channel of information for our listeners. We do this by choosing a pronoun whose character places additional constraints on their referents, satisfaction of which provides our listeners with a second "cognitive fix" on the referent, usually one that is utterance and speaker-independent.

Let's return to our example of the graduate students in the lounge talking about John Searle. Suppose now it is not a deluded me but Searle himself who walks in on the conversation, characteristically undeluded and combative. He hears the remark that Searle is a closet dualist, and he wishes to deny this. He needs to refer to himself, and say that he is not a dualist. He could say, "X is a not a dualist," The students would learn that there is a person Searle intends to refer to, who is not, or at least believed by Searle not to be, a closet dualist. That's the only channel they would have; it would be as if Searle were playing "Twenty Questions," challenging the students to figure out who X is. Or he could use a "he" that is anaphoric on the ongoing conversation. Two channels: the person the speaker intends to refer to, and the person we have been referring to. Or he could say "I." Two channels: the person the speaker intends to refer to, and the speaker himself. Normally, someone in Searle's position would use the first person. In that case considerations of relevance would lead the students to suppose that the speaker was Searle, the person whose metaphysical beliefs were under discussion (or at least thought himself to be Searle).

Let's suppose Searle intends for the students to realize that he is saying something about himself, that the very person they see and hear is the person said not to be a closet dualist. His various ways of referring put different "cognitive burdens" on the students; that is, require them to know different things, in order to end up thinking the thoughts he wants them to think. If he refers to himself merely as "X," they'll have a large burden, with no clear route other than asking a questions to get to the right end point. If he uses "he" anaphorically, they will realize he is talking about Searle, but will have to recognize him visually, or perhaps recognize his voice, to come with the right thought. But if he says "I" then they simply have to recognize which of the persons in the room made the remark, and assume he is being relevant.

Keeping the cognitive chains we require short and reasonable is a skill that goes beyond knowing language. Children and some adults lack it, using "this" and "that" and "that man" and the like to refer to things that their interlocutors can't hope to identify. Some people can manage in face to face conversation, but don't have the ability to alter their plans when talking on the phone, where more stage-setting is typically required.

## 1.5 True Demonstratives and directing intentions

By true demonstratives I will mean "this" and "that" and phrases built from them, and pronouns such as "he" and "she" used demonstratively. When a speaker uses such a pronoun with a communicative intention, his plan will typically include the following:

1. An object that the speaker is thinking about and wishes to refer to.
2. A role $R$ he takes this object to be playing in his life—for example, being the cup he is looking at, or being the car he remembers, or being the cigar he is holding—such that the demonstrative phrase in question can be used to refer to an object playing that role. The intention to refer to the object that plays this role is the *directing intention.*

3. A role $R'$ that the speaker takes the object to have in the interlocutor's life, or that it easily could have with a bit of re-orientation and reasoning on the interlocutor's part, that will open a useful channel of information and possibly action for the interlocutor. Some examples: being the cup he will see if he follows my gaze; being the car he can ask me about; being the cigar he will see if he looks at me.
4. Some plan for a cognitive path from the mode of reference to the mode of presentation, that the listener is likely to be able to follow.

Suppose I have just poured coffee for each of us. You come in the room; I point to one of the cups and say, "That cup has your coffee." The cup in question is the object I am thinking about and wish to refer to. I have a memory of this cup; I can think about it when I am not looking at it. I have a way of recognizing the cup, perhaps by its position on the counter, perhaps by some characteristic marking. The word "that" doesn't impose many constraints; I could simply say "That cup has your coffee" without turning and looking at the cup; I would have said something true, but possibly not in the most helpful way. You would have only one channel open to the cup; it is the one I refer to. This might be enough; by assuming that what I say is true, you can figure out which cup, if there are few enough coffee-filled cups.

My goal is to get you into a state in which you can pick up the right cup and drink from it; this means seeing it and knowing which of the cups you can see it is. To be helpful, and to minimize the cognitive burden on you (especially before your first cup of coffee) I would position myself so that I can see the cup, and so that you can see me and which cup I am looking at; if that's not going to be so easy I might point.

I'll call the cup I remember A. So I want to refer to A, and say about it, that it is the cup your coffee is in. I want thereby to convey to you the information necessary for you to go and pick up the right cup; I want you not only to believe that A is the cup with your coffee in it, but to believe it in a certain way, so that you are looking at A, and believing of it, as the cup you are looking at, that it has your coffee in it. It will not suffice to simply say, thinking of A, "that cup has your coffee in it." You will be able to think of A as "the cup JP is referring to," but that's not too helpful. I further constrain the cup by looking at it and perhaps nodding or pointing; you follow my gaze, or my point, and realize that A is one of the cups that I could be looking at or pointing to; if there are a few enough cups, and only one of them has coffee, that should do it.

There is plenty of room in this scenario for me to make mistakes, and to refer to some cup other than the one I intended to. However, some delicate issues arise which we need to consider.

Suppose it is like this. I remember a certain cup, A, the one into which I poured the coffee meant for you. Now as long as I don't turn around, pick out a cup with my eye-gaze or point, and so forth, it seems I can hardly fail to successfully refer to this cup by thinking about it, remembering pouring the coffee into it, and saying "That cup is the one your coffee is in." But instead I turn around, and fix on a certain cup, B, that I wrongly take to be A. Perhaps I have misremembered where on the counter cup A was; perhaps someone has moved it aside and put another cup in its place, so I am right about where A was but wrong about where it is. For whatever reason, the cup

I'm looking at, and directing your gaze towards, is B and not A. Something has gone wrong, but exactly what?

Given that I am the speaker, we have (at least) these two propositions in play:

(1) $\exists x$ $x$ is a cup & I remember putting coffee in $x$ & $x$ contains your coffee;

(2) $\exists x$ $x$ is a cup & I am looking at $x$ & $x$ contains your coffee;

Given further that A is the cup I remember and B is the cup I am looking at, we have:

(3) A contains your coffee.

(4) B contains your coffee.

(1) and (3) are true; (2) and (4) are false.

So what was my plan?

- I intended to refer to A *by* referring to the cup I was looking at; I succeeded in referring to the cup I was looking at, but not in referring to A thereby. So I said something false.
- I intended to refer to A with "that" and did so, but I misled you, because of my mistake, as to which cup I was referring to. So I said something true.

I clearly intended to refer to A, and I clearly intended to convey to you that the cup I saw, and directed your attention to, was A. But did I intend to refer to A *by* referring to the cup I saw? It seems like there are two different plans of reference that I might have in mind. One is simply to use "that cup" to refer to the cup I am thinking of; the attempt to direct your attention to a certain cup, that I took to the one I was thinking of, is, so to speak, and additional project. Return to the first case, where I just casually say "that cup has your coffee," in a relatively unhelpful way. Then you ask which one, and I turn and point. The current possibility is as if those two acts were compressed into one time frame; they still are two different plans, and the plan of identifying which cup I have, or am, referring to isn't a part of the plan to refer.

The second possibility is that my plan is to refer to A, the cup I remember, by referring to B, the cup I see. Here the helpful aspect of my act is not ancillary to the referring, but an aspect of it.

A third possibility seems more likely than either of these, however, and that is that the questions of *which* cup I refer to, and which proposition I express have no answer, because the question of which plan I had in mind has no answer. My overall goal was to provide you with information about which cup was yours. As a means to that end, I had to refer to the cup I thought was yours. Given my true view that your cup was the cup I remembered, and my false views that the cup I remember was the cup I saw, and that by saying "that cup" I could refer to both the cup I remembered filling and the cup I saw, my plan didn't need to distinguish between these two methods of achieving my goal.

Nevertheless, in this case we would probably say that I said something false, that your coffee was in cup B. Our ordinary concept of "saying" has a forensic aspect. I misled you into believing that cup B contained your coffee; I am responsible for your coming to have that false belief. Korta and I develop a concept of *locutionary content* that ignores the forensic aspect of saying, so that the locutionary content of an utterance is determined by the speaker's referential plan and the objective circumstances, disregarding affects, fortunate or unfortunate, on interlocutors, for which the speaker may be responsible. I intended to refer to a cup that meets conditions no cup actually meets, since there is no cup that is both the cup I remember and the cup I see. Hence, in this case, my utterance has no locutionary content at the referential level.

## 1.6 Names

What is the semantic contribution of an ordinary proper name? In the 1970's, Keith Donnellan, Saul Kripke, and David Kaplan convinced many of us that proper names were "directly referential," or "rigid designators." When I say "George Bush appears tired and discouraged," the contribution "George Bush" makes to the proposition I express is simply George Bush himself. What I say, the proposition I express, is true in worlds in which he appears tired and discouraged. The descriptions I might have of him, or expect that you could provide for him, are not constituents of the proposition I express.

My view of how names work is as follows. When someone is given a name, say at baptism, a permissive convention is established. When George Bush was named "George Bush," his parent established a convention that permits people to refer to their child with that name. But "George Bush," like most proper names, has been assigned to more than one person; at the time he was born, the most famous George Bush was his father. If we think of each convention as establishing a new meaning for the name, then most proper names are very ambiguous. It is a rather special kind of ambiguity, which I call "nambiguity."[3]

When I say "George Bush appears tired and discouraged," my plan is to refer to the President, and express a proposition about him. I plan to do that by exploiting the permissive convention his parents established. We can abstract from the particular convention I exploit, to get a reflexive account of the truth-conditions of my utterance $u$:

$\exists C \exists x$ ($C$ is a convention that permits people to refer to $x$ with "George Bush" & the speaker of $u$ exploits $C$ & $x$ appears tired discouraged.)

This is what I can plan on my interlocutors grasping, based only on the assumption that they know English. If we were watching television, and George W. Bush was appearing with his father George H.W. Bush, I wouldn't be able to count on my interlocutors knowing which convention I was intending to exploit, and it would be helpful to add something that makes this clear, perhaps by saying "George W. Bush" or "George Bush the younger" or something like that.

Cognitively, we use names to identify internal files we keep about people, places and things. Typically names are associated with information that isn't tied to current perception. A typical file for a person I know well will contain information that helps me recognize them and information that helps me interact with them in fruitful ways, facts about them that differentiate them from other people.

As with indexicals and demonstratives, we use proper names to open up a channel

[3] In *Reference and Reflexivity* I develop a theory of "notion-networks" to handle various problems, such as empty names, but I'll leave that aside for present purposes.

of information to the person we refer to. Although the various descriptions you may have of George Bush do not make it into the proposition I express, they are likely quite relevant to my overall goal in saying what I do. I want you to add to your file on the President that he appears tired and discouraged. Perhaps you have claimed that he is oblivious to the effects that various policies have had, and I want to convince you that he is not. Perhaps I think it will cheer you up to think that he is depressed. My goal is to have a particular effect on your mind, to effect the file you have on George Bush.

Suppose now we are having dinner, and I say, "Please pass John Perry the salt." That would sound rather pompous. To pass someone the salt, you need to think of them in terms of their location relative to you; the simplest cognitive path is provided by my saying "Please pass me the salt," since you can see that I am the person speaking. If I use my name, I presuppose that you know my name, and even if I am sure that you do, it sounds pompous. None of the particular things you know about me under the name "John Perry" are relevant to what I want you to do. It suffices that you know that the person who wants the salt is sitting across the table from you. Imposing the extra cognitive burden, rather than just saying "Please pass me the salt," and hence sounds pompous.

If we don't recognize the semantic contribution of names, that is highlighted at the reflexive level of analysis, many of the ordinary things we do with names can seem rather mysterious. If I meet you for the first time at a party, I can tell you my name by saying "I am John Perry." Saying "I am I" or "John Perry is John Perry" wouldn't work very well. But all three alternatives express the same proposition, on the assumption that "I" and "John Perry" are both devices of direct reference. The important difference emerges at the reflexive level. You realize that what I say is true only if there is a convention that permits reference to the speaker, the person talking to you, with the name "John Perry."

## 1.7 Conclusion

I have argued that by distinguishing between the referential content of an utterance and various reflexive or utterance-bound contents it may have, we can treat a number of phenomena about the pragmatics of reference in an illuminating way. This argues in favor of the proposal that Kepa Korta and I make about the relation between pragmatics and semantics. The semantic value of an assertive utterance is its utterance-bound truth-conditions, given the meanings of the expressions used in the language employed by the speaker. Further specification of content, taking into account issues of ambiguity, nambiguity, precision and vagueness, and other issues requires what we call "near-side" pragmatics, that is, broadly Gricean reasoning in the service of intention discovery. Levinson's "Gricean Circle" is avoided, since the utterance-bound content can serve as the input to this reasoning.

## References

Carston, Robyn. 2002. *Thoughts and utterances*. Oxford: Blackwell.

Korta, Kepa and John Perry. 2006a. Three demonstrations and a funeral. *Mind and Language* 21 (2):166–186.

Korta, Kepa and John Perry. 2006b. Varieties of Minimalist Semantics. *Philosophy and Phenomenological Research* LXXIII (3):450–458.

Korta, Kepa and John Perry. 2007a. Radical minimalism, moderate contextualism. In G. Preyer and G. Peter, eds., *Content and Context. Essays on Semantics and Pragmatics*. Oxford: Oxford University Press.

Korta, Kepa and John Perry. 2007b. The Pragmatic Circle. *Synthese* forthcoming.

Levinson, Stephen C. 2000. *Presumptive Meanings*. Cambridge: MIT Press.

Perry, John. 2001a. *Reference and Reflexivity*. Stanford: CSLI Publications.

Recanati, François. 2004. *Literal Meaning*. Cambridge: Cambridge University Press.

Sperber, D. and D. Wilson. 1986-1995. *Relevance: Communication and Cognition*. Blackwell: Oxford.

# 2

# Singular Propositions, Quasi-singular Propositions, and Reports

Eros Corazza

In this paper I shall argue that we do not need to appeal to quasi-singular propositions (i.e., propositions made up both of objects and properties and the modes of presentation under which they are conceived) to deal with two powerful theses:

- that indexicals (and proper names) are directly referential terms; and
- that we cannot always substitute *salva veritate* coreferring terms embedded in attitude reports

I shall show that the quasi-singular propositions approach faces a dilemma. Either:

- it is a mere notational variant on a version of the singular propositions approach and, in that case, the friend of the quasi-singular proposition strategy commits the *fallacy of misplaced information* (asking for a single entity, a proposition, to be the provider of all the relevant information) and the *fallacy of dislocated information* (filling in information where in fact there is none). Or,
- it forces us to give up semantic innocence—the thesis that terms do not switch reference when they are embedded in attitude reports

To state my point I shall focus on Recanati's (1993) influential work, based on the notion of a quasi-singular proposition.

Here is the way in which I shall proceed. In section 1, I shall propose and defend the theory of direct reference and show how the Fregean theory faces difficulties in handling indexical expressions. In order to state my point, I will focus on the influential papers of Kaplan (1989) and Perry (1977). In the second section, I shall expose Evans' (1983) argument against Perry's interpretation of Frege's theory of indexicality and Evans' claim that Perry's conception is but a notational variant of Frege's. In section 3, I shall discuss the theory which appeals to quasi-singular propositions and show that, if one accepts Evans' notational variant argument, then the quasi-singular propositions theory is also a notational variant of Frege's. Finally, in the last section I shall show

*Meaning, Intentions, and Argumentation.*
Kepa Korta and Joana Garmendia (eds.).

how the position that appeals to quasi-singular propositions either forces us to give up semantic innocence or is a mere notational variant on the position appealing to singular propositions and ways of believing them. In that case, the friend of quasi-singular propositions commits both the fallacy of misplaced information and the fallacy of dislocated information.

## 2.1 Indexical Thoughts and Singular Propositions

Uses of indexical expressions—e.g.: 'I,' 'here,' 'today,' 'now,' etc.—fix the reference according to the context in which they are uttered. With a change in the context of use a change in reference is likely to occur. Their linguistic meaning can be represented as a function taking as argument a context and giving as value a referent. Thus the meaning of the first-person pronoun corresponds to something like, "the agent of the utterance," the linguistic meaning of the second-person pronoun would be "the addressee of the utterance" and the linguistic meaning of 'now' would be "the time of the utterance." Roughly, the linguistic meaning of an indexical is a rule stating how to use it. If one looks in the dictionary for the entry under 'I,' one reads that "it is used to refer to the speaker or writer." Kaplan calls this meaning *character* and Perry *role*:

> The character of an expression is set by linguistic *conventions* and, in turn, determines the content of the expression in every context. Because the character is what is set by linguistic conventions, it is natural to think of it as *meaning* in the sense of what is known by the competent language user. (Kaplan (1989, p. 505))

> When we understand a word like 'today,' what we seem to know is a rule taking us from an occasion of utterance to a certain object. 'Today' takes us to the very day of utterance, 'yesterday' to the day before the day of utterance, 'I' to the speaker, and so forth. I shall call this the role of the demonstrative. I take the context to be a set of features of an actual utterance, certainly including time, place, and speaker, but probably also more. ... Clearly we must grant 'today' a *role*, the same on both occasions of use. And we must, as clearly, give it different values on two occasions. (Perry (1977, p. 6))

The value of an indexical expression is what ends up in the proposition expressed by the utterance in which the indexical appears. Intuitively, the proposition expressed corresponds to what is said. For this reason, Perry's and Kaplan's theory of indexicals is considered to be a version of the direct reference theory, as it has been popularized by (among others) Marcus, Donnellan, Kripke, Wettstein as well as Perry and Kaplan themselves. One of the main tenets of the direct reference theory is that singular terms (e.g. proper names and indexicals) contribute to expressing singular or Russellian propositions, i.e. propositions having the referents themselves as constituents. This does not preclude, however, indexicals having a descriptive meaning, which the referent must satisfy. The linguistic meaning of an indexical is given by a description (e.g. "*the* time of the utterance," "*the* agent of the utterance," etc.) that the referent must satisfy, but this meaning (unlike Frege's notion of sense), is not what gets into what is said and communicated. The latter are *singular* propositions; whereas the constituents of Fregean thoughts are senses or modes of presentation under which the referents are conceived:

> Directly referential expressions are said to refer directly without the mediation of a Fregean *Sinn*. What does this mean? There are two things it might mean. It might mean that the relation between the linguistic expression and the referent is not mediated by the corresponding propositional component, the content of what-is-said. This would be directly contrary to Frege, and it *is* what I meant. But it also might mean that *nothing* mediates the relation between the linguistic expression and the individual. So stated, this second interpretation is a wildly implausible idea. And it is contrary to the development of the notion of character which occurs in the text. This is *not* what I meant. (Kaplan (1989, p. 568))

Moreover, it has been argued (Perry and Kaplan) that no Fregean account of indexicals can be satisfactory, for Frege's sense/reference distinction falls apart when we look at how indexicals work. To illustrate this point, let us suppose that the first-person pronoun comes equipped with a sense, which determines its reference. Adopting Frege's terminology, when I say 'I,' I grasp a sense which determines *me* as the referent; when you say 'I,' you grasp a sense which determines you as referent, and so on. The sense we grasp (henceforth: mode of presentation, MP) is what we come to be aware of when we understand an expression (as such, it is the bearer of cognitive value) and is a constituent of a thought, the bearer of truth value. Following Frege, the mode of presentation I grasp when I think of myself in *prima persona* differs from the one you grasp when you think of yourself *via* 'I':

> Now, everyone is presented to himself in a particular and primitive way in which he is presented to no one else. So, when Dr Lauben has the thought that he was wounded, he will probably be basing it on this primitive way in which he is presented to himself. And only Dr Lauben himself can grasp thoughts specified in this way. But now he may want to communicate with others. He cannot communicate a thought he alone can grasp. Therefore, if he now says 'I was wounded,' he must use 'I' in a sense which can be grasped by others, perhaps in the sense of 'he who is speaking to you at this moment'; by doing this he makes the conditions accompanying his utterance serve towards the expression of a thought. (Frege (1918, p. 42))

Furthermore, the sense one associates with one's use of the first-person pronoun does not always correspond with his/her own conception, whatever this turn out to be. To stress this point, we can borrow Putnam's famous twin-Earth thought experiment. On Earth and twin-Earth everything is qualitatively similar, down to the last molecule. When on Earth I say "I am F," on twin-Earth, my twin, who is qualitatively indistinguishable from me, also says "I am F." Both my twin and myself use the first-person pronoun. Since we are so similar, we have the same conception of ourselves. We think, if you like, of ourselves in the same way. Imagine now that the way in which we think of ourselves, i.e. the conception we have of ourselves, constitutes the sense we associate with 'I;' in this case, the sense does not help us to determine the referent, for when my twin uses 'I' he refers to himself, whilst when I use it I refer to myself. Each refers to himself because each of us uses the first-person pronoun. Although we have the same self-conception, we do not refer to one another. To bring this point home and down to earth we can use a Castañeda-Perry inspired example. Someone, Jon, can believe that he is Hume and that he wrote the *Treatise*. When Jon thinks of himself, he thinks of himself, among other things, as the author of the *Treatise*. Hume too thinks of himself as the author of the *Treatise*. But when Hume says "I wrote the *Treatise*," he says something true whilst when Jon utters this very sentence, he says something false. So far, the general moral seems to be that 'I' refers without the mediation of a Fregean sense, for if reference were mediated by a Fregean sense both Hume and Jon would refer to the same person when they used 'I,' i.e., they would refer to whoever happens to satisfy the sense associated with 'I' (in our example, the author of the *Treatise*).

In short, we face the following dilemma: either the sense of 'I' is not the conception we have of ourselves, or sense is not what determines reference. On the basis of similar considerations, Perry (1977) convincingly argued that we cannot find a satisfactory notion of sense which can determine the reference of expressions like 'I' or 'today.' The main reason is that these expressions have a constant meaning which does not change according to the context of use, a Fregean sense *qua* what determines reference must differ each time an indexical use picks out a different referent. To escape this problem, one could equate an indexical linguistic meaning with an incomplete sense which must be completed in the context the indexical is used (see Perry (1977)). Only the latter, the complete sense, can play the role of a Fregean sense and be both what determines reference and what gets into the thought expressed. The problem this conception faces is that an indexical linguistic meaning (character or role) in a given context gives us a referent, not a sense. But only senses can be part of incomplete senses. As Russell pointed out, we cannot go from reference to sense.

> Such a sense [the sense completer], it seems, would have to be intimately related to the sense of a unique description of the value of the demonstrative in the context of utterance. But where does such a description come from? 'Today' seems to get us only to a day. And a day does not provide a particular description of itself. (Perry (1977, p. 11))

Since indexicals take different values on different occasions, different senses must be supplied. So, an indexical cannot be regarded as an abbreviation for an appropriate description. It is worth noticing that the problem for a Fregean theory of indexicality subsists whether or not we assume that the sense completer is given by a description of the referent or by a non-descriptive mode of presentation. As we now will see, the main problem is that the sense of an indexical cannot be furnished independently of the context of utterance, and context gives us referents, not senses.

## 2.2 The Notational Variant Argument and Quasi-Singular Propositions

Evans (1981) was well aware of the fact that contexts furnish referents and not senses. He thus questioned the very idea that only *senses* can complete senses. In doing so, he gives up the (Fregean) view that only senses end up in the thought expressed by an utterance containing indexical expressions. Evans argues that Perry's account and Frege's are *notational variants*:

> Perry has a positive proposal about ways of entertaining thoughts, one which links them to the 'roles' of meanings of demonstrative expressions of natural language. ... If Perry is to be able to report S's epistemic situation, his belief reports must be more complex than just a simple relational statement between a subject and a P-thought [a thought consisting of a certain object and an incomplete sense of a concept expression]; the way

in which the thought is apprehended must come in as well. Perry uses locutions like "By entertaining the sense of 'I,' S apprehends the thought consisting of Hume and the sense of '($\xi$) is hot,"' and so perhaps he has in mind some such constructions as:

(17) S apprehends-in-way-$w$ $\langle x$, sense of '($\xi$) is F'$\rangle$.

But surely this is now a notational variant of Frege's approach, at best. Where Frege would write:

(18) S believes $\langle x, w$, Sense of '($\xi$) is F'$\rangle$,

Perry will write:

(19) S believes-in-way-$w$ $\langle x$, sense of '($\xi$) is F'$\rangle$,

or "S believes, by apprehending such-and-such a sense, the thought consisting of $x$ and the sense of '($\xi$) is hot."'(Evans (1981, pp. 317-8), the numeration is Evans')

In short, according to Evans, where Perry thinks of 'I' as having a constant meaning which determines a reference according to the context of use, Frege, properly understood (that is, understood as Evans understands him), would consider 'I' to have a sense made up by the constant meaning *and* the referent. A sense can thus be viewed as a compound entity made up of a meaning (a partial sense or MP) and a referent. In other words, Perry analyses the utterance of a sentence like "I am F" into two factors:

- the thought constituted by the modes of presentations of 'I' and the predicate 'F,' and
- the proposition (singular or Russellian) made up by the referent of 'I' and the property $F$.[1]

On the other hand, Evans does not distinguish between the thought (or proposition) expressed and the modes of presentation under which the propositional constituents are conceived. An indexical thought is thus made up, amongst other things, of the indexical modes of presentation and their referents. This kind of thought has also been made familiar under the label *object-dependent* (*Russellian* or *de re*) *thought.* To illustrate Perry's and Evans' accounts, let us consider Sue's utterance:

(1) I am happy

Perry analyzes (1) in two components:

(1) a. $\langle MP_{'I'}, MP_{happy}\rangle$ & $\langle$Sue, the property of being happy$\rangle$

where '$\langle MP_{'I'}, MP_{happy}\rangle$' represents the thought Sue entertains in thinking that she herself is happy and $\langle$Sue, the property of being happy$\rangle$ is the singular proposition expressed by (1).[2] On the other hand, Evans' analysis would be:

[1] I intentionally ignore the fact that, in his 1977 paper, Perry does not speak of singular propositions and proposes a somewhat hybrid position, where a thought or proposition (the P-thought as Evans characterizes it) is constituted by the object referred to by the indexical expressions and the senses of the concept words. In his subsequent writing, Perry adopts the notion of singular proposition. The fact that I ignore Perry's 1977 hybrid position does not undermine, however, the force of my argument.

[2] In his more recent works, Perry characterizes his view as *Critical Referentialism.* According to this view, a single utterance expresses several propositions. There are thus several levels of content associated with a single utterance. In 1988, Perry distinguished between the proposition created and the proposition expressed by an utterance: "The proposition expressed by my utterance [You are spilling coffee] is

(1) b. $\langle\langle MP_{I'}, \text{Sue}\rangle; \langle MP_{happy}, \text{the property of being happy}\rangle\rangle$

which is the (*de re*) thought Sue entertains in her thinking that she is happy.

Following Schiffer (1978), I shall refer to (1b) as a quasi-singular proposition. It is a *singular* proposition insofar for it contains objects and properties, and it is *quasi*-singular because it also contains the modes of presentation under which these objects and properties are thought about. I shall use 'quasi-singular propositions' and 'object-dependent (*de re* or Russellian) thoughts' as synonymous.[3] Quasi-singular propositions should capture both the insight of direct reference (in particular, the idea that singular terms refer without the mediation of Fregean senses and contribute the object into what is said) and the Fregean insight (the view that distinct terms convey different cognitive values).

It is worth noticing that, in Perry's analysis, the first conjunct of (1b) is the bearer of cognitive value while the second conjunct is the bearer of truth value. Evans' analysis seems closer to Frege's conception inasmuch as the bearer of cognitive value and the bearer of truth value is the same entity, i.e. a quasi-singular proposition. According to Perry, we are facing an instance of what he terms *the fallacy of misplaced information*, i.e. the idea that all the information conveyed by an utterance must come from the proposition expressed (see Perry (1988, p. 195). Perry is also right in pointing out that Evans' position constitutes a departure from Frege's, just as his own does:

> If objects, rather than modes of presentation of them, figure in Evans' thoughts, then they represent the same *sort* of departure from Frege's theory as do the "thoughts as information" that I proposed. (If not the proposal remains completely obscure). There is no reason for me to reject Evans' suggestion as being a more radical departure from Frege than my own. It is a departure for Frege disavowed such hybrids. (Perry (1977, p. 23))

that Ellsworth is spilling coffee. The proposition created by it is that its speaker is addressing someone who is spilling coffee. Both can be regarded as singular propositions, one about Ellsworth, one about my utterance." (Perry (1988, p. 197). More recently Perry (2001) characterizes the proposition created as the *reflexive truth condition* of the utterance while the proposition expressed the *incremental* or *pure truth condition*. Roughly, the former have to do with linguistic meaning—i.e. what a competent speaker must know in order to correctly use the language—, while the latter are what is said/communicated by the utterance. What is said is also characterized as the *official content* of the utterance. The reflexive truth condition of an utterance like (1) "Clark Kent can fly" is: There is an individual $x$ and a convention $C$ such that, (i) $C$ is exploited by (1), (ii) $C$ permits one to designate $x$ with 'Clark Kent' and (iii) $x$ can fly. The incremental truth conditions correspond to the singular proposition *That Clark Kent can fly*. The reflexive truth conditions of an utterance containing an indexical like (2) "I can fly" [said by Clark Kent] are: There is an $x$ such that; (i) $x$ is the agent of (2); (ii) $x$ can fly. The incremental truth conditions are, again, given by the singular proposition *That Clark Kent can fly*. With this distinction in hand, Perry claims that he can solve the traditional (Frege-inspired) puzzles concerning cognitive significance. Without doubt, the incremental/reflexive distinction constitutes both a development and a refinement in Perry's theory. The reflexive truth-conditions are what allows us to classify the modes of presentations and thus the thoughts via which the referents are conceived. The basic idea, i.e. that the thought must be distinct from the proposition expressed, is thus preserved and Perry's difference from Evans' neo-Fregean conception is even more striking.

[3]Recanati (1993, Ch. 3), for instance, distinguishes between quasi-singular propositions *qua de re* thoughts and quasi-singular propositions *qua* what gets communicated. The subject part of the former is made up of objects and token modes of presentation, which are psychological and unsharable, while the subject part of the latter consists of objects and type (or linguistic) modes of presentations. For my argument, though, I do not need to adopt Recanati's distinction.

Recanati (1993) takes seriously the notational variant argument. But he also takes seriously direct reference, as it has been popularized by Perry and Kaplan. He argues, however, that the modes of presentation that are found in quasi-singular propositions are *truth-conditionally irrelevant*:

> [T]here does not seem to be any substantial difference between saying that there is a distinction between the (singular) proposition expressed and the (quasi-singular) proposition thought, only the latter involving a mode of presentation of the reference, and saying that the mode of presentation occurring in the thought is non-descriptive in the sense of truth-conditionally irrelevant. (Recanati (1993, p. 47))

Hence, when we come to compute a thought's truth value, we somehow have to extract the worldly entities (i.e. the object and properties) of the quasi-singular proposition. To illustrate this point, let us consider Tully's utterance:

(2) I am Roman

(2) expresses the quasi-singular proposition (or *de re* thought):

(2) a. $\langle\langle MP_{'I'}$, Tully$\rangle$; $\langle MP_{Roman}$, the property of being Roman$\rangle\rangle$

(2) is true iff Tully is Roman, that is, if the singular part of the quasi-singular proposition obtains. This amounts to saying that (2) is true only if the singular proposition,

(2) b. $\langle$Tully, the property of being Roman$\rangle$

is true. This mirrors Frege's way of telling the story: we can say that the thought (2a) is true iff it refers to (2b) and (2b) obtains.[4] One could argue that I am putting the cart before the horse: the genealogy goes the other way. First, we express a singular proposition and, only then, after expressing a singular proposition, do we add modes of presentation to it. If quasi-singular propositions come into the picture in this way, however, they seem to be artificial and *ad hoc*. That is, they are mere artifacts which come into play only *after* singular propositions, and modes of presentation have done their work. In short, the quasi-singular propositions friend faces a dilemma: either quasi-singular propositions are built up by putting together the singular proposition and the modes of presentation through which the former is expressed *or* quasi-singular propositions are what get directly (straightforwardly) expressed by an utterance. To have an interesting theoretical status, quasi-singular propositions ought to be that which are primarily and directly expressed by an utterance. If so, quasi-singular propositions, like Fregean thoughts, are that which an agent expresses, and thinks, in a communicative interchange and/or thinking episode. They are also the bearers of truth value.[5]

---

[4] I am not assuming, like Frege, that thoughts refer to truth values. But this has often been considered (e.g. Dummett (1981, pp. 175ff.)) to be a thesis we can give up without undermining Frege's general semantics.

[5] This is close to Recanati's picture. He argues (1993, pp. 47ff.) that the semantic content of a sentence is not exhausted by a singular proposition. This claim constitutes a departure from direct reference, insofar as the semantic content is a *de re* thought, a quasi-singular proposition. This departure, though, should not undermine the notational variant argument, for this argument has been conceived (see Evans) to capture the insights of direct reference (i.e., the content/character(role) distinction) within a Fregean framework. The goal of this argument is to make a single entity be the bearer of both cognitive value and truth value.

The natural question which comes to mind is, what are the *de re* modes of presentation that get into the thought? If modes of presentation are that which an agent thinks and what triggers her behavior, then modes of presentation *qua* thought constituents, ought to be tokens. They must be, to borrow Perry's terminology, cognitive particulars. A way to cash out such modes of presentation within the quasi-singular propositions approach is to follow Peacocke (1981) and argue that a token mode of presentation is obtained by indexing a mode of presentation *type* with an object. If $MP$ is a mode of presentation type, then $MP_x$ will be the token mode of presentation obtained by indexing the type $MP$ with the object $x$:

> '[self$_{Peter}$]' denotes the token MP obtained by indexing with Peter that type of way of thinking of something under which any person can think of himself, and under which no one else can think of him. (Peacocke (1981, p. 190))

Following these considerations, it seems that we can capture the insight of Perry's and Kaplan's approach (the singular proposition approach) within a Fregean framework. It suffices to say that the *de re* mode of presentation expressed by an indexical is a compound mode of presentation made up by the character (or role) and the object this character picks out in the given context. This is, indeed, the core of the notational variant argument.

It is worth mentioning that the notational variant argument has been used by Evans only once. In his further work on indexical thoughts, Evans never referred to this argument again. McDowell (1984, note 15) claims that the notational variant argument is "a slip on Evans' part." McDowell's skepticism concerning the notational variant argument rests on the thesis that *only senses complete senses*. As we saw, Evans explicitly rejects this thesis. In fact, this thesis must be rejected if the notational variant argument is to work. If McDowell is right, however, Fregean thoughts cannot be equated with quasi-singular propositions:

> It may seem ... that one could capture the effect of a Fregean conception of *de re* thoughts in terms of a special kind of Russellian proposition: Russellian propositions with both *res* and characters as constituents. On this view, an ordered pair of res and characters might represent a *de re* sense: such an item certainly depends on the *res* for its existence, and it determines, but is not determined by, a *Bedeutung* of the appropriate sort, namely the *res*. However, although this suggestion mimics aspects of a genuinely Fregean position, the resemblance is only superficial. This suggestion secures a *de re* nature for these 'thoughts' only by violating Frege's doctrine that thoughts are senses with senses, not *Bedeutungen*, as constituents. (McDowell (1984, p. 104))

Indeed, McDowell's proposal is more consonant with Frege's framework, insofar as thoughts are considered to be constituted by modes of presentation and not by the referents these modes of presentation are presentations of. This view is thus in clear disaccord with the direct reference picture, which holds that singular propositions (and not thoughts) are the objects of an attitude.

If we follow McDowell's proposal, then if our aim is to capture Frege's insight when we come to explain attitude ascriptions, either we must give up semantic innocence (i.e., the thesis that expressions do not change reference when embedded in attitude reports), or we give up the Fregean treatment of attitude reports (i.e., that an attitude report is exhausted by a relation between an agent and a thought):

> Since Frege, philosophers have become hardened to the idea that content-sentences in talks about propositional attitudes may strangely refer to such entities as intensions, propositions, sentences, utterances, and inscriptions. What is strange is not the entities, which are all right in their place (if they have one), but the notion that ordinary words for planets, people, tables, and hippopotami in indirect discourse may give up these pedestrian references for the exotica. If we could recover our pre-Fregean semantic innocence, I think it would seem to us plainly incredible that the words "The earth moves," uttered after the words "Galileo said that," mean anything different, or refer to anything else, than is their wont when they come in other environments. (Davidson (1968, p. 108))

## 2.3 Quasi-Singular Propositions and Beliefs Reports

Frege's treatment of attitude ascriptions has the merit of elegance. Within his framework, we easily find a solution to Frege's puzzle—the puzzle of substitution *salva veritate* of coreferring terms embedded in ascriptions. We can, for instance, block the inference:

(3) Sue believes that Tully is Roman

(4) Tully = Cicero

Thus:

(5) Sue believes that Cicero is Roman

Frege's solution, though, forces us to give up semantic innocence, for expressions appearing within attitude reports switch reference; their referent is no longer the object they refer to when appearing in simple sentences, but instead their ordinary senses. That is, in attitude reports expressions have their ordinary sense as their referent. Adopting Frege's framework, (3) can be regimented as:

(3) a. BEL(Sue, $\langle MP_{Tully}, MP_{Roman}\rangle$)

and (5) as:

(5) a. BEL(Sue, $\langle MP_{Cicero}, MP_{Roman}\rangle$)

where BEL is a dyadic relation relating the attributee to the thought referred to by the that-clause. Clearly, (3a) and (5a) do not attribute to Sue the same belief and hence they can differ in truth value. So, 'Tully' and 'Cicero,' in (3) and (5), cannot be substituted *salva veritate.*

On the other hand, if we assume that an attitude ascription is exhausted by a relation between a subject and a (singular) proposition, (3) gets regimented as:

(3) b. BEL(Sue, ⟨Tully, the property of being Roman⟩)

and (5) as:

(5) b. BEL(Sue, ⟨Cicero, the property of being Roman⟩)

where BEL is the a dyadic relation relating the attributee to the singular proposition referred to by the that-clause. In so doing, we save semantic innocence, for 'Tully' and 'Cicero' do not change reference when embedded in an attitude report, but we are unable to solve Frege's puzzle, i.e., to block the substitution *salva veritate* of coreferring terms appearing in attitude reports, for (3) and (5) cannot differ in truth value.

If we accept the notational variant argument, we can regiment (3) as:

(3) c. BEL(Sue, $\langle\langle MP_{Tully}$, Tully$\rangle$; $\langle MP_{Roman}$, the property of being Roman$\rangle\rangle$)

and (5) as:

(5) c. BEL(Sue, $\langle\langle MP_{Cicero}$, Cicero$\rangle$; $\langle MP_{Roman}$, the property of being Roman$\rangle\rangle$)

where BEL is a dyadic relation relating the attributee to the quasi-singular proposition referred to by the that-clause. Since in (3) and (5) Sue is related to two distinct quasi-singular propositions, (3) and (5) do not ascribe to her the same beliefs. Hence, we can deal with Frege's puzzle.

What, though, about semantic innocence? At first, it seems that 'Tully' and 'Cicero' do not change reference when embedded: the referent (Tully) gets into the proposition. But when embedded, these terms also perform another function. They specify the mode of presentation under which Sue thought of Tully. Recanati goes this way. He argues that, in an ascription, we enrich the singular proposition expressed by the that-clause. Since attitude ascriptions are highly context sensitive, the singular proposition can be enriched in many different ways:

> The process in question is a specific process of enrichment which I call 'quasi-singularization'; it takes us from the (singular) proposition expressed by the embedded sentence to a (quasi-singular) thought-content including a contextually provided mode of presentation. (Recanati (1993, p. 354))

This is puzzling. Either the quasi-singular propositions approach is theoretically interesting *or* it is a mere notational variant on the singular propositions approach. To play an interesting theoretical role, quasi-singular propositions should be that which is directly expressed and thought in *oratio recta* contexts. If so, we can assume that, with an ascription, we relate the attributee to the quasi-singular proposition she thought in her thinking episode. When Sue says: "Tully is Roman," she expresses a quasi-singular proposition and when we report "Sue said that Tully is Roman," we relate Sue to the quasi-singular proposition she expressed with her utterance. To see this point, consider attributions of 'I'-thoughts. When Sue utters (1)[I am happy], she expresses the *de re* thought (1b) [$\langle\langle MP_{'I'}$, Sue$\rangle$; $\langle MP_{happy}$, the property of being happy$\rangle\rangle$]. In reporting Sue's utterance, we usually say:

(6) Sue believes that she (herself) is happy

where 'she (herself)' is what Castañeda calls a *quasi-indicator*; it attributes to Sue a use (possibly only an implicit use) of 'I.' According to the quasi-singular propositions approach I have discussed, (6) can be regimented as:

(6) a. BEL(Sue, $\langle\langle MP_{'I'}$, Sue$\rangle$; $\langle MP_{happy}$, the property of being happy$\rangle\rangle$)

where BEL is a dyadic relation relating Sue with the thought referred to by the that-clause 'she (herself) is happy.' In so doing, we relate Sue to the thought she expressed with her utterance, i.e., (1). Hence, it seems that we do not need to appeal to the process of enriching singular propositions when dealing with attitude reports; at least, we do not have to appeal to it when dealing with the attribution of indexical thoughts.[6]

Notice that 'she (herself)' in (6) *refers* to the *de re* mode of presentation '$\langle MP_{I'}$, Sue$\rangle$' which is the ordinary sense of 'I.' 'She (herself)' can thus be viewed as the specific term which, in an *oratio obliqua* construction, enables the reporter to refer to the indirect sense of 'I.' But if 'she (herself)' in (6) refers to the (*de re*) mode of presentation '$\langle MP_{I'}$, Sue$\rangle$,' are we not jeopardizing semantic innocence? That is, are we not assuming that embedded expressions refer to their customary senses instead of their customary referents? The following chart should represent how the quasi-singular proposition picture fits within the Fregean framework of attitude ascriptions.

(6)

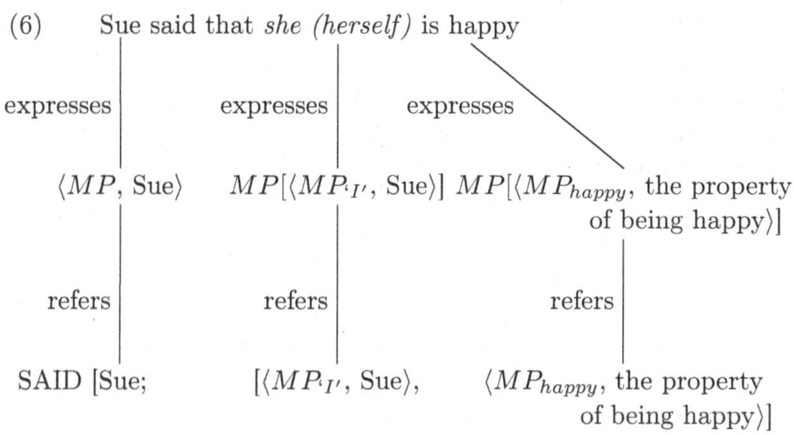


'$MP$ $[\langle MP_{I'}$, Sue$\rangle]$' and '$MP[\langle MP_{happy}$, the property of being happy$\rangle]$' are the indirect senses of, respectively, 'she(herself)' and 'is happy' which refers to the ordinary senses '$\langle MP_{I'}$, Sue$\rangle$' and '$\langle MP_{happy}$, the property of being happy$\rangle$.' As this chart makes clear, we give up semantic innocence within the Fregean framework insofar as embedded expressions do not refer to their ordinary referents, but instead to their customary modes of presentation. However, the friend of quasi-singular propositions could argue that, since *de re* modes of presentation are made up of partial senses and objects, we save semantic innocence. Embedded expressions refer (also) to the singular parts (i.e., the wordily entities such as objects and properties) of the mode of presentations. In other words, since the singular part of a mode of presentation does not change whether the term expressing it appears in an *oratio recta* or an *oratio obliqua* construction, the friend of quasi-singular propositions can claim that s/he saves semantic innocence. Is this a plausible answer?

[6]The story may be different when we deal with attributions involving proper names. On the one hand, we could argue that the quasi-singular proposition we obtain by the process of enrichment is made up by the referent and the proper name. That is, the process of enrichment goes as follows: $\langle$Cicero$\rangle$ $\rightarrow$ $\langle$Cicero, 'Cicero'$\rangle$ (see Recanati (1993, p. 374)). On the other hand, we could argue in favor of a free enrichment insofar as the embedded name may characterize only the way the reporter thinks of the referent and be silent on the way the attributee thought of it, the latter being contextually specified. (Recanati argued this way: personal communication.) As we shall soon see, it seems to me that both ways of telling the story show that the quasi-singular propositions approach and the triadic approach are notational variants.

Moreover, the friend of quasi-singular propositions faces the well-known *proliferation of senses* problem. The Fregean picture is committed to the view that, in multiple embedded contexts, a term expresses the indirect sense of the indirect sense ... and refers to the indirect sense of the indirect sense ... of the customary sense. It is difficult, if not impossible, to tell what an indirect sense is, let alone what the indirect sense of an indirect sense is.[7] Recanati does not go down this path; instead, he tries to salvage semantic innocence:

> [I]t would seem desirable to *preserve* the principle of Innocence since, other things being equal, a semantic theory which conforms to it is simpler and more elegant than one which does not. (Recanati (1993, p. 327))

Furthermore, Recanati claims that that-clauses, like simple sentences, are enriched and become quasi-singular propositions. The same pragmatic processes may occur whether or not a clause is embedded into a psychological prefix; these are the processes characterized as quasi-singularization. As I understand it, the quasi-singularization process corresponds, roughly, to a pragmatic enrichment. A that-clause, like a simple sentence, expresses a singular proposition, which gets pragmatically enriched and becomes a quasi-singular proposition. It is for this reason that Recanati believes that his position is consonant with semantic innocence:

> Note that we need not give up Innocence, on that account. Firstly, I am not saying that referential terms behave *differently* when they occur in the embedded parts of belief sentences. Optional p-processes [roughly, pragmatic processes] may come into play when a simple sentence is uttered in isolation (even though no implicit ascription of belief is made). Secondly, the typical p-process which explains failures of substitutivity in belief contexts is quasi-singularization, and it can be maintained that the embedded sentence in such cases does express the same proposition it would if not embedded. (Recanati (1993, p. 357))

[7]A referee suggested that one could avoid the proliferation of senses problem by assuming Zalta's PLUG function, which can be used to construct propositions. Since this function makes abstract entities out of abstract entities, we can use it to construe more and more complex propositions. If we consider the following example:

(i) John believes that Mary believes that Tully is an orator

the quasi-singular proposition view can be represented as follows. The quasi-singular proposition is composed of $\langle MP_{Tully}$, Tully$\rangle$ and $\langle MP_{beinganorator}$, being an orator$\rangle$. PLUG takes these two pairs and gives a new abstract object, i.e. the proposition in question: $\langle\langle MP_{Tully}$, Tully$\rangle$, $\langle MP_{beinganorator}$, being an orator$\rangle\rangle$. In his attitude, John is related to a proposition that is obtained from the application of PLUG to $\langle MP_{Mary}$, Mary$\rangle$, $\langle MP_{tobelieve}$, to believe$\rangle$ and $\langle\langle MP_{Tully}$, Tully$\rangle$, $\langle MP_{beinganorator}$, being an orator$\rangle\rangle$. This process gives us the following proposition: $\langle\langle\langle MP_{Mary}$, Mary$\rangle$, $\langle MP_{tobelieve}$, to believe$\rangle$, $\langle\langle MP_{Tully}$, Tully$\rangle$; $\langle MP_{beinganorator}$, being an orator$\rangle\rangle\rangle\rangle$. We thus do not need modes of presentation of modes of presentation in order to build up new propositions. We have ordinary referents and their modes of presentation, from which we construct propositions. This way we manage to reconstruct truth-conditions for propositional attitude reports without the need of modes of presentation of modes of presentation. Without doubt, more should be said about this suggestion and yet it suffices to say that, even if it does not crumble under the proliferation of senses charge, it does not seem to account for the semantic innocence desideratum. Zalta assumes that in a *de dicto* report the attributee is not related to a singular proposition *simpliciter*, but instead to a singular proposition containing an abstract individual: "The *de dicto* readings of attitude reports involve the same two-place relation between persons and propositions, except that in these cases, the proposition signified contains abstract rather than ordinary constituents" (Zalta (1989, p. 460)).

Why, though, must the enrichment processes that Recanati appeals to contribute to the proposition expressed and/or referred to by a that-clause? I.e. why must this process be a process of quasi-singularization? Why does this process not merely contribute *additional information*, which need not end up into the proposition referred to by a that-clause? As far as I understand, the friend of singular propositions can still maintain that that-clauses do refer to singular propositions, yet they contribute—together with pragmatic implications and enrichment—to specify the third relatum of an attitude ascription.

If Evans is right in arguing that Perry's position is a notational variant of Frege's, then *a fortiori* the quasi-singular propositions is nothing but a notational variant as well. If so, quasi-singular propositions do not seem to make a substantial contribution to the traditional direct reference view, which appeals to singular propositions and ways of entertaining them. Why should we merge the *what* (is believed) and the *how* (it is believed) into a single, hybrid entity like a quasi-singular proposition? In other words, the following two pairs of reports are notational variants of one another:

- BEL(Sue, ⟨Tully, the property of being Roman⟩; ⟨$MP_{Tully}$, $MP_{Roman}$⟩)
- BEL(Sue, ⟨⟨$MP_{Tully}$, Tully⟩; ⟨$MP_{Roman}$, the property of being Roman⟩⟩)

- BEL(Sue, ⟨Sue, the property of being happy⟩; ⟨$MP_{I'}$, $MP_{happy}$⟩)
- BEL(Sue, ⟨⟨$MP_{I'}$, Sue⟩; ⟨$MP_{happy}$, the property of being happy⟩⟩)

The only difference is that, in the quasi-singular proposition representation, BEL is viewed as a dyadic predicate, while within the singular propositions approach it is a triadic predicate relating the attributee, a (singular) proposition and the thought the attributee entertains when believing the proposition picked up by the that-clause. This difference, though, should not undermine the notational variant argument. It is a minor and negligible difference which, as we shall soon see, does not jeopardize the notational variant argument.

No doubt, a story must be told to explain how an attitude report can refer both to the proposition expressed by the that-clause *and* the thought under which the latter is entertained.[8] This story is, of course, very interesting insofar as it concerns the logical form of attitude ascriptions. I am not, however, going to deal with this problem here.[9] It suffices to say that the friend of the singular propositions approach may tell exactly the same story as the friend of the quasi-singular propositions approach; in particular, one can tell the very same story Recanati tells. Following Recanati, the singular proposition referred to by the that-clause gets enriched by modes of presentation. The enrichment process is pragmatic in nature and, according to the context of the report, such and such a mode of presentation is made salient and ends up in the quasi-singular proposition the attributee is related with. The friend of the singular propositions view can appeal to the very same enrichment procedure. The only difference will be that, instead of speaking of enriching singular propositions, one will speak of characterizing (i.e. furnishing) the

[8] Besides, we should decide whether the thought *qua* what gets into a belief report is made up by types of or tokens of modes of presentation. This question, though, is not relevant to my argument.

[9] I dealt with the logical form of attitude ascriptions in Corazza (1995, 1998, 2004).

modes of presentations that made up the third relatum of BEL, i.e., the thought *via* which the singular proposition is believed.

## 2.4 The Fallacy of Dislocated Information

In favor of the thesis that the quasi-singular propositions approach is but a notational variant on the singular propositions approach, I invite you to consider so-called de re (or relational) ascriptions. In a *de re* ascription, we cannot appeal to a quasi-singular proposition to be the referent of the that-clause. Consider:

(7) Sue believes that *I* am happy.

'I' can but refer to the reporter, say Tim. 'I' does not (and cannot) attribute to Sue the particular mode of presentation that she entertained in believing that Tim is happy. In line with the principle of semantic innocence, "I am happy" in (7) should express the same proposition it expresses in a direct discourse construction. Hence, according to the quasi-singular propositions approach, it expresses the *de re* thought $\langle\langle MP_{`I'}$, Tim$\rangle$, $\langle MP_{happy}$, the property of being happy$\rangle\rangle$. But in his attribution, Tim is not relating Sue to this *de re* thought. As a matter of fact, Sue *cannot* think of Tim using the mode of presentation $\langle MP_{`I'}$, Tim$\rangle$. The natural solution seems to be to quantify over modes of presentation and argue that (7) is of the form:

(7) a. $(\exists mp)$ BEL(Sue, $\langle\langle mp$, Tim$\rangle$, $\langle MP_{happy}$, the property of being happy$\rangle\rangle$),

where the quasi-singular proposition that Sue is related to is not fully specified. Once again, this move seems to be a shortcut of the singular propositions approach. For the latter would regiment (7) as:

(7) b. $(\exists mp)$ BEL(Sue; $\langle$Tim, the property of being happy$\rangle$; $\langle mp$, $MP_{happy}\rangle$).

The moral seems to be that, when we come to explain belief reports, the theorist who appeals to quasi-singular propositions (e.g. Recanati) is left with a dilemma: either (i) her/his account is a mere notational variant of the one that appeals to singular propositions and ways of believing them *or* (ii) s/he gives up semantic innocence and argues that embedded expressions refer, after all, to modes of presentation, i.e. the *de re* modes of presentation expressed by their *oratio recta* counterpart. In that case s/he will face the proliferation of senses problem. The following chart should summarize the two different ways in which modes of presentation can enter the picture. While the first chart is faithful to the Fregean spirit, the second is more consonant with the direct reference story I presented.

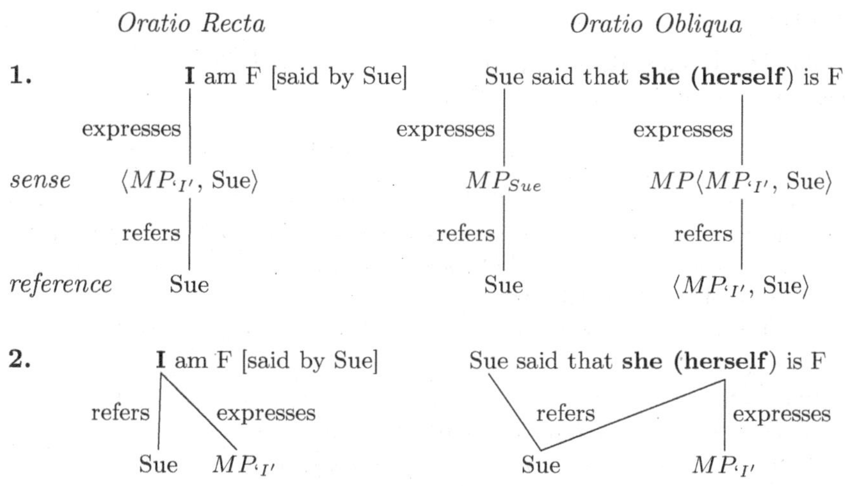


As I argued, if the friend of quasi-singular propositions claims that modes of presentation enter into the proposition in the way represented by the second chart, then her/his position is a notational variant of the view according to which that-clauses refer to singular propositions and, in addition, signal the mode of presentation under which the propositional constituents are thought of. If, on the other hand, the friends of quasi-singular propositions argue that that-clauses refer to quasi-singular propositions, as chart 1 shows, then her/his position is committed to the view that terms appearing in *oratio obliqua* constructions do not have their ordinary referents, but instead their ordinary modes of presentation, as referents. Since embedded terms switch reference, this position, like Frege's, gives up semantic innocence. Moreover, as the chart shows, if one adopts the singular propositions view, then one does not commit oneself to the distinction between indirect senses and ordinary senses. If Recanati is right in claiming that his position does not force him to give up semantic innocence and, therefore, does not face Frege's proliferation of indirect senses problem, then his position can be represented by the second chart. If so, his quasi-singular propositions view is nothing but a notational variant of the singular propositions view I proposed.

To end and summarize this section, I claim that the enrichment strategy, which takes as input singular propositions and gives as output quasi-singular propositions, commits *the fallacy of dislocated information.* As we saw in discussing the neo-Fregean attitude, Perry claims that the view which looks for all the relevant information in a single place commits *the fallacy of misplaced information.* A byproduct of this fallacy is the view which tries to compress all the available information into a single entity (e.g. into a quasi-singular proposition). This strategy commits the fallacy of dislocated information. It is like a detective that, when s/he does not find the evidence s/he is looking for at a given scene, contaminates the scene by introducing the relevant information s/he needs in order to prove her/his case. Our detective, like the friends of quasi-singular propositions, commits the fallacy of dislocated information.

## Acknowledgments

For comments I would like to thank Mark Kago, Kepa Korta, Jérôme Pelletier, François Recanati and an anonymous referee for CSLI Publications.

## References

Corazza, Eros. 1995. *Référence, Contexte, et Attitudes*. Paris-Montréal: Ed. Vrin/Bellarmin.

Corazza, Eros. 1998. She*: Pragmatically imparted or semantically encoded? In F. Orilia and W. J. Rapaport, eds., *Thought, Language and Ontology—Essays in Memory of Héctor-Neri Castañeda*, pages 217–234. Dordrecht: Kluwer.

Corazza, Eros. 2004. Essential Indexicals and Quasi–Indicators. *Journal of Semantics* 21(4):341–74.

Davidson, Donald. 1968. On Saying That. *Synthese* 19:130–46. Reprinted in D. Davidson, 1984. *Inquiries into Truth and Interpretation.* Oxford University Press, Oxford.

Dummett, Michael. 1981. *The Interpretation of Frege's Philosophy.*. Oxford: Duckworth.

Evans, Gareth. 1981. Understanding demonstratives. In *Collected papers*, pages 291–321. Oxford: Oxford University Press.

Frege, Gottlob. 1918. Thoughts. In N. Salmon and S. Soames, eds., *Propositions and Attitudes*, pages 33–55. Oxford: Oxford University Press.

Kaplan, David. 1989. Demonstratives: An Essay on the Semantics, Logic, Metaphysics, and Epistemology of Demonstratives and Other Indexicals. In J. Almog, J. Perry, and H. Wettstein, eds., *Themes from Kaplan*, pages 481–614. New York: Oxford University Press.

McDowell, John. 1984. De Re Senses. In C. Wright, ed., *Frege: Tradition and Influence*, pages 98–109. Oxford: Blackwell.

Peacocke, Cristopher. 1981. Demonstrative Thought and Psychological Explanation. *Synthese* 49:187–217.

Perry, John. 1977. Frege on Demonstratives. *The Philosophical Review* 86(4):474–95. Reprinted in J. Perry 2000. *The Problem of the Essential Indexical and Other Essays.* Stanford: CSLI Publications, 1-26.

Perry, John. 1988. Cognitive Significance and New Theories of Reference. *Noûs* 22:1–18. Reprinted in J. Perry 2000. *The Problem of the Essential Indexical and Other Essays.* Stanford: CSLI Publications, 189–206.

Perry, John. 2001. *Reference and Reflexivity*. Stanford: CSLI Publications.

Recanati, François. 1993. *Direct Reference*. Oxford: Blackwell.

Schiffer, Stephen. 1978. The Basis of Reference. *Erkenntnis* 13:171–206.

Zalta, Edward. 1989. Singular Propositions, Abstract Constituents, and Attitudes. In J. Almog, J. Perry, and H. Wettstein, eds., *Themes from Kaplan*, pages 455–78. New York: Oxford University Press.

3

# On Perry's Relative Truth-conditions

LUIS M. VALDÉS-VILLANUEVA


## Abstract

This paper has two main parts. In the first one my aim is to show that Perry's contention that the concept of the truth-conditions of an utterance is a relative concept faces several problems. In particular, I argue that Perry's reflexive truth-conditions are in fact *preconditions* that an utterance must meet in order to have truth-conditions rather than *genuine* truth-conditions. In the second part, I reflect on what I call *Reichenbach's Curse* and conclude that the price paid by Perry in order to avoid it—empty contents—is possibly too high.


## 3.1 Varieties of Truth-Conditions

John Perry's claim that the concept of the truth-conditions of an utterance is a relative concept is probably the touchstone of Perry's approach to semantics—what he calls "Critical Referentialism" or "Reflexive/Referential" account. This is the heroic attempt to merge into a single theory the "best of two worlds": the best of referentialism and the best of descriptivism. "On this view," says Perry in his paper, "there are many levels of content corresponding to the various things one can take as given when one talks of the truth-conditions of an utterance" (Perry (2001b, p. 1)).[1] Contents are tied to truth-conditions in the following way. A statement's *content*—where "statement" means a particular utterance, written or spoken, of a declarative sentence—is a proposition that incorporates the conditions under which the statement is true. Furthermore, Perry warns us not to confuse contents with meanings: *contents* belong to particular utterances whereas *meanings* do belong to types of expressions; meaning is what the rules of

[1]Perry's picture about this debate runs as follow: "The key concept in the debate between referential and descriptive approaches to the meaning of names and indexicals is that of content: *what is said* and *what is believed.* Referentialists rely on intuitions about content to make their case. Descriptivists complain that the referentialists' candidates for content cannot deal with the co-reference and no-reference problems. The innovation of the present treatment is to provide a family of contents, that meet the needs of both referentialists and descriptivists" (Perry (2001a, p. 17)).

*Meaning, Intentions, and Argumentation.*
Kepa Korta and Joana Garmendia (eds.).

language associate with simple and complex expressions. It is in this sense that one can say that truth-conditions are also relative: given the connection between contents and truth-conditions, different levels of content will give rise correspondingly to different levels of truth-conditions.

### 3.1.1 A continuum of facts

By saying that the concept of the truth-conditions of an utterance is a relative concept Perry means that instead of thinking about the truth-conditions of an utterance *simpliciter* we should conceive the truth-conditions of an utterance *given* several facts about it. There is, one could say, a *continuum* of facts about any given utterance. At one end of this continuum we have almost no facts given about a particular utterance, and at the other extreme almost all the facts might be taken as given. The number and quality, so to speak, of the facts given in each case would determine the content and the associated truth-conditions of the particular utterance. To begin with, let me say that I can envisage some difficulties in "opening the cage" of truth-conditions. It seems to me that we should provide some way or another of putting an end to the foreseeable increasingly finer content discriminations. On the contrary, we would indeed have a very cheap way of buying contents. I suppose that Perry would need to use here a peculiar Occam's razor for stopping this multiplication of contents when, for example, they would no longer have any explanatory use. In any case, this is not the important issue that I wish to address here. Therefore, I will not insist on this particular point in my comments.

Perry is anxious to distinguish between what he calls "reflexive truth-conditions" and "incremental truth-conditions" (Perry (2001b, p. 6)).[2] "Reflexive truth-conditions" are conditions *on the utterance itself*, truth-conditions that we get simply by fixing the meaning of the utterance. However, "incremental truth-conditions" are conditions *not* on the utterance itself, but truth-conditions *on the subject matter of the utterance.* They state some conditions on the world given that we know *more* additional facts about the utterance. In Eros Corazza's example the *reflexive* truth-conditions on the utterance:

(1) You are the only person from Switzerland teaching Philosophy at the University of Nottingham,

are:

(2) Given that (1) is an utterance of the English sentence "You are the only person from Switzerland teaching Philosophy at Nottingham," and given its syntax, and given the usual meaning of the words in English, (1) is true if and only if the addressee of (1) is the only person from Switzerland teaching Philosophy at Nottingham (Perry (2001b, p. 6)).

But the *incremental* truth-conditions are:

(3) Given that (1) is an utterance of the English sentence "You are the only person

[2] In fact, Perry distinguishes (Perry (1997, 2001a,b)), following a suggestion by Arthur Burks (1949), different levels of content and, therefore, different levels of truth-conditions. Nevertheless, I will almost ignore them here (I will only refer in passing to the difference between reflexive, indexical and other kinds of content) because I assume that they are not relevant for the points I am making here.

from Switzerland teaching Philosophy at Nottingham," and given its syntax, and given the usual meaning of the words in English, *and given in addition that Eros is the addressee of (1)*, (1) is true if and only if the addressee of (1) is the only person from Switzerland teaching Philosophy at Nottingham.
(Perry (2001b, p. 6)).

It seems very easy to see that the incremental truth-conditions of utterance (1) are its reflexive truth-conditions *plus* knowledge of additional facts about (1), for example that the addressee in (1) is the man Eros Corazza.

Perry's point about his concept of relative truth-conditions can perhaps be better grasped if we examine one of the examples in Perry (1997, p. 600) (slightly modified). Suppose that you are at an international philosophical meeting at the University of Nottingham, you do not speak a word of French and, during the usual welcome party, someone, mistaking you for Eros Corazza, talks to you:

(4) Vous êtes le seul philosophe suisse à cette Université.

Then, that same person whispers to you in a rather stammering English: "Aren't you?" You understand *just* the last sentence (the question), and given that you do not desire to make new acquaintances (in fact, you are anxious to meet for the first time a very famous philosopher attending the conference) you simply nod and go away. Taking everything into account, specially the last question uttered in English, there is no special problem for assuming that you took for granted that the utterance of your French-speaking colleague was a statement—an alternative way of saying that he has uttered something with which you could agree or disagree. Of course, *given the ordinary philosophical concept of the truth-conditions of an utterance* (a species of *incremental* truth-conditions, the "official" content as Perry sometimes says), one cannot say that you did grasp the truth-conditions of the proposition expressed by the utterance (again, its "official" content). However, Perry continues, you could list a series of conditions such that, were they true, the content of the utterance, *given the story I told you*, would be true. Let's call $m$ the *message* that the unknown speaker tried to convey to you in uttering (4). Such conditions would be:

(**m**) $m$ is true if there is a proposition $P$ such that in the language in which $m$ is written, its words have a certain meaning, and in the context in which $m$ was delivered, words with that meaning express $P$ and $P$ is true. (Or, for the sake of brevity: $m$ is true if and only if its words express some proposition $P$ and $P$ is true.[3])

Perry claims that (**m**) does not state the truth-conditions most philosophers would be thinking about when they talk about the truth-conditions of $m$. Presumably, they have in mind that some particular person—the addressee in this particular utterance—is the only Swiss national teaching Philosophy at the University of Nottingham and (**m**) does not establish such conditions for $m$ to be true. Nonetheless, he asserts that (**m**) states truth-conditions for $m$ "given certain facts about it," namely "given only the barest facts

[3] I take it for granted that $m$ consists of words from a particular language, with a particular meaning in the context they were uttered provided that $m$ is a statement.

about it, *that* it is a statement" (my italics) (Perry (1997, p. 600)).

### 3.1.2 Truth conditions and incremental truth-conditions are not at the same level

And now here is my first complaint. I think it is rather misleading to conceive the list that states the truth-conditions (**m**) as something standing at the same level (having the same status) as a list that states the incremental truth-conditions. According to Perry, the difference between (**m**) and such a list of incremental truth-conditions is *simply* that in the latter cases we add knowledge of more and more facts.[4]. Certainly, he acknowledges that it is not only a matter of the number of facts involved; facts of different *kinds* are involved: "The philosophical concept of truth-conditions corresponds to the case in which one knows a lot about *m*: in this case the conditions will pertain to the world outside *m*, not to *m*, itself" (Perry (1997, p. 600)). However, Perry does not seem to consider that this circumstance could introduce an important discrimination between *kinds* of truth-conditions. I mean: the circumstance that the so-called "philosophical truth-conditions" corresponds to the case in which such conditions belong to the world outside the utterance is considered by Perry as a *mere accident.* Nonetheless I am inclined to defend, given the different kinds of facts taken into account in each case, that reflexive truth-conditions could be truth-conditions only "by courtesy." (And I don't believe that this would be an unjustified *parti pris* in favour of "official" content). True, conditions listed in (**m**) are such that, were they true, *m* would be true. But there is perhaps much more to say on this matter than the mere acknowledgement of this fact, and Perry's treatment of the subject seems to me rather cursory.[5] For, in what sense does (**m**) give truth-conditions for *m*?

### 3.1.3 Conditions and preconditions

In order to explain my position here, let's make a brief digression. There is a famous proposition in Wittgenstein's *Tractatus* that runs as follows:

6.32 The Law of Causality is not a law but the form of a law.

According to the author of the *Tractatus*, the Law of Causality is not the form of a particular law, but the form of any law of a certain kind. Presumably, this amounts to saying that a sentence such as "Everything has a cause" does not say anything about the world—here "say" has the force of "state"—, it does not say which causal relations actually hold, but says that we assign causes the way we do as opposed to other ways. The Law of Causality, so to speak, is a *precondition* of our describing the world the way we do. This could be clearer if we consider what Wittgenstein says at 6.3611:

---

[4]"If your High-School French started to return to you, you must reason as follows, 'Given that the language of *m* is French, and given the meaning of 'Vous êtes le seul philosophe suisse à cette Université' in French, and given the fact that the author of *m* intended to use the word 'vous' to refer to that person (addressing him), *m* is true if and only if that person is the only Swiss national teaching at the University hosting the conference" (again adapted to my example, Perry (1997, p. 600))

[5]Perry says of a possible Kaplanian rejoinder that it "is clearly relying on the robustness of our intuitions about a certain concept which he (Kaplan) identifies in three ways: as *what he said*, as *the proposition expressed*, and as *the content of his utterance*" (Perry (2001b, p. 4)). But he is doing more or less the same thing when he tries to justify that (**m**) does state the truth-conditions for (4) "if we use that term in the ordinary way." Later on, I will have more on this matter.

> [...] When, for example, we say that neither of two events (which mutually exclude one another) can occur because there is *no cause* why the one should occur rather than the other, it is really a matter of our being unable to describe *one* of the two events unless there is some sort of asymmetry. And if there *is* such an asymmetry, we can regard this as the cause of the occurrence of the one and of the non-occurrence of the other.

Let us explain this with a very simple example. Suppose that at a time *t* you get a particular chemical reaction *R* under a certain set of conditions *C*. But at *t'* you get a different reaction which is incompatible with *R*, let's say *RI*, and, apparently, such a reaction is produced under *exactly the same conditions C*. In this case, it seems that we would be forced to admit that *RI* occurred *without any cause*. However, the fact that the Law of Causality should be interpreted as a precondition of our describing the world the way we do means that any difference between two events—even the fact that the two events are *two different events*—can, in principle, be considered as *the* difference we need in order to avoid the conclusion that something could happen without a cause. The *mere fact* that *R* and *RI* occur at *two different times* could count as the cause of the occurrence of *RI* and the non-occurrence of *R*. This would account for the fact that "Everything has a cause" does not say anything about the world but is rather taken for granted in our way of talking about the world: *any* difference between any two events—including the fact that they are not the same event—can be taken as the cause for the occurrence of one of them and the non occurrence of the other.

Now, according to Perry (**m**) gives truth-conditions for the message conveyed by the particular utterance (4) *given the mere fact* that this utterance is a statement. Of course, the utterance has some unique features of its own, but its only *relevant* feature for its truth-conditions *as given in* (**m**) is that it is a statement. Compare with the following: in the *Elements* of Euclid one can find the famous proof of the theorem that the three angles of a triangle are equal to two right angles. The proof is based on the construction of a particular and concrete diagram of a particular and concrete triangle. Nevertheless, one can conclude that the proven proposition holds for *any* triangle. Even though, the proof is based on the construction of a particular triangle, the theorem holds for *any* triangle in this sense: the properties involved in the proof are properties belonging to a particular triangle *in virtue of the fact that it is a triangle* and not a triangle *with some particular features*. Although we could argue that the theorem says something about a particular triangle, it would be misleading to think that it says what it does in virtue of the particular properties of the particular triangle used in the proof. It says something about it by stating a condition on *any* triangle and, in this way, it does not state anything peculiar to that particular triangle. The theorem is based on—I hope I will be allowed to say—a *conceptual truth* about triangles and not about facts on the triangle constructed in the execution of the proof.

In the same way (**m**), one could freely admit, states something about the truth-conditions of the message in (4), given that it says something about giving the truth-conditions of *any* statement, and (4) is a statement. However, by this very same fact, one can say that (**m**) does not give the truth-conditions for (4) *qua* particular utterance; (**m**) is not giving what should be the case in order for (4) to be true as opposed to the truth-conditions of, let's say, "Vous êtes le seul philosophe qùebecquois à cette Université," or

"La neige est blanche." In the same vein as "The Law of Causality is not a law but the form of a law," (**m**) is not a statement of (a variety of) truth-conditions of utterance (4), but the form that should take any indication of truth-conditions of *any* utterance which is a statement. In *Tractarian* terms (**m**) would be an attempt to state what can only be shown. I would not go so far; rather I would be happy with a much more modest conclusion: that (**m**) indicates the *precondition* for "giving the truth-conditions of an utterance that states something," much in the same way as the properties of any triangle are the precondition of our talking about a particular triangle of any kind. The so-called "incremental truth-conditions" are horses of a different colour: they are cases in which we *do state* something about particular utterances fulfilling the above precondition. However, if my characterisation of (**m**) as a precondition for giving truth-conditions is plausible, then my contention that (**m**) does not give truth-conditions for (4) will not be question begging, but a mere result of the differences in kind between establishing (a) the precondition for giving truth-conditions for *any* utterance which states something *whatever it could be*, and (b) stating something about individual utterances which state something *in concreto*. Therefore, the multifarious varieties of content (reflexive, indexical, etc.) cannot be, in my opinion, "systematic extensions" (Perry (2001a, p. 19)) of "official (mainly referential) content."

Perry could retort by saying that my objection is a mere restatement of the "official" view about truth-conditions. For, if reflexive truth-conditions are in fact conditions that an utterance must meet in order to be true and they *do* state how the world must be in order for the *utterance* to be true, how can I justify—philosophical prejudices excepted—my contention that they do not deserve the title of truth-conditions? I think Perry is playing some kind of trick here. He is asking us to consider a *particular* utterance like (4), an utterance that, given the story he told us, is true if and only if condition (**m**) is obtained. Then, he applies the following principle: the X-conditions of a thing are the conditions that a thing must meet in order to be X; (**m**) gives the conditions that (4) must meet in order to be true; therefore (**m**) gives truth-conditions of the particular utterance (4) (Perry (2001b, p. 5)). Of course, (**m**) does not give *the* truth conditions for (4), but nevertheless it gives—this is Perry's contention—*a variety* of truth-conditions ("reflexive truth-conditions") for it, *if we use the term in the ordinary way*. Now, it is a fact that (4) *is* a statement; it could have been, let's say, an order or a request. But this very fact is not something independent of "having truth-conditions": to be a statement is conceptually tied to the idea of an utterance expressing a proposition that, taken into account the context of the utterance, can be true or false. If I am right, this condition in (**m**) is simply empty; for what (**m**) really says is that (4) is true if and only if it is something susceptible to be true *and* it is in fact true. Using Perry's way of reasoning: if the X-condition of a thing is the condition that a thing must meet in order to be X, and the first condition in (**m**) gives the condition that (4) must meet in order to have truth-conditions; the first condition in (**m**) gives the condition for having truth-conditions of the particular utterance (4); that is: the first condition in (**m**) gives the *precondition* for (4) having truth-conditions. Nonetheless now it appears that (**m**) merely says that (4)—the message conveyed by it—is true if and only if it is true, the result one could expect if features used for giving the supposed truth conditions of utterance (4) are not peculiar to it. (For (**m**) only states that *m* is true if and only if it *can be true* and it *is* true that is trivially equivalent to *m* is true if and only if *m* is true.) Of course, I am not denying Perry the right to *stipulate* that the preconditions of having truth-conditions could be called truth-conditions, but one should admit that this is a different discussion.

### 3.1.4 Levels of informational content

Similar problems could appear with the notion of the informational content of an event. In *Reference and Reflexivity* (Perry (2001a, pp. 21ff)), Perry says that the content he ascribes to utterances should be interpreted in naturalistic terms, so to speak *à la* Dretske-Fodor. By "informational content of an event" he understands "what the world must be like in order for the event to have occurred. Such content is relative to constraints or laws, they are the source of the 'must' in 'must be like"' (Perry (2001a, p. 22)). Adapting again an example by Perry: this morning I found several letters on my desk at my office in the university. This event is an indication that someone was in my room early morning delivering the post. The constraints, laws, etc. alluded to by Perry work as follows: I know that postal items do not travel spontaneously to my desk and that they do not appear in my office by magic. Given such constraints, laws, etc., we can say that the state of my desk *contains information* about the previous delivery of my post. But if I know that a porter delivers my post every morning, that the porter is in fact the woman called Elena, and so on, the state of my desk will tell me that a porter was in my room delivering the post, that Elena was in my room delivering the post, that Elena is not yet on holiday..., and so on. Now, in my opinion this is part and parcel of the varieties of truth-conditions because of the link between content and truth-conditions. For a statement's content is simply the proposition which includes the conditions under which the statement is true. And this proposition, naturalistically interpreted, derives from the informational content of states and events. Given that informational content is relative to "constraints, laws and particular facts," propositions will vary accordingly between a *minimum* and a *maximum* of informational content. In principle, we could think of a minimum set of constraints, such that, for each event, they would provide us just with the *informational content that is common to any event giving informational content.* Aquinas' "*Aliquid movetur*," "Something happens" or whatever of this kind, could be utterances expressing what the world must be like in order for *any* event to have occurred. I mean: something like to these two utterances will have a content derived from the informational content of a particular event that has as informational content the form of any event. However, as in the case of the purported reflexive truth-conditions and much for the same reasons as in (**m**), it would be misleading to consider such "informational content" at the same level as, for example, "Elena was in my room delivering the post." The difference here would be not a matter of having a particular number of constraints; it would rather be a matter of the *kind* of constraints you have. Again, there must be a difference that is very easily overlooked if we adopt an "egalitarian" stance towards informational content. The referentialist would be glad to say that the difference is between having constraints (and therefore, informational content) and having no constraints at all and, therefore, no informational content. Or, if you prefer, it would be a difference between having constraints and having *empty* constraints on a particular content. And "empty constraints" probably could not determine a particular level of content from among indefinitely many levels of content. I would not say so much, but I believe that there is a core of truth in the referentialist's query. Again, it points to the differences in kind between varieties of informational content. For example, that everything has a cause could count as a constraint on informational content only "by courtesy" because it would be the precondition of any event having informational content.

## 3.2 Reichenbach's Curse

### 3.2.1 Token-reflexive expressions and reflexive content

In his *Elements of Symbolic Logic*, Hans Reichenbach developed—starting from an original idea by Bertrand Russell—his famous conception about a particular class of individual-descriptions constructed by reference to other individuals: "the class of descriptions in which the individual referred to is the act of speaking" (Reichenbach (1947, p. 284ff)). Between the special words indicating this reference Reichenbach lists "I," "you," "here," "now," "this" and devices such as tenses of verbs because they determine time using as the "reference point" the time when the words are uttered. Roughly speaking, the main idea is this. A word is defined as a class of tokens that are *equisignificant* rather than a class of words that are similar, for example, in shape. Therefore, a token-reflexive word is one "which refers to the corresponding token used in an individual act of speech or writing" (Reichenbach (1947, p. 284)). Token-reflexive words could be defined in terms of the expression "this token." Take, for example "I" in

(5) I am a philosopher;

the meaning of "I" would be the same as "the person who utters *this token*," where "*this token*" refers to the token of "I" in (5); "now" would mean the same as "the time at which *this token* is uttered," where "*this token*" refers to the token of "now" in a sentence, and so on. Obviously, each token of "this token" refers to a different token—a different set of noises or ink marks. Reichenbach's view is a very attractive account of indexicals but it is plagued with an endemic problem, which I will call Reichenbach's Curse: it *gets wrong*[6] the subject matter of token-reflexive sentences (the sentences in which there is a reflexive word). For suppose that Perry utters (5). Nobody would deny then that he is referring, and attracting the attention of his hearers, to himself, to the man John Perry, *and* to his utterance (5). However, there is no sensible way of interpreting Perry's utterance (5) as *saying*—even partially—that he is referring to the token of "I" that he is uttering. No doubt, when Perry refers to himself by means of a token-reflexive expression such as "I," this works by attracting attention to himself by means of the token of "I." But the latter is not the same as asserting that part of what Perry is saying by "I" in (5) is that he is referring to this very token of "I."

[6]This point is very similar to Frege's in "Ueber Sinn und Bedeutung." When trying to account for the difference in cognitive value between "$a = a$" and "$a = b$" he considers what would happen if the subject matter of both statements were the signs "$a$" and "$b$" themselves (the "metalinguistic" account). Frege explicitly objects to this result because it gets the subject matter of the two statements wrong: "a sentence like '$a = b$,"' he says, would no longer refer to a matter of fact but rather to our manner of designation; no genuine knowledge would be expressed by it."

Perry's critical referentialism makes use of Reichenbach's analysis. This is a terrific idea because in principle it seems to provide a coherent way of talking about descriptive content in the case of sentences containing indexicals. Perry's way of avoiding Reichenbach's Curse is to deny that "I" and "the person who utters *this token*" have the same meaning because, he says, "I" refers and "the person who utters *this token*" describes. Nevertheless, the good news in token-reflexive account is that "the person who utters *this token*" gives, at least, part of the meaning of "I" in giving the condition of designation that the English language associates with "I."[7] That is: if $\phi$ is an utterance of "I," the condition of designation for $\phi$ is *being the speaker of* $\phi$.[8] In this way, the proposition associated with (5) would be

(6) that *the speaker of* $\phi$ is a philosopher.

(6) gives the *reflexive* content of utterance (5) and this is called "reflexive" because it is about the utterance (5) itself. In fact, reflexive content is only a genus of which indexical content is a species. (For, take the identifying condition of "I"; such a condition is reflexive; generally, the indexical content is reflexive content given that reflexive identifying conditions are incorporated in the content. However, reflexive identifying conditions are only a species of reflexive content: "the particular case in which reflexivity is exploited by meaning.") One can say: (6) is tied to the truth-conditions of utterance (5) itself, but it is not part of what Perry is saying when uttering (5). But the referential content of (5) is

(7) that **Perry** is a philosopher,

and (7) is about the *man* John Perry, and its content has to do with the man John Perry being a philosopher: that is what Perry says in uttering (5). From this it follows that truth-conditions linked to (7) have to do with what is said. Furthermore, it is very easy to see why (6) and (7) should be quite different: for the sets of worlds in which (6) and (7) are true will be quite different. It goes without saying that an utterance such as

(8) You are a philosopher,

made by me addressing Perry has the same referential content as (5) but different reflexive (indexical) content, and so on. The distinction between reflexive (indexical) and referential content would have at least two effects. First, it seems to avoid what I called Reichenbach's Curse because reflexive (indexical) contents are not part of what is said. In utterance (5) Perry does not say that the person using "I" is a philosopher, but he says that he, the man Perry, is a philosopher even though he says this using a token with reflexive content. Second, the distinction will provide, among other things, for cases of co-referential and empty names. If the notion of truth-conditions is relative to some given facts, there will be varieties of truth-conditions tied to multiple relative

[7] This seems to be obvious, Perry says, if we reflect on what we undesrtand by hearing (5) without knowing who is uttering it.

[8] Here italics mean that we are talking about an identifying condition on the speaker of $\phi$, a condition that is instantiated by at most one object. The general proposition that the speaker of $\phi$ is a philosopher should be distinguished from the singular proposition that **the speaker of** $\phi$ is a philosopher, where the bold type indicates that the only individual satisfying the description is a philosopher. In this point, I am simply following Perry's notation.

contents naturalistically explained in turn via the notion of informational content. The cognitive significance of language could be explained by different reflexive contents of utterances with the same referential content. Empty names would need an additional notion of content—network content—"between reflexive and official [referential] content" working in a similar way as the well known causal chains in the direct reference account of proper names.

### 3.2.2 Perry's dilemma

So far, so good. But, does Perry in fact avoid Reichenbach's Curse? And, if our answer is "yes," how does he achieve such a result? Consider the two following propositions (written according to the above conventions):

(9) That *the person the speaker of (1) is addressing* is the only person from **Switzerland** teaching Philosophy at the university of **Nottingham**.

(10) That **Eros** is the only person from **Switzerland** teaching Philosophy at the university of **Nottingham**.

Both (9) and (10) give truth-conditions for (1). The difference is that (9) gives reflexive truth-conditions for (1) as result of fixing its meaning, whereas (10) gives truth-conditions for (1) as result of fixing its meaning *plus* the relevant contextual fact that **Eros** is the man that the speaker of (1) is addressing. Is there any reason for preferring (10) instead of (9) as the proposition expressed by (1)? Perry dismisses a possible Kaplanian rejoinder on the basis that (9) could have been a different proposition—we could have said a completely different proposition (let's say about François Recanati)—had the context of utterance (1) been different. Now, Perry apparently makes a change of tack asking the possible objector: Does (9) give us truth-conditions for (1)? And his answer is: of course it *does*. For, if the conditions specified in (9) are met, utterance (1) will be true. Does (9) give the *right* truth-conditions for (1)? Perry considers the possible objection that (9) does not provide us with either necessary or sufficient conditions for the truth of (1). True, it does not give us the right truth-conditions for (1) *provided that* what we have in mind is the proposition actually expressed by (1), that is: (10). But, Perry asserts, "I am asking about the truth-conditions of (1), the utterance itself" and "(9) gives us conditions on the actual world which must be met if utterance (1) is to be true [...]. If (9) is true, (1) will be, and vice versa" (Perry (2001a, p. 5)).

It is obvious from the previous section of this paper that my opinion is that Perry is moving very fast here. A crucial (and, I think, obscure) step in his argument against a Kaplanian critic is, as suggested before, Perry's complaint that such critic is "relying on the robustness of our intuitions about a certain concept which he [Kaplan] identifies in three ways: as *what he said*, as *the proposition expressed* and as *the content of his utterance*." At this point, Perry introduces by way of a question his notion of reflexive (indexical) content relying, more or less on the same kind of intuition as Kaplan. To the question "Does (9) give us truth-conditions for (1)?" the answer should be, according to Perry, "I think it does, in a perfectly clear sense." But note that this only works if we accept as a starting point that there are varieties of truth-conditions and all of them stand *at the same level*. (In fact, Perry takes the referential truth-conditions as the core notion of truth-conditions and he considers that other varieties of truth-conditions are "extensions" of the core notion.) However, when we ask for the reason behind this extension we are again left with "the robustness of our intuitions." For what Perry has to say is: "[...] we use that term ["truth-conditions"] in the ordinary way"[9] (Perry (2001b, p. 5)). Once this step is taken, the road is open to what I have called the *egalitarian* notion of truth-conditions and therefore, I am afraid, to overlooking the differences in kind between the supposed varieties of truth-conditions.

And here is my diagnosis. Perry faces a dilemma once he adopts a Reichenbach-like element in his approach to semantics. If he is to avoid Reichenbach's Curse he must escape the conclusion that the identifying condition *the person the speaker of (1) is addressing* is part of the subject matter of (1), or that the whole utterance (1) is itself part of such subject matter. Or, what amounts to the same: Perry must escape the conclusion that the speaker of (1) is talking about the way the English word "you" works or about the utterance (1) itself. At this point, he must make a choice. He could have taken the path of remaining faithful to the "official" concept of truth-conditions, trying to solve the problems along the lines of, let's say, Kaplan or perhaps using notions such as "presupposition" or anything from this constellation of concepts (a difficult task, I guess.) But Perry is a referentialist, more precisely, he is a *critical referentialist*, but a referentialist nonetheless. Therefore, he takes the path of considering the notion of truth-conditions as a relative concept, *given that any non-referentialist truth-conditions are extensions of the core referentialist notion.* Reflexive truth-conditions, for example, are just a species of the continuum of truth-conditions linked to reflexive contents. In this way, it seems that Reichenbach's curse has been overcome. For if someone points out that (9) is the proposition expressed by (1) Perry could reply that although (9) gives in fact (reflexive) truth-conditions for (1), *it is not* the proposition expressed by (1). (The proposition expressed by (1) is (10)). In fact, (9) just gives truth-conditions *on utterance (1) itself* and therefore our problem evaporates.

### 3.2.3 Reichenbach's Revenge

Nonetheless, there also exists Reichenbach's Revenge. For, what is really the meaning of "*to give the truth-conditions on the utterance (1) itself*"? One can rule freely that (9) is not the proposition expressed by (1) at the price of ignoring the differences in kind between (9) and (10) alluded to in part I. However, to extend the notion of truth-conditions in order to cover reflexive contents appears rather as a *verbal* manoeuvre: of course (1) is true if it has the (reflexive) content (9) and it is true that the pronoun "you" works that way in English. But the fact that "you" works precisely that way is neutral regarding the particular person selected in each utterance. The actual working of "you" is, so to speak, a precondition of (1) having "referential" truth-conditions and, therefore, the oddity of talking here of truth-conditions when what we have is, in fact, a

[9] In fact, the term "truth-conditions" is not an ordinary term, it is a term of art, and it is at least a dubious enterprise to try to judge the uses of it by ordinary standards. The first use of this term as a term of art probably occurs at §32 of the first volume of Frege's *Grundgesetze*: "Every such name of a truth-value *expresses* a sense, a *thought*. Namely, by our stipulations it is determined under what conditions the name denotes the True. The sense of this name—the *thought*—is the thought that these conditions are fulfilled."

precondition of having truth-conditions for each every and particular utterance in which "you" appears. But if the arguments given in the first part of the paper (1.1-1.1.4) are sound, I would be entitled to claim that Perry's proposal is very close to saying that (9) lists (partially) empty truth-conditions. Not because they are not referential truth-conditions, but because they are preconditions for the expression concerned to have truth-conditions. And here is Reichenbach's Revenge: Perry can rule that (9) is not the proposition expressed by (1) and it is not part of what the speaker of (1) says; this is his way of avoiding Reichenbach's Curse. Now, if I am right, this amounts to saying that the contents linked to the supposed truth-conditions are (partially) empty contents too. However, probably empty contents are not contents at all or, at least, it is very dubious that they could fulfil the requirements that any candidate to play the role of cognitive content must meet. But this is a different question that I cannot address here.

## Acknowledgments

I would like to thank my colleagues Alfonso García Suárez and Jorge Rodríguez Marqueze and the anonymous referee for their valuable suggestions. Mrs. Penny Metcalffe's help was definitive for fixing my rather oscillating English.

## References

Burks, Arthur. 1949. Icon, Index and Symbol. *Philosophy and Phenomenological Research* 9:673–689.

Perry, John. 1997. Indexicals and demonstratives. In B. Hale and C. Wright, eds., *A Companion to the Philosophy of Language*, pages 586–612. Oxford: Blackwell.

Perry, John. 2001a. *Reference and Reflexivity*. Stanford: CSLI Publications.

Perry, John. 2001b. Reference, Reflexivity and Indexicality. paper read at the First International Workshop on Semantics, Pragmatics and Rhetoric (SPR-01), Donostia/San Sebastián.

Reichenbach, Hans. 1947. *Elements of Symbolic Logic*. New York: The Macmillan Company.

Wittgenstein, Ludwig. 1961. *Tractatus Logico-Philosophicus*. London: Routledge and Kegan Paul. (With a new translation by D. F. Pears and B. F. McGuiness).

4

# Fiction and Deception: How Cooperative is Literature?

SALVATORE ATTARDO

"The tragic poet is an imitator, and, therefore, like all other imitators, he is thrice removed (...) from the truth." (Plato, *Republic* X, 597e)

Plato famously called for the expulsion of writers from the Republic under the charge that they were liars, an effective, if somewhat ham-fisted, way of posing the epistemological question of the status of fictional discourse in relation to non-fictional (factual) discourse.

This paper is concerned with this question, but not exclusively. I will briefly consider the idea that fiction is made of pro-social lies and then move on to speech act theory and the idea that fiction is non-cooperative. The central points around which my approach revolves are that both lies and fiction merely pretend to produce cooperative utterances (the difference being that lies are deceptive, of course).

I will then proceed to complicate the issue by considering a host of genres in which fictionality and factuality are mixed and, in short, the fact that the boundary between factual and fictional narrative is blurred. This is a traditional problem for the theory of narrative, since it is both difficult to differentiate between truth and fiction, and a pretense theory of fiction needs an algorythm to switch back and forth (and has been attacked for lacking it). I argue, in a somewhat partisan way, that the approach to pragmatics that I have been developing in the past years happens to provide an answer to both problems (the principle of non-cooperation and the "optimal" approach, respectively).

I close with two issues: why do we care so much about literature, to the point of involving matters of life and death in issues that concern fictional subjects, and why are we so interested in it? I argue that the willingness of accepting non-cooperative text comes from the human desire for narrative, because narrative imposes causality on the world.

I would like to stress a significant point: I see my contribution to the issue of the

*Meaning, Intentions, and Argumentation.*
Kepa Korta and Joana Garmendia (eds.).

pragmatics of literature as providing a way out of some problems of the commonsensical (and hence) widely adopted view of fiction as "pretense." I make no claim of having "discovered" the pretense approach and certainly do not claim that what follows is a complete treatment of any of the issues it addresses. In my eyes, the value of what follows is that it answers, using contemporary pragmatic tools, some very old questions.

## 4.1 Literature as lies

My argument is simply this: that we might as well concede that Plato is correct in telling us that mimetic art is imitation and hence falsification (i.e., not truth), but that the consequence that he draws (and that are usually drawn) do not follow, because telling a lie is not a problem. Lies are not intrinsically ethical acts. The ethical nature of a lie is determined by the goals of the liar. There are pro-social lies and there are egoistic lies (and most fall somewhere in between). Thus a literary lie (which is non-cooperative) may be said for cooperative goals (entertaining, educating, recreating, distracting, etc.). In Attardo (1997b) I review the distinction between cooperation for the sake of communication (locutionary, i.e., linguistic goals) and cooperation for the sake of extra-linguistic goals (perlocutionary, i.e., extra-linguistic goals). Hence literature is non-cooperative (locutionarily) but cooperative (perlocutionarily).

Moreover, the debate on fiction vs. non-fiction has focused primarily if not exclusively on truth (or lack thereof). However, there are other ways of being non-cooperative, i.e., by violating other maxims.

### 4.1.1 Disclaimer

As we have seen, Plato set the stage for the consideration of literature within the parameter of truth (and its opposite: lies). The literature on lying and deception is quite large. Reviewing it would require a separate paper. So, I will have to limit myself to a few blunt statements, which I hope have the strength of common sense to back them up. Similarly, I will not attempt a complete review of those who have already said what I will claim on any specific point. This too would require a separate paper. Nor will I attempt, for similar reasons, a summary of all that has been written on fiction (either in philosophy or in literary criticism).

### 4.1.2 Lies

Let me start by stating very clearly that most of the literature on lying comes from philosophy and, more precisely, from ethics. The problem is: how wrong is it to lie and, subordinately, when is it acceptable to lie, if ever? As one can imagine, in order to decide when it may be OK to lie, one has to determine what a lie is.

Within linguistics, the best known account of lies is Coleman and Kay's (Coleman and Kay (1981, p. 28)) which can be summed up in the following three aspects:

1. S believes $p$ to be false
2. In saying $p$ S intends to deceive H
3. $p$ is false

which basically encode a "folk" view of lies (or in other words: this is how untrained people think of lies). However, it can be shown that points 1 and 3 do not hold.

That points 1 and 3 do not hold was already known in antiquity: for example, Augustine notes that one can lie by telling what is objectively true and knowing that to be the case. Moreover, one can lie by omission, i.e., by not saying something: hence there is no $p$ that can be false. In general, we now recognize that one can lie by implicature, i.e., by letting H draw inferences that are false.[1]

Hence, what is left is S's intention to deceive. So, we can reach the definition of a lie as some meaning that S intends H to retrieve (either propositionally, or inferentially) which S believes to be false (the latter stipulation is added to rule out error). Here things are complicated by the fact that a well formed lie has to be uttered with the intention to deceive. However, a book labeled "fiction" can hardly be said to have been "uttered" (in a broad sense of uttering) with the intention to deceive the readers into thinking that the events related in the book actually happened. See section (4.2).

Barnes (1994) in fact, maintains that since literary works are clearly labeled as such, their authors are not lying. Clearly, fiction is not deceptive, in the sense that it is clearly labeled in the para-text (Genette (1987)) as such. So, in a sense, Barnes' remark (which is quoted here only for its representativeness) is disingenuous: the (implied) author does his/her best to try to convey the illusion of factuality, using a gamut of tools, ranging from naive direct addresses to the reader to embedded narrators, who implicitly attest the factuality of the events, and more broadly speaking by using realism, which is a sort of warranty of (potential at least) factuality. It is only with extremely sophisticated authors such as Sterne, Pirandello, or Robbe-Grillet that the realist illusion is exploded (and of course Sterne and Pirandello still can be counted as realists at the meta-level).

So, literary authors want their readers to believe the stories they read, at least while they are reading them, and most frequently beyond that (see the whole idea of art being "true" to life or that art can "teach."). Moreover, often literary works are understood to refer to real-world facts, and their authors as making statements that apply to the real world: consider Bulgakov's *Master and Margarita* which obviously describes fantastic events (the devil's rampage through Moscow) but also obvioulsy denounces Stalinism (and because of that was never published in his lifetime). Similarly, but in a totally different context, Rushdie's novel *Satanic Verses* resulted in a fatwa calling for his (non-fictional) death. Nor is this phenomenon limited to modernity: it is reported that a wave of suicides followed Goethe's *The Sorrows of Werther.*

### 4.1.3 Literature as licensed lying

Here, Raskin's idea of "licensed lying" comes in handy: essentially, Raskin (1992) says, under certain circumstances, it is societally expected that a certain amout of lying will take place. Sophisticated members of the society will be aware of this fact and take it into account when interacting. Thus, for example, in a sales situation, the participants will be aware of the fact that the seller will try to represent the item to be sold under the best possible light and that quite possibly this will involve some amount of lying.

It is easy to apply the idea of licensed lying to literature: essentially, the reader of a novel enters into a tacit agreement with the author: the reader will suspend disbelief for

[1] Incidentally, this can be a problem for the stipulation, common in the field, that lies have to be propositional. This can be repaired by assuming that implicatures are ultimately propositional.

the duration of the novel in exchange for entertainment, cathartic emotional activation, or other pleasurable feelings elicited by literary texts.

But if that is the case, and I believe it is, where does all the fuss come from? I believe that there are two factors at play: one—the simplest one—is that the ethical treatment of lying has muddied the waters. The second one is that the idea of licensed lying, while correct, is not the end of the story.

Let's consider the first issue: is lying morally wrong? The answer is (as is the case in most interesting questions): it depends. It has been clear since the earliest treatments of lying that some lies are good. We even have the term "white lie" to indicate a lie that is acceptable (often with the connotation that it concerns a matter of small importance). It is also a well known fact that a significant part of politeness consists of not telling unpleasant truths (or mitigating them). However, consider a somewhat extreme example: suppose that one were in a position to save the lives of a thousand innocent persons by uttering a lie (for the sake of the argument, let the lie be a real lie, not a white lie, or any attenuated form of lying). Clearly, one would be justified in lying. It follows that lies are not morally either right or wrong: it is the goals of the liars that make the lies morally acceptable or inacceptable. See Scheibe (1980) on the moral irrelevance of lying.[2]

But what of the claim that lying is always damaging of the interests of H (who has a permanent goal of knowing the truth (Castelfranchi and Poggi (1998)))? That is true, but irrelevant: agents have contrasting goals all the time. There is nothing special about the goal of having the truth rather than, say, more food. Agents constantly struggle with other agents.

So, let's recapitulate: Plato may be right that literature is made of lies. But these lies are uttered to a sophisticated audience who fully expects that they will be lied to; and in any case, even if they were duped by the lies, the goals of the literary authors are positive and hence no moral stigma should be attached to the fact that they lie to their audience.

But what of the fact that some members of the audience take literary works to be factual reports (witness Orson Welles' panic-inducing radio production of the *War of the Worlds*)? Those cases don't really concern us, because the moment that I take a literary work to be a factual report, I no longer treat it as a literary work at all.

### 4.1.4 Is licensed lying all there is to literature?

Let us turn now to the second issue: is it the case that licensed lying is all there is to literature? I believe that this is not the case.

My argument is based on the following observations:

- Even fiction is not totally fictional: many aspects of it are veridic; for example, in the Sherlock Holmes' stories, London exists, Baker Street exists, etc. It is only Holmes and Watson that do not exist factually and of course the events they purportedly took

[2]Interestingly, the effects of an action have no bearing on its moral status: suppose that I give a piece of chocolate to another person, who is allergic to it, while I am not aware of this fact. The allergic person is akrasic, eats the chocolate and becomes severely ill. I bear no moral responsibility for his/her actions (note that if the person were a child, the situation would be different). Thus lies told with good intentions may have disastrous effects and vice-versa.

part in. A better description of the status of the fictional world would be a blended counterfactual mental space between reality and a counterfactual space in which Holmes and Watson exist. In other words: the author sets up a counterfactual space in which all non-factual elements of a story are present (this may be a very sparcely furnished space, or an elaborate description); what we think of as fiction is *always* a blended space between the "reality" mental space and the counterfactual mental space. A fiction containing exclusively counterfactual (fictional) elements would be uninterpretable, since we would have no rules of inference, except very general morphosyntactic ones: consider Carroll's *Jabberwocky*). This is related to, but different from, the observation that many utterances in a fictional text are not fictional (see below).

- the desire to be "taken in" by the recipients of literature, which I argue goes well beyond the "willing suspension of disbelief" of Coleridgian memory. This may well be an evolutionary remnant of a trait that gave some sort of evolutionary advantage to those humans who could build narratives (i.e., could find causal connections) and believed those narratives (for example, to find food).[3]
- the existence of a host of more or less recently labeled genres that blur the boundary between fiction and factual narrative. This is called "creative non-fiction." (CNF)

**We want literary works to be true**

This may be controversial, but normal people (I am ruling out literary critics and other outliers in the bell curve of education) firmly assume that literature must be true. And this is true today, as much as it was millennia ago, in our so-called sophisticated, post-modern ironical societies. I base this claim on an acute observation, which I owe to Umberto Eco (2005): recently there has arisen a small cottage industry of books[4] that argue for or against the Christologic thesis at the center of " *The Da Vinci Code*," a rather poorly written but captivating mystery by Dan Brown (2003). Eco's occasion for writing was the publication by an authoritative Catholic figure of one such book refuting the *Da Vinci Code*. Eco's point was this: why bother refuting a work of fiction unless a significant number of people take the fiction seriously (i.e., as non fiction)? Further examples of this attribution of factuality to fiction can be found in Pinker (1997, p. 538–539).

In short, it takes extensive training (roughly a PhD) to eradicate the idea that literature tells the truth. And when one has finally accepted the fact that literature is not truthful, there arise all sorts of genres (known in the US as "creative non-fiction") which base in large part their attraction on the truthful nature of their "stories." Thus, travel writers purport to tell the truth about their adventures, when the mere selection of facts to report, while inevitable, fictionalizes the objective-report-of-experience: consider that taping a conversation and transcribing it comes nowhere close to producing anything even remotely redable, let alone literarily pleasant (and this may be the greatest lesson to be learned from Conversation Analysis).

[3] I am skeptical of evolutionary accounts of cognitive facts, as they seem to boil down to finding a story that rings true, and as we shall see, humans are very good at finding stories and enjoy this way too much. This is not to say that evolutionary accounts of cognitive functions do not have a certain plausibility.

[4] A search on Amazon.com reveals some 30 books on the subject and as many downloadable articles.

## Creative non-fiction

Despite claims to it being a new genre, CNF has always existed, Thucydides' (between 460 and 455 BC–circa 400 BC) *History of the Peloponnesian War* and Xenophon's (c. 427-355) *Anabasis* are probably the best known early example of the "genre."

**Definition of CNF** A brief survey of definitions of CNF nets the following results:

- actual facts/events as subject matter
- literary techniques
  - characterization
  - author's engagement
  - literary voice
  - polished language
  - story/narration
- artistic vision (Dobler (2005), Druker (2005))

**How cooperative is CNF?** It is fascinating to see that the definitions of CNF focus on the factuality and truthfulness of the genre (understandably, since this is the only definitory difference from regular fiction), thus highlighting by default the theoretical assumption of fundamental untruthfulness of regular creative writing. However, note how they give only to take away, so to speak, since in the next breath they note that "literary" techniques such as characterization may override the committment to factuality: thus a narrator would presumably feel free to condense different meetings with one character, edit his/her words, change the temporal order of facts, etc. to achieve a better literary effect (assuming for the sake of the argument that the author is still committed to factual truth).

But let us ask ourselves the obvious question: how factual is writing, any writing, be it creative or not? In fact, this is a misleading question. Consider this: no description of an actual event will ever match the event in its phenomenological complexity. Any representation underdetermines the represented. Even the most skilled of writers had to choose what to write about. This choice means the exclusion of all the other things that he/she could have written about.[5]

Critical debate on CNF is not primarily interested in factuality (let alone cooperation), but some interesting issues from our perspective emerge nonetheless. Let me quote a couple of more or less recent discussions[6] which argue for the erosion of the bound-

[5]The same applies, mutatis mutandis, to mechanical recording of any kind: microphones capture only a range of sounds, cameras have to aimed, recording has to be started and ended, etc. Even in a milieu such as the Internet, where all exchanges and documents are potentially archivable, any selection of material to be presented as "the work" will reintroduce the arbitrariness of selection. No-one can read/vision/listen to the totality of information produced even for a single hour. But let us imagine a sci-fi scenario in which some machine records all the perceptions of an individual A and broadcasts them to another individual (B): would we then have an absolutely objective reporting on the comings and goings of subject A? Yes. But it would take exactly one hour of B's life to experience one hour of A's life. It is an interesting question if that would be considered "art," since it would be indistinguishable from living A's life. It is reported that after Jack Kerouac's success with *On the Road*, people took to taping Neal Cassady's (the real life inspiration for the Neal Moriarty character) speech in the hope of transcribing it. The result was useless.

[6]I am grateful to Ann Amicucci for directing me to these sources on the fictionality of travel writing.

aries between fiction and non-fiction, e.g., Packard (1990), Sherrill (2000). Holland and Huggan (1998) very clearly point to the free admixture of fact and fiction in the genre of travel writing, speaking of a "license" of "entertaining fraud" (7), of "freely mix[ing] fact and fable" (9), and of a "license to exaggerate or even to invent" (Ibid.). Sherrill (2000) even more forcefully argues that "in the case of the new American picaresque [i.e., autobigraphical travel narrative] heavy lines between the 'real' and the 'created,' the 'genuine' and the imagined, the autobiography and the novel , fact and fiction, cannot be confidently drawn" (Sherrill (2000, p. 73); see 73-80 for further examples and discussion.)

Nor is the admixture of fact and fiction limited to travel writing. Historical memoirs also blend fact and fiction. Consider the example of Edmund Morris' biography of Ronald Reagan (*Dutch*, 1999) which contains several fictional characters, including an alter ego of Morris, who are not identified as fictional in the footnotes of the book (incidentally, the outcry[7] that followed the publication is itself interesting, since it reveals that the biography of a living president is not considered appropriate for historical novelization). Nowhere is the fictional nature of the book acknowledged (the subtitle is "A memoir of Ronald Reagan"), except for a passage in the back flap which identifies "a literary technique whereby, in the earlier chapters (...) Morris's [sic] biographical mind becomes in effect another character in the narrative, recording long-ago events with the same eyewitness vividness (and absolute documentary fidelity) (...)" A few lines below this technique is defined as "a new biographical style" in a direct quote by the author.

Another (auto-)biographical example is *I, Rigoberta Menchú* (Menchú (1983)), made more complex by the fact that the story was claimed to have been recorded (literally, with a tape recorder) by a French anthropologist, Elisabeth Burgos-Debray; who, however, claims not to have added or altered any matter of substance. Menchú's book was revealed to contain several episodes which were not factual: for example, the author had not been present at her brother's death (Stoll (1999); see also Arias (ed.) (2001)). It is clear that the factual nature of the Guatemalan army's oppression of the indigenous populations is not in question, but that Menchú departs from the factual truth for effect.

### 4.1.5 A referentialist (mini)theory of fiction.

At this point, my reader may well be wondering what my definition of fiction is, given that I have argued that there is no clear boundary between the two, in terms of literary genres. Indeed, in order to account for the distinction between fiction and factual narrative, we need to have recourse to a philosophical, not a literary notion. Obviously, a simple referential semantic theory will do the trick: a factual narrative is one which describes events, objects, states of affairs, etc. that exist in the real world. A fictional narrative describes entities that do not (either entirely or more probably partially) have a referent in the real world.[8] Needless to say, there are plenty of ontological issues that

[7] For example, Masur (1999), "Dutch is deliberately deceptive and undeniably bad history," and that is not a particularly negative review.

[8] Non-Referentialist "theories" of fiction go back at least to Frege, (see Cebik (1984, p. 41)). A good formulation can be found in Park, quoted in Cebik (1984, p. 41) "To call X a fiction is to indicate that the words and the sentences in the linguistic products are not used to refer to the real world." I will not try to address the issue of whether fictional sentences are false (Russell, Quine), or neither true nor false (Strawson, Ryle) (see Eaton (1972, p. 164)).

surround a theory of this kind, but for my purposes in this context it is perfectly adequate. I will mention possible worlds, in what follows. Let me make it clear that a possible world account is entirely compatible with the naive referentialist (mini)theory I have invoked: any possible world representation will have one world conveniently labeled "reality": all factual reports refer to entities within this world.

### 4.1.6 Fiction as a language game

A basic encyclopedia definition (Wikipedia) of (non-)fiction reads:

> Non-fiction is an account or representation of a subject which is presented as fact. This presentation may be accurate or not; that is, it can give either a true or a false account of the subject in question. It is one of the two main divisions in writing, particularly used in libraries, the other being fiction. Essays, journals, documentaries, scientific papers, photographs, biographies, textbooks, technical documentation like user manuals, diagrams and journalism are all common examples of non-fiction works and fiction within any of these works is usually regarded as dishonest. Other works can legitimately be either fiction or non-fiction, such as letters, magazine articles, histories, websites, speeches and travelogues. Although they are mostly either one or the other it is not uncommon for there to be a blend of both, particularly non-fiction with a dash of fiction for added spice.

Let us note the naive assumption that fiction does not incorporate factual information. However, in their naiveté, the Wikipedians make a very significant point: "fiction within any of these works [non-fiction] is usually regarded as dishonest." This is a fundamentally important point: the pragmatic (in a non-linguistic sense) attitude toward fiction and non-fiction is the real matter at stake: the speaker of factual narrative/text is held to a moral/practical standard, that can be punished socially ("dishonest"). Conversely, the author of fiction escapes any such prosecution (for example, Nicholson Baker's *Checkpoint* (2004) describes a character's case for killing George W. Bush, the president of the United States. Mr. Baker is still free to go as he pleases).

So, to quote Wittgenstein, when we tell a fictional story we engage in a different language game (*Sprachspiel*) than when we make up a story (Wittgenstein (1953, p. 11)). The rules of the language game are different if we want to engage in fiction or factual narration, just like soccer and rugby have different rules for handling the ball with your hands.

Does this mean that we sink into a free-for-all social constructivism? Not really, because the referentialist mini-theory of fiction anchors factuality to naive-referentialism. Note of course that naive referentialism fares pretty badly under the withering criticism of Perry (2001). But here I am using referentialism not as a foundation for semantics, but, much more modestly, factuality.

## 4.2 Speech Acts and Literature

Having addressed, however in a limited and partial fashion, the issues of fictionality and truth, it is time to broaden our perspective to a more pragmatic perspective. As is well known, Austin and Searle see literature as a "parasitic" or "aetiolated" (Austin (1962, p. 104), Searle (1969, p. 57, 78-79)) use of language.[9]

[9] Searle (1969, p. 78) speaks of a "let's-pretend mode of discourse."

Searle's *The Logical Status of Fictional Discourse*, first published in 1974-75, then in Searle (1979), develops a speech act approach to literature and fiction.[10] He distinguishes between literature (which he claims is a "family resemblance" category), which is essentially a social construct and lacks a central defining feature, and fiction, which he sets out to analyze. Searle's main point is that the speaker (in its usual broad sense which includes writers, poets, etc.) of a work of fiction "pretends[11] to perform a series of illocutionary acts" (1979, p. 65). Given this definition, he further argues that the "identifying criterion" of fictionality therefore must "lie in the illocutionary intentions of the author" (65).[12] Petrey (1990, p. 67-68) takes exception with this claim. I tend to agree with Petrey, in this case, because (as we have seen) the boundary of fictionality is porous and texts that start out as factual are redefined under pressure from (some of) their readers as (partially) fictional. The opposite case holds as well: texts which were intended as fictional become factual (e.g. Jules Verne's submarine). The best way to put this issue may be (Brown and Steinmann (1978, p. 149)) point that texts are fictional due to the intention of their author but are *taken* as such due to a decision of their audience.[13]

Since an author is pretending to produce an illocutionary act, he/she "has no committment whatever as regards [the] truth" of his/her utterance (1979, p. 59).[14] Tellingly, Searle's account of fiction brings it very close to lies: "what distinguishes fiction from lies is the existence of a separate set of conventions which enables the author to go through the motions of making statements which he knows to be not true even though he has no intention to deceive" (1979, p. 67). To put it simply: lies are fictions told with the intention to deceive. So, according to Searle, fictions and lies work like this:

(intention to deceive (intention to pretend (intention to mean)))

Finally, Searle addresses the issue that "most fictional stories contain non-fictional

[10]Other approaches include Eaton's "translocution" (Eaton (1972, 1973, p. 171)) in which the author "speaks through" the characters: "thereby avoiding the necessity of making liars" of the authors (Eaton (1973, p. 229)).

[11]Searle lists several quasi-synonyms to "pretend" ("acting as if, going through the motions, imitating") to make the point that the terminology "pretense" matters little. It should be noted that I make no ontological commitment (or lack thereof) to the existence of the objects referred to in the pretend act of fiction. Crittenden (1991, p. 45-52) lists a number of problems with a theory of pretend reference. My claim is merely that the speaker pretends to cooperate, at some level, not necessarily all of them. On the ontological status of fictional objects and more generally artistic ones, see Varzi (2005, p. 89-103).

[12]"What makes it a work of fiction is, so to speak, the illocutionary stance that the author takes toward it" (Searle (1979, p. 65)).

[13]It should be noted that the view of fiction as a pretend speech act is not original, in the sense that considering fiction a "pretense" is esentially a commonsensical approach, which, as mentioned above, was adopted by Frege and many others (see a review in Schmidt (1976, p. 162-162), but in fact goes back much further and is ultimately related to the Platonic view discussed in the opening of this essay. On Searle's conception of fiction and how to expand it (see Fotion (2003)). The Derridian "critique" of speech act theory is outside the purview of this paper. For a discussion of Derrida's general position vis-à-vis linguistics (see Attardo (1993a)). For a discussion of Derrida's views in relation to Austin, see Petrey (1990, p. 131-146) which has some discussion of the Searle/Derrida polemic. For a highly tendentious Derridian view of the issue, see Robinson (1997). For a very stimulating explanation of the different frameworks that Searle and Derrida operate from, see Mulligan (2003).

[14]Fiction is the "performing [of] utterance acts with the intention of [...] suspend[ing] the normal illocutionary committments of the utterances" (1979, p. 68).

elements" (Searle (1979, p. 72)) or, to put it differently, "sometimes the author of a fictional story will insert utterances in the story which are not fictional and not part of the story" (73-74). Searle's explanation is that not all the text of a "work of fiction" is fictional (i.e., a fictional text may include factual information). Petrey (1990, p. 66-67) objects to this claim because it would force the reader to an impossibly complex shifting in and out of fictionality. I believe that this objection is rebutted by the Non-Cooperation Principle (NCP; see below 4.4). The same goes for the other criticism that Petrey addresses to Searle, namely the lack of a heuristic for when to apply the suspension of illocutionary conventions (i.e., how does the reader know when to switch to a fictional interpretation?). Once more, the NCP's provides a set of heuristics independently motivated that handle this problem (i.e., switch to fiction when you encounter information incompatible with your representation of reality and return to reality as soon as possible).

I claim, along the lines of Austin, Searle, and Ohmann (1971), that "the writer pretends to report discourse"; see also Brown and Steinmann (1978, p. 150). Pratt objects[15] specifically to Ohmann's definition because " if we are to use these characteristics to define literature, they must be shown to be unique to literature. And they are not" (Pratt (1977, p. 91)) insofar cases such as hyperbole, teasing, kidding around, imitations, verbal play, hypothetical discourse, planning, imagining, fantasizing, irony, insulting, etc. would fall under the same aegis. But of course Pratt is wrong because we are *not* to use these critieria to differentiate literature from non-literature, simply because one cannot in principle do so (see, for example, Searle's claim reported above that "literature" does not have a defining feature). Similarly, Schmidt (1976) and Fish (1980) both reject Searle's approach because it cannot separate literature from non-literature on the grounds of fictionality. The objection is irrelevant: there's no reason to believe that fictionality and literature are coextensive. In fact, fictionality is present in a great many non-literary works: for example, the US government's documents claiming the presence of weapons of mass destruction in Iraq were certainly fictional but hardly literary.

Pratt's (1977) own account[16] of literature using speech acts claims that the author of a text (the actual person who writes/invents the text) is flouting Grice's CP and communicating an implicature that the text is worth reading, focusing on, or, in short, being perceived as a literary work. The characters, and most notably the narrator, may opt out the CP or even violate it occasionally, but at the level of the grand speech act of the telling of the story/writing the work, the author is implicating, through a flout (Pratt (1977, pp. 165, 178, 191, 217)).

This thesis is patently wrong, because it presupposes what it claims to demonstrate. If anything, the physical author of a text (to differentiate him/her from the implied author) is ostensively displaying the existence of the text. Pratt presupposes what needs to be demonstrated, i.e., that the physical author agrees with, stands by, or at least is responsible for what the fictional characters in the text do/say. To use her own example, suppose that I read Robbe-Grillet's *La jalousie* and I deduce from the text that it is

[15] Although she agrees with the analysis per se: "I think such an analysis is in itself correct" (Pratt (1977, p. 173)).

[16] Written before Searle's pretense account was widely available.

a clever implication of a psychological state of mind of a paranoid narrator. First, Mr. Robbe-Grillet, the actual author of the novel, has strongly and publicly decried any such psychologizing reading. Fine, one could argue, the author is simply mistaken, and the text or its implied author are implicating the paranoid reading. But this requires attributing to the (implied) author an intentional stance toward the text (i.e., that the author meant the text to be read as such). However, in a strict Gricean paradigm (or post-Gricean, the same argument would apply to weak-implicatures, see Sperber and Wilson (1986)) we can only proceed with this attribution iff we can assume that the author is following the CP (or relevance). But in the case of literature, humor, lies, etc. we have *prima facie* evidence that the author is precisely *not* doing so. Hence, no such attribution of intentionality may subsist. What is left is the possibility that the text signifies ostensively, i.e., naturally. I return to this idea below (section 4.5.2).[17]

So, recapping, if fiction is a pretend speech act, it shares a very significant trait with lies and other non-cooperative covert acts: they all pretend to perform some cooperative act, while in fact pursuing a different agenda. Herein, must the truth of the Platonic condemnation of mimetic art be found.

## 4.3 Is there a CP for literature?

Pratt (1977, p. 147 and passim) claims that literature has "different standards" than regular speech: "the standards of quantity, quality, and manner for display texts differ from those that Grice suggests for declarative speech acts." Elsewhere, Pratt has noted that narratives must have tellability, which goes beyond relevance, in that it includes a fourth feature, beyond the first three that define relevance:

1. truth
2. non-obvious truth
3. "relate somehow to the discourse in progress and to the addressee" (Pratt (1977, p. 134))
4. "tellability must represent state of affairs that are held to be unusual, contrary to expectations, or otherwise problematic." (136)

But Pratt goes further than that: "a description of literary speech acts will, at least in some cases, have to take into account both the CP and maxims as defined for the work's genre and the CP and maxims as defined by the fictional speaker's utterance" (Pratt (1977, p. 203)) Readers familiar with humor theory will immediately recall Raskin's (Raskin (1985, p. 100-104)) CP for jokes.

[17]Interestingly, talking about jokes, Pratt says: "there are contexts where it is appropriate for the fiction/non-fiction line to remain completely undefined. This is often the case for jokes. The stand-up comedian (...) makes no committment whatever to the truth of his anecdote. (...) The question of veracity simply doesn't seem to matter that much when the point of the utterance is understood to be pleasure." (Pratt (1977, p. 97)). It is unclear why, if in the case of jokes the hearer is left to puzzle out the fictiveness of the possible world of the text on the basis of "if it is implausible enough" (ibid.), in the case of a novel, we are to accept that the author means what he/she says. Note also in passing that implausibility is simply not a good criterion to determine factuality. It is plausible enough that this morning I had a breakfast of toast and orange juice. I did not. This is not to say that *prima facie* plausibility is not a good heuristic of factuality.

I have argued against proliferating CPs elsewhere (Attardo (1999, 2000a)) and my own pragmatic model merely requires the presence of a "principle of non-cooperation" which describes the rational ways of non-cooperating.

A different tack to essentially the same erroneous conclusion, is that the rules of the CP are somehow "suspended" (e.g., Fotion speaks of putting the "rules of language use," which are very close to the CP, "in deep freeze" and of "suspending" them; (Fotion (2003, p. 37)). The problem with the suspension idea is that, while the activation of the suspension has some plausibility, no one ever discusses how the rules are re-activated. A different approach is to simply see the CP as always active and the speakers negotiating its constraints against other principles (such as the NCP) also always active. This approach will remind people of optimality theory and that's indeed why I have referred, not too seriously, to my approach as Optimal Pragmatics.

## 4.4 NCP

The facetiously named non-cooperative principle (NCP), claims that violations of the CP are not random, but they follow certain rational rules, The NCP attempts to propose some of these rules. As a first approximation, the Least Disruption Principle (LDP) has been proposed. The LDP seems to be subordinate to the NCP.[18] The LDP's wording is as follows: Super-maxim: Minimize your violation of the CP;

1. limit your violation of the CP to the smallest possible conversational unit (one utterance, one conversational turn, one speech exchange);
2. try to link the entire CP-violating unit to the rest of the interaction, for example by finding a certain appropriateness to the CP-violating unit;
3. limit your violation of the CP to smallest possible distance from its requirements;
4. if you must violate a maxim do so in the direction that is expected by your audience (i.e., say what your audience wants to hear).[19]

A significant connection between the theory of pragmatics I have been elaborating and possible worlds analysis of fiction comes from Ryan's (1980) "principle of minimal departure" which states that "we construe the world of fiction and counterfactuals as being the closest possible to the reality we know. This means that we will project upon the world of the statement everything we know about the real world, and that we will make only those adjustments which we cannot avoid" (p. 406). As is obvious Ryan's minimal departure is a special case of my own "least disruption" principle (and would fall under point 3). I was not aware of Ryan's work when I proposed the LDP.

Ryan's minimal departure and the least disruption principles neatly handle the admixture of fictionality and factuality in literature, with a general heuristic that roughly boils down to "assume that anything that is not *prima facie* fictitious is factual."

[18] It is unclear at this time if there are aspects of the NCP that the LDP does not cover; if this should turn out not to be the case, the two would be indistinguishable.

[19] Cf. Castelfranchi and Poggi (1998, p. 139) "a cognitive agent prefers to conserve favored knowledge and to reject the disliked one." My formulation was arrived at independently.

## 4.5 How cooperative is fiction?

I will argue that fiction (and literature in general) is non-cooperative.[20] Let me address first two objections, an obvious and a subtle one. The obvious objection first: since H must cooperate with S for the literary text to "get through" so to speak, it would follow that the exchange is cooperative.[21] That some degree of cooperation is necessary in any exchange is true but irrelevant: in a lie H and S must cooperate to the extent that the liar must get his/her lie across. That does not render the exchange cooperative. Once more, the distinction between locutionary cooperation and perlocutionary cooperation (Attardo (1997b)) comes to the rescue: lies (and literature) are locutionarily cooperative (if that, as we'll see, as in fact they may pretend to be locutionarily cooperative) but perlocutionarily non-cooperative. Here then the source of the objection: when one reads a novel or a poem one wants to be deceived ("willing suspension of disbelief") and one is aware of the literary frame (in a Goffmaninan sense), hence one is not being deceived.

Indeed, part of this objection is corrrect: the goals of the deception in the case of lies and in the case of literature are radically different: a liar lies (usually) for his/her benefit, which often corresponds to our loss (in a zero sum game); hence the social stigma on lies. Conversely, a novelist lies for our benefit (enjoyment, entertainment, etc.). In other words, the goals of the liar are usually antisocial, whereas those of the novelist are prosocial. Note that the second part of the argument in my objection above is self-defeating: if I agree to be deceived I am still being deceived.[22] So, fiction is non-cooperative, in that it is deceitful, albeit for prosocial goals.

On to the subtle objection: in order for the literary text (fictional or not) to function there must be much more than a passive acceptance of the text as true or "willingly suspended": the writer and the reader must collaboratively build the meanings of the text, largely but not exclusively through inferential means, hence they must collaborate. Indeed, this is true, but it is true of all texts, not just of literary or otherwise sophisticated texts: this is the great lesson that the current debate about the semantics/pragmatics boundary has taught us.[23] Hence, we are left exactly where we were before: all texts enroll the hearer in the co-creation (the negotiation) of meaning(s). Some texts then turn out to refer to non-existant entities.

But my point is that fiction, literature, etc. is non-cooperative in more ways that just by being about non-existant facts.

In fact, fiction violates the CP in many ways. Consider the following examples, which

[20]Surprisingly, Pratt makes the following claim: "there are a a great many types [of illocutionary acts], including natural narrative and literature, whose purpose is not a maximally effective exchange of information in the Gricean sense." (Pratt (1977, p. 131)), which is tantamout to claiming that fictional narratives are NCP, and hence that we cannot assume their veracity, referentiality, etc. Cf. also the claim that "deviance" from the generic norms of narrative is "noncooperation" (214).

[21]E.g., Brown and Steinmann (1978, p. 155) "Producing and interpreting fictional discourse—like most authentic language use—involve a cooperative effort."

[22]A masochist may ask a sadist to whip him/her; that does not make the whipping not painful. The masochist enjoys the pain. Note the negation (and hence the meta-status) present in the folk-definition of the concept of pain as not-pleasure, well captured in the old joke: Masochist to a sadist: "Hurt me." Sadist: "No."

[23]And before them those authors, such as Umberto Eco, who married pragmatics and text-theory, see Eco (1979).

are not meant to be exhaustive:

- suspense: a fairly obvious example, but a revealing one. By witholding information on the outcome of the plot (a clear violation of the maxim of quantity and possibly relevance) S produces an effect of expectation and forces H to attend to the text against H's will (consider cliff hangers, which often delay the satisfaction of H's desire to know "what happened" by periods of time ranging from few seconds to several months). An interesting issue, is that "tellability" can be achieved artificially, so to speak, by introducing suspense in otherwise unremarkable facts: for example, if one summarizes the plot of Jane Eyre as "Jane Eyre meets Rochester and marries him," the tellability is pretty low. Bronte's art is to insert 38 chapters between the two facts. Strategic witholding of information is even more crucially significant in some genres, such as humor, detective mysteries, and thrillers.
- style: a reductive, but partially on target, view of style as a departure from an unmarked form of language (Barthes' *degré zero*) gets right the fact that all non directly explicit forms of language from novel metaphors to irony, via tropes, etc. require extra processing (and thus are violations of the maxim of manner). In fact, Shklovski's "estrangement" sees one of the central tools of literary writing as a systematic violation of the maxim of manner (which could be re-worded as "be familiar").
- non-communicative aspects of language: there are several aspects of language including alliteration, rhyme, assonance, etc. which are clearly not geared toward the transmission of information (this is a slippery area: let me retreat to a very elementary definition of transmission of information as recoverability of intention—it is clear that whatever, if any, the goals of the author in alliterating or rhyming, no propositional meaning can be recovered by attributing him/her an intention because the intention cannot be recovered[24]).

### 4.5.1 Fiction, non-cooperation, and mode adoption

In Attardo (2000b, 2001), I introduced the idea of mode adoption. I cannot go into the details of the definition, especially on how it differs from the Austinian *uptake* and *taking up*. Let it suffice to define it as the recognition of the illocutionary force of an utterance and then the performance of another speech act having the same type of inferential path, but not necessarily the same illocutionary force. Thus, responding ironically to an ironic turn is mode adoption, but laughing, or responding seriously to it are not. Needless to say, a hearer is free to mode adopt or not.

My argument here is that irony and fiction allow (or even strongly suggest) mode adoption, whereas humor and lying do not.[25] Certainly, one can respond with a joke to a joke, but the preferred response is appreciation of the joke (possibly followed by another humorous turn). With fiction and irony, refusal to mode adopt is definitely dispreferred: imagine a situation in which one would complain to a story teller about the factual nature of his/her tale, which is similar to the situation in which an ironical

[24] The perspicuous reader will have realized that I am avoiding taking position on whether sound symbolism may carry meanings.

[25] In the case of lying, definitely not, since the eventuality of mode adoption would mean the failure of the liar to have his/her lie go undetected.

turn is responded to at face value (but not ironically).

In this aspect, then, the violation of cooperation within fiction differs from the violations of humor and lying: the violations of cooperation in fiction are announced and agreed to, in fact, mode adopted, whereas the violations of humor are not mode adopted and not (always) announced; the violations of lying are definitely not announced and (hopefully, for the liar) not mode adopted. In Attardo (1997a) I proposed the idea of a continuum of cooperativeness, which this suggestion returns to.

### 4.5.2 Why do we take fiction seriously?

The conclusion that fiction is non-cooperative, leads to a possible objection: if fiction is non-cooperative, how can people attach such significance to it (recall Rushdie's fatwa, Goethe's suicides, etc.)? In other words: how can literature communicate anything if it is fictional?[26] Moreover, As Cebik notes, those who claim that fiction may communicate true propositions have "largely ignored what makes such derivations possible" (Cebik (1984, p. 102)).

I wish to suggest that this is because of a number of features of the metacommunicative status of fiction.

- All fiction, when it is identified as such, carries the metamessage: "this is fiction." This metamessage has a corollary, which is also a metamessage: "It is appropriate to speak of X in the context of Y" where X is the subject matter of the fictional event and Y is the setting of the fictional event (ultimately, the text). This explains Khomeini's fatwa: Khomeini would not have objected to a novel ridiculing Buddha or President Carter. What Khomeini objected was the metamessage "It is appropriate to speak of Mohammed in the context of a grotesque text." Note how suddenly his behavior becomes perfectly rational.[27]
- Fiction communicates through its presuppositional basis. I have made this claim in relation to jokes (Attardo (1993b)) but Cebik (1984, p. 44) and others have made the same claim within philosophical approaches to fiction. Cebik (1984) argues at length that the possibility for fiction to express true propositions, which are "almost invariably generalizations about human experience or nature" (101) arises from "generalizations," which "emerge indirectly" (125) and are presupposed or implied by the fictional texts (129).

  Suppose I say *p* i.e., "La marquise sortit à cinq heures" and that *p* is false. It still follows that there is a marchionness and that she went out, albeit not at five o'clock. In other words, the presuppositions of a sentence communicate despite its falsehood (witness the problem in defending oneself from the question: "have you stopped beating your wife?") Needless to say, in the case of fiction the very presupposition of existence may be false, but the default is clearly the opposite. As we have seen in section (4.4) the reader of a fictional text works with a basic heuristic, provided by the NCP, along the lines of "whatever not clearly fictional is assumed to be factual."[28] For

[26] The alert reader will recognize here essentially the same argument I developed in Attardo (1993b) in the context of the communicative value of humor.

[27] Not that I agree with literally putting authors to death for literary crimes, although—should the idea catch on—I have a little list I'd like to put up for consideration.

[28] Actually, the strategy is more complex: for any entity *e*

example, a friend recently told me that eggplant was introduced into Italian cooking via Jewish cuisine. I asked for the source of this bit of information and she mentioned, without any hesitation, that she had read it in a novel.[29]

- Allegorical readings: there exists a very ancient approach to the reading of texts that attributes them allegorical or symbolic meanings, see for example Dante's theory of the four meanings of the *Divine Comedy.* This allows Dante to make theological and ethical points that hold factually, while not necessarily claiming factuality for his trip.
- Disregard the metamessage: odd as it may seem, many readers choose to simply ignore the metamessage "this is fiction" and take the text at face value. In a sense, they act as if there existed a maxim along the lines of "all novels are *à clef*" and "all stories are true." This is the case of the readers of the *Da Vinci Code.*

## 4.6 Why do we crave narratives?

It still remains a mystery why humans should be so interested in narratives. We can agree with the assessment that "theories that seek to explain why we are attracted to (...) fictions and whether we learn from them have produced no consensus and no adequate overall account" (Steen and Owens (2001, p. 289)).

Essentially the various attempts at explaining the unquestionable attraction of narratives have either focused on the positive effects of the exposure to narratives (learning, examplar nature of the texts, or the cathartic nature of the exposure), or on the presumed evolutionary advantages of a species that has the capacity to produce narratives.

Of course, the best known proponent of the cathartic interpretation of literature is Aristotle's *Poetics.* A contemporary example of cathartic approach to literature is Pratt's. She claims that display texts are designed to serve a "communicative purpose" of "verbally representing states of affairs and experiences which are held to be unusual or problematic in such a way that the addressee will respond affectively in the intended way, adopt the intended evaluation and interpretation, take pleasure in doing so, and generally find the whole undertaking worth it" (Pratt (1977, p. 148)). There's not much to add here, except that presumably this is the basis of the preference for realism in art: without the belief that the events being represented really happened we would emote less. This is why, for example, comedians always claim that the funny stories they relate really happened to them.

Pinker's (Pinker (1997, pp. 539-542)) "instruction" view corresponds to the "disregard the metamessage" strategy, mentioned above: it consists of taking fiction as an approximation of reality. His "recreation" side is similar to Freud's "wish fulfiment." A

---

1. if $e$ is already in $PW_R$ (where $PW_R$ is the possible world labeled "reality") then assume its factuality (Eco (1989, p. 63))
2. if $e$ is not already in $PW_R$assume factuality in the possible world of the text ($PW_t$) (without necessarily trying to reconcile $PW_t$ with $PW_R$; see Eco (1989, pp. 68-69))
3. assume that $PW_t = PW_R$
4. if $e$ conflicts with anything in $PW_R$ assume fictionality
5. unless the description of $e$ is a better "theory" of $e$ in which case revise $PW_R$ to include $e$.

[29] This seems indeed to be factual: see Capatti and Montanari (2003, p. 42).

related strategy is to see the value of literature in it being a dry run for reality: already Groos (1898) had argued that play served as practice of adult behavior. Along these lines, fiction provides "models of behavior" (Carroll (1999)) or "thought experiments[30]" (Hobbs (1990)).

Steen and Owens argue that pretend play is evolutionarily advantageous because it "is designed to solve a particularly complex adaptive problem, that of improving performance on a task in the absence of the normal eliciting conditions. Pretense allows the young mammal or child to make use of affordances in its environment to devise learning situations that are safe, readily available, and developmentally appropriate" (Steen and Owens (2001, p. 297)).

My feeling is that all these approaches are correct, in the sense that narrative does all those things, but limited, in the sense that narrative does not just do those things. I think we need to go deeper. Carroll's view that literature provides "a sense of psychological order" (Carroll (1999, p. 170)) is intriguing, but he elaborates his claim as meaning that with narratives "we regulate our complex cognitive machinery. It contributes to personal and social development and to the capacity for responding flexibly and creatively" which is, in my mind, a by-product of the real function of narratives, which is to organize cognition.

My hunch, which at this point I can do no better than support with a few generally intriguing but obviously inconclusive examples, is that narratives are central to human cognition. To put it differently: to be human is (also) to be able to tell a story.[31] To some extent, the lexicon is a collection of encapsulated little stories (scripts, in some terminology; think of the word "alimony" which presupposes a whole story: a woman meets a man, they get married, they later divorce and one of the two is forced to pay a certain sum of money by a court). The concept of causality, clearly basic for human cognition, is better understood as a deterministic model (hence narrative) than as a Bayesian one (Pearl (2000, p. 26-27)). Ontogenetically, naratives occur very early. Children as young as 3 or 4 years can produce chronological narratives connected by "and" which become common by age 5 (Peterson and McCabe (1983)). I myself have observed a child of two invent a (very simple) chronological narrative.

Narratives are satisfying because they provide order: they give us the impression (illusion) that things fit "nicely" into a pattern.[32] They give us "meaning,"[33] so to speak.

[30]"Situations that are more or less possible, but not actual, are set up and in a carefully controlled framework the author and the readers can explore the consequences of these situations" (Hobbs (1990, p. 39)).

[31]Obviously cognition precedes narration. But where syntax is, narrative is not far away.

[32]If something happens, it is consolatory to be able to fit it into a narrative arc, with a beginning, a middle and an end. This is especially true of we can build in some moral to the story, some learning that results from it. Witness Labov (1972) "a good coda [conclusion] ... leaves the listener with a feeling of satisfaction and completeness that matters have been rounded off and accounted for."

[33]As in 'the meaning of life is... '. I am told that there is an affinity between this point and the late Paul Ricoeur's approach to narrative. This is both surprising and reassuring to me.

## References

Arias (ed.), Arturo. 2001. *The Rigoberta Menchú controversy*. Minneapolis, MN: University of Minnesota Press.

Attardo, Salvatore. 1993a. Derrida and Saussure. Working Papers in Linguistics Vol. 3, Northeastern Illinois University, Chicago: Illinois.

Attardo, Salvatore. 1993b. Violation of Conversational Maxims and Cooperation: The Case of Jokes. *Journal of Pragmatics* 19(1):537–558.

Attardo, Salvatore. 1997a. Competition and Cooperation: Beyond Gricean Pragmatics. *Pragmatics and Cognition* 5:1:21–50.

Attardo, Salvatore. 1997b. Locutionary and Perlocutionary Cooperation: The Perlocutionary Cooperative Principle. *Journal of Pragmatics* 27:753–779.

Attardo, Salvatore. 1999. The place of Cooperation in Cognition. In *European Conference of Cognitive Science (ECCS'99)*. Siena, Italy.

Attardo, Salvatore. 2000a. Covert speech acts and their meaning. In J. C. R. Alan D. Manning, Heather Judson and J. Young, eds., *Proceedings of the 1999 Deseret Language and Linguistics Society Simposium*, pages 202–217. Provo, UT: Brigham Young University.

Attardo, Salvatore. 2000b. Irony as relevant inappropriateness . *Journal of Pragmatics* 32:793–826.

Attardo, Salvatore. 2001. On the pragmatic nature of irony and its rhetorical aspects. In E. Nemeth, ed., *Pragmatics in 2000. Selected papers from the 7th International Pragmatics Conference*, pages 52–66. Antwerp: IPrA.

Austin, J. L. 1962. *How To Do Things With Words*. Oxford/New York: Oxford University Press.

Barnes, J. A. 1994. *A Pack of Lies: Towards a sociology of lying*. Cambridge: Cambridge University Press.

Brown, Robert L., Jr and Martin Steinmann, Jr. 1978. Native readers of fiction: a speech-act and genre-rule approach to defining literature. In P. Hernadi, ed., *What is Literature?*, pages 141–160. Bloomington, IN: Indiana university Press.

Capatti, Alberto and Massimo Montanari. 2003. *La cucina italiana: storia di una cultura*. New York, NY: Columbia UP. Engl. translation by Aine O'Healy. (*La cucina italiana: storia di una cultura, 1999*).

Carroll, Joseph. 1999. The Deep Structure of Literary Representations. *Evolution and Human Behavior* 20:3:159–173.

Castelfranchi, Cristiano and Isabella Poggi. 1998. *Bugie, finzioni e sotterfugi*. Roma: Carocci.

Cebik, L. B. 1984. *Fictional Narrative and Truth. An Epistemic Analysis*. Lanham, NY: University Press of America.

Coleman, Linda and Paul Kay. 1981. Prototype Semantics: The English Word *Lie*. *Language* 57:1:26–44.

Crittenden, Charles. 1991. *Unreality. The Metaphysics of Fictional Objects*. Ithaca/London: Cornell University Press.

Dobler, Bruce. 2005. Bruce dobler's creative nonfiction compendium. http://www.pitt.edu/bdobler/readingnf.html.

Druker, Phil. 2005. What is creative non-fiction. http://www.class.uidaho.edu/druker/ nonfic.html.

Eaton, Marcia. 1972. The truth value of literary statements. *British Journal of Aesthetics* 12:163–174.

Eaton, Marcia. 1973. Liars, ranters, and dramatic speakers. In B. R. Tilghman, ed., *Language and Aesthetics*, pages 43–64. Kansas State University Press. Reprinted in Morris Philipson and Paul J. Gudel, (eds.) 1980. *Aesthetics Today.* MeridianBooks.

Eco, Umberto. 1979. *Lector in Fabula.* Milan: Bompiani.

Eco, Umberto. 1989. Small Worlds. *Versus* 52/53:53–70.

Eco, Umberto. 2005. Il codice colpisce ogni giorno. *L'espresso.* http://www.espressonline.it/eol/.

Fish, Stanley. 1980. *Is There a Text in This Class?.* Cambridge, MA: Harvard University Press.

Fotion, Nick. 2003. From speech acts to speech activity. In B. Smith, ed., *John Searle*, pages 34–51. Cambridge: Cambridge University Press.

Genette, Gerard. 1987. *Seuils.* Paris: Seuil. Trans. Jane E. Lewin. *Paratexts: Thresholds of interpretation.* Cambridge: Cambridge University Press. 1997.

Hobbs, Jerry. 1990. *Literature and Cognition.* Stanford, CA: Center for the Study of Language and Information.

Holland, Patrick and Graham Huggan. 1998. *Tourists with Typewriters: Critical Reflections on Contemporary Travel Writing.* Ann Arbor: University of Michigan Press.

Masur, Kate. 1999. Edmund morris's dutch: Reconstructing reagan or deconstructing history? *Perspectives.* December. http://www.historians.org/perspectives/issues/1999/9912/.

Menchú, Rigoberta. 1983. *Me llamo Rigoberta Mechú y así me nació la concencia.* Barcelona: Argos Vergara. Engl. tr. *I, Rigoberta Menchú. An Indian Woman in Guatemala.* London: Verso, 1984. Edited by Elisabeth Burgos-Debray.

Mulligan, Kevin. 2003. Searle, Derrida, and the ends of phenomenology. In B. Smith, ed., *John Searle*, pages 261–286. Cambridge: Cambridge University Press.

Ohmann, Richard. 1971. Speech Acts and the Definition of Literature. *Philosophy and Rhetoric* 4:1–19.

Packard, Robert. 1990. *Refractions: Writers and Places.* New York: Carroll and Graf Publishers.

Pearl, Judea. 2000. *Causation. Models, Reasonnig and Inference.* Cambridge: Cambridge UP.

Perry, John. 2001. *Reference and Reflexivity.* Stanford, CA: CSLI.

Peterson, C. and A. McCabe. 1983. *Developmental psycholinguistics: Three ways of looking at a child's narrative.* New York: Plenum Press.

Petrey, Sandy. 1990. *Speech Acts and Literary Theory.* New York/London: Routledge.

Pinker, Stephen. 1997. *How the Mind Works.* New York: W.W. Norton.

Pratt, Mary Louise. 1977. *Toward a Speech-Act Theory of Literary Discourse.* Bloomington, IN: Indiana University Press.

Raskin, Victor. 1985. *Semantic mechanisms of humor.* Dordrecht: D. Reidel.

Raskin, Victor. 1992. Using the powers of language: Non-casual language in advertising, politics, relationships, humor, and lying. In E. L. Pedersen, ed., *Proceedings of the 1992 Annual Meeting of the Deseret Language and Linguistic Society*, pages 17–30. Provo, UT: Brigham Young University.

Robinson, Douglas. 1997. Speech acts. In M. Groden and M. Kreiswirth, eds., *The John Hopkins Guide to Literary Theory and Criticism.* Baltimore, MD: John Hopkins University Press.

Ryan, Marie Laure. 1980. Fiction, Non-Factuals, and the Principle of Minimal Departure. *Poetics* 9:403–422.

Scheibe, Karl. 1980. In defense of lying: on the moral neutrality of misrepresentation. *Berkshire Review* 15:15–24.

Schmidt, Sigfried J. 1976. Toward a pragmatic interpretation of "fictionality.". In T. A. van Dijk, ed., *Pragmatics of Language and Literature*, pages 161–178. Amsterdam: North Holland.

Searle, John. 1969. *Speech Acts: an essay in the philosophy of language*. Cambridge: Cambridge University Press.

Searle, John. 1979. *Expression and Meaning*. Cambridge: Cambridge University Press.

Sherrill, Rowland. 2000. *Road-Book America: Contemporary Culture and the New Picaresque*. Urbana: University of Illinois Press.

Sperber, Dan and Deirdre Wilson. 1986. *Relevance*. Cambridge, MA: Harvard University Press.

Steen, Francis F. and Stephanie A. Owens. 2001. Evolution's pedagogy: An adaptationist model of pretense and entertainment. *Journal of Cognition and Culture* 1:4:289–321.

Stoll, David. 1999. *Rigoberta Menchú and the Story of All Poor Guatemalans*. Boulder, CO: Westview Press.

Varzi, Achille. 2005. *Ontologia*. Milan: Laterza.

Wittgenstein, Ludwig. 1953. *Philosophische Untersuchungen*. Oxford: Blackwell.

# 5

# Failures, Omissions, and Negative Descriptions

ACHILLE C. VARZI

## 5.1 Introduction

A long-standing tradition in the linguistic and philosophical literature—mostly rooted in the work of Donald Davidson (1980)—holds that the distinction between objects and events is central to the way we talk. If we say that John is smart, what we say is true or false according to whether a certain *object* (a person) is or is not smart, but if we say that John's walk is leisurely, what we say is true or false according to whether a certain *event* (a walk) is leisurely or not. The first statement is about John; the second is about something else—not about John himself but about something he is performing. Likewise, if we say that John watered the plants carelessly, our statement is about John but also about his action: we are saying that John did something to the plants, and we are saying of what he did—his watering of the plants—that *it* was careless.

This view is not uncontroversial but I am happy to go along with it, at least conditionally. The question I am interested in concerns the scope of the view. Assuming that events form a genuine ontological category, shall we say that a good inventory of the world ought to include "negative" events—things that didn't happen—along with positive ones? After all, we often seem to be talking about such things, too. We speak of John's walk with the same easiness with which we speak of the talk he was supposed to give, the nap he did not take, the party he failed to organize. Davidson himself was candid about this: "We often count among the things an agent does things he does not do", he wrote (Davidson (1985, p. 217)). Yet this may offend our ontological scruples. If John did not actually do those things, why should we include them in an inventory of the *actual* world? Besides, how would we go about identifying such non-doings? Is the talk John was supposed to give (but did not give) the same as the talk I would have liked him to give? Is it the same as the talk you would have liked? The same as the talk he can still give tomorrow? And how many things did John fail to do when he failed to give his talk? Surely he also failed to please the organizers, as he failed to sit on that

*Meaning, Intentions, and Argumentation.*
Kepa Korta and Joana Garmendia (eds.).

chair, or to turn on the overhead projector. And surely he also failed to do many other things he could have done at that very same time: he didn't go jogging, didn't water the plants, didn't check his email. Would all of these non-doings deserve a place in our inventory of the world?

I do not think so. In a way, speaking of non-occurring events is like speaking of non-existing objects, and my inclination is not to take these manners of speaking at face value.[1] We often speak *as though* there were such things, but deep down we may want our words to be interpreted in such a way as to avoid serious ontological commitment. For example, we may say that reference to Harry Potter or to the golden mountain is to be understood within the context of a fictional story, a pretense, a game of make-believe, and we may likewise say that reference to the things John didn't do is to be understood within the context of a suitable fictional scenario. It is true that Harry Potter wore round glasses insofar as that is true *according to* J. K. Rowling's narrative; similarly, it is true that John's canceled talk was on metaphors (say) insofar as that is true *according to* certain counterfactual speculations about how the world might or should have been.

Alas, non-occurring events appear to be more resistant to Occam's razor than the analogy with non-existing objects might suggest. Not only do we often speak *as though* there were such things. We often speak in such a way as to suggest that reference to or quantification over non-occurrences is to be taken strictly and literally. Typical examples include statements such as 'John often doesn't go jogging' or 'Mary saw John not leave', whose Davidsonian logical forms appear to require a straight commitment to actions that John failed to perform. Or think of what we say when we engage in causal talk. We say that John's failure to turn off the gas caused an explosion, that his omitting the cutlery from the wedding list made Mary angry, or that the main cause of the fire in the forest was lack of rain. How can we uphold to the view that causation is a relation between events (a view that has many advantages over its competitors) and yet deny that sometimes the terms of a causal transaction involve failures, omissions, events that did *not* happen?

The point of this paper is to outline a way of resisting such difficulties on behalf of the view according to which the only events to be seriously countenanced are the positive ones—those that actually feature in the history of the world. This involves articulating two distinct but related ideas. First, there is the idea that in some cases a "negative" event (a non-leaving) just *is* an ordinary, positive event (a staying); it is a positive event under a negative description. Second, there is the idea that not all causal explanations are reports of causation. When we mention John's failure to turn off the gas as an explanans of why there was an explosion (for example), we do not say *what* caused the explosion. We do not mention any of the relevant causes. We just remark that one *sort* of event that was supposed to occur, and whose occurrence would have prevented the explosion, did not in fact occur.

[1] The "ontological scruples" mentioned above parallel Russell's scruples concerning the reality of Meinongian *possibilia*, and the worries about ontological proliferation parallel Quine's worries about the "identity conditions" for *possibilia* (see Russell (1905) and Quine (1948), respectively).

## 5.2 Events and Their Descriptions

Let us begin with the first idea: in many cases, "negative" events are just ordinary, "positive" events under a negative description. My reasons for thinking along these lines stem from a general consideration concerning the semantics of our event talk.

Events, I take it, are particulars, or so we are supposed to think if we accept a broadly Davidsonian framework (see Davidson (1970)). They are unrepeatable entities located in space and time, and we can *describe* any such entity in various ways, just as we can describe any particular object in various ways. I say: John is the right person for Mary. You say: Tell me more about him—and I elaborate: "He is smart, he likes traveling, and he is fond of jogging". You say: John took a walk last night. I say: Tell me more about it—and you elaborate: "It was a long and leisurely stroll in Central Park, before dinner, with his friend Sue, and Mary got really angry about it". The pronoun 'it', here, just as the pronoun 'he' in the previous scenario, is all we need to carry the reference back to the entity we were talking about. Similarly, just as we can *refer* to an object by means of a number of different descriptions, each of which relies on certain properties that the object possesses, so we can refer to an event by means of descriptions that may vary depending on the context and the purpose of our discourse. We can refer to John by his proper name or we can identify him by saying 'Mary's boyfriend', 'my smart colleague', or 'the president of the jogging club', and we can likewise identify what he did last night by saying 'John's walk in Central Park', or 'John's leisurely promenade with Sue', or 'the cause of Mary's anger'.

To be sure, people have different intuitions in this connection. Since John could have walked alone, whereas he could not have gone for a promenade with Sue all by himself, some are inclined to say that 'John's walk' and 'John's promenade with Sue' must refer to distinct events by virtue of Leibniz's law: those terms are not substitutable *salva veritate*. Likewise, if Mary got angry, not because John went for a walk, but because he went with Sue, some are inclined to say that 'the cause of Mary's anger' does not refer to John's walk but to his promenade with Sue, which should therefore be treated as a distinct event. I disagree with such intuitions. Surely not every description of what John did last night may be equally adequate in every context, but that is not to say that he did many things at once: different descriptions may have different senses and may therefore serve different purposes, yet their actual referent may coincide. Thus, although it is true that in a possible world in which John went for a lonely walk the description 'John's promenade with Sue' would not apply, it doesn't follow that such a description fails to pick out John's walk in this world. (Compare: although it is true that 'the number of planets' could pick out a number other than 9 in different worlds, it doesn't follow that it fails to pick out the number 9 in this world.) Likewise, although it would be silly to *explain* why Mary got angry by describing what John did as a mere walk, it doesn't follow that the walk is not the cause of Mary's anger: causal explanations are language-sensitive but causal reports are semantically transparent (see Davidson (1967)). (Compare: 'John's walk with Sue caused Mary's anger' vs. 'John's walk with my neighbor caused Mary's anger': the former statement may be better suited as an explanatory report, especially if you don't know that Sue is my neighbor, but this doesn't imply that John did two things: walking with Sue *and* walking with my neighbor.) In short, I think we should be careful not to assume that the expressions we use to identify actions and other events tell the whole truth about those actions and events: just as an object's description can be very partially informative, and even misleading for certain purposes, so an event's description can be partially informative and misleading. As Jonathan Bennett (1988) put it, there is no way we can "read off" the nature of an object or the nature of an event from the words we use to refer to them.

With this picture in place, it is obvious that among the many ways in which we can pick out an event, there are some that may be broadly classified as negative descriptions. John took a walk in Central Park. Really, he was all dressed up for jogging, and he would have jogged with his friend Tom had Sue not joined him. That was the plan. So, depending on the context, you might want to refer to John's walk, not as a walk but as a non-jogging. It was a walk, so it was not a jog, so it was a non-jogging, and that may very well be the bit of information about John's doing that you may want to convey in your description of it. His walk caused Mary's anger because of Sue's presence? Then we'd better refer to it explicitly as a promenade with Sue. John's walk caused Tom's complaint because they were supposed to go jogging together? Then we might want to refer to it, not as a walk or a promenade, but as a non-jogging. There may be linguistic noise here. When using negative descriptions, we might be inclined to go for expressions that do not qualify as perfect nominals. In English, the cause of Tom's complaint is best described, not as John's non-jogging, but as John's not jogging, and this latter expression is a gerundial. It has a verb that is still "alive and kicking inside it", as Zeno Vendler (1967, ch. 5) famously put it. And if Vendler is right, and Bennett with him, gerundial nominals do not strictly speaking pick out events: they typically pick out facts, or states of affairs. It is indeed unclear whether English admits of any grammatically decent examples of negative event descriptions that pass the Vendler-Bennett test (see Bennett (1988, p. 148)). But never mind that: to the extent that we *intend* to refer to an event, the point is clear enough: by speaking of John's not jogging we are not referring to a negative action; we are referring to what John actually did—his walk—by mentioning a salient property that it lacked. A negative description has a negative sense, not a negative referent.

I suggest that precisely this sort of account applies to the putatively problematic cases mentioned above, which involve hidden quantification rather than explicit event reference.[2] Suppose I say

(1) Mary saw John not leave.

According to a standard analysis, due to Jim Higginbotham,[3] naked infinitive perceptual reports require a Davidsonian analysis. In particular, a statement such as (1) would be analyzed as[4]

(1′) $\exists e$(Non-leaving($e$, John) & Saw(Mary, $e$)).

---

[2]Here I elaborate on Tovena and Varzi (1999).

[3]See Higginbotham (1983) and the discussion in Neale (1988).

[4]Strictly speaking, since Mary's seeing is itself an event, the fully spelled out logical form of (1) should involve two bound variables: $\exists e \exists e'$(Non-leaving($e$, John) & Seeing($e'$, Mary, $e$)). For simplicity, here and below I will ignore such details if they are not relevant.

Does this mean that by uttering (1) I am committing myself to a negative event that Mary saw, i.e., a non-leaving, a leaving that John did not take? Some people think so,[5] but I surely don't. Surely Mary could only see what John actually did, unless she was hallucinating. For instance, suppose John walked upstairs rather than leaving. Then that is what Mary saw: she saw him walk upstairs. And I could report this fact by uttering (2) instead of (1):

(2) Mary saw John walk upstairs.

In that case the correct analysis would be

(2′) $\exists e(\text{Walking-upstairs}(e, \text{John}) \,\&\, \text{Saw}(\text{Mary}, e))$.

That I appeal to a negative characterization in (1) and a positive characterization in (2) doesn't mean that the variable $e$ must pick out two distinct events in the two cases. It picks out the same event under two different descriptions, and which description is more appropriate is a pragmatic question. For instance, suppose everybody expected John to leave. Then (1) is much more effective as a report of what happened than (2). It is more effective because the negative attribute 'non-leaving' conveys a salient piece of information, whereas 'walking-upstairs' does not. Sometimes we do exactly the same when it comes to speaking of objects. If I say

(3) Mary saw a non-philosopher,

then I am characterizing what Mary saw with the help of a negative attribute. Surely that doesn't mean that Mary saw a negative entity. In fact, if I knew more I could be more explicit, as in

(4) Mary saw a guy 7.1 feet tall, wearing glasses, a blue tie, and a hat.

Yet this need not be the best way of reporting what Mary saw. If, as we may suppose, Mary was attending a philosophy conference, then the negative attribute 'non-philosopher', though less informative, picks out a feature of the person Mary saw that is much more salient than his height and look, so in that context (3) may well be more effective than (4). The case of (1) versus (2) is exactly parallel. And the parallel is confirmed by the fact that in both cases we can go on and ask: Tell me more. Tell me more about this non-philosopher. "Well, he was a guy 7.1 feet tall, wearing glasses, a blue tie, and a hat". Tell me more about what Mary saw. "Well, she saw John walk upstairs, on the sly, without saying a word, while nobody else was looking". Just as with the walk that was not a jogging, we can always switch from a negative characterization to a positive one, and vice versa: we choose our words depending on the message we wish to convey.

Indeed, one further reason to reject the thought that a negative attribute picks out a negative event is that often there is no clear-cut criterion for saying whether an attribute is negative. Consider

(5) John stayed whereas Tom left.

The connective 'whereas' suggests that staying and leaving are to be understood as opposite. But which is positive and which negative? If everybody left with Tom, then

[5] Here I disagree with Przepiórkowski (1999), for instance.

what John did could be described equally well (if not better) as a non-leaving. However, if everybody stayed with John, then it is what Tom did that could be described negatively as a non-staying. Obviously both options are equally plausible, so the opposition between staying and leaving cannot be construed ontologically, as a conflict between being and non-being. Nor can we choose between the two options on purely semantic grounds. The choice depends on the context, so it is a function of pragmatic factors at large.

At this point it should be clear how other problematic cases can be handled along similar lines. Consider

(6) What happened at the end is that Sue didn't kiss John.

Henriette de Swart takes statements such as this to provide evidence for the existence of negative events—in this case, a non-kiss by Sue (see de Swart (1996, p. 229)). Presumably this is because, on a standard analysis, the logical form of (6) implies the existential statement

(7) $\exists e$(Non-kissing($e$, Mary, John)).

But so what? On the face of it, what happened at the end, $e$, must be something perfectly positive, ontologically speaking. It must be something that did happen. John didn't tell us, so we don't know. Perhaps Sue just said "Good night", or "Thanks for the pleasant walk". Perhaps she hopped into a taxi cab without saying a word. Who knows? What we know, based on what John told us, is that whatever she did, it was not a kiss. And since we are starting to feel judgmental about this whole story, we are happy to accept this characterization as a good characterization of what happened, uninformative as it may be in all sorts of respects.

Here is another typical case where we seem to be quantifying over negative events:

(8) John often doesn't go jogging.

Stockwell, Schachter, and Partee[6] take statements such as (8) to provide counterexamples against Lakoff's claim that "one cannot assert the frequency of an event that does not occur" (Lakoff (1965, p. 172)). I see why one might be tempted to view it that way, but I disagree. That is, I agree with Lakoff. For one thing, it seems to me that statements such as (8) should not to be construed as quantifying over events at all, whether positive or negative. Consider first

(9) John often goes jogging.

On the face of it, in (9) we are quantifying over certain *times*—over evenings, say—and we are saying that there are many such times during which John goes jogging. In other words, we are quantifying over the open formula

(9′) Evening($t$) & $\exists e$(Jogging($e$, John) & During($e, t$)).

But then (8) should be handled similarly. In (8) we are again quantifying over certain times—evenings—and we are saying that there are many such times during which John does *not* go jogging: we are quantifying over the formula

(8′) Evening($t$) & $\sim \exists e$(Jogging($e$, John) & During($e, t$)).

[6]Stockwell et al. (1973), ex. (49b). Compare Horn (1989, p. 54), de Swart (1996, p. 230), and Przepiórkowski (1999, p. 241).

There is nothing here that should suggest the repeated occurrence of a negative event. On the other hand, if we took such statements to be truly quantifying over events, then again I see no reason to suppose that the quantification in (8) ranges over *negative* events. What did John do yesterday evening? He went for a walk with Sue. What did he do the evening before? He went to the bookstore with Mary. And on Tuesday he went to see the Yankees play. All of those things are things that John actually did, and they all took place in the evening. We may describe them directly, as I have just done, or we may describe them indirectly as doings that are not joggings—as non-joggings. That is not very informative. But for someone like Tom, who loves jogging, it may be enough. And it may be perfectly all right for Tom to summarize the picture by saying that John often doesn't go jogging. John is the president of the jogging club, so in the evening he shouldn't engage in all those non-joggings—whatever they are.

## 5.3 Omissions, Failures, and Causation (I)

If all of this is correct, then some major evidence in support of an ontology of negative events appears to founder in the light of the sense/reference distinction. To repeat the slogan, a negative description has a negative sense, not a negative referent. At least, this is what I want to suggest *vis-à-vis* the sorts of argument to the contrary based on simple considerations of logical form.

Now, can we say the same also when it comes to the second sort of argument offered in this connection, namely the argument from causation? "Every causal situation develops as it does as a result of the presence of positive factors alone", says David Armstrong (1999, p. 177) and I agree. Yet our ordinary way of speaking—and much philosophical talk, too—suggests that the driving forces of nature also include failures, omissions, and the like. Can we resist that suggestion by exploiting the idea that *prima facie* negative causes are just positive causes under a negative description?

To some extent we can. I have already hinted at the idea above, but let me spell it out more explicitly. On a Davidsonian semantics, singular causal statements are best construed as statements involving a causal relation between events, not as statements involving a causal connective or other propositional devices (see Davidson (1967)). For example, the statement

(10) John's walk with Sue caused Mary's anger.

is to be construed as having the following logical form (modulo uniqueness):

(10′) $\exists e \exists e'(\text{Walk}(e, \text{John}, \text{Sue}) \ \&\ \text{Anger}(e', \text{Mary}) \ \&\ \text{Caused}(e, e'))$.

Accordingly, consider now a causal statement that appears to involve a negative event, such as

(11) John's non-jogging caused Tom's complaint.

The corresponding logical form would be

(11′) $\exists e \exists e'(\text{Non-jogging}(e, \text{John}) \ \&\ \text{Complaint}(e', \text{Tom}) \ \&\ \text{Caused}(e, e'))$.

At this point one may be inclined to maintain that $e$, the cause, must be a negative event, but I would simply say that $e$ is a positive event described negatively. We know what John did: he took a leisurely walk with Sue. So that is what caused Tom's complaint (besides Mary's anger). The reason why we may not want to put it that way is that the statement

(12) John's walk with Sue caused Tom's complaint.

is likely to convey the wrong message. As Bennett points out, "in general, truths about causes will be assertible only if they report causes that are salient—that is, stand out as notably significant, surprising, or the like" (Bennett (1995, p. 133)). To put it differently, the reason why we are inclined to assert (11), but not (12), is that the latter statement would lack explanatory force. The statement would be true, because John's walk with Sue and John's non-jogging with Tom are one and the same event under different descriptions, and causal reports are semantically transparent. So the logical form of (12),

(12′) $\exists e \exists e'(\text{Walk}(e, \text{John}, \text{Sue})\ \&\ \text{Complaint}(e', \text{Tom})\ \&\ \text{Caused}(e, e'))$.

would be materially equivalent to that of (11). When reporting causal facts, however, we are generally interested in *explaining* why something happened, and the adequacy of an explanation does not only depend on the truth of what is said. When it comes to an explanation, we must also make sure we describe the cause in a way that proves informative given the relevant background of shared knowledge and presuppositions, as with every act of communication; otherwise we would violate a major Gricean maxim.[7] Compare: if the only non-philosopher at the conference was a guy with a blue tie, then it is true that seeing a non-philosopher surprised Mary if and only if it is true that seeing a guy with a blue tie surprised her. But if we want to explain *why* Mary was surprised, given that she was at a philosophy conference, then we should say 'non-philosopher', not 'guy with a blue tie'. Likewise, if we want to explain why Tom complained last night, we should describe what John did in a way that brings out the fact that it didn't measure up to Tom's expectations. Tom expected John to go jogging, and it is the fact that John's action turned out to be something *else* than a jog that explains the complaint. That is why (11) is better than (12). In fact, that is why (11), but not (12), translates naturally into the familiar jargon of causal explanations:

(11″) Tom complained *because* John did not go jogging.
(12″) Tom complained *because* John went for a walk with Sue.

That John's action was a walk with Sue—or that it took place in Central Park, before dinner, and so on—may be more informative than its not being a jog, but that information explains nothing when it comes to Tom's complaint.

So here is how the account would go in a nutshell. We sometimes construe a causal report as a causal explanation, but in order for the explanation to be successful we must use a description of the cause that conveys the right sort of information. Exactly what counts as the right sort of information depends on the context. And in certain contexts,

[7] See Grice (1975, p. 45): "Make your conversational contribution such as is required, at the stage at which it occurs, by the accepted purpose or direction of the talk exchange in which you are engaged". Of course, I do not mean to suggest that the value of a causal explanation is always reducible to simple matters of pragmatics. For instance, Hempel (1965) famously emphasized that scientific explanations are meant to be as objective and non-pragmatic as the laws and theories on which they rest. But our concern here is with ordinary explanations, hence the usual Gricean maxims apply.

negative descriptions are just more informative, causally, than positive descriptions.[8] They are in the negative, but they nonetheless pick out a perfectly "positive" cause.

Unfortunately we cannot leave it at that. As it turns out, this sort of account works well in some cases, but in other cases it can hardly be pressed. Consider the following:

(13) John's failure to turn off the gas caused an explosion.
(14) The main cause of the fire in the forest was lack of rain.

What is the positive cause negatively described in (13)? What did John do that may be blamed for the explosion? Surely he left the gas on, but that sounds more like a positive description of John's failure than a negative description of something he actually *did*. And what is the cause of the fire negatively described in (14) as lack of rain? On the face of it, in cases such as these it doesn't help to say that we have a negative description of a positive event, because we have no clue as to what that event could be. Indeed, as Higginbotham (2000, p. 74) remarked, in cases such as these there doesn't seem to be *any* particular event that we are describing negatively. Any Davidsonian analysis of (13) along the lines of

(13′) $\exists e \exists e'(\text{Non-turning-off}(e, \text{John, the gas}) \;\&\; \text{Explosion}(e') \;\&\; \text{Caused}(e, e'))$.

would therefore seem to commit us to the existence of a cause $e$ that is strictly and literally negative: a failure, an omission, a non-doing by John. Similarly for (14). Appealing to the pragmatics of speech acts seems to be of no help, for the problem is not that we tend to construe such causal reports as causal explanations; the problem arises with their being causal reports in the first place.

## 5.4 Omissions, Failures, and Causation (II)

Here is where the second idea advertised at the beginning enters the picture. I actually want to deny that such statements are genuine causal reports. In other words, I want to deny that (13) is correctly analyzed as having the logical form in (13′)—and similarly for (14) and the like. The right thing to say, I think, is that such statements are *just* causal explanations. And if that is what they are, then the problem does not arise at all.

The idea comes from recent work by Helen Beebee (2003). Consider: What reasons are there to regard such statements as genuine causal reports? One reason, of course, is that they explicitly involve the word 'caused', or 'cause', but this doesn't take us very far. What reasons are there to suppose that such words are always to be taken strictly and literally? The main reason, Beebee says, is that we are generally inclined to think that whenever we engage in causal talk, we do so by speaking of causes and effects. I have said that we should pay attention to the distinction between causal reports (of the form '$e$ caused $e'$') and causal explanations (of the form '$A$ because $B$'), but I have also said that there is a close connection between the two: typically, a causal explanation is a certain way of reporting the existence of a causal nexus, a way of reporting a causal

[8] If you like facts, you may want to say that whereas causation is a relation among events, causal explanations relate facts. When it comes to fact descriptions, differences in logical power create differences of referent. But one does not need a fact ontology to cash out the distinction: one can just say that causal explanations relate statements. And when it comes to statements, what you see is what you get.

interaction in which the cause and the effect are described in a suitable fashion given the relevant background of shared knowledge and presuppositions. This is misleading, for it suggests that there must always exist a correspondence between cause and explanans, on the one hand, and effect and explanandum, on the other—which is not the case. Indeed, there is no reason to think that a causal explanation should *always* mention the cause explicitly. If we know the cause of a certain event, and we know it under a description that fits the bill, then we can rely on this knowledge to produce a successful explanation, as with (11) and (11″). But the converse need not hold. If I say

(15) Tom complained because nobody went jogging with him,

I am offering a perfectly reasonable explanation of Tom's complaint. And it is a *causal* explanation: it answers a why-question, as opposed to a how- or a what-question. Yet (15) is silent about the actual cause of Tom's complaint: there is no mention, direct or indirect, of the specific event that brought it about, which is to say John's walk.

David Lewis has a nice way of making this point succinctly (see Lewis (1986), section III.) A causal explanation, he says, aims to provide some information about the "causal history" of a certain event *e*, and there are many ways of providing such information: we can do so by citing a cause of *e* (in which case the goodness of our explanation depends primarily on the words we use to pick out that cause), but we may also provide information that relates only indirectly to *e*'s cause. What matters is that the information provided fills in a significant gap in what we know about the causal history of *e*. We may, for example, say that *e* occurred because a certain *type* of event occurred, without specifying any particular instance. Or we may say that the causal history of *e* includes several events of such-and-such types, related to one another in such-and such ways. The information we provide about a causal history may range from very specific to very abstract. And in some cases it may be so abstract as to concern, not what the causal history includes, but what it does not include. There is no event of someone's jogging with Tom in the causal history of his recent complaint—*that* is why he complained. (Compare also what John may have said in response to Mary's request for an explanation of Sue's presence last night: "Why was she at the park when I went there before dinner? Just a coincidence, Mary, believe it or not".[9]) Of course, this is not to say that all explanatory information is of equal value: the more directly and completely we can describe the causal history of an event, the more likely we are to succeed in our explanatory efforts. But never mind that. The point to be stressed is simply that we need not and often do not aim at such completeness.

So, now, to go back to our main example, consider the following four statements:

(16) There was an explosion because Mary turned on the light.
(17) There was an explosion because somebody turned on the light.
(18) There was an explosion because nobody turned off the gas.
(19) There was an explosion because John didn't turn off the gas.

Following Beebee (and Lewis), I would say that only (16) may be regarded as a causal explanation in which the cause of the explosion is mentioned explicitly. Only (16) says something directly informative about the causal history of the event in question, or so we

[9]The example is adapted from Lewis (1986, p. 220).

may suppose. The other statements are less and less informative: (17) makes a general existential statement about what the causal history includes, whereas (18) and (19) only say something about what the causal history does *not* include: it includes no event of somebody's turning off the gas, and more specifically no event of John's turning off the gas. It follows that only (16) can be matched by a corresponding causal statement:

(16′) Mary's turning on the light caused an explosion.

As with (11), here it doesn't really matter whether we use the 'caused' language or the 'because' language: in both cases we are giving a description of what led to the explosion, and a description that is explanatorily adequate. Perhaps we can say the same about (17), which can be rephrased as

(17′) Somebody's turning on the light caused an explosion.

though here I wouldn't be so sure. With (18) and (19), however, the situation is clearly different: as with (15), there we are offering perfectly reasonable explanations of why a certain event took place—causal explanations. Yet, because such explanations are silent about the actual cause of that event, we cannot rephrase our statements as causal reports *stricto sensu*. We are not saying what events feature in the causal history of the explosion; rather, we are saying what (sort of) event is *missing* from that history. If you wish, we can add that the explanatory value of such statements lies in the truth of the corresponding counterfactuals:

(18′) Had somebody turned off the gas, there would have been no explosion.
(19′) Had John turned off the gas, there would have been no explosion.

But this is not to say we can now apply a counterfactual analysis of causation backwards, so to say, and generate in each case a matching causal statement.[10] Causal statements concern events that feature in the history of this world; counterfactuals concern what goes on in other worlds. And although we can counterfactualize about this world by considering how things might have gone had certain events not taken place, we cannot work our way backwards and infer how things actually went from the way they might have gone. We cannot infer that the actual world contains a non-occurrence $e$ from the fact that $e$ occurs in some counterfactual world, just as we cannot infer that the actual world contains a non-existing Pegasus from the fact that Pegasus exists in some non-actual world. You need not be a Russellian to block the inference. To put it differently, the counterfactual analysis of causation requires conditionals whose antecedents are negative statements: had a certain event *not* occurred, some other event would not have occurred either. The antecedents in (18′) and (19′), by contrast, are in the affirmative, so their logical form does not match the analysis—period.

Incidentally, I am focusing on cases putatively involving negative causes because these are the most interesting and widely discussed cases,[11] but let me stress that a perfectly

[10]The counterfactual analysis of causation comes from Lewis (1973). Of course, the analysis itself has been subjected to various criticisms and refined accordingly (see Collins et al. (2003)), but never mind: the main criticisms concern cases of preemption or overdetermination, so in the present context they could be ignored.

[11]Not only in philosophy and linguistics; there is also a large literature in the law. See for instance Hart and Honoré (1985).

parallel story could be told with regard to putative cases of negative *effects*. Only, in those cases we would hardly speak of "explanations" in the strict sense. We should not speak of the "causal history" of an event but, rather, of its "causal future". Just to give the gist of it, suppose I say

(20) John didn't turn off the gas because he left for a walk.

Then what I am offering is not a causal report of what happened. In fact, what I am saying is silent about what happened: I am not saying what events followed from John's leaving for a walk—that there was an explosion, for example. All I am saying is that a certain type of event, which was supposed to take place in the ordinary course of things, did not in fact happen. And this is all that is required in order to apply the analysis offered above, *mutatis mutandis.*

At this point it should be clear how we can bring all of this to an end. We started out by saying that the truth of a causal statement such as

(13) John's failure to turn off the gas caused an explosion

appears to commit us to the existence of a negative event: John's failure to perform a certain action. We should now say that the problem does not arise, for we should deny the truth of (13). That statement is not true because the subject term, 'John's failure to turn off the gas', fails to refer. What is true is the corresponding explanatory statement

(19) There was an explosion because John didn't turn off the gas,

and if you insist also the corresponding counterfactual in (19′). But the truth of these statements is independent of (13) and does not entail a commitment to John's failure as such. Indeed, if we apply a Davidsonian analysis to the explanans, i.e., to the statement

(21) John didn't turn off the gas,

what we get is not a quantification over a negative event. All we get is the negation of a perfectly ordinary quantification, hence something totally free of ontological commitments:

(21′) $\sim \exists e(\text{Turning-off}(e, \text{John}, \text{the gas}))$.

## 5.5 Concluding Remarks

As I have said, in offering this account I am basically following Helen Beebee, though I'd like to remain neutral on the ontology underlying our explanatory talk. Perhaps here is where facts enter the picture, as Beebee suggests. But perhaps we can just bypass the issue and rest content with Davidson's claim that 'because', unlike 'cause', is truly a sentential connective relating pairs of statements. Otherwise it's hard to see why we shouldn't take all of this as evidence for the view that 'cause' *is* like 'because' and that the causal relata are facts rather than events (as argued for instance by Hugh Mellor (1995). Beebee (2003, p. 293) has her reasons for not accepting this view. Let me now conclude with two remarks concerning the overall plausibility of the account.

First, why are we inclined to assert (13), if (13) is not true? Why do we speak as in (13), if the proper way to phrase things is (19)? Sarah McGrath (2005, p. 129) pointed out that we cannot just appeal to conversational maxims here, and she is right: the maxim of relevance may explain why we do not utter certain truths, not why we do utter certain falsehoods. So how can we explain our inclinations concerning such falsehoods as (13)?

The answer, I think, does lie in a fact about our conversational practices, though a general fact that goes beyond the scope of a Gricean theory. The fact is, we often speak loosely. Indeed, we tend to speak loosely especially when it comes to keeping track of our ontological commitments. When speaking with the vulgar, we may say that there is a difference in age between John and Mary without thereby implying that there are such things as age differences. If necessary, we can rephrase our statement more carefully by saying, for instance,[12]

(22) Either John is older than Mary or Mary is older than John.

We may say that a slice of cheese contains many holes without thereby implying that there are such things as holes. If pressed, we could rephrase our statement more neutrally by saying, for instance,[13]

(23) That slice of cheese is multiply-perforated.

Likewise with (13), I submit. We like the language of causation and we tend to use it freely when it comes to the task of offering explanations. Sometimes this is perfectly all right, as we have seen: it is all right when we actually know the cause of the event whose occurrence we are trying to explain and we know it under a suitable description. Sometimes, however, this is just speaking with the vulgar. If we don't know the relevant cause, for example, then obviously we are not in a position to produce a genuine causal report. We can only produce a causal explanation; we can provide *some* information about the causal history of the event, including negative information to the effect that certain events did not take place. If pressed, that is how we should speak. If pressed, we should rephrase a statement such as (13) by uttering (19) instead. It's just that usually we are not pressed. Usually we don't pay attention to such nuances because usually we don't care about the metaphysical underpinnings of what we say. We tend to speak loosely, and that is a fact about which not even philosophers can complain. What really matters is that we know how to regiment our talk if the need arises.

The second remark concerns a dual worry. Not only are we inclined to assert (13) even though, strictly speaking, (13) is false. We are also inclined to deny

(24) There was an explosion because I didn't turn off the gas

even though, strictly speaking, (24) is true. After all, not only does the causal history that led to the explosion include no event of John's turning off the gas; it includes no event of my turning off the gas, either. Still, had I turned off the gas, there would not have been an explosion. So why are we willing to offer (19) as an explanation, or even (18), but not (24)?

The answer, I think, is once again part and parcel of the general theory of explanation I have been assuming throughout. I have said that the goodness of an explanation is to be weighed against the relevant background of shared knowledge and presuppositions, as with every act of communication. Accordingly, relevance constraints and standards of

[12]The example is from White (1956, pp. 68–69)).

[13]This example is from Lewis and Lewis (1970).

normality apply, not only when we construe a causal statement as a causal explanation, as with (11) versus (12), but also when we put forward a causal explanation explicitly, as with (19) versus (24). Here again I agree with Beebee: the *truth* of a causal explanation does not depend on the moral question of who is to be blamed for what happened; but its *adequacy* does so depend (Beebee (2003, p. 307)). Thus, it is true that there was an explosion because I didn't turn off the gas, for it is true that had I turned off the gas, the explosion would not have occurred. It's just very hard to imagine that someone would be *satisfied* with that explanation: everybody expected John to turn off the gas, which is to say that everybody expected an event of that sort to take place. That no such event took place, as per (19), is therefore significant to an assessment of the causal history of the explosion. It is also significant that nobody turned off the gas, as in (18), although that leaves us with nobody to blame. That no event of *my* turning off the gas took place, however, is completely irrelevant. I don't even know John and I don't know where he lives, so why blame me? Otherwise we might as well blame God for everything. Surely enough, whenever something goes wrong, God could have done something to prevent it. Yet that would be a very poor explanation of *why* that went wrong, *pace* a certain way of telling the story of the world.

## Acknowledgments

This paper brings together two previous papers of mine (Varzi (2006b,a)). I am thankful to the respective editors and publishers for allowing me to re-use the material in the present form.

## References

Armstrong, D. M. 1999. The Open Door. In H. Sankey, ed., *Causation and Laws of Nature*, pages 175–185. Dordrecht: Kluwer.

Beebee, H. 2003. Causing and Nothingness. In Collins et al. (2003), pages 291–308.

Bennett, J. 1988. *Events and Their Names*. Oxford: Clarendon Press.

Bennett, J. 1995. *The Act Itself*. Oxford: Clarendon Press.

Collins, J., H. Hall, and L. A. Paul (eds.). 2003. *Causation and Counterfactuals*. Cambridge (MA): MIT Press.

Davidson, D. 1967. Causal Relations. *Journal of Philosophy* 64:691–703. Reprinted in Davidson (1980), pages 149–162.

Davidson, D. 1970. Events as Particulars. *Noûs* 4:25–32. reprinted in Davidson (1980), pages 181–187.

Davidson, D. 1980. *Essays on Actions and Events*. Oxford: Clarendon Press.

Davidson, D. 1985. Reply to Bruce Vermazen. In B. Vermazen and M. B. Hintikka, eds., *Essays on Davidson: Actions and Events*, pages 172–76. Oxford: Clarendon Press.

de Swart, H. 1996. Meaning and Use of *not ... until*. *Journal of Semantics* 13:221–263.

Grice, H. P. 1975. Logic and Conversation. In P. Cole and J. L. Morgan, eds., *Syntax and Semantics, Vol. 3: Speech Acts*, pages 41–58. New York: Academic Press.

Hart, H. L. A. and T. Honoré. 1985. *Causation in the Law*. Oxford: Clarendon Press. 2nd ed.

Hempel, C. 1965. Aspects of Scientific Explanation. In C. Hempel, ed., *Aspects of Scientific Explanation and Other Essays in the Philosophy of Science*, pages 331–496. New York: Free Press.

Higginbotham, J. 1983. The Logic of Perceptual Reports: An Extensional Alternative to Situation Semantics. *Journal of Philosophy* 80:100–127.

Higginbotham, J. 2000. On Events in Linguistic Semantics'. In J. Higginbotham, F. Pianesi, and A. C. Varzi, eds., *Speaking of Events*, pages 49–79. New York: Oxford University Press.

Horn, L. R. 1989. *The Natural History of Negation*. Chicago: Chicago University Press.

Lakoff, G. 1965. *Irregularity in Syntax*. New York: Holt, Reinhart & Winston.

Lewis, D. K. 1973. Causation. *Journal of Philosophy* 70:556–567.

Lewis, D. K. 1986. Causal Explanation. In D. K. Lewis, ed., *Philosophical Papers: Volume II*, pages 214–240. Oxford: Oxford University Press.

Lewis, D. K. and S. R. Lewis. 1970. Holes. *Australasian Journal of Philosophy* 48:206–212.

McGrath, S. 2005. Causation by Omission: A Dilemma. *Philosophical Studies* 123:125–148.

Mellor, D. H. 1995. *The Facts of Causation*. London: Routledge.

Neale, S. 1988. Events and "Logical Form". *Linguistics and Philosophy* 11:303–321.

Przepiórkowski, A. 1999. On Negative Eventualities, Negative Concord, and Negative Yes/No Questions. In T. Matthews and D. Strolovitch, eds., *Proceeding of Semantics and Linguistic Theory 9*, pages 237–254. Ithaca (NY): CLC Publications.

Quine, W. V. O. 1948. On What There Is. *Review of Metaphysics* 2:21–38.

Russell, B. 1905. On Denoting. *Mind* 14:479–493.

Stockwell, R., P. Schachter, and B. Partee. 1973. *The Major Structures of English*. New York: Holt, Rinehart & Winston.

Tovena, L. M. and A. C. Varzi. 1999. Events and Negative Descriptions. In *Sinn und Bedeutung 1999. Fourth Annual Conference of the Gesellschaft für Semantik*, pages 71–73. Düsseldorf: Heinrich-Heine Universität.

Varzi, A. C. 2006a. Omissions and Causal Explanations. In J. Quitterer and F. Castellani, eds., *Agency and Causation in the Human Sciences*. Paderborn: Mentis Verlag. (To appear).

Varzi, A. C. 2006b. The Talk I Was Supposed to Give. In A. Bottani and R. Davies, eds., *Modes of Existence. Papers in Ontology and Philosophical Logic*. Frankfurt: Ontos Verlag. (To appear).

Vendler, Z. 1967. *Linguistics in Philosophy*. Ithaca (NY): Cornell University Press.

White, M. G. 1956. *Toward a Reunion in Philosophy*. Cambridge (MA): Harvard University Press.

6

# The Case for Core Meaning

MANFRED KIENPOINTNER

## 6.1 Introduction

In this paper the assumption of a language-specific, context-independent core meaning of words and sentences will be defended. To justify this assumption, some old and some more recent arguments in favour of core meaning will be taken up. These arguments have been brought forward by representatives of European Structuralism (Jakobson, Coseriu, Pottier) or Generative Grammar (Katz, Jackendoff), but also in more recent treatises on semantics (Wierzbicka, Goddard). The more general theoretical background for my arguments is the theory of language developed by Coseriu (1958, 1973, 1988, 1990, 1994).

In the following sections, I will first discuss the relationship between core meaning and contextual meaning (cf. section 2), secondly, the relationship between literal meaning and core meaning (cf. section 3) and thirdly, some of the most important pro and counter arguments in relation to core meaning will be discussed (cf. section 4 and 5). But before doing that, I would like to briefly mention three issues I cannot treat in enough detail due to limits of time.

The first issue concerns the vexed problem of choosing an adequate metalanguage for semantic description. The second issue concerns the distinction between encoded and inferred aspects of meaning, or alternatively, between structuralist code models and Gricean inferential models of communication. The third issue concerns the problem of ambiguity of linguistic expressions. As far as these issues are concerned, I have to content myself with the following three remarks. The first remark is on metalanguage and somewhat longer.

Early semantic metalanguages like Katz' markerese (cf. Katz (1972, 1980, 1981)) have received strong and convincing criticism (cf. e.g. Eco (1975, pp. 140 ff.), Eco (1985, pp. 91 ff.); Lyons (1977, pp. 334 ff.); Lyons (1995, pp. 107 ff.); Heringer (1978, pp. 77 ff.); Lakoff (1987, p. 205); Blank (2001, pp. 23 ff.)). The meaning of lexemes and sentences cannot be described adequately with sets of 'universal' semantic markers and distinguishers. For example, the 'notorious' noun *bachelor* has been described as (cf. Katz (1980, p. 61)):

*Meaning, Intentions, and Argumentation.*
Kepa Korta and Joana Garmendia (eds.).

(1) Engl. *bachelor*: {(Physical object), (Human), (Adult), (Male), (Single)}

However, the bracketed meta-linguistic expressions are hard to interpret and cannot easily be distinguished from the corresponding expressions in natural languages. They also involve problems of infinite regress and hidden circularity. Therefore, some linguists have given up the postulates of universality, non-circularity and finiteness of markerese. They simply consider the semantic features as expressions of a particular natural language which are used metalinguistically. That is, semantic features can be seen as convenient abbreviations given in place of more adequate and/or more comprehensive descriptions of meaning (cf. Coseriu (1973, pp. 14 ff.); Lyons (1977, I, pp. 334 ff.)). More specifically, Pottier (1992, p. 73) characterizes the "sème" ("seme", "marker", "semantic feature") as a short periphrastic discourse. This discourse describes the meaning of an expression with as many words of a natural language as are necessary for the clear distinction of the relevant semantic features:

> De notre point de vue, le sème doit se dire avec autant de mots de la langue naturelle qu'il faut pour bien mettre en relief le trait distinctif relatif à l'ensemble considerée. La dénomination de sème est un discours périphrastique à vocation métalinguistique

Convenient as it is, this practice of simply using expressions of a particular natural language A as a semantic metalanguage increases the danger of a perspective which is biased as to the semantic structures of A.

To overcome these deficiencies of earlier semantic metalanguages, Wierzbicka has tried to construct a truly universal metalanguage (called NSM = Natural Semantic Metalanguage). Wierzbicka (1999, p. 36), Wierzbicka (2001, p. 239) restricts the number of metalinguistic expressions to about sixty elements, among them, for example, *I, you, person, thing, people, this, one, two, some, many, good, bad, big, small, think, feel, say, do, make, feel, believe, have, not, because, if, now, here, very, like,* etc. She explicitly excludes all more specific and/or technical lexical items which would make the semantic description incomprehensible for lay people, circular or biased towards one particular language. Moreover, and most interestingly, Wierzbicka formulates her semantic descriptions as full sentences, which together form a coherent text. This makes it possible to describe emotion terms of a language as a prototypical scenario. For example, with the help of NSM, Wierzbicka (1999, p. 88) describes the basic meaning of the English adjective *angry* as follows:

(2) X was angry (with Y)

a. X felt something because X thought something
b. sometimes a person thinks about someone:
c. this person did something bad
d. I don't want this person to do things like this
e. I want to do something because of this
f. when this person thinks this, this person feels something bad
g. X felt something like this
h. because X thought something like this

As far as the difficult problem of the universality of the semantic metalanguage is concerned, Wierzbicka's NSM seems to be an important step forward. However, there remain many theoretical and practical problems. One of the more practical problems is the fact that Wierzbicka's definitions are so long and cumbersome. But she is ready to admit that, for practical reasons, further expressions of a language beyond NSM could be used, as long as they are always conceptually simpler than the defined expressions. Further, these expressions ultimately have all to be defined via NSM (= the principle of "reductive analysis", cf. Wierzbicka (1985, p. 45)). As a practical and more realistic example of the reduction of meta-linguistic vocabulary, the Longman dictionary of contemporary English can be mentioned (cf. LDOCE (2003, p. xi)). In this dictionary, only 2000 words are used as a descriptive metalanguage. The definition of *angry* in the LDOCE (2003, p. 49) runs as follows:

(3) Engl. *angry* "feeling strong emotions which make you want to shout at someone or hurt them because they have behaved in an unfair, cruel, offensive etc. way, or because you think that a situation is unfair, unacceptable etc"

One of the theoretical problems of NSM is the status of the semantic primitives. It can be doubted whether "think" and "want" are indeed simple concepts which would not be in need of further explication and/or definition. Furthermore, the alleged universality of the semantic primitives remains controversial at our present state of rudimentary knowledge about the thousands of languages of the world (for a reply to critics of NSM cf. Goddard (1998)).

As to the second issue, I would like to content myself with the observation that code models and inferential models do not exclude each other and could be integrated into a comprehensive semantic theory. For example, Sperber and Wilson (1986), two distinguished scholars favouring an inferential model of communication, have no problem with the assumption that inferential processes of understanding take encoded meaning as their starting point (cf. Wilson and Sperber (2004, p. 607). Relying on the "Communicative Principle of Relevance", that is, "Every ostensive stimulus conveys a presumption of its own optimal relevance", and more specific communicative principles and strategies, listeners/readers can infer further information beyond the encoded literal meaning on the basis (cf. also Carston (1999)).

As to the third issue, the difficult problems of homonymy, polysemy and free contextual variation have to be dealt with (cf. Lyons (1995, pp. 54 ff.); Cruse (1997, pp. 50 ff.); Blank (2001, pp. 103 ff.)). It could be claimed that there are hardly any truly "monosemic" expressions (Gibbs (1994, p. 41); Recanati (2004, p. 135)) and that, therefore, it is not possible to define one core meaning or a small finite number of core meanings. This does not mean, however, that core meanings become infinite. The cases of homonymy, polysemy and free contextual variation pose differing challenges in this respect.

The easiest case for the defence of core meaning is homonymy (on different types of homonymy cf. Lyons (1995, p. 55)). In the case of homonymy, we are dealing with two or more formally identical, but semantically distinct lexemes, which belong to totally different semantic domains or fields (cf. English examples such as the homophones *knight* vs. *night*, or the homographs *bank* vs. *bank*). This fact prevents the necessity of assuming two or more core meanings because we are actually dealing with two ore more different lexemes, each of them having one core meaning. This becomes especially evident if homonyms (homophones or homographs) belong to different word classes. The following slightly modified example (French *verre/ver/vert/vers*) is taken from Kallmeyer (1974, p. 117):

(4)

| Form | Homophones | Homographs (Homophones) | Word Class | Core meanings |
|---|---|---|---|---|
| | <verre> | | Noun | "glass" |
| | <ver> | | Noun | "worm" |
| [vɛr] | <vert> | | Adjective | "green" |
| | | <vers> | Preposition | "towards" / "around" |
| | | <vers> | Noun | "verse" |

In the case of polysemy, formally identical expressions have two or more meanings which are semantically similar and/or belong to the same semantic field. A similar, further criterion for distinguishing polysemy from homonymy is introduced by Blank (2001, p. 111): The meanings of polysemic lexemes are connected by semantic relations, while this is not the case with the meanings of homonymic lexemes (cf. also Lyons (1995, p. 58)). Hence, in the case of polysemy, one and the same lexeme has two or more meanings. However, the number of meanings can be restricted according to the number of lexemes connected by language-specific semantic relations with the polysemic lexeme (e.g. by being antonyms, hyponyms, cohyponyms etc. of the lexeme). According to this criterion, the polysemic Spanish noun *mujer* could be assigned the following three core meanings (cf. García Hernández (2003, pp. 123 ff.)): 1. *mujer* vs *hombre* ("female human being"), 2. *mujer* vs *niña* "adult woman", 3. *mujer* vs *marido* "married woman".

Both homonymy and polysemy have to be distinguished from free contextual variation of meanings (e.g. *woman* : "woman with a driving licence", "woman who knows four languages", "woman who has received the Nobel Prize" "woman living abroad" etc.etc.), which is indeed infinite. Only free contextual variation seriously challenges the assumption that there is a strictly limited number of core meanings and must be explained in a way that rescues core meaning (cf. below section 2). Similar arguments apply to the ambiguity of syntactic constructions (phrases, sentences) with clearly distinct meanings (cf. Chomsky's well-known examples *the shooting of the hunters, Flying planes can be dangerous* or *John is eager to please*).

## 6.2 Core Meaning and Contextual Meaning

How can free contextual variation of meanings be explained without giving up the idea of core meaning? Of course, they have to be derived somehow from core meaning. This must be done in a way that the core meanings either appear directly in texts or, if they do not manifest themselves directly, at least underlie the contextual meanings in a way that the latter can be derived from them. Coseriu (1988, pp. 188 ff.) distinguishes three types of relationships between core meanings and contextual meanings, which may have to be supplemented with further types. Here, I only discuss the two most important and frequent types.

The first and most frequent case is characterized by the fact that the core meaning is implied by all more specific contextual meanings (cf. Recanati's (2004, pp. 24 ff.) term "enrichment"). Thus the core meaning forms part of the meaning of the contextually specified expressions (cf. Figure 1):

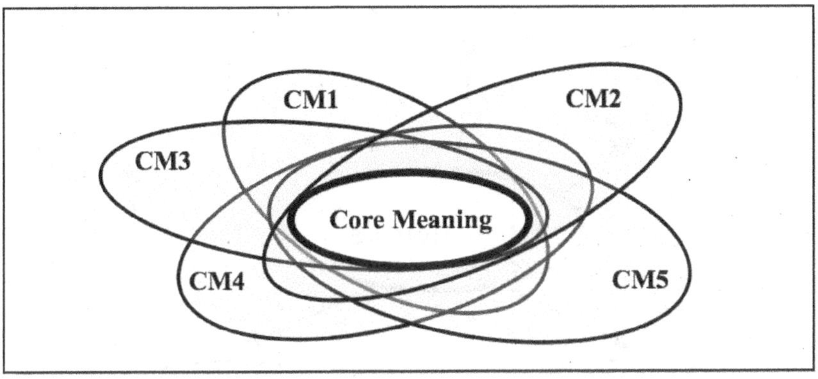


ABBREVIATIONS: CM1, CM2, ..., CM5=CONTEXTUAL MEANINGS 1-5
FIGURE 1

In other words, the core meaning partially 'contains' the contextual meanings, which are additionally specified by features of the context. The contextual meanings, in turn, entail the core meaning. This can be exemplified with the core meaning of grammatical morphemes. Coseriu (1988, p. 188) mentions the Spanish Imperfect Tense, which can refer to present, past or future events, to momentary or repeated activities and to real or fictitious events. All these contextual variants, however, imply a core meaning which can be defined as "inaktuelles Präsens", that is, "a present which is not actual" (ibid.).

Similar examples are provided by lexical morphemes such as English *love* or Latin *amor* and Greek *eros* (cf. Kienpointner (1996a, 1999, 2006)). The core meaning of the noun *love* could be approximately given as follows (cf. also Kövecses (1988, pp. 58 ff.), LDOCE (2003, pp. 962 ff.); OED (1992)):

(5) Engl. *love*: "A strong feeling of affection or liking for someone or something. If this feeling concerns a person, it is combined with sexual attraction and/or a strong feeling of caring about this person. If you experience love, you want to be close to the person you love and you want to be approved by him/her. If this feeling concerns a thing or activity, it is a strong feeling which you experience when you like something very much. This thing or activity gives you pleasure and

enjoyment."

This core meaning is implied by countless contextual variants such as "romantic love", "tender love", "passionate love", "altruistic love", "Platonic love", "love of nature", "love of music", "love of tennis", etc. In English, these variants are lexicalized, for example, in the following hyponyms of *love: affection* = "tender love"; *ardour* = "passionate love"; *charity/devotion* = "altruistic/dedicated love"; *lust, wantonness, lewdness, lasciviousness* = "sensual love".

A far more complicated case is the derivation of contextual meanings in cases where the core meaning is not part of the contextual meanings, but motivates them (cf. Recanati's (2004, p. 26) term "transfer") (cf. Figure 2):

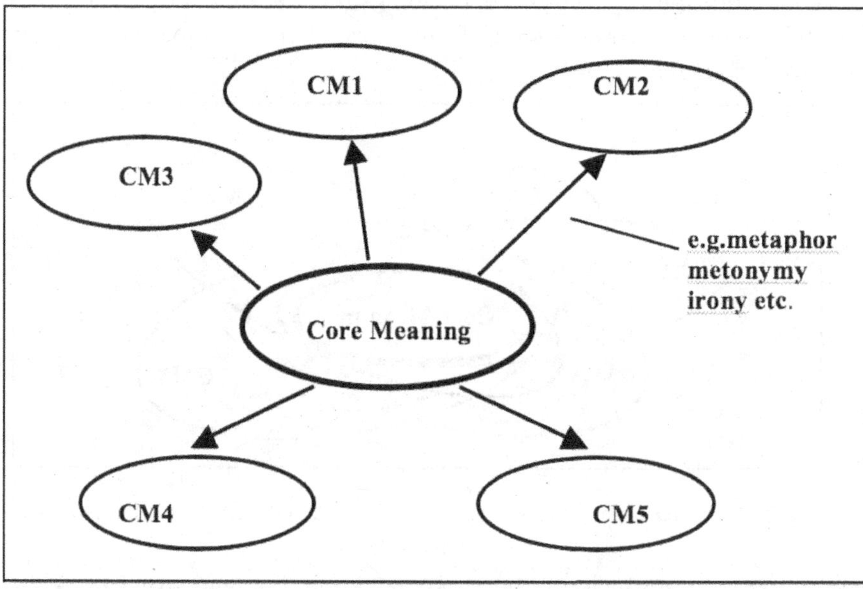


FIGURE 2

Again, Coseriu (1988, pp. 189 ff.) gives the example of a grammatical morpheme, namely, the diminutive suffix in Latin and several Roman languages. In this case, the contextual meanings of the suffix such as affection, tenderness, irony or sarcasm (cf. Spanish *amiguito, hombrecito, profesorcito*) can be motivated by the core meaning, that is, "(objective) diminishment (in size or quantity)") (cf. *casa* ("house") → *casita* ("small house")). The contextual meanings do not contain the core meaning as a part. The contextual meanings in this case can even occur in cases where the core meaning cannot apply at all, for example, when you ironically call a big house *casita* (*¡Qué casita!*). Similarly, mass nouns (*agüita* (lit. "little water"),*vinito* (lit. "little wine")) or pronouns, adjectives and adverbial phrases occur in the diminutive form (*todito, mismito, de rodillitas*). Differently from the contextual meanings, however, the core meaning can occur in all cases where the objects referred to can be small. In these cases the diminutive meaning appears independently from context. This differs from the emotional or ironic variants of the diminutive form, which are totally dependent on their respective contexts (Coseriu (1988, p. 190)):

(6) "Objective diminution": Independent of Context:
e.g. Span. *casita, bosquecito, arbolito, profesorcito, ratoncito, elefantito* etc. ("small house", "small wood", "small tree", "little professor", "small mouse", "small elephant" etc.)
"Emotional, ironic, evaluative diminution": Dependent on Context:
e.g. Span. *casita* ("irony", when used in relation to a huge palace); *profesorcito* ("affection" or "admiration", when used by his mother or close friends; "dislike" or "contempt", when used by colleagues who don't like the professor etc.)

Therefore, the core meaning "objective diminution" can motivate the various emotional meanings ("subjective diminution"): Small things tend to involve emotional judgements, either positively or negatively. In a similar way, Kiefer (2004, p. 341) explains the use of diminutives in Hungarian: "The semantic meaning of the diminutive suffix is in all cases 'small, a little'; that meaning can be modified or added to in various speech situations that are accounted for within pragmatics" (e.g. *újságocska* "little newspaper", that is, not a serious, well-known one; or *a szép szájacskádat* "your nice little mouth", used between lovers; cf. Kiefer (2004, p. 338 f.).

Note, however, that Dressler and Merlini-Barbaresi (1994, p. 396; 2001, pp. 43 ff.), while making a distinction between (morpho-)semantic and (morpho-)pragmatic aspects of diminutives in English, German and Italian, argue against the possibility of motivating the pragmatic meaning [non-serious] with the semantic meaning [small]): 1. Not all uses of diminutives can be motivated with the semantic meaning. 2. In first language acquisition, the pragmatic meaning is developed first. 3. Diachronic changes are better explained on basis of the pragmatic meaning. While these are strong arguments against the assumption of [small] as the core meaning of diminutives, the case for core meaning is not weakened by them: After all, a core meaning ([non-serious]) is assumed by Dressler/Merlini-Barbaresi, albeit a different one. As far as lexical items are concerned, the following example can illustrate how the use of metaphor and paradox can 'enrich' the core meaning of lexemes in a persuasive way. The French advertisement line

(7) French *Son silence est la plus belle des symphonies* (Le Figaro, 30.9.89, p. 51) ("Its silence is the most beautiful of all symphonies")

refers to the Opel Omega. The implied claim is that this car makes almost no noise (or else effectively protects the driver from exterior traffic noises). For the driver, always bothered by the ubiquitous noise of modern traffic, this silence becomes almost like a beautiful symphony, thus enhancing the attractiveness of the Opel Omega for potential purchasers. It is perfectly clear that the core meaning of the French *silence* ("silence") has not been permanently changed by this paradoxical/metaphorical contextual enrichment ("a combination of silence and beautiful music"). However, contextual metaphorical extensions of the core meaning can become permanent. For example, *mouse* as "a small object connected to a computer by a wire, which you move with your hand to give instructions to the computer" LDOCE (2003, p. 1074) or metonymical modifications of the core meaning such as *sails* standing for "sail boats" or *love* standing for the "loved person/object" have become conventionalized. By now, they are a second (third etc.) core meaning (for a description of the diachronic semantic processes leading to these derived meanings, cf. Coseriu (1990, p. 270); Blank (2001, pp. 70 ff.)).

It could be argued that in all these cases the term "core meaning" is inadequate because there is no longer a common "core" which would be implied by all contextual meanings. However, the direction of motivation is always asymmetrical (cf. Recanati (2004, p. 28)): From the core meaning to the metaphorically (etc.) related contextual meanings, and not vice versa. This justifies the derivation of the metaphorical, metonymical, hyperbolic, ironic etc. meanings from the core meaning.

Moreover, the distinction between core meanings and metaphorically (or metonymically etc.) derived contextual meanings is not as hopeless a distinction as Gibbs (1994, p. 42) wants it to be. For instance, the difference between

(8) *The newspaper weighs five pounds (= "publication")* and

(9) *The newspaper fired John (= "publisher")*

clearly relies on a contextually given metonymical reading of *newspaper* in (9). This is also the reason why the core meaning underlying the use of *newspaper* in (8) is placed as the first entry in dictionaries (cf. LDOCE (2003, p. 1106)). Of course, contextual meanings can become conventionalized to a degree that they can develop into second, third etc. core meanings (cf. above). This does not in general prevent, however, the recognizability of core meanings. Nor does it prevent the existence of an asymmetric relation between primary, or core meanings, and secondary, or contextual meanings. Moreover, most of the time innovative metaphorical or metonymical specifications do not immediately change the core meanings of linguistic expressions (cf. Coseriu (1990, pp. 259 ff.), cf. also below, section 3).

Finally, from a methodological point of view, it is most important to stress that semantic features of core meaning have to be empirically verified as to their direct or indirect manifestation in texts, and not as to their appearance in reality, that is, as properties of extra-linguistic objects and states of affairs.

## 6.3 Literal Meaning and Core Meaning

Before turning to the arguments concerning core meaning, I have to add a few remarks to clarify the concept of "literal meaning", which is closely related to the notion of "core meaning" (cf. Gibbs (1994, pp. 27 ff.)). This concept can be understood in many different ways. Here it is understood as the purely language-specific meaning of words and sentences, without any contextually added, and hence more specific semantic properties. Literal meaning in this sense is equivalent to core meaning.

"Literal meaning" in this sense, however, is not to be confused with referential or truth-conditional meaning. The referential and truth-conditional aspects of meaning are also, and quite mistakenly, often called "literal meaning". But the reference of lexical items and the truth/falsity of sentences cannot be judged without presupposing some prototypical usage of the respective expressions. This prototypical usage inevitably involves some default assumptions and background knowledge about the context and the speech situation within which the linguistic expressions are used (cf. Recanati (2004, pp. 141 ff.)).

This is also the reason why Katz's (Katz (1980, p. 14)) attempt to find a criterion for isolating the literal meaning of sentences by imagining an "anonymous letter situation" is no real way out of this problem. In this situation, one receives an anonymous letter with only one sentence and "with no clue whatsoever about the motive, circumstances of transmission, or any factor relevant to understanding the sentence on the basis of its context of utterance" (ibid.). Eco (1985, pp. 122 ff.) has shown quite convincingly, however, that in this situation it would not only be important what is said or written, but also what is not conveyed. This also happens in similar, more realistic situations of oral communication, where only one speaker has access to some relevant information and utters only one sentence. The readers or listeners of 'contextless' sentences would immediately start to infer missing information starting from default assumptions about the intention and the identity of the anonymous writer or the speaker with privileged access to information. The problem is that literal meaning cannot be isolated by imagining a fictitious communicative use of linguistic expressions. Literal meaning can only be isolated by looking how the semantic structures of a language manifest themselves in texts and how these manifestations differ from one language to another.

Finally, "literal meaning" has often been opposed to "figurative meaning". The latter is the meaning appearing in figures of speech such as metaphor, metonymy, hyperbole, irony, understatement etc. However, in spite of the attempts of Dubois et al. (1970) to define it, there is no 'neutral' or 'zero' variety of a language. First of all, there is an extremely large number of conventionalized figures of speech appearing in all varieties of a natural language. As I have already stated above, a figurative usage can be conventionalized to the degree that the metaphorical, metonymical meaning is connected with the respective expressions irrespective of context and situation. This is the case in the following figurative use of the verb *to explode*, which is explicitly mentioned in dictionaries and has become another core meaning:

(10) Engl. *to explode* = "to suddenly express strong feelings such as anger" (cf. LDOCE (2003, p. 549))

Furthermore, it has been shown (cf. Gibbs (1994, pp. 75 ff.)) that judgments of ordinary speakers about the literality of linguistic expressions differ according to the definitions of literal meaning they are given before they are asked to judge certain words or sentences (e.g. "literal meaning" = "conventional meaning", "literal meaning" = "meaning normally expressed in relation to certain subject matters/situations/institutions", "literal meaning" = "non-metaphorical meaning", "literal meaning" = "truth-conditional meaning" etc.). These findings at the same time confirm, however, that speakers' judgments have to be dealt with very cautiously. The meta-linguistic intuitions of native speakers tend to be rather vague and confused (cf., however, Recanati's (2004, p. 79) methodological remarks on the "availability" of literal and derived meanings for ordinary native speakers).

## 6.4 Arguments against Core Meaning

In what follows, a survey of the most important arguments against (the assumption of the existence of) core meaning will be given. Most of these arguments are closely related, but they are separated here for practical purposes of presentation:

**1. Argument:** It is not possible to make a clear distinction between dictionary meaning and encyclopedic meaning, that is, between meaning exclusively known through linguistic competence and meaning which is accessible only through knowledge about the extra-linguistic world (cf. Eco (1975, pp. 70 ff.), Eco (1985, pp. 140 ff.), Haiman (1980)). As encyclopaedic knowledge is virtually endless, the existence of (a finite number of) core meaning(s) seems to become impossible. Furthermore, processing the meaning of words and sentences, we need to have access to general background knowledge about the world. Otherwise, the precise meaning of compounds like *typewriter table* could not be constructed (Gibbs (1994, p. 35); Recanati (2004, pp. 139 ff.)).

**2. Argument:** The meaning of words and sentences cannot be isolated from the influence of contextual factors. In isolation, words only have a "potential for reference", core meaning is a secondary phenomenon and only an abstraction deduced from textual meaning. The latter is the primary phenomenon both as far as language acquisition and discourse comprehension is concerned. This has often been claimed within text linguistics (cf. e.g. Kallmeyer (1974, pp. 119 ff.)) or other linguistic and philosophical theories of "contextualism" (cf. Recanati (2004, pp. 140 ff.)). Taking into account contextual factors seems to make it impossible to establish a core meaning (or, in the case of polysemic words or ambiguous sentences: a few core meanings) because the contextual meanings are virtually endless. Again, the existence of core meaning according to this view is impossible.

**3. Argument:** Some representatives of the reference theory of meaning and truth-functional semantics deny that language-specific meaning exists at all (cf. Russell (1949),Quine (1971)). In this perspective, lexical items refer to extra-linguistic objects and the meaning of declarative sentences is their truth-value rather than some language-specific core meaning. Variants of this perspective (cf. Putnam (1975)) assume that only the reference of linguistic expressions is stable and fixed by the best available expert knowledge (e.g. *water* = $H_2O$). As to the meaning of linguistic items, Putnam claims that it consists of a set of markers and stereotypes. Stereotypes are defined as a set of common sense assumptions about extra-linguistic objects held by lay people (e.g. *water* = "natural kind", "liquid", "colorless", "transparent", "tasteless", "thirst-quenching" etc.; cf. Putnam (1975, p. 269)):

(11) *water*

| SYNTACTIC MARKERS | SEMANTIC MARKERS | STEREOTYPES | EXTENSION |
|---|---|---|---|
| mass noun; concrete | natural kind; liquid | colorless; transparent; tasteless; thirst-quenching; etc. | $H_20$ (give or take impurities) |

Putnam assumes that in most cases the markers and stereotypes are defeasible, which makes the existence of a stable core meaning impossible.

**4. Argument:** This emphasis on reference and truth has been criticized by Wittgenstein (1975) and his followers (e.g. Heringer (1978, 1999); Recanati (2004, p. 146)), who replaced reference theory with a use theory of meaning. However, as a consequence of this replacement, a new criticism of core meaning arises: The complexities of the use of linguistic expressions can never be fully captured without taking into account the extra-linguistic contexts of linguistic usage, for example, the nonverbal activities and the institutions within which linguistic utterances are embedded. Again, core meaning seems to be impossible in this view.

**5. Argument:** Ordinary language philosophy, speech act theory and linguistic pragmatics have stressed that to use language means to perform actions, "to do things with words". The assumption of static or stable core meanings does not seem to fit into a pragmatic view of language as a dynamic process of interaction. In this view, meanings are created, reproduced, but also negotiated, modified and changed within dialogue. Therefore, they are not existing as abstract entities prior to and independent of discourse (cf. Verschueren (1981, 1999), Deppermann (1999)).

**6. Argument:** Prototype semantics, a more recent tradition within the study of meaning (cf. Rosch (1978)), has assumed that borderlines among many (though not all: Lakoff (1987, p. 150)) categories are fuzzy. In the case of fuzzy categories it is hard to draw a sharp line between members of neighbouring categories. The resulting semantic continuum between two categories seems to make a discrete description of core meanings impossible. Furthermore, it has been assumed that there is no minimal set of necessary and sufficient properties shared by all members of a category. Again, this makes it impossible to describe the core meaning of a category as a limited number of semantic properties. Moreover, according to the cognitive perspective, meaning is primarily organized according to cognitively relevant scenes/scripts or idealized cognitive models rather than language-internal structures (cf. Fillmore (1977b), Lakoff (1987)).

**7. Argument:** The cognitive theory of metaphor, as developed by Lakoff, Johnson, Kövecses and others, assumes that abstract concepts such as "love", "anger" or "theory" are basically understood metaphorically. Therefore, these concepts cannot be defined by non-metaphorical semantic properties (cf. Lakoff (1987, 1996, 2005), Lakoff and Johnson (1980), Kövecses (1988, 2000, 2002)). Hence, an independently defined core meaning does not seem to be possible in these cases.

There is no way to deny that these are important arguments which, taken together, make a very strong case against core meaning. Nevertheless I am convinced that 1. Some of these arguments can be refuted, 2. Others are right in some respect, but can be integrated into a comprehensive theory of meaning which still leaves a place for core meaning (cf. Lyons (1991, p. 23)), and 3. Still others arise out of misunderstandings and a failure to distinguish different layers and aspects of meaning.

To show this, I first need to introduce a threefold distinction between aspects of meaning developed by Coseriu. This threefold distinction is one of the main strengths of Coseriu's comprehensive theory of meaning, because it helps to avoid some of the problems and misunderstandings mentioned above (cf. the similar, but not identical threefold distinction made by Recanati (2004, p. 21)). Coseriu (1994, pp. 63 ff.); Coseriu and Geckeler (1981, p. 54) distinguishes between meaning in the narrow sense ("Bedeutung" = language-specific meaning), reference ("Bezeichnung" = meaning as reference to extra-linguistic objects and states of affairs) and sense ("Sinn" = context-specific meaning at the text or discourse or speech act level; note that this definition of "sense" clearly differs from the one established by Lyons (1995, p. 80): "the set, or network, of sense-relations that hold between it and other expressions of the same language"). As summarized in Figure 3, these three aspects of semantics relate to language, reality and discourse, respectively:

**Linguistic Semantics:**

| **Meaning** | **Reference** | **Sense** |
|---|---|---|
| (Language) | (Reality) | (Discourse) |

FIGURE 3

In this way, Coseriu does not claim that linguistic semantics has to deal primarily, let alone exclusively, with one of these three types of meaning. Both structural semantics (the description of language-specific meaning), reference theory (the description of various types of reference to extra-linguistic objects, for example, definite reference, indefinite reference, generic reference etc.) and text semantics/pragmatics find their place in this comprehensive theory of semantics (cf. also the arguments against reductionism in semantic theory advanced by Lyons (1991, p. 23)). The description of core meaning has to be complemented with descriptions of the many ways of referring to reality, including truth-conditional semantics, and descriptions of contextual meanings at the text or discourse level (cf. Asher (1999); Blutner (2002)). A similarly broad semantic theory, distinguishing both ("virtual", context-independent) meaning and ("actual", context-specific) sense, is established in Beaugrande and Dressler (1981, p. 88) and in Wunderlich (1991, p. 33).

Moreover, according to Coseriu, the language-specific meaning of an expression has to be described for one and the same "functional language". A functional language is a structurally homogeneous variety of a "historical language" such as English, German or Turkish. Historical languages are complex entities structured by an "architecture of language" comprising diatopic, diastratic and diaphasic varieties (i.e. dialects, sociolects, and stylistic varieties). If this distinction is not taken into account, many pseudo-problems of semantics arise, such as the existence of synonyms having a different form but exactly the same core meaning. For example, it is impossible to find substantial semantic differences between pseudo-synonyms such as *piss* and *urine* or *rabbit* and *bunny*, apart from their differing connotations. However, these connotations do not arise from the semantics of the lexical items, but from their belonging to specific varieties of a language.

Now one could still ask critically: Why is it necessary to consider an independent level of core meaning at all, if language-specific meaning is only a small part of the whole story anyway and if it can hardly be separated from referential and contextual meaning? In the following, I would like to deal with the seven arguments against core meaning listed above in order to answer this critical question.

## 6.5 Arguments for Core Meaning

### 6.5.1 Dictionary and Encyclopaedia

As far as the first argument is concerned, the following two things have to be conceded: 1. In many cases it is indeed hard to draw a clear line between dictionary meaning and encyclopaedic meaning (cf. Wierzbicka (1985, p. 141); Pottier (1992, p. 75); Kleiber (1998, p. 49)). 2. In many cases is it not even possible to draw a line at all.

This does not mean, however, that the distinction between dictionaries and encyclopaedias has to be given up. Even critics of the distinction such as Haiman and Gibbs concede that the distinction has to be made somehow out of practical reasons:

> [...] the distinction between dictionaries and encyclopedias, while theoretically untenable, has the happy property of working very well in practice (cf. Haiman (1980, p. 355))

> On a practical level, it makes sense to keep the dictionary entry for *horse* rather brief and to put most of the remaining information about horses in an encyclopedia (cf. Gibbs (1994, p. 28))

There is no doubt that we cannot dispense of dictionaries. But there are also important theoretical arguments for maintaining the distinction between dictionary meaning and encyclopaedic meaning.

First of all, in spite of the many problems to draw a precise line between core meaning and encyclopaedic meaning, there are criteria for doing this in a principled way (pace Cruse (1997, pp. 19 ff.)). Wierzbicka (1985, pp. 113 ff.; 139 ff.) has suggested the following basic criterion: Core meaning is what adult speakers of a language have to know as a "concept minimum" to count as competent members of a speech community. Even as far as technological knowledge about the structure and function of cars and bicycles is concerned, "there is a limit to the technical ignorance compatible with linguistic competence" Wierzbicka (1985, p. 117). At the same time, competent speakers of a language do not need to be experts in some particular field: "[N]o specialized knowledge can be regarded as part of the meaning" Wierzbicka (1985, p. 41).

Furthermore, representatives of structural semantics such as Coseriu (1973, pp. 26 ff.); Coseriu (1990, pp. 252 ff.) and Lyons (1977, I, pp. 287 ff.); Lyons (1995, pp. 100 ff.) are willing to concede that large portions of the lexicon of everyday language are accessible only via encyclopaedic knowledge. This is true, for example, for thousands of lexemes belonging to biological and mineralogical nomenclatures such as the following English terms

(12) Engl. *finch, robin...*; *bass, cod...*; *elm, ash...*; *larkspur, narcissus...*; *garnet, amethyst* etc.

or the corresponding German lexical items

(13) Germ. *Fink, Rotkehlchen...*; *Barsch, Kabeljau...*; *Ulme, Esche...*; *Rittersporn, Narzisse...*; *Granat, Amethyst* etc.

Therefore, some of the respective lexical items do not have a (full) dictionary meaning at all (cf. also similarly Jackendoff (1990) on the perceptual domain of vision).

But at least for some very well-known subsections of the biological nomenclature, purely semantic descriptions can be given, which do not contain expert knowledge. Wierzbicka has shown this for dozens of expressions of everyday vocabulary such as *cat, dog, horse, tiger, apple, pear*, etc. Wierzbicka (1985, p. 146 ff.). Moreover, there are many other parts of the lexicon which are definable by language-specific knowledge alone, for example, nouns from the semantic fields of family members, emotions or furniture, adjectives in the fields of age, space and temperature, verbs of motions, speech act verbs, space and time adverbials, prepositions, conjunctions, discourse particles etc. (cf. Coseriu (1973), Coseriu and Geckeler (1981), Wierzbicka (1985, 1991)). The same holds for grammatical morphemes (e.g. tense, aspect, case etc.; as to the core meanings of Russian case morphemes, cf. Jakobson (1974) and Wierzbicka (1980)).

Below, I will give one example. At the same time, I will try to solve the problem that the rather long descriptions in Natural Semantic Metalanguage (NSM) could not be used for practical lexicographic purposes. Therefore, I try to modify and reduce Wierzbicka's (Wierzbicka (1985, p. 167)) description of *cat* in a way which makes the respective dictionary entry both semantically exhaustive and quantitatively more manageable. The ideal of reductive analysis can be maintained insofar as it would be possible to define all the lexemes I have used as 'shortcuts' of semantic description (e.g. "domestic", "whiskers" etc.) via NSM. Thus the inevitable length of descriptions relying exclusively on NSM can be avoided. The description in (14) is a compromise between the long and cumbersome description of *cat* in NSM (more than one printed page!) and the short description in LDOCE, which surely does not cover the conceptual minimum all native speakers have (cf. example (15)):

(14) Engl. *cat* : "a small domestic animal (male or female; the male cat is called *tomcat*) which is soft and furry, has a round head with whiskers and pointed ears, sharp teeth, four legs with sharp claws and a long tail [HABITAT, SIZE, APPEARANCE].

Cats like to be clean, licking their body to keep it clean. They chase little animals and birds whose meat they could eat. They move quickly, without noise and in an elegant way. They can see in the dark. Cats make characteristic sounds: They meow, they purr if they are happy, they spit if they are angry. They are rather independent animals, unlike dogs they do not do what people would tell them to do [BEHAVIOUR].

Most people like them as pets and consider cats to be useful and nice domestic animals. Cats are thought to be lazy and to like to be comfortable, but to fight for what they want to get [RELATION TO PEOPLE]"

(15) Engl. *cat* : "a small animal with four legs that people often keep as a pet. Cats sometimes kill small animals and birds" LDOCE (2003, pp. 230 ff.)

A few comments on (14) are in order to point out potential theoretical problems for semantic theory. Strictly spoken, only a small part of (14) is "core meaning" in the sense of purely language-specific meaning. This part probably includes

1. the features "small domestic animal";
2. the fact that in English, the general term *cat* is both used for male and female cats, whereas there is a specific term for the male cat, *tomcat* (cf. similarly German *Katze* vs *Kater*; in Roman languages such as Italian or French, it is the other way round: *gatto* vs *gatta*, *chat* vs *chatte*; on such "inclusive oppositions" cf. Coseriu and Geckeler (1981, p. 48)):

(16)

| ENGLISH | GERMAN | FRENCH | ITALIAN |
|---|---|---|---|
| *tomcat* masc. | *Kater* masc. | *chatte* fem. | *gatta* fem. |
| *cat* | *Katze* | *chat* | *gatto* |

3. the "lexical solidarity" (cf. Coseriu (1967), Coseriu and Geckeler (1981, p. 56)) between *cat* and *meow*, *purr* and *spit*. Here, language-specific syntagmatic semantic structures can be observed: *Cats meow, Dogs bark, Horses neigh, Ducks quack* etc.

The other parts of the semantic description in (14) can be justified as core meaning in a broader sense. However, they are not parts of the semantic system of the English language, but of the norm. The norm is the level of language which is mere traditionally fixed, statistically most frequent, but not necessarily functional, that is, distinctive in relation to other expressions of the language (cf. Coseriu and Geckeler (1981, p. 54)). Now what is usually said about cats, albeit not necessarily so, can be integrated into a description of the lexeme *cat* which tries to capture the norm. This includes the most frequent semantic variants and the most frequent uses of *cat* in sentences and discourse (cf. Coseriu (1990, p. 257)).

The inclusion of frequently used, "expected" Cruse (1997, pp. 18 ff.) but not necessary properties comes close to the suggestion of Verschueren (1981, p. 334), Lyons (1995, p. 116) and Kleiber (1998, p. 80) to take prototypical properties of lexical items into account (cf. below, section 5.6.). However, Coseriu's point of view in this respect is linguistic rather than cognitive.

### 6.5.2 Core Meaning and Context

The second argument can be countered with the following observations: It is true that there is no upper limit of free contextual variants of meaning. But not all senses (contextual meanings) found in texts have equal status. Most, if not all of them can be related to one or a few core meanings of lexical items or sentences. The contextual meanings can be shown to be dependent on this core meaning or these few core meanings (cf. above, section 2 and Coseriu (1988, pp. 188 ff.)). Of course, it has to be shown with the help of authentic empirical material, that the potentially infinite contextual meanings can indeed be derived from one or a few core meaning(s). Core meanings are not Platonic "abstract objects" (pace Katz (1981)). For example, some central elements of the lexical field "age" in Classical Latin are the following six adjectives which are assigned their respective semantic features (cf. Coseriu (1990, p. 263)). The following overview is based on the revised description in Kienpointner (1996b):

(17) Lat. *vetus, novus, vetulus, novellus, senex, iuvenis*

| | |
|---|---|
| *senex*<br>[advanced age]<br>[of human beings] | *invenis*<br>[young age]<br>[of human beings] |
| *vetulus*<br>[advanced age]<br>[of animals/plants] | *novellus*<br>[young age]<br>[of animals/plants] |
| *vetus*<br>[advanced age]<br>[of any entities] | *novus*<br>[young age]<br>[of any entities] |

The empirical plausibility of these semantic structures can be shown by their direct manifestation in many Latin texts (for examples cf. Kienpointner (1996b)). Apparent exceptions like

(18) Lat. *homo novus, vetus gladiator, canis senex*

can be explained by the fact that *novus* in *homo novus* ("upstart", "parvenu") does not contain the semantic feature [young age], but [person who has very quickly acquired a highly prestigious position of political power]. Nor does *vetus* in the noun phrase *vetus gladiator* have the feature [advanced age], but rather: [experienced]. Finally, *canis senex* can be an anthropomorphic, metaphorical extension of *senex* to a domestic animal, whose faithfulness and loyalty is highlighted by this metaphor. Alternatively, *canis* and *senex* can be combined in certain text genres like fable, where animals are regularly assigned human properties.

Interestingly enough, these attempts to explain contextual meanings by deriving them from core meanings plus additional (sometimes metaphorical) features provided by context, situation or text genre have clear parallels in cognitive linguistics. They come close to Lakoff's distinction between central subcategories of a category and non-central extensions of these central subcategories. Lakoff (1987, pp. 83 ff., 104 ff.) explains the differences between central and non-central cases of *mother* and the Japanese classifier *hon* as effects of a "radial structure":

(19) Engl. *mother* (central case: the woman who gave birth to the child, supplied her half of the child's genes, nurtured the child, is married to the father, is one

generation older than the child and its legal guardian) vs *stepmother* (who didn't give birth or supply the genes, but is currently married to the father), *adoptive mother* (who didn't give birth or supply the genes, but is the legal guardian and is obliged to provide nurture) as well as *birth mother, foster mother, biological mother* etc.

(20) Jap. classifier *hon* (central case: used for classifying rigid long, thin objects like sticks, canes, pencils, candles, trees, ropes, hair etc.) vs *hon* in non-central cases, that is, used for classifying the following entities: martial art contests (where long/thin staffs and swords are used), hits in baseball (due to the straight trajectories of the ball and the form of the baseball bat, which is long, thin and rigid), telephone calls (transmitted by wires, which are long, thin objects) etc. etc.)

The underlying categories are "radial categories" (cf. Lakoff (1987, p. 84)):

> The category of *mother* in this culture has what we will call a *radial structure*. A radial structure is one where there is a central case and conventionalized variations on it which cannot be predicted by general rules. [...] We are limiting radial structures only to cases where the variations are conventionalized and have to be learned.

Following Lakoff, Rainer (2003) uses the concept of radial structures to explain central and non-central types of derivation with the Spanish suffix *-azo*. The central type means "blow, stroke, etc. with an x", e.g. *acotazo* "blow with a whip" (*acote*), and "continues to be by far the most important and productive one" (Rainer (2003, p. 198)). From this type, metaphoric and metonymic extensions are derived, for example, *bogotazo* ("riot in Bogotá"), *cañonazo* "shot with a cannon" (*cañón*), *jeringazo* "injection with a syringe" (*jeringa*) etc.

Of course, the theoretical perspectives of Coseriu, Lakoff and Rainer are totally different. On the one hand, we have a language-specific perspective looking for contrasts between core meaning and contextual meanings (Coseriu), on the other hand, a cognitive perspective looking for cognitive mechanisms in human thought (Lakoff), or a perspective of word formation denying the possibility of a core meaning and explaining non-central cases of a word formation type as "semantic fragmentation" (Rainer (2003, p. 198)). However, we can observe a striking similarity in distinguishing and deriving non-central cases from central cases of a certain semantic type.

A further weakness of the second argument has to do with the fact that some specific examples of arguments using contextual variation against core meaning are potentially fallacious. These examples, which are given to refute an assumed core meaning, are based on a circular argument. First an alleged, but much too specific core meaning is given, then it is shown that certain semantic features of this core meaning can be absent in perfectly normal contextual uses. However, sometimes a more abstract or a more aptly formulated version of the core meaning would not be refuted by these examples.

Coseriu (1990, pp. 256 ff.) discusses Fillmore's example of the alleged core meaning of *to climb*: "to move", "upwards", "clambering". The non-prototypical counter examples of *The monkey is climbing down the flagpole* and *The snail is climbing up the flagpole* are intended to show that the assumed features "upwards" and "clambering" can be deleted. Using also Spanish examples, however, Coseriu (1990, p. 256) demonstrates that differently from Spanish *trepar* (roughly, = "to climb upwards"), Engl. *to climb* could be defined in a more abstract way (cf. e.g. the definition of *to climb* "to move vertically usually upwards, usually with effort" in the FrameNet Database: http://framenet.icsi.berkeley.edu; 4.11.2005). In this way, the alleged counter examples do not refute semantic features of core meaning.

For instance, if instead of "para arriba" (= "upwards") and "ayudándose con las manos y los pies o con las patas" (= "clambering", that is, "using hand and feet or paws") the features "sobre un plano vertical o inclinado" (= "along a vertical or slanting surface") and "agarrándose con las extremidades" (= "clinging to something with one's extremities"), not only the monkey's climbing down the flagpole, but also the snail's climbing up and the contextual uses of still other expressions, such as Spanish *plantas trepadoras* ("twiners", "climbers", that is, climbing plants) can be easily explained. Thus the core meaning is no longer 'refuted':

(21) *to climb* : [to move][along a vertical or slanting surface][clinging to something with one's extremities]
(Described in this way, the verb is applicable to the movement of human beings and animals such as monkeys, upwards and downwards, as well as to the movement of other animals, even snails, and plants)

Still other uses of *to climb* such as

(22) *The plane climbed to 30,000 feet*

could still be subsumed under the core meaning, while sentences such as

(23) *The temperature climbed into the 90s or*

(24) *The stock market climbed 50 points today*

could be explained as contextually derived metaphorical meanings. It is true that metaphorical meanings by definition cannot be subsumed under the core meaning "on the basis of a common semantic denominator" (Gibbs (1994, p. 44); cf. also Rainer (2003, pp. 206 ff.)). However, it remains quite clear that there is an asymmetry: The metaphorical meanings depend on the core meaning and can be derived from it or motivated by it, but not vice versa (cf. above, section 2).

This does not mean that the only way to 'rescue' core meanings is always to rely on more abstract definitions nor that these definitions necessarily become abstract to a degree that they are not falsifiable (contrary to what Gibbs (1994, p. 43) seems to believe; cf. also Recanati (2004, p. 140)). Sometimes, the contextual variants have even to be explained by making the core meaning more specific. The legendary definition of the noun *bachelor* is such a case. Fillmore (1977b, pp. 67 ff.) and Lakoff (1987, pp. 70 ff.) have argued that the current definition "male, adult, unmarried" does not hold (or only hold given idealizing assumptions). There are non-prototypical examples such as the Pope, Tarzan (before meeting Jane), unmarried homosexuals etc., who would not normally be called "bachelors". This may be true for the standard definition, but not for an improved one which replaces the feature "unmarried" by "who, being able to marry, has not done so or has ceased to do so". This is Coseriu's (Coseriu (1990, pp. 247, 255)) definition of the analogous Spanish example *soltero* (= *bachelor*):

(25) Span. *soltero* : [varón], [adulto], [que, pudiendo casarse, no lo ha hecho aún o ha dejado de hacerlo]( "male, adult (person), who, being able to marry, has not done so or has ceased to do so")

Still another weakness of the second argument results from the fact that it would be hard to explain how we understand each other in everyday communication if we indeed had to deal with an infinite number of senses. To take one further example: It is true that there are many contextually specified variants of the meaning of *red.* Gibbs (1994, p. 39) (cf. also Recanati (2004, p. 138 f.)) lists five senses:

(26) Engl. *red*: "(a) tawny when predicated of a skin type, (b) pinkish red when predicated of potatoes, (c) orange when predicated of hair, (d) purply when predicated of wine, (e) pinkish red when predicated of wood" (Gibbs correctly adds "and so on")

This is intended as a counter argument against the assumption of a set of mentally stored 'literal' meanings, because such an assumption would run into problems with the limits of processability. But actually this is a counter argument against the assumption of an infinity of contextual meanings. These would hardly be processable without the assumption of a more central, relatively stable core meaning underlying and explaining the more peripheral or specific senses in certain verbal and situational contexts (cf. Beaugrande and Dressler (1981, pp. 89 ff.) on the relative stability of "virtual meaning"). In the case of the adjective *red,* the specific senses could all be derived from the core meaning "the color thought of as the color of blood" (cf. Wierzbicka (1985, p. 18)):

(27) Engl. *red*: "the color thought of as the color of blood" (cf. also LDOCE (2003, p. 1374): *red* "having the colour of blood")

The more specific shades of "red" can be derived from the additional semantic information provided by the colour of the object referred to in a specific context. Note that Coseriu (1990, p. 254) does not assume that basic colour terms are analysable within the framework of structural semantics. However, he acknowledges that at least some colour terms or the semantic field of colour terms as a whole could be partially analyzed.

The relevance of core meaning for speaking and understanding also explains that it plays a central role in Levelt's model of speech production (Levelt (1989, p. 9)). An adult speaker with a normal speech rate produces some 150 words per minute and normal educated speakers of English actively use about 30.000 words (Levelt (1989, p. 199)). In order to explain the enormous speed of access to lexical items Levelt postulates parallel processing, but also the existence of core meanings of "lemmas" (= the syntactic and semantic part of entries in the mental lexicon). The meaning of a lexical item is defined as "the set of conceptual conditions that must be fulfilled in the message for the item to become selected", for example "to ingest for nourishment or pleasure" in the case of the English verb *to eat* (Levelt (1989, p. 182)).

Furthermore, in order to explain "convergence", that is, our success in choosing the right lexical item for a concept, Levelt introduces three principles which all involve core meaning Levelt (1989, p. 213):

> *The uniqueness principle* No two lexical items have the same core meaning. [...]

> *The core principle* A lexical item is retrieved only if its core condition is satisfied by the concept to be expressed. [...]
>
> *The principle of specificity* Of all the items whose core conditions are satisfied by the concept, the most specific one is retrieved.

Of course, using the concept of core meaning, Levelt does not deny the huge theoretical problems connected with the description of core meaning: "[T]he problems about the precise structure of theses conceptual specifications are horrendous" Levelt (1989, p. 197). But it can be argued that core meaning and lexical fields play an important role in language processing (cf. also Lutzeier (1993, pp. 207 ff.)), although there are also psycholinguistic models denying the existence of a core meaning (cf. Recanati (2004, p. 147) on models supporting (core) "meaning eliminativism").

### 6.5.3 Core Meaning, Reference, and Truth

The third argument, namely, that meaning is equivalent to reference or truth, can be refuted by a comparison of semantic structures across or within languages. As core meaning is language-specific by definition, this comparison across languages is highly important as far as methodology is concerned. These structures can have the same reference, but nevertheless differ considerably as to their meaning. In the following: 1. semantic differences at the lexical level, 2. contrasting syntactic and semantic sentence structures, 3. differing semantic roles and finally, 4. differing entailments of sentences will be chosen as illustrative examples.

Lexemes in different languages can clearly differ semantically while the reference remains the same. For example, the meaning of a lexeme L1 in language A can be more specific than the meaning of the corresponding lexeme L2 in language B. Here are a few examples: Latin *avunculus/patruus* and English *uncle*, English *sky/heaven* and German *Himmel*, French *louer*, Engl. *rent (out)* and German *mieten/vermieten*, Latin *senex/vetulus/vetus* and English *old*/German *alt* (for further examples cf. Blank (2001, pp. 130 ff.)). These lexemes can be used to refer to the same objects, properties and activities in the real world, but they clearly differ in meaning:

(28)

Lat. *avunculus* ("maternal uncle") ↖
Engl. *uncle* ("maternal or paternal uncle")
Lat. *patruus* ("paternal uncle") ↙

Furthermore, also within one and the same language, lexemes/sentences can differ semantically, but refer to the same object or state of affairs. This can be illustrated by Frege's (Frege (1975, p. 41)) well-known example of Germ. *Morgenstern/Abendstern* ("morning star/evening star"). Moreover, many lexical units or even whole word classes seem not to refer to anything specific in the real world or some possible world (cf. discourse particles, interjections, or greetings etc.), but still have language-specific meaning (cf. Wierzbicka (1985, p. 15)).

Similar arguments apply to the sentence level. Sentences having the same truth value clearly differ in meaning across languages. This has been acknowledged also by philosophers who distinguish between "extension" (reference; Frege's "Bedeutung") in the real world or in possible worlds and "intension" (roughly equivalent to meaning; Frege's "Sinn") (cf. Frege (1975, p. 41); Carnap (1972, pp. 23 ff.), Lewis (1970, p. 23)).

More specifically, languages often express the same state of affairs in a (slightly) different perspective or conceptualize semantic roles in differing ways. For example, in the semantic domain of possession, syntactic constructions can foreground or background the possessor by assigning different syntactic functions to the possessor. These functions can be roughly ordered according to the following hierarchy (taken slightly simplified from Lehmann et al. (2000, p. 10)):

(29) Subject > Direct Object > Indirect Object > Adjunct > Adnominal function

This hierarchy and further semantic hierarchies (e.g. Human > Non Human Animate > Inanimate etc. or Agent > Patient) establish the difference between "person prominence" languages (e.g. many Indo-European Languages) and "relation prominence" languages (e.g. Turkish, Yucatec Maya) in the realm of possession (cf. Lehmann et al. (2000, p. 16)). The distinction can be illustrated with the following examples (The Yucatec example is quoted according to Lehmann et al. (2000, p. 52)):

(30) Engl. *I have money.*

(31) Germ. *Ich habe Geld.* ("I have money")

(32) Lat. *Habeo pecuniam.* ("Have-1.SG. money", that is, "I have money")

(33) Lat. *Mihi est pecunia.* (that is, "To me is money")

(34) Turk. *Param var.* ("Money-POSS.1.SG. exists", that is, "My money exists")

(35) Yuc. *Yàan teen tàak'in.*
EXIST me money (that is, "Exists to me money")

(36) Yuc. *Yàan in tàak'in.*
EXIST POSS.1.SG money (that is, "My money exists")

Abbreviations: POSS = Possessive; 1 = $1^{st}$ person; SG = singular; EXIST = Existential

These examples show how languages differ in characterizing the possessor in a more or less person prominent or relation prominent way. Whereas English and German assign the highly person prominent syntactic function "subject" to the possessor, in Latin there is at least one other highly frequent construction, where the possessor is assigned the less person prominent function "indirect object". In Turkish, the possessor appears still less person prominent as adnominal function (a possessive suffix (*-m*) as an adnominal suffix of the possessed noun *para* "money") and in Yucatec Maya, as an indirect object or, alternatively, as an adnominal function (an attribute (*in*) to the possessed noun *tàak'in* "money"). At the same time, these examples show that the sentence meaning is language-specific because it ultimately is composed on the basis of the meanings of the constituents of the sentence (words, grammatical morphemes, phrases). As all example sentences basically refer to the same state of affairs and can have the same truth value, language-specific meaning cannot be equated with reference or truth value.

The difference between meaning and reference at the syntactic level can also be shown as far as semantic roles or theta roles are concerned.

Semantic roles such as Agent, Patient, Benefactive, Instrument have often been equated with "reference roles". Reference roles refer to real world entities and relationships rather than to semantic roles in the narrow sense, namely, "language-specific roles" ("sprachlich-begriffliche Rollen", cf. Coseriu (1987, p. 189)). Coseriu does not deny the importance of dealing with reference roles within grammar. But he is right in stressing that we refer to extra-linguistic entities through language, that is, through the lexical and grammatical means of the conceptualization of reality within particular languages Coseriu (1987, p. 186). Not making this distinction at all would lead to the counter-intuitive result of claiming that the only "role differences" between languages concern formal expression. However, forms have functions, and neglecting or ignoring these language-specific functions would reduce linguistic semantics to some kind of reference theory or truth-conditional semantics, which already has been shown to be counter-intuitive by examples (30) to (36).

If we look at some early analyses of "semantic" roles within modern linguistics, it becomes quite clear that these contributions indeed reduce language-specific conceptualizations of reference roles to differences in material expressions within one language or several languages (cf. García Hernández (2003, p. 122)). In this respect, see examples (37-39), (40-41) and (42-43). Fillmore (1968, p. 25) classifies both *the key* and *with the key* in (37-39) as Instrument (= INSTR). Similarly, Helbig and Buscha (1991, p. 636) classify both *mit dem Messer* and *das Messer* in (40-41) as Instrument. Finally, Foley and Valin (1984, pp. 56 ff.) classify both *against the wall* and *the wall* in (42-43) as Locative (= LOC):

(37) *John opened the door* [$_{INSTR}$ *with the key*].

(38) [$_{INSTR}$ *The key*] *opened the door.*

(39) *John used*[$_{INSTR}$ *the key*] *to open the door.*

(40) Germ. [$_{INSTR}$ *Das Messer*] *schneidet das Brot.* ("The knife cuts the bread")

(41) Germ. *Er schneidet das Brot* [$_{INSTR}$ *mit dem Messer*]. ("He cuts the bread with the knife")

(42) *The man hits the cane* [$_{LOC}$ *against the wall*].

(43) *The man hits* [$_{LOC}$ *the wall*] *with the cane.*

Arguing against this oversimplification, Coseriu correctly stresses that different forms in individual languages usually encode differing semantic functions. For example, Latin ablative forms with or without the preposition *a(b)* can be used to distinguish the reference roles Agent (= AG) and Force (= FO) in passive clauses. In this way, the respective Latin ablative forms express non-animate causes of events in a less "agent-like" way. In German passive clauses, both Agent and Force can be encoded with the prepositional adjunct *von* + NP, although the prepositional adjunct *durch* + NP is more commonly used for Force (cf. Kühner and Stegmann (1962, p. 495); Helbig and Buscha (1991, p. 173 f.)):

(44) Lat. *Oppidum*[$_{PPAbl}$ AG *a Caesare deletum*] *est.* ("The city was destroyed by

Caesar")

(45) Lat. *Oppidum* [$_{NPAbl}$ FO *eruptione Vesuvii*] *deletum est.* ("The city was destroyed by the eruption of the Vesuvius")

(46) Germ. *Die Stadt wurde* [$_{PPDat}$ AG *von Caesar*] *zerstört.* ("The city was destroyed by Caesar")

(47) Germ. *Die Stadt wurde* [$_{PPAcc/Dat}$ AG *durch den/von dem Ausbruch des Vesuvs*] *zerstört.* ("The city was destroyed by the eruption of the Vesuvius")

Similarly, in the following sentences, the Latin perspective portrays the soldiers as Recipients (= REC; a noun phrase in the dative case) of the consul's arrangement of the cavalry, whereas in the German translation, the infantry is constructed as the local Direction (= DIR; a prepositional phrase in the accusative case) of the consul's positioning of the cavalry:

(48) Lat. *Consul equites revocatos circumdedit* [$_{NPDat}$ REC *peditibus*]. (Liv. 21.55.3) ("The consul positioned the re-called cavalry around the infantry")

(49) Germ. *Der Konsul stellte die zurückbeorderte Reiterei* [$_{PPAcc}$ DIR *rings um die Fußsoldaten*] *auf.* (*Der Konsul stellte die ... Reiterei den Fußsoldaten ringsum auf) ("The consul positioned the re-called cavalry around the infantry")

In the meantime, there is a widespread consensus (cf. Fillmore (1977a, pp. 74 ff.); Fillmore (2003, p. 462); Jackendoff (1990, pp. 135 ff.; 198 ff.; 297, note 4) that differences in sentence structure (within or across languages) have to be dealt with by assigning different semantic descriptions, for example, differing semantic roles, to the respective arguments. This is also the case in the following examples, where *hay* is portrayed more directly affected (as Theme or Patient) in (50) than in (51), where it is portrayed as Instrument. The same holds for *the students* in (52), where they are described as Patients of the teaching, while they are the Recipients of the teaching in (53):

(50) *Bill loaded hay on the truck.*

(51) *Bill loaded the truck with hay.*

(52) *Harry teaches the students French.*

(53) *Harry teaches French to the students.*

The examples given above have shown that meaning cannot be reduced to reference and/or truth: There is a level of language-specific meaning apart from reference and/or truth, which has to be described by linguistic semantics (cf. also the complex model of Blank (2001, p. 132)). Still, the following question remains: What are the precise limits of language-specific core meaning at the sentence level? If Katz's anonymous letter situation is not accepted as a criterion (cf. above, section 3) for separating literal meaning from contextual meaning, it is hard to see what a sentence means apart from context and situation. And how is the closely related difficulty of distinguishing between analytic and synthetic sentences to be solved? This distinction has been brilliantly and devastatingly criticized by Quine (1971, pp. 22 ff.). Finally, the definition of core meaning at the sentence level involves the difficulty of distinguishing between direct and indirect speech acts.

In this respect, I would like to concede that it is not possible to draw a sharp borderline between analytic and synthetic aspects of sentence meaning. However, as in the corresponding case of the distinction between dictionary and encyclopaedia, the concession that there are borderline cases needs not lead to the conclusion that the distinction between analytic and synthetic sentences has to be given up completely. Again, the comparison of languages shows that it would be counterintuitive not to acknowledge the clear difference between sentences which are true on the basis of their meaning alone, and others which can be true or false. It would be counterintuitive because the translation of the respective sentences reveals clear differences as to their status as analytic (contradictory) or synthetic sentences in different languages (cf. also Carnap (1972, p. 31)):

(54) Germ. *Diese Katze ist ein Männchen.* ("This cat is male") SYNTHETIC

(55) Germ. *Diese Katze ist ein Weibchen.*("This cat is female") SYNTHETIC

(56) Ital. *Questa gatta è un maschio.* ("This cat is male") CONTRADICTORY

(57) Ital. *Questa gatta è una femmina.* ("This cat is female") ANALYTIC

I do not assume, however, that illocutionary types can be determined on the basis of core meaning alone (cf. Sökeland (1980, p. 41)). Only with the help of some background knowledge and a default context can we determine whether a declarative, an interrogative or an imperative sentence is a statement, a question or a request/command, respectively. Searle (1982, p. 142) still calls a sentence meaning, which has been enriched by a minimal extra-linguistic context, a "literal meaning", but this seems to be too broad a notion of literal or core meaning (cf. also Wilson and Sperber (2004) on "explicature" in Relevance Theory, Wunderlich (1991, pp. 37 ff.) on "Äußerungsbedeutung"/"utterance meaning", Blutner (2002, p. 52) on "pragmatic strengthening" and Recanati (2004, pp. 23 ff.) on "primary pragmatic processes" of saturation and enrichment). Speech acts belong to the level of discourse. According to the terminology of Coseriu (1994, pp. 63 ff.), they 'have sense' (or 'make sense'), which is established both by linguistic and extra-linguistic context. We are dealing with "utterance meaning" rather than with "sentence meaning" in the narrow sense, with "text sentences" rather than with "system sentences" (cf. Lyons (1995, p. 234 ff., 260 f.)).

On the other hand, some aspects of the propositional content of sentences seem to remain stable across different types of illocutionary types and can be derived from the core meaning of sentences alone. Hence, these aspects of the meaning of sentences, the "propositional structure" could be equated with their core meaning (cf. Wunderlich (1991, p. 33) similar notion of "Satzbedeutung"/"sentence meaning" and Recanati (2004, p. 6) on sentence meaning as a "semantic skeleton" underlying truth-conditional meaning and communicative meaning ). What is the propositional structure of a sentence? The propositional structure is based on the predicate, the lexical items used as arguments and satellites of the predicate, their semantic roles and the global syntactic and semantic structure of the sentence. If these language-specific factors remain unchanged, some semantic entailments are valid across different types of speech acts. If we compare languages with differing propositional structures, the (in)validity of these semantic entailments can change drastically.

In this respect, I agree with Katz (1980, pp. 228 ff.) that the following entailments are semantically valid irrespective of context and across differing speech acts within one and the same language because they are based on the propositional structure of the sentences (but cf. the differences between English and Latin). However, I do not agree with his assumption that basic illocutionary types such as "assertion", "question" and "request" can be established out of context (cf. also Wunderlich (1991, pp. 46 ff.)):

(58) John is having a nightmare. ⇒ John is having a dream.

(59) Is John having a nightmare? ⇒ Is John having a dream?

(60) I request that you eat breakfast. ⇒ I request that you eat a meal.

(61) Peter loves his uncle ⇒ Peter loves the brother of his mother.

(62) Peter loves his uncle ⇒ Peter loves the brother of his father.

(63) Lat. Petrus avunculum suum amat. ⇒ Petrus fratrem matris suae amat.
("Peter loves his maternal uncle") ("Peter loves the brother of his mother")

(64) Lat. Petrus patruum suum amat. ⇒ Petrus fratrem patris sui amat.
("Peter loves his paternal uncle") ("Peter loves the brother of his father")

(65) Lat. Petrus avunculum suum amat. *⇒ Petrus fratrem patris sui amat.
("Peter loves his maternal uncle") ("Peter loves the brother of his father")

(66) Lat. Petrus patruum suum amat. *⇒ Petrus fratrem matris suae amat.
("Peter loves his paternal uncle") ("Peter loves the brother of his mother")

Explanations: "⇒" = "semantically entails"; "*⇒" = "does not semantically entail". Semantic entailment is not to be confused with material implication ("p → q") because of the paradoxes of material implication. These arise from the fact that in classical propositional logic "p → q" is only false if "p" is true and "q" is false, that is, any false proposition "p" materially implies any true proposition "q" and "p" and "q" need not be semantically related to each other.

I would like to conclude these rather long remarks on core meaning, reference and truth with some critical observations concerning the semantic theory of Putnam (1975). Language-specific semantic properties belonging to the core meaning are not defeasible stereotypes in the sense of Putnam. That is, to a certain degree core meaning is independent of reference (cf. García Hernández (2003, p. 128); and besides, reference itself is not independent of contextual reinterpretations; cf. Recanati (2004, p. 146)).

As far as language-specific meaning is concerned, it can remain stable for a while even if the common reference of linguistic expressions has been proven to be wrong. The thought experiments of Putnam (e.g. cats which display all stereotypes of normal cats, but actually are robots) concern reference and not meaning. Katz (1981, p. 145) adduces the counter example of *witch*, which still has strong and stable negative connotations, although it has become quite clear that the women accused, tortured and killed as witches have been the innocent victims of fundamentalist beliefs and sexist institutions. Compare Katz's definition of *witch* with the quite similar one in LDOCE (2003, p. 1895):

(67) *witch*: "woman possessing supernatural powers by virtue of a pact with an evil spirit"

(68) *witch*: "a woman who is supposed to have magic powers, especially to do bad things"

Similarly, it has become quite clear that the German word *Walfisch* (lit. "whale fish") refers to a species of the genus "mammal" and not to a kind of fish. Nevertheless, the word *Walfisch* is still used in contemporary German (beside the synonymic noun *Wal*), and sometimes is even anaphorically substituted by the noun *Fisch* ("fish"), as in the following text *Der Walfisch* (written 19.9.2001 by the Swiss author Franz Dodel, *1949):

(69) **Der Walfisch** *[...]* ***Wale*** *sind dem Menschen gegenüber äusserst friedlich und schon der antike Schriftsteller Plinius berichtet davon, dass Delphine (die ins Reich der* ***Zahnwale*** *gehören) einen Menschen vor dem Ertrinken zu retten vermögen, indem sie diesen —wie ihre Jungen— an die Wasseroberfläche drängen, was sie allerdings auch mit einer vollgesogenen Luftmatratze tun. Derselbe Autor berichtet von* ***Pottwalen****, die damals noch ins Mittelmeer schwammen. Von denen soll sich einer zur Regierungszeit des Kaisers Septimus Severus in den neuerstellten römischen Hafen von Ostia verirrt haben, was die Römer zur Simulation einer Seeschlacht animierte. Der riesige* ***Fisch*** *zertrümmerte mit seiner Schwanzflosse kurzerhand einige Militärboote und verschwand vor den Augen der konsternierten Armee ins offene Meer.*

At the sentence level, examples such as *The sun is rising/The sun is going down* are still perfectly normal, although by now we know that the earth moves around the sun and not vice versa.

This relative immunity of core meaning—as far as changes in reference are concerned—can also be shown with the help of several linguistic tests (cf. Cruse (1997, p. 17); Kleiber (1998, pp. 89 ff.)). These tests show that not all semantic features can be deleted without the result of producing unacceptable sentences (but cf. the criticism of Levelt (1989, p. 212) and Coseriu (1990, p. 164), who correctly argue that (some of) these tests sometimes do not work properly and are not able to distinguish language-specific semantic properties from those known by encyclopaedic knowledge):

(70) ?*This is a cat, but it isn't an animal.*

(71) ?*This is a cat, but it is an animal.*

(72) ?*This cat is an animal.*

### 6.5.4 Core Meaning and the Use Theory of Meaning

As to the fourth argument, it has to be conceded that the description of core meaning by no way exhausts the richness of usage of linguistic expressions, which always and inevitably involves verbal and nonverbal contexts (situations, cultural institutions, history etc.). Within use theory, the meaning of a word is defined as its use in a language (cf. Wittgenstein (1975, p. 41)). The use of an expression is fixed via the rules of usage within a speech community, also called a "language game" by Wittgenstein. A language game consists of verbal and non-verbal activities (cf. Wittgenstein (1975, p. 19)). Therefore, a comprehensive description of use involves more than a short semantic definition. It should be at least as long as a "short story", as Heringer (1999, p. 39) aptly remarks:

> Ziel semantischer Theorien scheinen oft Definitionen...Aber eine Bedeutung ist eine lange Geschichte. Und um davon wenigstens etwas zu erfassen, braucht es wenigstens eine short story...Nur die detaillierte Darstellung des Gebrauchs offenbart die konstitutive Rolle eines Wortes für die Kultur, für die Weltansicht, für uns.

However, the description of core meaning within structural semantics and the comprehensive description of the use of linguistic expressions within a use theory of meaning do not exclude each other. The description of core meaning can be seen as the minimal set of usage rules, which is necessary, but not sufficient for producing and understanding linguistic expressions in everyday communication.

Furthermore, the use theory of meaning provides another argument against reference theories of meaning such as the one suggested by Putnam (1975), because even experts often disagree about the reference of linguistic expressions (cf. Kienpointner (1992, p. 97 ff.); Gibbs (1994, p. 37)). This becomes especially clear in the case of ideologically controversial lexical items where it is implausible to assume that there is one and only one 'objective' reference, for example lexemes like *freedom, justice, democracy*, etc. In these cases, we often engage in 'semantic fights' and/or argumentative discourse to justify our rules of usage (on the complex relationship between language, ideology and argumentation cf. Kienpointner (1996c, 2003)). However, while we often disagree on the ideological aspects and applications of these lexemes, we agree on their core meaning (cf. García Hernández (2003, p. 127 f.)). The following remarks by Wittgenstein (1975, p. 139) could be interpreted in this way, namely, as a distinction between the controversies concerning the reference or truth of linguistic expressions and the uncontroversial agreement as far as the core meaning or the system of language is concerned:

> "So sagst du also, dass die Übereinstimmung der Menschen entscheide, was richtig und was falsch ist?" —Richtig und falsch ist, was Menschen sagen; und in der Sprache stimmen die Menschen überein. Dies ist keine Übereinstimmung der Meinungen, sondern der Lebensform.

Therefore, meaning cannot be simply equated with 'objective' (expert) reference. Words are not 'labels' which are attached to objects: Rather, according to Wittgenstein, a language is the irreducible background, not only for the use of lexical items and their definition, but also for judgments about the truth or falsity of statements (Wittgenstein (1975, p. 139)). This basic assumption is summed up by Heringer (1978, p. 12):

> The use theory gives up the idea that words, like labels, are attached to objects given in the world. There is no need here to assume such a pre-established world. The description of speech acts can demonstrate, rather, that different social groups make different assumptions about the world by referring to different objects or by referring differently.

Finally, use theory has also rightly criticized the primary interest of philosophers in the truth of assertive sentences. The enormous number of different speech acts (questioning, requesting, ordering, reproaching, promising, excusing, advising, warning, threatening, arguing, greeting, etc.) necessitates a language theory which takes the multiplicity of "language games" into account (cf. Lyons (1995, p. 182)).

### 6.5.5 Core Meaning and Pragmatics

The fifth argument correctly insists that the meaning of lexemes and sentences is created, recreated and changed by speakers/listeners. It must not be 'reified' as existing independent of human actors. This argument is correct insofar as linguistic structuralism, as inspired by Ferdinand de Saussure, indeed had a far too static concept of meaning. Therefore, such structuralist approaches run into problems as far as the dynamics of communicative processes and semantic change is concerned (cf. Verschueren (1999, p. 147 ff.); Asher (1999)). Furthermore, it favoured a view of language which is somehow imposed on the individual speaker (cf. Saussure (1968, p. 30); I have to refrain from discussing the problems of reconstructing the 'original' Saussure):

> En séparant la langue de la parole, on sépare du même coup: 1° ce qui est social de ce qui est individuel; 2° ce qui est essentiel de ce qui est accessoire et plus ou moins accidentel. La langue n'est pas une fonction du sujet parlant, elle est le produit que l'individu enregistre passivement.

However, Coseriu holds a thoroughly dynamic view of language, claiming that dialogical interaction is the essence of language: "La esencia del lenguaje se da en el diálogo" (Coseriu (1958, p. 40); cf. Dressler (2004, p. 14)). The (semantic) system of a language in this perspective is not a static structure, but the result of the continuous realization of its structure by its speakers. It also becomes clear that Coseriu would not at all want to 'reify' the system as an entity which is independent of the speakers.

In this view, the (semantic) system of a language exists because "it is done" by the speakers and listeners of a speech community ("el sistema existe porque se hace"; Coseriu (1958, p. 154)). The relative stability of the structures of the language system is due to the fact that most of the time we "reproduce" the system. This is the reason why pragmaticians such as Jef Verschueren acknowledge that these semantic processes produce "relatively stable cores of meaning" (Verschueren (1999, p. 123)).

Quite often, however, we do not reproduce the system without modifications or even change it considerably. If these changes get conventionalized to a degree that the innovative context-specific uses are generalized all over a speech community (nowadays often through the influence of the mass media), the language system has been changed. More specifically, the core meaning can be changed when contextual (e.g. metaphorical, metonymical etc.) meanings become conventionalized.

In the long run, language is constantly "being created through change": "La lengua se hace mediante el cambio" (cf. Coseriu (1958, p. 160)). This insight leads to Coseriu's somewhat hyperbolic bon mot "Language change does not exist" (cf. Coseriu (1983, p. 53)), which has to be understood with this theoretical background in mind.

Linguistic pragmatics and structural semantics could agree, therefore, on a division of labour. Unlike structural semantics, pragmatics does not primarily deal with core meaning. Like text linguistics, pragmatics is dealing with context-specific "sense", that is, the richness of the use of language, the infinity of contextual meanings realized in speech acts and discourses of various genres.

### 6.5.6 Core Meaning and Prototype Semantics

Prototype semantics has been welcomed as a breakthrough in semantics, a new approach capable of solving many of the vexed problems of semantics discussed above. However, as Coseriu (1990) has shown in his thorough criticism of cognitive semantics in general, and prototype semantics in particular, the problem with this approach is that it actually does not deal with language-specific meaning, but with reference and/or discourse semantics. The fact that meaning and reference are confused weakens most of the criticism of cognitive semantics against "checklist views of meaning", "definition by a list of the necessary and sufficient properties of a concept" etc. This will be illustrated with the help of a few examples.

The fuzziness of categories and the enormous difficulties of justifying lists of necessary and sufficient properties, which together would define the essence of an entity, indeed pose serious problems. But these difficulties concern theories of reference, not the description of core meaning. It is indeed hard to discern the precise border line between day and night, cold and cool, red and pink, light blue and dark blue etc., but this does not apply to the clearly distinct meanings of the respective English and Russian lexemes. Even if we disagree about whether it is day or night or whether some object is red or pink, we presuppose the semantic distinctions created by the respective lexemes (vgl. Coseriu (1973, p. 30 f.); García Hernández (2003, p. 127)):

(73) Engl. *day* vs *night*

| *day* | *night* |
|---|---|
| Referential Continuum | |

(74) Engl. *red* vs *pink*

| *red* | *pink* |
|---|---|
| Referential Continuum | |

(75) Russ. *sinij* ("dark blue") vs *goluboj* ("light blue")

| *sinij* | *goluboj* |
|---|---|
| Referential Continuum | |

Furthermore, even the meaning of a referentially vague concept "can be portrayed in discrete terms" (Wierzbicka (1985, p. 17)). This includes particles used as hedges such as *rather*, for example, in the clause

(76) *Mary is rather tall.*

Wierzbicka (1985, p. 17) provides the following definition for the meaning of *rather* in this sentence:

> Mary is such that if I had to say either Mary is tall or Mary is not tall wanting to say what is true I would rather say (i.e. I would prefer to say) Mary is tall.

Nor is 'semantic necessity' the same as logical or referential necessity (cf. Katz (1972, pp. 182 ff.), Wierzbicka (1985, p. 60)). If in a particular language a semantic feature is part of the meaning of a lexeme (e.g. [animal] in the meaning of *cat*) or if a sentence is analytically true because the subject is a hyponym of the predicate (*Cats are animals*), these language-specific facts are not refuted by pointing out that there could be cases in the real world where the feature is absent or that the sentence could be falsified (because cats actually are robots) (cf. also Kleiber (1998, p. 90)). In spite of Quine's (Quine (1971, p. 22)) elegant bon mot, core meaning and ontological essence are not to be confused (on Aristotle's relation to modern structural semantics cf. Wierzbicka (1985, pp. 84 ff.); Coseriu (1990, pp. 276 ff.); Kienpointner (1992, pp. 117 ff.)):

> The Aristotelian notion of essence was the forerunner, no doubt, of the modern notion of intension or meaning. [...] Meaning is what essence becomes when it is divorced from the object of reference and wedded to the word.

It is, however, one of the important achievements of prototype semantics to have experimentally demonstrated again and again that there are prototype effects: That is, not all members of a category are equally cognitively salient for informants. This insight, however, is an important insight concerning human cognition and categorization, not a fact which would concern language-specific core meaning. Cognitively, a sparrow or an eagle is more salient as a member of the category bird than a hen, let alone a penguin or an ostrich. Semantically, however, the nouns *sparrow, eagle, hen, penguin* and *ostrich* all belong equally to the semantic class of birds (cf. Coseriu (1990, p. 248)).

A further important insight of prototype semantics, namely, that there are pertinent, prototypical, though not necessary properties of lexical items, should be taken into account for practical lexicographic purposes. As I have tried to show above (cf. section 5.1), it could also be integrated in the framework of Coseriu's semantic theory. Prototypical properties, that is, pertinent, but not necessary semantic features could be integrated into semantic descriptions of core meaning because they belong to the set of properties most frequently and/or most typically ascribed to members of a category in everyday language. That is, these properties belong to the norm of a language system, though not to the semantic system itself.

A final remark is in order, however, to stress once more the necessity of the clear distinction of cognitive aspects of meaning described with concepts such as scenes and frames, scripts and idealized cognitive models, and purely language-specific aspects of meaning. The cognitively relevant aspects typically exceed the language-specific aspects. The typical "commercial event" as a scene involves more people, objects and transactions than are realized in a specific sentence structure of a natural language (cf. Fillmore (1977b, pp. 58 ff.); Fillmore et al. (2002); Lehrer (1993, pp. 152 ff.)). Hence it can be concluded that the meanings of all linguistic expressions imply the existence of corresponding concepts, while the converse is not true. Therefore, not all potentially relevant and cognitively important aspects of meaning are encoded within semantic structures, for example, lexical fields, of a language.

Furthermore, differences which are cognitively relevant are encoded in the lexical system of some languages, but not all languages. For example, in English, French and German, the concept "bird" is lexically realized with one item, *bird, oiseau* and *Vogel*, respectively. But in Spanish and Portuguese, there are two lexical items, *ave* ("big bird") and *pájaro/passaro* ("small bird") (cf. Coseriu (1990, p. 253); Blank (2001, p. 52)):

(77) Engl. *bird*/Germ. *Vogel*/French *oiseau* vs Span. *ave* ("big bird")/*pájaro* ("small bird")

Again, this makes a distinction between language-specific core meaning and elements within cognitive models indispensable.

### 6.5.7 Core Meaning and the Cognitive Theory of Metaphor

The cognitive theory of metaphor holds that human thought is deeply metaphoric: "Our ordinary conceptual system, in terms of which we both think and act, is fundamentally metaphorical in nature" (Lakoff and Johnson (1980, p. 3). To have recognized and described the enormous importance of metaphor for human thought is one of the major achievements of the cognitive theory of metaphor, although Lakoff and Johnson were not the first to have had this important insight (cf. Ricoeur (1975)). But more than this, representatives of the cognitive theory of metaphor have also argued that definitions of lexical items such as emotion terms cannot be given without taking into account and using metaphorical models within the definition. And indeed, Kövecses (1990, pp. 15 ff.) is correct when he criticizes the fact "that the core alone cannot capture the totality of our experiences in connection with given aspects of the world (like the emotions, for example)". Furthermore, it is true that many conventional metaphors have become lexicalized to a degree that it makes sense to consider them as part of the core meaning of lexical items (cf. the example already mentioned above, namely, *to explode*, which can also conventionally mean "to be very angry").

But this does not mean that abstract concepts cannot be defined or understood without metaphors. To deny this would mean that there are no essential semantic differences between abstract lexemes like *love, hate* and *anger* and the concrete lexemes or noun phrases used for defining them, such as *fire, wild animal, boiling liquid in a container* (cf. Stöckl (2004, p. 207)). Furthermore, the definitions of abstract concepts given by structural semanticists such as Coseriu and Geckeler, but also by Wierzbicka (2002) and Goddard (2004) have demonstrated that it is possible to define core meanings of emotions and other abstract entities in a non-metaphoric way (cf. above).

Even more important is the following criticism of the cognitive theory of metaphor. Lakoff and Johnson (1980), seeing metaphor almost exclusively as a phenomenon of thought, underestimate the important influence of language-specific meaning for the creation of metaphors. For example, the various degrees of anger encoded in the German lexemes *Ärger, Zorn, Wut* (from "slight anger" to "fury, rage") influence the way in which the metaphor ANGER IS MADNESS is (not) compatible with these abstract concepts (cf. German *Wutanfall* vs. **Ärgeranfall, *ärgerschäumend*):

(78) German *Ärger* ("slight anger"), *Zorn* ("strong anger"), *Wut* ("furious anger")

(79) German *Wutanfall* ("a fit of anger"), *wutschäumend* ("foaming with rage") vs *?Zornanfall, ?zornschäumend* vs **Ärgeranfall, *ärgerschäumend*

Similarly, in Turkish, there are two lexemes for "love", namely, *sevgi* ("love in general"; Redhouse (2000, p. 660): "love, affection") and *aşk* ("passionate love"; Redhouse (2000, p. 54): "love, passion"). Differently from *sevgi*, *aşk* has ambivalent, sometimes clearly negative connotations and, consequently, is used for metaphoric conceptualizations such as LOVE IS MADNESS or for negative aspects of roads, paths etc. in the conceptual metaphor LOVE IS A JOURNEY. The same lexeme *aşk* also appears in negatively evaluated metonymic effects of passion, namely, blindness (cf. Yurtbaşi (1993); Redhouse (2000)):

(80) Turk. *Aşk başta karar etse, akıl firar eder.* ("If (passionate) love settles down in the head, reason flees")

(81) Turk. *Aşkın yolu dikenlidir.* ("The path of (passionate) love is thorny")

(82) Turk. *Aşk gözleri kör eder/Aşk kör yapar.* (lit. "(Passionate) Love makes (the eyes) blind")

One of my Turkish informants, asked to describe the noun *aşk*, wrote the following highly ambivalent description of *aşk*:

(83) *Aşkın her zaman güzel olduğuna da inanmiyorum. Bazen acı veriyor insana ama her şey yolundaysa, mükemmel bir şey. Aşk ve kıskançlık çok yakın kavramlar.* ("I don't believe that passionate love is nice all the time. Sometimes it hurts human beings, but if everything is all right it is an excellent thing. Passionate love and jealousy are concepts which are very close to each other")

However, there are also positive aspects of *aşk*, as can be seen in the following instance of the conceptual metaphor LOVE IS A FLOWER:

(84) *Eğer hayat çicekse aşk kokusu.* ("If life is a flower, love is its scent")

These language-specific facts should be taken into account also by cognitive semanticists because they have clear effects on the selective use of conceptual models of metaphor such as ANGER IS MADNESS or LOVE IS MADNESS/LOVE IS A JOURNEY/LOVE IS A FLOWER (on language and culture-specific aspects of (active) metaphor cf. also Goddard (2004), Kienpointner (2004)).

This criticism directed against the cognitive theory of metaphor does not prevent theories of core meaning from assigning metaphoric language use a central place in the functioning of language. Coseriu even situates the creation of metaphors at the very heart of human language: There are no reasons for metaphoric creativity in language because metaphoric creativity is inherent in the definition of language (cf. Coseriu (1956, p. 26)):

> Pero ¿cuáles son las razones de la creación metafórica en el lenguaje? O mejor: ¿pueden investigarse las razones íntimas de la creación lingüística? Evidentemente no, puesto que la creación, la invención, es inherente al lenguaje por definición.

Wierzbicka (1985, p. 57) (cf. also Wierzbicka (2002)) states in a similar vein:

> [...] the word <u>hat</u> is extended to 'party hats' or [...] the word <u>mother</u> is extended to adoptive mothers, because natural language is economical, elastic and adaptable to new situations and new conceptualizations. The possibility of creative usage is inherent in its functioning.

## 6.6 Conclusion

To sum up, I would like to conclude that a strong case for core meaning can indeed be made, although this does not mean that the criticism of core meaning discussed above has been proven wrong in all respects. But more often than not, recent semantic theories complement rather than replace a description of core meaning. The comprehensive theory of meaning developed by Coseriu seems to be able to integrate many of the frameworks mentioned above, while still assigning core meaning an important place within linguistic semantics. It does seem possible, at least in many cases, to assign a relatively stable core meaning to words, phrases and sentences, which either subsumes contextual variants or else can motivate them, serving as the point of departure from which contextual variants can be derived.

Any kind of reductionism in semantic theory should be avoided and a division of labour of different semantic approaches (e.g. structural semantics, reference theory, truth conditional semantics, use theory, pragmatic approaches, relevance theory, prototype semantics) should be developed.

## References

Asher, N. 1999. Discourse structure and the logic of conversation. In K. Turner, ed., *The Semantics/Pragmatics Interface from Different Points of View*, pages 19–48. Oxford: Elsevier.

Beaugrande, A. De and W. U. Dressler. 1981. *Einführung in die Textlinguistik*. Tübingen: Niemeyer.

Blank, A. 2001. *Einführung in die lexikalische Semantik für Romanisten*. Tübingen: Niemeyer.

Blutner, R. 2002. Lexical semantics and pragmatics. In F. Hamm and T. Zimmermann, eds., *Semantics*, pages 27–58. Hamburg: Buske.

Carnap, R. 1972. *Bedeutung und Notwendigkeit*. New York: Springer.

Carston, R. 1999. The semantics/pragmatics distinction: A view from relevance theory. In K. Turner, ed., *The Semantics/Pragmatics Interface from Different Points of View*, pages 85–125. Oxford: Elsevier.

Coseriu, E. 1956. *La creación metafórica en el lenguaje*. Montevideo: Univ. de la República.

Coseriu, E. 1958. *Sincronia, diacronia e historia*. Montevideo: Univ. de la República.

Coseriu, E. 1967. Lexikalische Solidaritäten. *Poetica* 1(3):293–303.

Coseriu, E. 1973. *Probleme der strukturellen Semantik*. Tübingen: Narr.

Coseriu, E. 1983. Language change does not exist. *Linguistica Nuova ed Antica. Rivista di linguistica classica medioevale e moderna* 1:51–63.

Coseriu, E. 1987. Bedeutung, Bezeichnung und sprachliche Kategorien. In E. Coseriu, ed., *Formen und Funktionen*, pages 177–198. Tübingen: Niemeyer.

Coseriu, E. 1988. *Einführung in die Allgemeine Sprachwissenschaft*. Tübingen: Narr.

Coseriu, E. 1990. Semántica structural y semántica "cognitiva". In *Jornadas de Filología [Homenaje al Profesor Francisco Marsá]*, pages 239–282. Barcelona: Universitat de Barcelona.

Coseriu, E. 1994. *Textlinguistik*. Tübingen: Narr.

Coseriu, E. and H. Geckeler. 1981. *Trends in Structural Semantics*. Tübingen: Narr.

Cruse, D. A. 1997. *Lexical Semantics*. Cambridge: Cambridge Univ. Press.

Deppermann, A. 1999. Semantic shifts in argumentative processes: A step beyond the fallacy of equivocation. In F. H. van Eemeren et al., eds., *Proceeding of the Fourth International Conference of the International Society for the Study of Argumentation*, pages 123–128. Amsterdam: SicSat.

Dressler, W. 2004. Textlinguistik mit und ohne Kontext. Diskurs versus Text. In O. Panagl and R. Wodak/(Hg.), eds., *Text und Kontext*, pages 11–22. Würzburg: Königshausen and Neumann.

Dressler, W. and L. Merlini-Barbaresi. 1994. *Morphopragmatics*. Berlin: Mouton de Gruyter.

Dressler, W. and L. Merlini-Barbaresi. 2001. Morphopragmatics of diminutives and augmentatives. In I. Kenesei and R. Harnish, eds., *Perspectives on Semantics, Pragmatics, and Discourse*, pages 43–58. Amsterdam: Benjamins.

Dubois, J., et al. 1970. *Rhétorique générale*. Paris: Larousse.

Eco, U. 1975. *Trattato di semiotica generale*. Milano: Bompiani.

Eco, U. 1985. *Semiotik und Philosophie der Sprache*. Munchen: Fink.

Fillmore, Ch. 1968. The case for case. In E. Bach and R. Harms, eds., *Universals in Linguistic Theory*, pages 1–90. New York: Holt, Rinehart and Winston.

Fillmore, Ch. 1977a. The case for case reopened. In P. Cole and J. Sadock, eds., *Syntax and Semantics 8. Grammatical Relations*, pages 59–81. New York: Academic Press.

Fillmore, Ch. 1977b. Scenes-and-frames semantics. In A. Zampolli, ed., *Linguistic Structures Processing*, pages 55–81. Amsterdam: North-Holland.

Fillmore, Ch. 2003. Valency and semantic roles: the concept of deep structure case. In V. Ágel et al., eds., *Dependenz und Valenz*, pages 457–475. Berlin: De Gruyter.

Fillmore, Ch., C. F. Baker, and H. Sato. 2002. Seeing arguments through transparent structures. In *Proceedings of the Third International Conference on Language Resources and Evaluation (LREC)*, pages 787–791. Las Palmas: ELRA.

Foley, W. A. and R.D. Van Valin. 1984. *Functional Syntax and Universal Grammar*. Cambridge: Cambridge Univ. Press.

Frege, G. 1975. *Funktion, Begriff, Bedeutung*. Göttingen: Vandenhoeck and Rupprecht.

García Hernández, B. 2003. La semántica de Eugenio Coseriu: Significación y designación. In V. Orioles, ed., *Studi in memoria di Eugenio Coseriu*, pages 121–138. Udine: Centro Internazionale di Plurilinguismo.

Gibbs, R. 1994. *The Poetics of Mind*. Cambridge: Cambridge Univ. Press.

Goddard, C. 1998. Bad Arguments against Semantic Primitives. *Theoretical Linguistics* 24:129–156.

Goddard, C. 2004. The ethnopragmatics and semantics of 'active metaphors'. *Journal of Pragmatics* 36:1211–1230.

Haiman, J. 1980. Dictionaries and Encyclopaedias. *Lingua* 50:329–357.

Helbig, G. and J. Buscha. 1991. *Deutsche Grammatik*. Leipzig: VEB Verlag Enzyklopädie.

Heringer, H. J. 1978. *Practical Semantics*. Paris: Mouton.

Heringer, H. J. 1999. *Das höchste der Gefühle. Empirische Studien zur distributiven Semantik*. Tübingen: Stauffenburg.

Jackendoff, R. 1990. *Semantic Structures*. Cambridge/Mass.: MIT Press.

Jakobson, R. 1974. Beitrag zur allgemeinen Kasuslehre (Gesamtbedeutung der russischen Kasus). In R. Jakobson, ed., *Form und Sinn*, pages 77–124. München: Fink.

Kallmeyer, W., et al. 1974. *Lektürekolleg zur Textlinguistik*. Frankfurt: Athenäum. 2 ed.

Katz, J. J. 1972. *Semantic Theory*. New York: Harper and Row.

Katz, J. J. 1980. *Propositional Structure and Illocutionary Force*. Cambridge/Mass.: Harvard Univ. Press.

Katz, J. J. 1981. *Language and Other Abstract Objects*. Oxford: Blackwell.

Kiefer, F. 2004. Morphopragmatic phenomena in Hungarian. *Acta Linguistica Hungarica* 51/3–4:325–349.

Kienpointner, M. 1992. *Alltagslogik*. Stuttgart: Frommann-Holzboog.

Kienpointner, M. 1996a. Structural semantics and latin linguistics. In H. Rosén, ed., *Aspects of Latin*, pages 603–617. Innsbruck: Verlag des Instituts für Sprachwissenschaft.

Kienpointner, M. 1996b. Comment justifier la description structurale d'un champ lexical. In M. Fruyt and C. Moussy, eds., *Structures lexicales du latin*, pages 75–84. Paris: Presses de l'Université de Paris-Sorbonne.

Kienpointner, M. 1996c. Whorf and Wittgenstein. Language, world view and argumentation. *Argumentation* 10:475–494.

Kienpointner, M. 1999. Zum Wortfeld, Liebe-Haß' im Altgriechischen. In P. Anreiter and E. Jerem, eds., *Studia Celtica et Indogermanica*, pages 163–177. Budapest: Archäolingua.

Kienpointner, M. 2003. Ideologie und Argumentation in TV-Wahldebatten. In A. Deppermann and M. Hartung, eds., *Argumentieren im Alltag*, pages 64–87. Tübingen: Narr.

Kienpointner, M. 2004. Metaphern für Emotionen: Universalien oder Kulturspezifika? In L. Zybatow, ed., *Translation in der globalen Welt und neue Wege in der Sprach- und Übersetzerausbildung*, pages 61–91. Frankfurt/M.: Lang.

Kienpointner, M. 2006. Emotion terms in the recent history of the english language. In C. Mair, R. Heuberger, and J. Wallmannsberger, eds., *Corpora and the History of English*, pages 183–203. Heidelberg: Winter.

Kleiber, G. 1998. *Prototypensemantik. Eine Einführung*. Tübingen: Stauffenburg.

Kövecses, Z. 1988. *The Language of Love: The Semantics of Passion in Conversational English.* Lewisburg: Bucknell UP.

Kövecses, Z. 1990. *Emotion Concepts*. New York: Springer.

Kövecses, Z. 2000. *Metaphor and Emotion*. Cambridge: Cambridge Univ. Press.

Kövecses, Z. 2002. *Metaphor*. Oxford: Oxford Univ. Press.

Kühner, R. and C. Stegmann. 1962. *Ausführliche Grammatik der lateinischen Sprache. Satzlehre. Vol. 1*. Darmstadt: Wiss. Buchgesellschaft.

Lakoff, G. 1987. *Women, Fire and Dangerous Things*. Chicago: Chicago Univ. Press.

Lakoff, G. 1996. The metaphor system of morality. In A. Goldberg, ed., *Conceptual Structure, Discourse and Language*, pages 249–266. Stanford: CSLI Publications.

Lakoff, G. 2005. *Don't Think of an Elephant!*. White River Junction: Chelsea Green.

Lakoff, G. and M. Johnson. 1980. *Metaphors We Live by*. Chicago: Chicago Univ. Press.

LDOCE. 2003. Longman Dictionary of contemporary English (LDOCE). Harlow, Essex: Pearson.

Lehmann, Chr., Yong-Min Shin, and E. Verhoeven. 2000. *Person prominence and relation prominence. On the typology of syntactic relations with special reference to Yucatec Maya.* München: Lincom.

Lehrer, A. 1993. Semantic fields and frames: Are they alternatives? In P. Lutzeier, ed., *Studien zur Wortfeldtheorie/Studies in Lexical Field Theory*, pages 149–162. Tübingen: Niemeyer.

Levelt, W. J. M. 1989. *Speaking. From Intention to Articulation.*. Cambridge/Mass.: MIT-Press.

Lewis, D. 1970. General semantics. *Synthese* 22:18–67.

Lutzeier, P. R. 1993. Wortfelder als Kognitive Orientierungspunkte? In P. Lutzeier, ed., *Studien zur Wortfeldtheorie/Studies in Lexical Field Theory*, pages 203–214. Tübingen: Niemeyer.

Lyons, J. 1977. *Semantics*. Cambridge: Cambridge Univ. Press. 2 Vols.

Lyons, J. 1991. Bedeutungstheorien. In A. von Stechow and D. Wunderlich, eds., *Semantik/Semantics*, pages 1–24. Berlin: de Gruyter.

Lyons, J. 1995. *Linguistic Semantics. An Introduction*. Cambridge: Cambridge Univ. Press.

OED. 1992. The oxford english dictionary (oed). Second Edition. On Compact Disk. Oxford: Oxford UP.

Pottier, B. 1992. *Théorie et analyse en linguistique*. Paris: Hachette.

Putnam, H. 1975. The meaning of 'meaning'. In H. Putnam, ed., *Mind, Language and Reality: Philosophical Papers. Volume 2*, pages 215–271. Cambridge: Cambridge University Press.

Quine, W. V. O. 1971. *From a Logical Point of View*. Cambridge/Mass: Harvard Univ. Press.

Rainer, F. 2003. Semantic fragmentation in word formation: The case of spanish —*AZO*. In R. Singh, S. Starosta, and S. Neuvel, eds., *Explorations in Seamless Morphology*, pages 197–211. New Delhi: Sage.

Recanati, F. 2004. *Literal Meaning*. Cambridge: Cambridge University Press.

Redhouse. 2000. The larger redhouse portable dictionary. English-Turkish, Turkish-English. Istanbul: SEV.

Ricoeur, P. 1975. *La métaphore vive*. Paris: Seuil.

Rosch, E. 1978. Principles of categorization. In E. Rosch and B. Lloyd, eds., *Cognitions and Categorization*, pages 27–48. Hillsdale: Sag Erlbaum.

Russell, B. 1949. On denoting. In H. Feigl and W. Sellars, eds., *Readings in Philosophical Analysis*, pages 103–115. New York: Appleton.

Saussure, F. de. 1968. *Cours de linguistique générale*. Wiesbaden: Otto Harrassowitz. Édition critique par R. Engler. Tome 1.

Searle, J. 1982. *Ausdruck und Bedeutung: Untersuchungen zur Sprechakttheorie*. Frankfurt/M.: Suhrkamp.

Sökeland, W. 1980. *Indirektheit von Sprechhandlungen*. Tübingen: Niemeyer.

Sperber, D. and D. Wilson. 1986. *Relevance: Communication and Cognition*. Blackwell: Oxford.

Stöckl, H. 2004. *Die Sprache im Bild - Das Bild in der Sprache*. Berlin: Mouton de Gruyter.

Verschueren, J. 1981. Problems of lexical semantics. *Lingua* 53:317–351.

Verschueren, J. 1999. *Understanding Pragmatics*. London: Arnold.

Wierzbicka, A. 1980. *The Case for Surface Case*. Ann Arbor: Karoma.

Wierzbicka, A. 1985. *Lexicography and Conceptual Analysis*. Ann Arbor: Karoma.

Wierzbicka, A. 1991. *Cross-Cultural Pragmatics. The Semantics of Human Interaction*. Berlin: Mouton-De Gruyter.

Wierzbicka, A. 1999. *Emotions across Languages and Cultures. Diversity and Universals*. Cambridge: Cambridge Univ. Press.

Wierzbicka, A. 2001. Leibnizian linguistics. In I. Kenesei and R. Harnish, eds., *Perspectives on Semantics, Pragmatics, and Discourse*, pages 229–253. Amsterdam: Benjamins.

Wierzbicka, A. 2002. The Semantics of Metaphor and Parable: Looking for Meaning in the Gospels. *Theoria et Historia Scientiarum* IV (1):85–106.

Wilson, D. and D. Sperber. 2004. Relevance theory. In L. R. Horn and G. Ward, eds., *Handbook of Pragmatics*, pages 607–632. Oxford: Blackwell.

Wittgenstein, L. 1975. *Philosophische Untersuchungen*. Frankfurt/M.: Suhrkamp.

Wunderlich, D. 1991. Bedeutung und Gebrauch. In A. v. Stechow and D. Wunderlich, eds., *Semantik/Semantics*, pages 32–52. Berlin: de Gruyter.

Yurtbaşi, M. 1993. *Türkisches Sprichwörterlexikon*. Ankara: Bilsev.

7

# Situations from events to proofs

TIM FERNANDO

**Abstract**. String representations of events are applied to Robin Cooper's proposal that propositions in natural language semantics are types of situations. Links with the higher types of proof-theoretic semantics are forged, deepening type-theoretic interpretations of Discourse Representation Structures to encompass event structures.

## 7.1 Introduction

Barwise and Perry's *situation semantics* sprang in no small measure from unhappiness with the possible worlds analysis (PW) of a proposition.

(PW) A proposition is the set of possible worlds in which it is true.

Proof-theoretic semantics (e.g. *intuitionistic type theory*, Martin-Löf (1984)) offers an alternative (PT) to (PW), replacing truth in a possible world by proof.

(PT) A proposition is the type of objects that prove it.[1]

Situation semantics is linked to intuitionistic type theory in Cooper (2005) on the basis of the following reading of Austin (1961) in Barwise and Perry (1983):

> a statement is true when the actual situation to which it refers is of the type described by the statement. (p. 160)

With this in mind, Cooper points to Ranta (1994) for applications of (PT) to linguistic semantics, including events in Davidson (1980).

> For non-mathematical propositions Ranta draws a parallel with Davidson's (1980) event-based approach. In type theory a proof of the proposition that *Amundsen flew over the North Pole* would be a flight by Amundsen over the North Pole. Mixing type theoretical and situation theoretical terminology we might say that a proof of this proposition is a situation in which Amundsen flew over the North Pole and that type theoretical propositions are types of situations. (Cooper (2005, p. 335))

[1]For present purposes, let us put aside any difference in meaning between "set" and "type" (except that the former is used chiefly in connection with truth conditions and the latter with proof conditions).

*Meaning, Intentions, and Argumentation.*
Kepa Korta and Joana Garmendia (eds.).

Cooper goes on to encode situations as type-theoretic records, noting along the way similarities with *Discourse Representation Theory* (DRT, Kamp and Reyle (1993)). The present paper aims to deepen these connections, focusing on temporal matters that are analyzed in DRT using *event structures*. It strays from intuitionistic type theory in adopting a computational model for events altogether different from the typed functional programming assumed in proof-theoretic semantics. Nonetheless, the resulting account is, I will argue, compatible with the spirit, if not with the letter, of Ranta (1994), Cooper (2005) and Kamp and Reyle (1993).

Compatibility with possible worlds semantics is a more tortuous affair. It will prove instructive to highlight two familiar principles associated with the view (PW) that a proposition is a set of possible worlds. The first, (CM), concerns the use Carnap and Montague make of possible worlds to bridge notions of intension (or sense) with extension (or reference).

(CM) Intension is a function from possible worlds to extensions.

The second, (TV), specifies the possible extensions of a sentence.

(TV) Sentences refer to one of two truth values.

If propositions are intensions of sentences, as we henceforth assume, then (PW) becomes an immediate consequence of (CM), (TV) and the equivalence between the space $2^W$ of functions from a set $W$ to the two-element set $2 = \{0, 1\}$ and the family $\mathsf{Pow}(W)$ of subsets of $W$. Barwise and Perry reject (TV) and an argument for (TV) they attribute to Davidson (among others) which they call "the slingshot, for reasons buried in the early history of situation semantics" (Barwise and Perry (1983, p. 24)). Instead, in situation semantics, a statement refers to a situation (as Cooper reminds us above). The switch here from sentences to statements hints at the context dependence of reference famously captured by Kaplan's notion of *character* (Kaplan (1979)) as a function from contexts to *contents*, the latter being the intensions characterized in (CM). In place of (CM), Barwise and Perry propose a "relational theory of meaning," an early form of which is put as follows.

> The leading idea of situation semantics is that the meaning of a simple declarative sentence is a relation between utterances and described situations. The interpretation of a statement made with such a sentence on a specific occasion is the described situation. (Barwise and Perry (1983, p. 19))

As is clear from Perry (1997), this passage leaves out later developments in situation semantics, including elaborations of utterances into pairs of situations (called discourse situations and connective situations). Compared to possible worlds, situations are much smaller; situations are partial in that, unlike possible worlds, they may fail to make an arbitrary sentence true or false.

Without aspiring to be fully faithful to any particular version of situation semantics, the present paper follows situation semantics in employing situations for two purposes:

(i) as alternatives to truth values in (TV), and

(ii) as alternatives to possible worlds in (CM).

This is not to say that we need only replace possible worlds and extensions in (CM) by situations for an account of what the intension of a sentence is. That account would be in direct conflict with propositions-as-types (PT), if intensions of sentences are, as we have agreed, propositions. To clarify matters, notice that (CM) implies (UR), assuming possible worlds in (CM) are relabeled "circumstances of evaluation."

(UR) The reference of a sentence is uniquely determined by the proposition the sentence expresses and the circumstances of evaluation.

Reducing circumstances of evaluation from possible worlds (in (CM)) to partial situations raises the question: could there not be propositions and circumstances of evaluation that together underdetermine reference, contradicting (UR)? We may, of course, hardwire existence and uniqueness of reference by throwing out circumstances of evaluation that lead to non-deterministic reference. But might such circumstances not be interesting in their own right? A plausible approach to ambiguity and presupposition failure is to explore the non-determinism possible in relations, as opposed to functions (from say, (CM) or, for that matter, Kaplan). That said, if we put ambiguity and presupposition failure aside, can we speak of "*the* described situation"?

No, or so Davidson argues in page 91 of Davidson (1967), where he considers sentence (S1).

(S1) Amundsen flew to the North Pole in May 1926.

Davidson cautions against thinking (S1) describes an event[2] because of potential complications with uniqueness; the sentence may describe several flights or "a kind of event." In any case, the crucial point for Davidson is that the sentence is true iff "there is an event that makes it true" (Davidson (1967, p. 91)). Here Davidson calls events proofs (inasmuch as what makes a sentence true is a proof). More generally, he associates certain action sentences $S$ with sets $E(S)$ of events such that

(1) $S$ is true iff there is an event $e$ such that $e \in E(S)$ .

Possible worlds do *not* appear in (1), the idea being that (1) is purely extensional, with events as particulars. Observe, however, that (1) may hold for quite unrelated pairs $S$ and $E(S)$. For instance, given any event $\hat{e}$, we can satisfy (1) by setting

$$E(S) \stackrel{\text{def}}{=} \begin{cases} \{\hat{e}\} & \text{if } S \text{ is true} \\ \emptyset & \text{otherwise} \end{cases}$$

independently of whether or not $S$ is remotely about $\hat{e}$. If the "actual" world were an event, we could, of course, choose that for $\hat{e}$, and claim that $S$ is in some sense about $\hat{e}$. Even then, however, the question remains: why speak of events if one, $\hat{e}$, will do?

In fact, we need more than one. An event may appear in many expressions as arguments to various predicates from which $E(S)$ is, in practice, formed. *Logical form* is central to Davidson (1967); it is unfortunate that (1) hides the logical form behind $E(S)$ and the possibility that $e$ occurs many places within that form. But what if that logical form has no structure, or rather, its structure is "atomic"? Proof-theoretic semantics provides interpretations of logical connectives but otherwise says nothing about the interpretations of atomic expressions (which are free of connectives). Whatever one may

[2]Throughout this paper, we follow Cooper in understanding events as situations.

think of logical atomism, there is considerable linguistic interest in developing what Parsons calls *subatomic semantics*, by which he means

> the study of those "formulas of English" that are treated as atomic formulas in most investigations of English. The main hypothesis to be investigated is that simple sentences of English contain subatomic quantification over events. (Parsons (1990, p. ix))

Significant aspects of subatomic semantics concern temporality. Indeed, it is difficult to see anything beyond the temporal traces of events in the event structures of Kamp and Reyle (1993).

A bit of temporal logic (aka Priorean tense logic) provides a glimpse of what the notions of intension, extension and circumstances of evaluation become below. Let $\hat{S}$ be the formula

$$\mathsf{previous}(\varphi) \quad \wedge \quad (\psi \ \mathsf{until}\ \chi)$$

over the atomic propositions $\varphi$, $\psi$ and $\chi$. Let us interpret $\hat{S}$ relative to a discrete timeline such as the integers (with well-defined previous and next moments). Under the standard Kripke semantics for temporal logic (e.g. Emerson (1992)), $\hat{S}$ is true at a moment $\mathsf{now}$ iff

$$\text{previous to } \mathsf{now},\ \varphi \text{ is true} \quad \text{and} \quad \psi \text{ is true from } \mathsf{now} \text{ until } \chi \text{ is true.}$$

Accordingly, an event proving $\hat{S}$ is a string of the form

$$\boxed{\varphi}\boxed{\mathsf{now}, \psi}\boxed{\psi}^{n}\boxed{\chi} \qquad (\text{for some } n \geq 0)$$

with length $(n+3)$, specifying $\varphi$ one moment before $\mathsf{now}$ and $\psi$ from $\mathsf{now}$ until $\chi$. We enclose snapshots in boxes and string these together into film strips. Using the notation in (1), we associate with $\hat{S}$ the event-type

$$\begin{aligned} E(\hat{S}) &= \boxed{\varphi}\boxed{\mathsf{now}, \psi}\boxed{\psi}^{*}\boxed{\chi} \\ &= \{\boxed{\varphi}\boxed{\mathsf{now}, \psi}\boxed{\chi},\ \boxed{\varphi}\boxed{\mathsf{now}, \psi}\boxed{\psi}\boxed{\chi},\ \boxed{\varphi}\boxed{\mathsf{now}, \psi}\boxed{\psi}\boxed{\psi}\boxed{\chi},\ \ldots\}\,. \end{aligned}$$

Next, we say a string $s$ *occurs in* a string $c$ if we can form $s$ from $c$ by selectively deleting boxes at the beginning and end of $c$, as well as various occurrences of formulas in $c$. For example,

(2) $\quad \boxed{\varphi}\boxed{\mathsf{now}, \psi}\boxed{\psi}\boxed{\chi}$ occurs in $\boxed{\varphi, \psi}\boxed{\varphi, \chi}\boxed{\mathsf{now}, \varphi, \psi}\boxed{\varphi, \psi}\boxed{\varphi, \chi}$

as can be seen by deleting everything underlined in

$$\underline{\boxed{\varphi, \psi}}\boxed{\varphi, \underline{\chi}}\boxed{\mathsf{now}, \underline{\varphi}, \psi}\boxed{\underline{\varphi}, \psi}\boxed{\underline{\varphi}, \chi}\,.$$

We can then relativize (1) to a circumstance of evaluation $c$, formulated as a string, by agreeing that

(3) $\quad S \text{ occurs in } c \quad \overset{\text{def}}{\Longleftrightarrow} \quad (\exists e \in E(S))\ e \text{ occurs in } c\,.$

It follows from (2) and (3) that

$$\hat{S} \quad \text{occurs in} \quad \boxed{\varphi, \psi}\boxed{\varphi, \chi}\boxed{\mathsf{now}, \varphi, \psi}\boxed{\varphi, \psi}\boxed{\varphi, \chi}\,.$$

$\hat{S}$ also occurs in

$$c_1 \quad = \quad \boxed{\varphi, \psi}\boxed{\mathsf{now}, \varphi, \psi}\boxed{\psi, \chi}\boxed{\varphi, \chi}\boxed{\varphi, \psi}\boxed{\varphi, \psi}$$

this time because

$$\fbox{$\varphi$}\fbox{now, $\psi$}\fbox{$\chi$} \text{ and } \fbox{$\varphi$}\fbox{now, $\psi$}\fbox{$\psi$}\fbox{$\chi$} \quad \text{both occur in} \quad c_1 \ .$$

We define the *c-extension of* $S$, $\text{ext}(S, c)$, to be the set of strings in $E(S)$ that occur in $c$

$$\text{ext}(S, c) \ \stackrel{\text{def}}{=} \ \{s \in E(S) \mid s \text{ occurs in } c\}$$

so that

$$S \text{ occurs in } c \quad \text{iff} \quad \text{ext}(S, c) \neq \emptyset \ .$$

As $\text{ext}(S, c)$ need not be a singleton $\{s\}$, we ought perhaps not speak of reference, leaving that to what Austin calls *demonstrative conventions*. If reference is not fixed in (3), then (3) must, of course, fall short of Barwise and Perry's reading of Austinian truth (quoted by Cooper). On the other hand, the intension/type $E(\hat{S})$ described by $\hat{S}$ above is in harmony with Kripke semantics for $\hat{S}$, formulated in terms of truth at worlds, insofar as every world $w$ is fully determined by a set $E_w$ of events, and

$$\hat{S} \text{ is true at } w \quad \text{iff} \quad E(\hat{S}) \cap E_w \neq \emptyset \ .$$

In place of the Carnap-Montague picture (CM) of intension as a function from possible worlds to extensions, the intension of $S$ is identified with the set $E(S)$ of possible values (extensions) of $S$, some subset of which get realized in a circumstance of evaluation.

The strings we build below are, in general, designed to ground the higher types of proof-theoretic semantics in finite observations over time (Fernando (2004)). But are we not, by working with strings, smuggling an assumption of discrete time that for all we know, is unfounded? In section 2, we link discreteness to the assumption that our observations are finite, and construct arbitrary event structures such as the real line from inverse limits of strings. Whereas events for Davidson are particulars, our strings are representations that can be embedded in incompatible circumstances of evaluation. In section 3, we study explicit and contextual entailments, treating strings as both extensions and circumstances of evaluation. These two roles of strings are related in section 4 to proof-theoretic semantics.

## 7.2 Event tokens and time in languages

Let us henceforth call a set of strings a *language* (following the custom in formal language theory) and temporal formulas *fluents* (following the custom in AI since McCarthy and Hayes (1969)). The strings we are interested in are sequences of sets of fluents, enclosed in boxes to reinforce the intuition of snapshots arranged into a movie. For example, we can portray the phrase *rain from dawn to dusk* by the set

$$\begin{aligned} & \fbox{$\mathit{rain},\ \mathit{dawn}$}\fbox{$\mathit{rain}$}^{*}\fbox{$\mathit{rain},\ \mathit{dusk}$} \\ = \ & \{\fbox{$\mathit{rain},\ \mathit{dawn}$}\fbox{$\mathit{rain}$}^{n}\fbox{$\mathit{rain},\ \mathit{dusk}$} \mid n \geq 0\} \end{aligned}$$

of strings $\fbox{$\mathit{rain},\ \mathit{dawn}$}\fbox{$\mathit{rain}$}^{n}\fbox{$\mathit{rain},\ \mathit{dusk}$}$ of length $n + 2$ that describe $n + 2$ successive moments of time (for $n \geq 0$), each with rain, the first at dawn and the last at dusk. The different values of $n$ support different levels of temporal granularity: the larger the $n$, the finer the grain. It is not obvious, however, that we should think of each of these

| | | | |
|---|---|---|---|
| $\varphi$ before $\psi$ | $\boxed{\varphi}\Box\boxed{\psi}$ | $\varphi$ after $\psi$ | $\boxed{\psi}\Box\boxed{\varphi}$ |
| $\varphi$ meets $\psi$ | $\boxed{\varphi}\boxed{\psi}$ | $\varphi$ met-by $\psi$ | $\boxed{\psi}\boxed{\varphi}$ |
| $\varphi$ contains $\psi$ | $\boxed{\varphi}\boxed{\varphi,\psi}\boxed{\varphi}$ | $\varphi$ finished-by $\psi$ | $\boxed{\varphi}\boxed{\varphi,\psi}$ |
| $\varphi$ started-by $\psi$ | $\boxed{\varphi,\psi}\boxed{\varphi}$ | $\varphi$ equals $\psi$ | $\boxed{\varphi,\psi}$ |
| $\varphi$ overlapped-by $\psi$ | $\boxed{\psi}\boxed{\varphi,\psi}\boxed{\varphi}$ | $\varphi$ finishes $\psi$ | $\boxed{\psi}\boxed{\varphi,\psi}$ |
| $\varphi$ overlaps $\psi$ | $\boxed{\varphi}\boxed{\varphi,\psi}\boxed{\psi}$ | $\varphi$ during $\psi$ | $\boxed{\psi}\boxed{\varphi,\psi}\boxed{\psi}$ |
| $\varphi$ starts $\psi$ | $\boxed{\varphi,\psi}\boxed{\psi}$ | | |

TABLE 1 Allen relations (Allen (1983)) as strings

infinitely many strings as distinct events. Surely we can reduce the infinite language to some finite core that captures its essence: three snapshots, $\boxed{rain,\ dawn}$, $\boxed{rain}$ and $\boxed{rain,\ dusk}$, arranged in a particular order. Indeed, it is tempting to reduce every string $\boxed{rain,\ dawn}\boxed{rain}^n\boxed{rain,\ dusk}$ with $n \geq 1$ to the string $\boxed{rain,\ dawn}\boxed{rain}\boxed{rain,\ dusk}$ of length 3. Let us define, in general, the *interval reduction* $\mathsf{ir}(s)$ of a string $s$ inductively

$$\mathsf{ir}(s) \stackrel{\text{def}}{=} \begin{cases} s & \text{if length}(s) \leq 1 \\ \mathsf{ir}(as') & \text{if } s = aas' \\ a\,\mathsf{ir}(a's') & \text{if } s = aa's' \text{ where } a \neq a' \end{cases}$$

(for all sets $a, a'$ of fluents), reducing a block $aa$ of two $a$'s to one, in line with the dictum "no time without change" (Kamp and Reyle (1993, p. 674)).

We can represent intervals by fluents and the thirteen basic interval relations of Allen (1983), listed in Table 1, by strings derived from ir and a natural form of conjunction between languages $L$ and $L'$. The *superposition $L\&L'$ of $L$ and $L'$* consists of the componentwise union of strings in $L$ and $L'$ of the same length

$$L\&L' \stackrel{\text{def}}{=} \bigcup_{n\geq 0}\{(a_1 \cup b_1)\cdots(a_n \cup b_n) \mid a_1\cdots a_n \in L \text{ and } b_1\cdots b_n \in L'\}$$

(Fernando (2004)). For example,

$$\begin{aligned} \boxed{rain,\ dawn}\boxed{rain}^*\boxed{rain,\ dusk} &= \boxed{\text{rain}}^+ \ \& \ (\boxed{dawn}\Box^*\boxed{dusk}) \\ &= \boxed{\text{rain}}^+ \ \& \ \boxed{dawn}\Box^+ \ \& \ \Box^+\boxed{dusk} \end{aligned}$$

where $L^+ \stackrel{\text{def}}{=} LL^*$ (and parentheses are suppressed, as & is associative). To loosen the tight temporal overlap between $L$ and $L'$ in $L\&L'$, we pad $L$ and $L'$ to the left and right by empty boxes $\Box$ (giving $\Box^*L\Box^*$ and $\Box^*L'\Box^*$) and then unpad their superposition. That is, we define the *loose superposition $L\&^{\Box}L'$ of $L$ and $L'$* by

$$L\&^{\Box}L' \stackrel{\text{def}}{=} \mathsf{unpad}(\Box^*L\Box^* \ \& \ \Box^*L'\Box^*)$$

where $\mathsf{unpad}(s)$ is $s$ with all initial and final $\Box$'s stripped off unless $s = \Box$

$$\mathsf{unpad}(s) \stackrel{\text{def}}{=} \begin{cases} s & \text{if } s = \Box \text{ or} \\ & \quad s \text{ neither begins nor ends with } \Box \\ \mathsf{unpad}(s') & \text{if } s = \Box s' \text{ or else if } s = s'\Box\ . \end{cases}$$

and $\mathsf{unpad}(L) \stackrel{\text{def}}{=} \{\mathsf{unpad}(s) \mid s \in L\}$. Now, we can generate the thirteen strings representing the Allen relations in Table 1 by

$$\begin{aligned}
\mathsf{ir}(\mathsf{ir}^{-1}(\boxed{\varphi}) \,\&^{\square}\, \mathsf{ir}^{-1}(\boxed{\psi})) &= \mathsf{ir}(\boxed{\varphi}^{+} \,\&^{\square}\, \boxed{\psi}^{+}) \\
&= \mathsf{ir}(\mathsf{unpad}(\square^{*}\boxed{\varphi}^{+}\square^{*} \;\&\; \square^{*}\boxed{\psi}^{+}\square^{*})) \\
&= \boxed{\varphi}(\square + \epsilon)\boxed{\psi} \;+\; \boxed{\psi}(\square + \epsilon)\boxed{\varphi} \;+ \\
&\quad (\boxed{\varphi} + \epsilon + \boxed{\psi})\boxed{\varphi, \psi}(\boxed{\varphi} + \epsilon + \boxed{\psi})
\end{aligned}$$

(where $+$ is choice/union and $\epsilon$ is the null string of length 0).

What about relations between more than two intervals? Take the real line $(\Re, <)$, used in van Lambalgen and Hamm (2005) with the admission that

> One cannot simply assume that we have a dense set of events in memory to derive from this that cognitive (and not just physical) time may be assumed to be continuous. It is much more reasonable to assume that density arises in the limit of adding more and more events, and that, at each stage, memory contains only finitely many events. (p. 12, extended version of Chapter 2 from `http://staff.science.uva.nl/~michiell/docs/ProofsTime.pdf`)

Let us suppose each real number is a fluent so that we can turn any finite sequence of real numbers

$$r_1 < r_2 < \cdots < r_n$$

into the string

$$\boxed{r_1}\square\boxed{r_2}\square \cdots \square\boxed{r_n}$$

with empty boxes as place-holders for the uncountably many points sandwiched between $r_i$ and $r_{i+1}$. We can construct $(\Re, <)$ from such strings through inverse limits that we can define for any set $\Phi$ of fluents ($\Re$ or not). Given a finite subset $X$ of $\Phi$, let $\rho_X : \mathsf{Pow}(\Phi)^* \to \mathsf{Pow}(X)^*$ be the function that maps a string $a_1 \cdots a_n$ of sets $a_i$ of fluents to its $X$-*restriction* $\rho_X(a_1 \cdots a_n)$ obtained by intersecting each $a_i$ with $X$

$$\rho_X(a_1 \cdots a_n) \;\stackrel{\text{def}}{=}\; (a_1 \cap X) \cdots (a_n \cap X) \; .$$

For example,

$$\rho_{\{r_2, r_4\}}(\boxed{r_1}\square\boxed{r_2}\square\boxed{r_3}\square\boxed{r_4}) \;=\; \square\square\boxed{r_2}\square\square\square\boxed{r_4} \; .$$

Next, we compose $\mathsf{ir}$ and $\mathsf{unpad}$ with $\rho_X$ to define

$$\pi_X(s) \;\stackrel{\text{def}}{=}\; \mathsf{ir}(\mathsf{unpad}(\rho_X(s))) \;=\; \mathsf{unpad}(\mathsf{ir}(\rho_X(s)))$$

so that, for instance,

$$\pi_{\{r_2, r_4\}}(\boxed{r_1}\square\boxed{r_2}\square\boxed{r_3}\square\boxed{r_4}) \;=\; \boxed{r_2}\square\boxed{r_4} \; .$$

A $\Phi$-*point* is a function $p$ from the set $Fin(\Phi)$ of finite subsets of $\Phi$ to

$$\bigcup_{X \in Fin(\Phi)} \mathsf{Pow}(X)^*$$

such that for every $X \in Fin(\Phi)$ and every subset $Y$ of $X$,

$$p(Y) \;=\; \pi_Y(p(X)) \in \mathsf{Pow}(Y)^* \; .$$

| | |
|---|---|
| ($P_1$) | $e < e'$ implies not $e' < e$ |
| ($P_2$) | $e < e' < e''$ implies $e < e''$ |
| ($P_3$) | $e \bigcirc e$ |
| ($P_4$) | $e \bigcirc e'$ implies $e' \bigcirc e$ |
| ($P_5$) | $e < e'$ implies not $e \bigcirc e'$ |
| ($P_6$) | $e_1 < e_2 \bigcirc e_3 < e_4$ implies $e_1 < e_4$ |
| ($P_7$) | $e < e'$ or $e \bigcirc e'$ or $e' < e$ |

TABLE 2 Postulates for event structures (Kamp and Reyle (1993, p. 667))

For example, each string $s \in \mathsf{Pow}(\Phi)^*$ is represented by the $\Phi$-point $p_s$ mapping $X$ to $\pi_X(s)$. More interestingly, we can represent the real line $(\Re, <)$ by the $\Re$-point $p^{\Re}$ where

$$p^{\Re}(\{r_1, r_2, \ldots, r_n\}) \stackrel{\text{def}}{=} \boxed{r_1}\Box\boxed{r_2}\Box\cdots\Box\boxed{r_n}$$

for any finite sequence $r_1 < r_2 < \cdots < r_n$ of real numbers. The moral here is that whether or not time is dense (like the reals or rationals), finite observations lead to discrete *observation* times. We can refine discrete orders arbitrarily, by working with languages and not simply strings in isolation. But the refinements will each be discrete, mirroring the step-by-step operation of computer programs (and instructions, in general), each step of which is decomposable into finer steps.

The preceding discussion assumes temporal moments/instants are given. An alternative approach described in Kamp and Reyle (1993) is to start with an *event structure* $\langle \mathsf{E}, <, \bigcirc \rangle$ consisting of a set $\mathsf{E}$ of events, and binary relations of temporal precedence $<$ and temporal overlap $\bigcirc$ satisfying postulates ($P_1$) – ($P_7$), listed in Table 2.[3] By ($P_7$), ($P_5$) and ($P_4$), we can define $\bigcirc$ from $<$ through the equivalence

$$e \bigcirc e' \quad \text{iff} \quad \text{neither } e < e' \text{ nor } e' < e\ .$$

In cases where $\bigcirc$ is $=$ on $\mathsf{E}$, $<$ is a linear order. But in general, we

(i) form sets of pairwise overlapping events, collecting them in

$$O(\bigcirc) \stackrel{\text{def}}{=} \{i \subseteq \mathsf{E} \mid (\forall e, e' \in i)\ e \bigcirc e'\}$$

(ii) lift $<$ existentially to $O(\bigcirc)$, defining for $i, i' \in O(\bigcirc)$,

$$i <^{O} i' \stackrel{\text{def}}{\Leftrightarrow} (\exists e \in i)(\exists e' \in i')\ e < e'$$

(iii) equate temporal instants with $\subseteq$-maximal elements of $O(\bigcirc)$

$$I(\bigcirc) \stackrel{\text{def}}{=} \{i \in O(\bigcirc) \mid (\forall i' \in O(\bigcirc))\ i \subseteq i' \text{ implies } i = i'\}$$

and say $e$ *occurs at* $i$ if $e \in i$.

**Theorem** (Kamp). *$<^{O}$ linearly orders $I(\bigcirc)$ and for each $e \in \mathsf{E}$,*

$$\{i \in I(\bigcirc) \mid e \in i\}$$

*is a $<^{O}$-interval (i.e. for all $i, j, k \in I(\bigcirc)$, if $e \in j$, $e \in k$ and $j <^{O} i <^{O} k$ then $e \in i$).*

[3] The first two postulates are superfluous. ($P_1$) is derivable from ($P_2$), ($P_3$) and ($P_5$); and ($P_2$) from ($P_3$) and ($P_6$).

How do event structures and Kamp's theorem above relate to $\Phi$-points? Given a $\Phi$-point $p$, let us form the triple $\langle \mathsf{E}^p, <^p, \bigcirc^p \rangle$ by collecting fluents with interval temporal profiles in

$$\mathsf{E}^p \stackrel{\text{def}}{=} \{\varphi \in \Phi \mid p(\{\varphi\}) = \boxed{\varphi}\}$$

and (with Table 1 in mind) setting

$$\varphi <^p \psi \stackrel{\text{def}}{\Leftrightarrow} p(\{\varphi, \psi\}) \in \boxed{\varphi}(\square + \epsilon)\boxed{\psi} \tag{4}$$

$$\varphi \bigcirc^p \psi \stackrel{\text{def}}{\Leftrightarrow} p(\{\varphi, \psi\}) \in (\boxed{\varphi} + \epsilon + \boxed{\psi})\boxed{\varphi, \psi}(\boxed{\varphi} + \epsilon + \boxed{\psi}). \tag{5}$$

for all $\varphi, \psi \in \Phi$. For instance, if $p$ is the point $p^{\Re}$ for the real line, then $\mathsf{E}^p$ is $\Re$, $<^p$ is $<$ and $\bigcirc^p$ is $=$ on $\Re$. It is easy to verify that for every $\Phi$-point $p$, $\langle \mathsf{E}^p, <^p, \bigcirc^p \rangle$ is an event structure.

How do we resolve the choices in (4) and (5)? Given an event structure $\langle \mathsf{E}, <, \bigcirc \rangle$, let us define a *compaction of* $\langle \mathsf{E}, <, \bigcirc \rangle$ to be an $\mathsf{E}$-point $p$ such that $\mathsf{E}$ is $\mathsf{E}^p$, $<$ is $<^p$, $\bigcirc$ is $\bigcirc^p$ and moreover,

$$p(\{e, e'\}) = \boxed{e}\boxed{\square}\boxed{e'} \quad \text{iff} \quad (\exists e'' < e')(\exists e''' \bigcirc e'')\ e < e''' \tag{6}$$

$$p(\{e, e'\}) \in \boxed{e}\boxed{e, e'}(\boxed{e} + \epsilon + \boxed{e'}) \quad \text{iff} \quad e \bigcirc e' \text{ and } (\exists e'' < e')\ e \bigcirc e'' \tag{7}$$

$$p(\{e, e'\}) \in (\boxed{e} + \epsilon + \boxed{e'})\boxed{e, e'}\boxed{e} \quad \text{iff} \quad e \bigcirc e' \text{ and } (\exists e'' \bigcirc e)\ e' < e'' \tag{8}$$

for all $e, e' \in \mathsf{E}$. The strings $\boxed{e}\boxed{\square}\boxed{e'}$ and $\boxed{e}\boxed{e, e'}$ pose a problem for the notion of temporal instants as maximal sets of pairwise overlapping events, as neither $\square$ nor $\boxed{e}$ is maximal

$$\square \subset \boxed{e} \subset \boxed{e, e'}\,.$$

To overcome this problem, let us introduce whenever $e < e'$,

(i) a fluent $\mathsf{past}(e')$ that stretches indefinitely back over the past of $e'$, and
(ii) a fluent $\mathsf{future}(e)$ that stretches indefinitely forward over the future of $e$.[4]

We can then flesh out $\boxed{e}\boxed{\square}\boxed{e'}$ to

$$\boxed{e, \mathsf{past}(e')}\boxed{\mathsf{future}(e), \mathsf{past}(e')}\boxed{\mathsf{future}(e), e'}$$

and $\boxed{e}\boxed{e, e'}$ to

$$\boxed{e, \mathsf{past}(e')}\boxed{e, e'}$$

satisfying (6) and (7) with $e'' = \mathsf{past}(e')$ and $e''' = \mathsf{future}(e)$. (For (8), $e'' = \mathsf{future}(e')$ will do.) To build $\mathsf{past}$ and $\mathsf{future}$ into an event structure $\langle \mathsf{E}, <, \bigcirc \rangle$, we extend

(i) every (finite or infinite) subset $X$ of $\mathsf{E}$ to

$$X_+ \stackrel{\text{def}}{=} X \cup \{\mathsf{past}(e) \mid e \in X \text{ and } (\exists e')\ e' < e\} \cup$$

[4]This is similar to the Walker instants described in chapter 2 of van Lambalgen and Hamm (2005) but without the assumption that the past and future sets are non-empty.

$$\{\mathsf{future}(e) \mid e \in X \text{ and } (\exists e')\ e < e'\}$$

(ii) $\bigcirc$ to overlap $\bigcirc_+$ on $\mathsf{E}_+$, setting for all $e, e' \in \mathsf{E}$,

$$e \bigcirc_+ e' \overset{\text{def}}{\Leftrightarrow} e \bigcirc e'$$

with $\mathsf{past}(e)$ and $\mathsf{future}(e)$ given by existential quantification

$$\mathsf{past}(e) \bigcirc_+ e' \overset{\text{def}}{\Leftrightarrow} (\exists e'' < e)\ e'' \bigcirc e'$$
$$\mathsf{future}(e) \bigcirc_+ e' \overset{\text{def}}{\Leftrightarrow} (\exists e'' > e)\ e'' \bigcirc e'$$
$$\mathsf{past}(e) \bigcirc_+ \mathsf{future}(e') \overset{\text{def}}{\Leftrightarrow} (\exists e'' < e)(\exists e''' > e')\ e'' \bigcirc e'''$$

and so on, and

(iii) $<$ to precedence $<_+$ on $\mathsf{E}_+$, defining $<_+$ to be the union

$$\begin{aligned} < \ \cup\ & \{(\mathsf{past}(e), e') \in \mathsf{E}_+ \times \mathsf{E}_+ \mid \text{not } \mathsf{past}(e) \bigcirc_+ e'\} \\ \cup\ & \{(e, \mathsf{future}(e')) \in \mathsf{E}_+ \times \mathsf{E}_+ \mid \text{not } e \bigcirc_+ \mathsf{future}(e')\} \\ \cup\ & \{(\mathsf{past}(e), \mathsf{future}(e')) \in \mathsf{E}_+ \times \mathsf{E}_+ \mid \text{not } \mathsf{past}(e) \bigcirc_+ \mathsf{future}(e')\} \end{aligned}$$

so that for all $x, y \in \mathsf{E}_+$,

$$x <_+ y \quad \text{iff} \quad \text{neither } x \bigcirc_+ y \text{ nor } y <_+ x \ .$$

One can show that for every subset $X$ of $\mathsf{E}$, $\langle X_+, <_+^X, \bigcirc_+^X \rangle$ is an event structure, where $<_+^X$ and $\bigcirc_+^X$ are the restrictions of $<_+$ and $\bigcirc_+$ to $X_+$, respectively

$$<_+^X \overset{\text{def}}{=} <_+ \cap\ (X_+ \times X_+) \quad \text{and} \quad \bigcirc_+^X \overset{\text{def}}{=} \bigcirc_+ \cap\ (X_+ \times X_+) \ .$$

We can then form a compaction $p$ of $\langle \mathsf{E}, <, \bigcirc \rangle$ as follows. Given a finite subset $X$ of $\mathsf{E}$, we linearly order the temporal instants in $\langle X_+, <_+^X, \bigcirc_+^X \rangle$ via Kamp's theorem, arranging the instants in increasing order $a_1 \cdots a_n$, and setting

$$p(X) \overset{\text{def}}{=} \pi_X(a_1 \cdots a_n) \ .$$

For the record,

**Theorem.** *Every event structure has a compaction.*

A projection $\pi_X$ filters out information beyond the bounded set $X$ of observations. The asymmetry ($\mathrm{P}_1$) of temporal precedence rules out event recurrence, in line with Davdison's conception of events as particulars. The event structure constructed from a $\Phi$-point $p$ leaves out fluents $\varphi$ such that $p(\{\varphi\}) \neq \boxed{\varphi}$. Take, for example, $\varphi$ to be *rain*. Or more abstractly, suppose

$$p(\{\varphi\}_+) = \boxed{\mathsf{past}(\varphi)}\boxed{\varphi}\boxed{\mathsf{future}(\varphi)} \ .$$

Then we would expect that for the negation $\overline{\varphi}$ of $\varphi$,

$$p(\{\overline{\varphi}\}) = \boxed{\overline{\varphi}}\boxed{\phantom{\varphi}}\boxed{\overline{\varphi}}$$

which implies $\overline{\varphi} \notin \mathsf{E}^p$. For partial snapshots, it is convenient to explicitly represent negations, stepping beyond event-occurrences within an event structure to event-types as languages.

## 7.3 Situation-types and constraints as languages

If we &-superpose $\boxed{\mathit{rain},\ \mathit{dawn}}\boxed{\mathit{rain}}^*\boxed{\mathit{rain},\ \mathit{dusk}}$ with $\square^+\boxed{\mathit{noon}}\square^+$, we get

$$\boxed{\mathit{rain},\ \mathit{dawn}}\boxed{\mathit{rain}}^*\boxed{\mathit{rain},\mathit{noon}}\boxed{\mathit{rain}}^*\boxed{\mathit{rain},\ \mathit{dusk}}$$

which filters out the string $\boxed{\mathit{rain},\ \mathit{dawn}}\boxed{\mathit{rain},\ \mathit{dusk}}$ of length 2, and fleshes out the remaining strings in $\boxed{\mathit{rain},\ \mathit{dawn}}\boxed{\mathit{rain}}^+\boxed{\mathit{rain},\ \mathit{dusk}}$ by including *noon* in the middle. To capture the growth of information here, let us say that $L$ *subsumes* $L'$ and write $L \trianglerighteq L'$ if the superposition of $L$ and $L'$ includes $L$

$$L \trianglerighteq L' \quad \overset{\text{def}}{\Longleftrightarrow} \quad L \subseteq L\&L'$$

(roughly: $L$ is at least as informative as $L'$ over the same temporal stretch). Conflating a string $s$ with the singleton language $\{s\}$, it follows that $L$ subsumes $L'$ exactly if each string in $L$ subsumes some string in $L'$

$$L \trianglerighteq L' \quad \text{iff} \quad (\forall s \in L)(\exists s' \in L')\ s \trianglerighteq s'$$

where $\trianglerighteq$ holds between strings of the same length related componentwise by inclusion

$$a_1 a_2 \cdots a_n \trianglerighteq b_1 b_2 \cdots b_m \quad \text{iff} \quad n = m \text{ and } a_i \supseteq b_i \text{ for } 1 \leq i \leq n\ .$$

For example, $\boxed{\varphi, \psi} \trianglerighteq \boxed{\varphi} \trianglerighteq \boxed{\varphi} + \boxed{\psi}$. As a type with instances $s \in L$, a language $L$ is essentially a disjunction $\bigvee_{s \in L} s$ of conjunctions $s$ (as is clear from the model-theoretic interpretations spelled out in Fernando (2004)).

To express requirements such as occurrences of *dawn* and *dusk* sandwich *noon*

$$\boxed{\mathit{dawn}}\square^*\boxed{\mathit{dusk}} \quad \Rightarrow \quad \square^+\boxed{\mathit{noon}}\square^+\ ,$$

let us define

(i) for any string $s$, a *factor of* $s$ to be a string $x$ such that $s = uxv$ for some (possibly null) strings $u$ and $v$, and

(ii) for any languages $L$ and $L'$, the *constraint* $L \Rightarrow L'$ to be the set of strings $s$ such that every factor of $s$ that subsumes $L$ also subsumes $L'$

$$L \Rightarrow L' \quad \overset{\text{def}}{=} \quad \{s \in \mathsf{Pow}(\Phi)^* \mid (\text{for every factor } x \text{ of } s)\ x \trianglerighteq L \text{ implies } x \trianglerighteq L'\}$$

(Beesley and Karttunen (2003), Fernando and Nairn (2005)). With $\Rightarrow$, we can define the *$\varphi$-bivalent* language

$$\square \quad \Rightarrow \quad \boxed{\varphi} + \boxed{\overline{\varphi}}$$

consisting of strings $a_1 a_2 \cdots a_n \in \mathsf{Pow}(\Phi)^*$ such that for each $i$ from 1 to $n$ (inclusive), $\varphi \in a_i$ or $\overline{\varphi} \in a_i$. While we may want to work with strings that do not belong to this language (allowing a string to be silent on $\varphi$), it makes sense to restrict our events to strings in the *$\varphi$-consistent* language

$$\boxed{\varphi, \overline{\varphi}} \quad \Rightarrow \quad \emptyset$$

requiring that no symbol in a string contain both $\varphi$ and its negation $\overline{\varphi}$. Similarly, to require that a fluent r occur at most once in a string, the constraint

$$\boxed{\mathrm{r}}\square^*\boxed{\mathrm{r}} \quad \Rightarrow \quad \emptyset$$

precludes the occurrence of r in two different positions in a string. We may impose this on r equal to some moment now or other.

A Reichenbachian approach to tense and aspect locates the event time $E$ relative to not only a speech time $S$ but also a *reference time* $R$ (Reichenbach (1947)). To see the point behind $R$, consider the pair (S2), (S3). (The oddness of (S3) is marked by the superscript $^?$.)

(S2) Pat left Dublin but is back (in Dublin).

(S3) $^?$Pat has left Dublin but is back (in Dublin).

In both (S2) and (S3), Pat's departure $L_0$ from Dublin

$$L_0 \stackrel{\text{def}}{=} \mathcal{L}(\text{Pat leave Dublin}) \trianglerighteq \boxed{\text{in}(p,d)}\Box^*\boxed{\overline{\text{in}(p,d)}}$$

(where the fluent in$(p, d)$ is read Pat-in-Dublin) precedes the speech time $S$

$$\begin{aligned} \mathcal{L}(\text{Pat left Dublin}) &\trianglerighteq L_0\Box^*\boxed{S} \\ \mathcal{L}(\text{Pat has left Dublin}) &\trianglerighteq L_0\Box^*\boxed{S}\,. \end{aligned}$$

$R$ allows us to distinguish $\mathcal{L}$(Pat left Dublin) from $\mathcal{L}$(Pat has left Dublin), coinciding with the end of $L_0$ in the former case

(9) $$\mathcal{L}(\text{Pat left Dublin}) \trianglerighteq \boxed{\text{in}(p,d)}\Box^*\boxed{\overline{\text{in}(p,d)}, R}\Box^*\boxed{S}$$

and with $S$ in the latter

(10) $$\mathcal{L}(\text{Pat has left Dublin}) \trianglerighteq \boxed{\text{in}(p,d)}\Box^*\boxed{\overline{\text{in}(p,d)}}\Box^*\boxed{R, S}\,.$$

In general, we apply aspectual and tense operators in sequence, forming, for instance,

$$\begin{aligned} \mathcal{L}(\text{Pat left Dublin}) &= \textsc{Past}(\textsc{Simp}(L_0)) \\ \mathcal{L}(\text{Pat has left Dublin}) &= \textsc{Pres}(\textsc{Perf}(L_0)) \end{aligned}$$

with tense operators for the past and present applied after operators for simple and perfect aspect. If an event with temporal projection $E$ is represented by a language $L$, we get three aspectual operators on $L$.

$$\begin{aligned} \textsc{Simp}(L) &\stackrel{\text{def}}{=} L \,\&\, \Box^*\boxed{R} && \text{(i.e. } E = R) \\ \textsc{Prog}(L) &\stackrel{\text{def}}{=} L \,\&\, \Box^+\boxed{R}\Box^+ && \text{(i.e. } R \text{ contained in } E) \\ \textsc{Perf}(L) &\stackrel{\text{def}}{=} L\Box^*\boxed{R} && \text{(i.e. } E < R) \end{aligned}$$

As a position from which to view the event represented by $L$, $R$ says in the case of $\textsc{Simp}(L)$, that the event has reached completion; in the case of $\textsc{Prog}(L)$, that it has *not* quite gotten there yet but is on its way; and in $\textsc{Perf}(L)$, that it is history. Tense then locates $S$ relative to $R$, coinciding with $R$ for the present

$$\textsc{Pres}(L) \stackrel{\text{def}}{=} (L \,\&^{\Box}\, \boxed{S}) \cap \text{`}R = S\text{'}$$

and coming after $R$ for the past

$$\textsc{Past}(L) \stackrel{\text{def}}{=} (L \,\&^{\Box}\, \boxed{S}) \cap \text{`}R < S\text{'}$$

where '$R = S$' is the set of strings

$$(\boxed{R} + \boxed{S}) \Rightarrow \boxed{R, S}$$

in which $R$ and $S$ co-occur, and '$R < S$' is the set of strings

$$(\boxed{R,S} + \boxed{S}\square^*\boxed{R}) \Rightarrow \emptyset$$

in which $R$ precedes $S$.

To account for the contrast between (S2) and (S3), it suffices that $\overline{\text{in}(p,d)}$ persist forward in $\mathcal{L}$(Pat has left Dublin)

(11) $$\mathcal{L}(\text{Pat has left Dublin}) \trianglerighteq \square^+\boxed{\overline{\text{in}(p,d)}, S}$$

but not in $\mathcal{L}$(Pat left Dublin)

(12) $$\mathcal{L}(\text{Pat left Dublin}) \ntrianglerighteq \square^+\boxed{\overline{\text{in}(p,d)}, S} \ .$$

If the postcondition $\overline{\text{in}(p,d)}$ of $L_0$ were to flow up to $R$, then we can derive (11) from (10) while respecting (12), given (9). Independent confirmation that $R$ is a barrier to persistence (forward) is provided by the non-entailment

$$\text{Pat was in Dublin} \quad \not\vdash \quad \text{Pat is in Dublin}$$

where

$$\mathcal{L}(\text{Pat was in Dublin}) \trianglerighteq \boxed{\text{in}(p,d)}^*\boxed{\text{in}(p,d), R}\square^*\boxed{S} \ .$$

If $\text{in}(p,d)$ were to spill past $R$ and over to $S$, $\boxed{\text{in}(p,d), S}$ would mean Pat is in Dublin.

We can express the persistence of an *inertial* fluent $\varphi$ by introducing a non-inertial fluent $\mathsf{f}\overline{\varphi}$ that marks the application of a force against $\varphi$. The constraint

$$\boxed{\varphi}\square \Rightarrow (\square\boxed{\varphi} + \boxed{\mathsf{f}\overline{\varphi}}\square + \boxed{R}\square)$$

then says that $\varphi$ persists to the next moment unless some force is applied against $\varphi$ or $R$ coincides with $\varphi$.[5] The persistence of the postcondition $\overline{\text{in}(p,d)}$ of $L_0$ in (11) arises from the assumption that *no* force is applied against the fluent at the end of $L_0$. Instances where a force is applied against the postcondition surface as cases such as (S4) of non-persistence.

(S4) Pat has been to Dublin ($\not\vdash$ Pat is in Dublin)

The formation of the Reichenbachian perfect extends the event's temporal stretch, yielding a situation greater than the event. To extract the information contained in a string, it is useful to relax the strict temporal match-up in

$$L \trianglerighteq L',.$$

[5] Forces that make $\varphi$ true appear in the backward persistence constraint

$$\square\boxed{\varphi} \Rightarrow (\boxed{\varphi}\square + \boxed{\mathsf{f}\varphi}\square)$$

stating that if $\varphi$ is true, it must have been so previously or else was forced to be true. The fluents $\mathsf{f}\varphi$ and $\mathsf{f}\overline{\varphi}$ were assumed identical in Fernando and Nairn (2005). Differentiating them allows us to formulate the constraint "succeed unless opposed"

(suo) $$\boxed{\mathsf{f}\varphi}\square \Rightarrow (\square\boxed{\varphi} + \boxed{\mathsf{f}\overline{\varphi}}\square)$$

saying an unopposed force on $\varphi$ brings $\varphi$ about at the next moment. Were $\mathsf{f}\varphi$ and $\mathsf{f}\overline{\varphi}$ the same, (suo) would have no bite (denoting, as it would, the universal language $\mathsf{Pow}(\Phi)^*$).

An early paper on the relevance of inertia to linguistics is Dowty (1986); later works include Steedman (2000) and van Lambalgen and Hamm (2005), where a different formal approach to inertia is pursued.

weakening its second argument $L'$ to the set $L'^{\Box}$ of strings in $L'$ with any number of leading and trailing $\Box$'s deleted or added

$$\begin{aligned} L'^{\Box} &\stackrel{\text{def}}{=} \Box^{*}\mathsf{unpad}(L')\Box^{*} \\ &= \{s \mid \mathsf{unpad}(s) \in \mathsf{unpad}(L')\} \ . \end{aligned}$$

We define *weak subsumption* $\underline{\blacktriangleright}$ by

$$\begin{aligned} L\underline{\blacktriangleright}L' &\stackrel{\text{def}}{\iff} L \unrhd L'^{\Box} \\ &\quad \text{iff} \quad \mathsf{unpad}(L) \subseteq L\&^{\Box} L' \ . \end{aligned}$$

Weak subsumption compares information content in the same way as $\unrhd$

$$L\underline{\blacktriangleright}L' \quad \text{iff} \quad (\forall s \in L)(\exists s' \in L') \ s\underline{\blacktriangleright}s' \ .$$

but without insisting that strings have the same length

$$s\underline{\blacktriangleright}s' \quad \text{iff} \quad (\exists s'') \ \mathsf{unpad}(s'') = \mathsf{unpad}(s') \text{ and } s \unrhd s'' \ .$$

Insofar as $L\underline{\blacktriangleright}L'$ says every instance of $L$ contains some instance of $L'$, it is natural to say $L'$ *occurs in* $L$ when $L\underline{\blacktriangleright}L'$. This generalizes the notion of occurrence discussed in the introduction.

Having weakened the second argument of $\unrhd$, we now strengthen its first argument with background contextual information encoded by a set $C \subseteq \mathsf{Pow}(\Phi)^{*}$ of strings. To illustrate, an event $L = \boxed{\text{rain,now}}$ of *raining now* updates a background

$$C \quad = \quad (\Box + \boxed{\text{rain}} + \boxed{\overline{\text{rain}}})^{+} \ \& \ (\Box^{+}\boxed{\text{now}}\Box^{+})$$

to give

$$C[L] \quad = \quad (\Box + \boxed{\text{rain}} + \boxed{\overline{\text{rain}}})^{*}\boxed{\text{rain,now}}(\Box + \boxed{\text{rain}} + \boxed{\overline{\text{rain}}})^{*} \ .$$

Evidently, neither the intersection $C \cap L$ nor the superposition $C\&L$ will do for the result $C[L]$ of updating $C$ by $L$. Combining $\cap$ and $\&$, let

$$\begin{aligned} C[L] &\stackrel{\text{def}}{=} \{s \in C \mid s\underline{\blacktriangleright}L\} \\ &= (L^{\Box}\&C) \cap C \ . \end{aligned}$$

Not only does context grow eliminatively, $C[L] \subseteq C$, but $C[L]\underline{\blacktriangleright}L$, so that we can strengthen $\underline{\blacktriangleright}$ to a relation $\vdash^{C}$ sensitive to $C$, defining

$$L \vdash^{C} L' \quad \stackrel{\text{def}}{\iff} \quad C[L]\underline{\blacktriangleright}L'$$

(Fernando (2006)).

## 7.4 On to proof-theoretic semantics

How do the relations $\unrhd$ and $\vdash^{C}$ square with proof-theoretic semantics? More notation is convenient. Given a string $c$ and a language $L$, let

(i) $E_L(c)$ be the set of strings in $L$ that $c$ subsumes

$$E_L(c) \stackrel{\text{def}}{=} \{s \in L \mid c \unrhd s\}$$

(ii) $\text{ext}(L, c)$ be the set of strings in $L$ that occur in $c$

$$\text{ext}(L, c) \stackrel{\text{def}}{=} \{s \in L \mid c \underline{\blacktriangleright} s\}$$

(iii) $e_L(c)$ be some element of $E_L(c)$ if $E_L(c) \neq \emptyset$ else $e_L(c) = c$, and
(iv) $e(L,c)$ be some element of $\text{ext}(L,c)$ if $\text{ext}(L,c) \neq \emptyset$ else $e(L,c) = c$.

It follows that

$$\begin{aligned} L \trianglerighteq L' \quad & \text{iff} \quad (\forall x \in L)\ E_{L'}(x) \neq \emptyset \\ & \text{iff} \quad (\forall x \in L)\ e_{L'}(x) \in L' \end{aligned}$$

and

$$\begin{aligned} L \vdash^C L' \quad & \text{iff} \quad (\forall x \in C)(\forall y \in \text{ext}(L,x))\ \text{ext}(L',x) \neq \emptyset \\ & \text{iff} \quad (\forall x \in C)(\forall y \in \text{ext}(L,x))\ e(L',x) \in L' \ . \end{aligned}$$

Adopting the familiar sequent format $\Gamma \longmapsto \Theta$ for an assertion (or judgment) $\Theta$ based on assumptions (or context) $\Gamma$, we might then express $L \trianglerighteq L'$ as

(13) $$x \in L \quad \longmapsto \quad e_{L'}(x) \in L'$$

and $L \vdash^C L'$ as

(14) $$x \in C,\ y \in \text{ext}(L,x) \quad \longmapsto \quad e(L',x) \in L' \ .$$

If we are to replace $e_{L'}(x)$ and $e(L',x)$ by terms $t(x)$ and $t'(x,y)$ that can be formed through a system of rules, we must beef $L'$ up to $E_{L'}(x)$ and $\text{ext}(L',x)$ respectively,[6] resulting in

(15) $$x \in L \quad \longmapsto \quad t(x) \in E_{L'}(x)$$

for (13) and

(16) $$x \in C,\ y \in \text{ext}(L,x) \quad \longmapsto \quad t'(x,y) \in \text{ext}(L',x)$$

for (14). In both (15) and (16), the first variable typed, $x$, relativizes the languages of all other terms appearing in the sequent ($L'$ in (15), and $L, L'$ in (16)). To isolate the variable $x$ to the left of $\longmapsto$, we can put (16) as

$$x \in C \quad \longmapsto \quad (\lambda y \in \text{ext}(L,x))\, t'(x,y) \ \in \ \text{ext}(L,x) \to \text{ext}(L',x)$$

with a function $(\lambda y \in \text{ext}(L,x))\, t'(x,y)$ to the right of $\longmapsto$. The example of $e(L',x)$ from (14) for $t'(x,y)$ suggests the function need not consult $y$ during its computation; the typing $y \in \text{ext}(L,x)$ serves simply to ensure that the search for a string in $\text{ext}(L',x)$ succeeds, provided $L \vdash^C L'$. At any rate, we need not worry about termination of the computation, so long as we bound the search to strings occurring in (or, in the case of $t(x)$, subsumed by) $x$.

With these functions in mind, let us call a function $f$ on strings over the alphabet $\mathsf{Pow}(\Phi)$ a $\trianglerighteq$*-map* if for all $s \in \mathsf{Pow}(\Phi)^*$, $s \trianglerighteq f(s)$. If we collect in $L \overset{\trianglerighteq}{\to} L'$ all $\trianglerighteq$-maps that send strings in $L$ to strings in $L'$

$$f \in L \overset{\trianglerighteq}{\to} L' \quad \overset{\text{def}}{\iff} \quad f \text{ is a } \trianglerighteq\text{-map and } (\forall s \in L)\ f(s) \in L'$$

then we can reduce $L \trianglerighteq L'$ to the non-emptiness of $L \overset{\trianglerighteq}{\to} L'$

$$L \trianglerighteq L' \quad \text{iff} \quad L \overset{\trianglerighteq}{\to} L' \text{ is inhabited (i.e. non-empty)} \ .$$

[6]This is because we can no longer rely on the fact that for all languages $L$ and strings $x$, $e_L(x) \trianglerighteq x$ and $e(L,x) \underline{\blacktriangleright} x$.

Weakening subsumption $\unrhd$, we define a function $f$ on strings over the alphabet $\mathsf{Pow}(\Phi)$ to be a $\blacktriangleright$*-map* if for all $s \in \mathsf{Pow}(\Phi)^*$, $s \underline{\blacktriangleright} f(s)$. Then $L \vdash^C L'$ reduces to the existence of a $\underline{\blacktriangleright}$-map from $C[L]$ to $L'$

$$L \vdash^C L' \quad \text{iff} \quad \text{there is a } \underline{\blacktriangleright}\text{-map } f \text{ such that } (\forall s \in C[L])\ f(s) \in L' .$$

We can go beyond any single (finite) string $c$ to a set $C$ of strings that approximates a world, assuming $C$ is $\underline{\blacktriangleright}$*-directed* in that for all $c, c' \in C$, there exists $c'' \in C$ such that $c'' \underline{\blacktriangleright} c$ and $c'' \underline{\blacktriangleright} c'$. Forming the union of their extensions

$$\text{ext}(L, C) \stackrel{\text{def}}{=} \bigcup_{c \in C} \text{ext}(L, c) ,$$

it is natural to modify (16) to

$$(17) \qquad x \in C,\ y \in \text{ext}(L, x) \quad \longmapsto \quad \hat{t}(x, y) \in (\exists z \in C)\,\text{ext}(L', z)$$

for which the problem is how to bound the variable $z$. Our approach of building an inference relation $\vdash^C$ by incorporating background assumptions $C$ into the first argument of $\underline{\blacktriangleright}$ shifts the complexity from proof terms $t, t', \ldots$ to $C$. Constraints $L \Rightarrow L'$ are useful in forming $C$, and involve $\unrhd$-maps insofar as

$$s \in L \Rightarrow L' \quad \text{iff} \quad \{x \in \text{Fac}(s) \mid x \unrhd L\} \unrhd L'$$

where $\text{Fac}(s)$ is the set of factors of $s$

$$\text{Fac}(s) \stackrel{\text{def}}{=} \{x \in \mathsf{Pow}(\Phi)^* \mid (\exists u, v \in \mathsf{Pow}(\Phi)^*)\ s = uxv\} .$$

There are variants of $\Rightarrow$ that apply to various cases of (17), described in Fernando and Nairn (2005), drawing on methods in Beesley and Karttunen (2003).

### Acknowledgments

This paper is an update on my invited talk at SPR 2001. I thank the organizers of that workshop and editors of this volume, especially Kepa Korta for his patience. I am grateful also to Yukinori Takubo, Takao Gunji, Ikumi Imani, Hiroshi Mito and Norihiko Ogata for much appreciated interest.

## References

Allen, J.F. 1983. Maintaining knowledge about temporal intervals. *Communications of the ACM* 26(11):832–843.

Austin, J.L. 1961. Truth. In J. Urmson and G. Warncock, eds., *Philosophical Papers*. Oxford University Press.

Barwise, J. and J. Perry. 1983. *Situations and Attitudes*. MIT Press, Cambridge, Mass.

Beesley, K.R. and L. Karttunen. 2003. *Finite State Morphology*. CSLI Publications, Stanford.

Cooper, R. 2005. Austinian truth, attitudes and type theory. *Research on Language and Computation* 3(4):333–362.

Davidson, D. 1967. The logical form of action sentences. In N. Rescher, ed., *The Logic of Decision and Action*, pages 81–95. University of Pittsburgh Press. Reprinted in [Dav80].

Davidson, D. 1980. *Essays on Actions and Events*. Clarendon Press, Oxford.

Dowty, D.R. 1986. The effects of aspectual class on the temporal structure of discourse: semantics or pragmatics? *Linguistics and Philosophy* 9:37–61.

Emerson, E.A. 1992. Temporal and modal logic. In J. v. Leeuwen, ed., *Handbook of Theoretical Computer Science*, vol. B: Formal Methods and Semantics, pages 995–1072. MIT Press.

Fernando, T. 2004. A finite-state approach to events in natural language semantics. *Journal of Logic and Computation* 14(1):79–92.

Fernando, T. 2006. Finite-state temporal projection. In *Proc. 11th International Conference on Implementation and Application of Automata (CIAA 2006)*, Lectures Notes in Computer Science 4094, pages 230–241. Springer-Verlag.

Fernando, T. and R. Nairn. 2005. Entailments in finite-state temporality. In *Proc. 6th International Workshop on Computational Semantics*, pages 128–138. Tilburg University.

Kamp, H. and U. Reyle. 1993. *From Discourse to Logic*. Kluwer Academic Publishers, Dordrecht.

Kaplan, D. 1979. On the logic of demonstratives. *Journal of Philosophical Logic* 8(1).

van Lambalgen, M. and F. Hamm. 2005. *The Proper Treatment of Events*. Blackwell.

Martin-Löf, P. 1984. *Intuitionistic Type Theory*. Bibliopolis, Napoli. Notes by Giovanni Sambin of a series of lectures given in Padua, June 1980.

McCarthy, J. and P. Hayes. 1969. Some philosophical problems from the standpoint of artificial intelligence. In M. Meltzer and D. Michie, eds., *Machine Intelligence 4*, pages 463–502. Edinburgh University Press.

Parsons, T. 1990. *Events in the Semantics of English: A Study in Subatomic Semantics*. MIT Press, Cambridge, MA.

Perry, J. 1997. Situation semantics. In *Routledge Encyclopedia of Philosophy*. London, Routledge.

Ranta, A. 1994. *Type-Theoretical Grammar*. Oxford University Press, Oxford.

Reichenbach, H. 1947. *Elements of Symbolic Logic*. London, Macmillan.

Steedman, M. 2000. *The Productions of Time*. Draft, ftp://ftp.cogsci.ed.ac.uk/pub/steedman/temporality/temporality.ps.gz. Subsumes 'Temporality,' in J. van Benthem and A. ter Meulen, editors, *Handbook of Logic and Language*, pages 895–935, Elsevier North Holland, 1997.

8

# A Compositional Account of Counterfactuals

NICHOLAS ASHER AND ERIC MCCREADY

### Abstract

This paper is to explore the meaning of counterfactuals. We first review our dynamic account of modal operators that is capable of accounting for both the phenomena noted by Veltman with respect to epistemic modals and also modal subordination. We then use this theory, together with an analysis of conditionals and irrealis mood, to give a fully compositional semantics of indicative and counterfactual conditionals. On our analysis, the distinction between counterfactual and indicative conditionals follows directly from the interaction between the semantics of these three semantic elements.

## 8.1 Introduction

Over the past twenty years with the advent of the "dynamic turn" in semantics, there have been numerous discoveries and theoretical proposals for modals in Romance and Germanic languages, as well as for conditionals and counterfactuals. But there has been little attempt to produce a compositional account of counterfactuals from an account of the meanings for the conditional and the modals, something which Kratzer (e.g., Kratzer (1977, 1981, 1986, 1991)) argued for convincingly but only carried out in her static framework for analyzing modalities.[1] Here we present a detailed, dynamic semantics for modals that leads to a new semantics for counterfactuals.

In a paper in the *Journal of Semantics*, we proposed a semantics that accounted for a variety of observations made about epistemic modals in natural languages. In particular we were concerned to formalize the observations concerning epistemic modals by Veltman (1996) together with the observations made by Roberts (1987, 1989) concerning the anaphoric properties of modals in discourse. We review these briefly below. When we wrote that paper, there were no proposals that could simultaneously capture both of these observations.

[1]Prominent exceptions to this generalization are Gillies (2003) and Kaufmann (2005). Gillies, however, does not consider the modal subordination use of modals and Kaufmann considers complementary interactions between conditionals and modals to the ones that we concentrate on.

*Meaning, Intentions, and Argumentation.*
Kepa Korta and Joana Garmendia (eds.).

Veltman's (1996) seminal paper on epistemic modals introduces the idea that epistemic possibilities conveyed with a modal like *might* interact dynamically with factual information introduced in a discourse. Factual information introduced into a discourse may rule out certain epistemic possibilities that might otherwise be present. Consider the following minimal pair.

(1) a. It might be sunny. It's not sunny.
    b. #It is not sunny. It might be sunny.

Veltman's examples show that epistemic possibilities are subject to what information has already been introduced in the discourse; once it has been established in the discourse that it is not sunny, it is no longer permissible to introduce the epistemic possibility that it might be sunny, as in (1b).[2] While some have claimed that (1b) has a reading according to which the speaker revises his contribution, we claim that revisions need much more linguistic marking than is possible in (1b). Like Veltman, we believe that (1b) remains very marginal even when one has the revision scenario in mind. An alternative is to adopt a pragmatic story on which an assertion of (1b) would be bad because it violates Grice's maxim of Quality: since the first sentence explicitly rules out the possibility of it being sunny, the second sentence is obviously false. Put another way, if the discourse is to be uttered, the speaker is not sincere in his utterance of one of the two sentences, since they are inconsistent. In any case, (1b) remains incoherent on an epistemic reading.[3]

The observation originally due to Roberts is that uses of modals may pick up and refine epistemic possibilities introduced by the use of modals in previous utterances. This phenomenon has come to be known as *modal subordination.* Consider for example the discourses in (2). Here the indefinites should be understood *de dicto*, as nonspecific indefinites under the scope of the modal.

(2) a. A wolf might walk in. It would eat you first.
    b. A wolf might walk in. # It will eat you first.
    c. A wolf might walk in. It might eat you first.

There is a striking difference between (2a) and (2b). In (2a) the use of the epistemic modal *would* enables the pronoun *it* to find its intended antecedent, the wolf introduced under the scope of the modal in the first sentence, while futurate *will* in (2b) does not allow this possibility. (2c) shows that the modal *might* has the same effect as *would*

[2] Some people, philosophers notably, claim that *might p* is ambiguous between the epistemic reading that says "for all that is known given the discourse so far, it's possible that *p*" and the metaphysical reading. We think that (1b) has–at best–a very marginal metaphysical reading, and so that it's pretty bad, whereas (1a) is felicitous on the preferred epistemic reading. We think that there is in fact a metaphysical reading in this variant of (1b): *It is not sunny. But it might have been sunny.* But this example has rather different properties in general.

[3] Introducing as an epistemic possibility something that has already been established in the discourse as in (1c) is also infelicitous, though much less so than (1b).

(1c) ? It is sunny. It might be sunny.

We take the second sentence of (1c) to be uninformative, and so we account for its oddness using a pragmatic principle of informativeness. But the second sentence of (1b) isn't uninformative; the discourse is epistemically unsatisfiable. One of the important goals, we think, of a theory of modals is to show why (1b) is so different from (1c).

in enabling the accessibility of the intended antecedent. Nevertheless, since *a wolf* occurs under the scope of the modal operator in these sentences, it is unavailable as an antecedent for the pronoun in nonmodal contexts, which is what standard dynamic semantics predicts. The accessibility of the antecedent under the scope of a modal to a pronoun also under the scope of a modal, however, was something that standard dynamic semantic accounts of anaphora as well as more traditional accounts could not predict; and the accounts of Roberts and later of Frank (1997) provided significant insights into the semantics of anaphoric expressions.

Roberts's observations extend in principle to various pairs of modals, though, we note, not all examples of modal subordination are equally good. More important for the purposes of this paper is that counterfactuals also can depend on *might* claims:

(3) A wolf might walk in. If it were to eat you first, I'd be unhappy, but not as unhappy as if it ate me first.

In fact many modals combine productively together with a conditional whose antecedent is adjusted for the appropriate mood to create counterfactuals of various kinds.

(4) a. If I were not to sleep tonight, I would topple over tomorrow (I might topple over tomorrow).
b. If I had not slept last night, I would have toppled over today.
c. What should be your mascot if you were a school? (Google)
d. If we were to get more serious, should I tell him my age? (Google)
e. If it were easy, anyone could do it (Google, *Converge Magazine*).

The ease with which modals and conditionals combine strongly suggests that we should try to build a compositional account of the semantics for counterfactuals. The slight differences in meaning between the different modals create different sorts of counterfactuals; for instance *should* and *would* don't have quite the same range of meanings; and nor do *could* and *might*. And not unexpectedly, there is a definite change in meaning between (4e) and the variant *if it were easy, anyone might do it*. Our goal in this paper is an account of the contribution of modal expressions to counterfactuals; more specifically, we will provide a compositional account of these constructions. The idea is that, with the right semantics for modals, the conditional, and the irrealis mood that appears in counterfactual constructions, a theory of counterfactuals will fall out in a compositional manner. We will in fact go further and in the last section suggest connections between counterfactuals and normality conditionals such as this one, showing how they are realized within our analysis.

(5) If someone never exercises, he is usually unhealthy.

## 8.2 An overview of our theory of modals

In this section we review the data that led us to adopt the particular account of modals that we do. We first look to see how modals behave with non modal discourse before looking to their interactions. An interesting use of the epistemic modal *would* concerns its effects as an agreement marker in discourse. In (6), B's utterance conveys that the content of A's utterance conforms to B's expectations, or, in other words, that in all of B's epistemic possibilities (before processing A's utterance) Kim's teasing Pat was something that was bound to happen.

(6) a. A: Kim teased Pat.
b. B: Kim would do that.

There are in addition many uses of 'polite would'. One is

(7) a. Who is Asher?
b. That would be me.

(8) a. What are you drinking?
b. I'd like a glass of champagne.

Such polite uses indicate a sort of scalar strength between $\phi$ and *Would* $\phi$ (*Would* and *Might* are operators in our formalization and are the counterparts of the English modals). More specifically, *Would* $\phi$ is weaker than $\phi$ and so clearly doesn't entail it. This is made even clearer by discourses like this one.

(9) a. A: Who drank the last beer?
b. B: That would be me.
c. A:'Would'?
d. B: OK, it was me.

The lack of entailment allows room for the politeness effect of (7b) and (8b).

We made the hypothesis that on this use, $\phi$ implies *Would* $\phi$. Our first reason for this is philosophical. On a certain idealization that we adopt here, the discourse context established through prior assertions represents what is the common ground and thus mutually believed by the conversation participants.[4] The epistemic possibilities through which the meaning of *would* is defined ought to reflect these convictions. Thus, if $\phi$ is part of the prior discourse context, our analysis should reflect that $\phi$ is true in all the epistemic possibilities. An epistemic understanding of *would* makes, in such a circumstance, *Would* $\phi$ true.

Does the usage of *would* reflect this conceptual point? We think it does. We have two pieces of evidence for this claim. The first comes from discourses like those in (10). Here we must understand *would* as similar to the instance in (6) above. If we do, the discourse in (10b) is perfectly sensible.

(10) a. ? John is at the party. He wouldn't be at the party.
b. ? John is at the party. He would be at the party.

(10a) is a flat out contradiction, unless the second sentence is understood as some sort of self-correction.[5] We admit that (10b) also sounds pretty odd; indeed we should predict that it's pragmatically odd since we take *Would* $\phi$ claims to be weaker than $\phi$. Thus, the second clause of (10b) is redundant. But at least some speakers balk at the claim that the first clause of (10b) entails the second. We think that is perhaps due to a temporal effect on the interpretation of *would*. *Would* has some element of past tense evaluation in it; it refers to epistemic possibilities just prior to the *now* of non modal

[4]Though see Asher and Gillies (2003) for a view of discourse context where this is not the case.

[5]Or unless we understand some sort of suppressed antecedent of a counterfactual as occurring there, for which there is little if any evidence.

discourse, though there are temporal dependences between modals in modal discourse. There is a feeling that *prior* to the extended "now" for the discourse and thus prior to update with $\phi$, *Would* $\phi$ should be true. $\phi$, that is, should not come as a surprise. At least for some speakers, there is a lag between update and readjustment of epistemic possibilities. Our model does not include times, so we cannot model the lag between update and readjustment. But aside from this complication, we take this inference to go through.

Next, consider the discourse in (11). Here it seems clear to us that the content $\phi$ of A's utterance is being used to correct to B's claim that $\neg$ *Would* $\phi$. If $\phi$ implies *Would* $\phi$, then we have a straightforward explanation of the two Corrections in terms of indirect proof or modus tollens.

(11) a. A: John stole some money from Mary.
b. B: He wouldn't do that.
c. A: Well he did.

This leads one to wonder about the relationship between *might* and *would*. Their semantics is strongly interconnected, and they appear to be weak duals, in the sense that one cannot have *Might* $p$ and *Would* $\neg p$. Similarly, most speakers baulk at *Would* $p$ but *Might* $\neg p$. Intuitions thus support that *Would* $p$ implies *Might* $p$.

(12) a. #John might come to the party but John would not come to the party.
b. #John would not come to the party but John might come to the party.

With this basic picture of *might* and *would* modals, we now review how they interact with conditionals; the kind of compositional semantics for counterfactuals we want to give must assign meanings to the various modals and to the conditional expressed *if ... then* and then see how those all combine together.[6] What sort of semantics ought the conditional itself to have? This is of course a question that many have worried over; but on the present view, the semantics of the conditional in counterfactuals should be exactly the same as that in so called "indicative" conditionals, in which the antecedent is in the indicative (as opposed to subjunctive) mood.

Indicative conditionals have interesting connection with the epistemic modals as Kratzer (1981) and Stalnaker (1975) noted long ago (for a discussion see Gillies (2004)), as well as a number of commonly agreed upon characteristics:

- they have Ramsey test like behavior and support *modus ponens*. (The Ramsey test refers to a theory of conditionals on which, in essence, a conditional is true if the consequent is true in any situation in which the antecedent is).[7]
- they support logical exportation (across the turnstile), in the sense that $\phi \Rightarrow (\psi \Rightarrow \chi) \models (\phi \wedge \psi) \Rightarrow \chi$ and vice-versa.
- they have a modal flavor—more specifically, they should obey the following equivalence: $\neg(\phi \Rightarrow \psi) \leftrightarrow (\Diamond(\phi \wedge \neg\psi)$

[6] A similar project is attempted by McCawley (1996), among others.

[7] This means that the consequent does not contain more information than the antecedent in the sense of dynamic semantics. A more formal definition of the Ramsey test is given in the main text below.

While the first two properties are obvious enough, the modal properties of ordinary conditionals require some comment. Consider the following interaction from Gillies (2004) between two detectives, A and B, who are investigating a crime at a mansion for which grounds staff consists of a driver and a grounds keeper.

(13) a. A: If one of the grounds staff committed the crime, then it was the driver.
b. B: No, it might have been the grounds keeper.

B's response *it might have been the grounds keeper* is a way of elaborating on his denial of A's claim; clearly we take B's response to explain *why* he thinks A's assertion is false. But if this is right, then the truth conditions of a conditional must involve the semantics of modals in some way, and that in turn means that conditionals involve epistemic possibilities.

### 8.2.1 Previous Accounts

To set the stage for our analysis, we sketch briefly how dynamic semantics fits into this enterprise. Dynamic semantics was designed to account for how the meaning of an utterance in a particular discourse context might change or contribute to that very discourse context. Accordingly, all dynamic semantic theories analyze the meaning of a sentence as a relation between contexts, an input context and an output context. Broadly speaking, contexts in dynamic semantics are sets of n-tuples consisting at least of a world, an assignment function, and often other things as well.[8] There are two broad parameters in the way dynamic semantics may describe the effects of an utterance on a context: first it may be *distributive* and define the effects of a sentence on each element of the context, or not (this is the *collective* view); secondly these effects may affect those elements of the context or not. If they don't, the semantics is called *eliminative*. DRT of Kamp and Reyle (1993) as well as DPL (Groenendijk and Stokhof (1991)) are examples of distributive semantics that are not eliminative, whereas Veltman's (Veltman (1985, 1996)) update semantics which he uses for his account of the modals, is eliminative but not distributive.

Let's take a look at Veltman's update semantics first. Contexts are understood as sets of worlds and the epistemic sense of *might* that is to be captured is one that surveys the possibilities common to the discourse participants who have accepted the information in the discourse so far. Thus, the picture is that as discourse proceeds the set of epistemic possibilities left open to the participants gradually narrows as they build up a common ground of information between them. When updating a context with a formula, we either eliminate worlds from that context that do not satisfy it or the formula operates as a "test" on the context as a whole. Formulas of the form *Might* $\phi$, *Would* $\phi$ and conditionals function as tests on the context. Here is the semantic clause for formulas of the form *Might* $\phi$:

- Veltman's account of *Might*:
- Let $\sigma$ be a set of possible worlds, $\phi$ a formula of a propositional language, $\|phi\|$ its usual modal interpretation, and $+$ the update operation. Then:

[8] In this paper we will use the notion of possible world in its ordinary sense as an evaluation point that gives a truth value to all well formed sentences of the formal language in a classical fashion. We do not investigate, here, a notion of epistemic possibility which may not be logically closed.

$$\sigma + Might\phi = \sigma \text{ if } \sigma \cap \|\phi\| \neq 0$$
$$= 0 \text{ otherwise.}$$

The idea is that an information state will pass the test of *Might* $\phi$ whenever $\phi$ is true in at least one world in the context. But updating contexts with factual information such as in (1c) will eliminate all those worlds that support the epistemic possibility that it is sunny, and so then attempting to update the information state with *it might be sunny* will yield an empty information state, a sign that something has gone wrong.

Veltman's semantics for modals naturally extends to a simple semantics for conditionals. Gillies (2004) analyzes conditionals as introducing tests on (Veltman-style) information states: a state $\sigma$ will pass $\phi \Rightarrow \psi$ iff $\sigma$ obeys the Ramsey test for this conditional—i.e.:[9]

- $\sigma + \phi + \psi = \sigma + \phi$.

von Fintel (2002) takes a more "dynamic" approach to counterfactuals, where added to a Lewis-style semantics is the idea that the set of modal possibilities relevant to the evaluation of the counterfactual dynamically evolve and expand to include possibilities that verify the antecedent of the counterfactual. One might think that *might* could be understood similarly as an expander of some background set of epistemic possibilities. This is known as the accommodation account of *might*, according to which *Might* $\phi$ expands the epistemic possibilities to make $\phi$ true (Gillies (2003)). The attractions of this view are that it offers a Lewisian semantics for counterfactuals, or one built on a semantics for conditionals like the one above, a solution for following pair of problematic examples.[10]

(14) a. If John were to come to the party, it would be fun.
b. But of course if John were to come to the party, he might have a heart attack and that wouldn't be fun.

On a standard Lewisian semantics for *might* counterfactuals, it is difficult to see how to make these two counterfactuals jointly satisfiable, as we show in more detail in section 4. An accommodation account of *might* offers hope of a satisfactory analysis of (14). However, the accommodation account needs to be strongly constrained, if we are to account for Veltman's original observations about *might*, which strongly suggest that *might* functions as a test on *existing* epistemic possibilities. Further, any compositional analysis of counterfactuals that adopts this view of *might* threatens to trivialize the semantics by making all *might* counterfactuals with a satisfiable consequent true, since it should always be possible to extend the set of modal possibilities to include those that support some satisfiable sentence. In our semantics we will reject an accommodation account of *might* and argue for a different analysis of (14).

Veltman's theory and Gillies's extension capture the data about the interactions between *might* sentences, conditionals and non modal sentences effectively. But they don't extend easily to capture other data about the modals, in particular the data on modal subordination or how modal statements interact dynamically. *Might* is just a

[9] This conditional should be distinguished from material implication $\rightarrow$. $\Rightarrow$ is the semantic representation of the natural language, *if-then* conditional.

[10] Thanks to Thony Gillies for these examples.

test on the whole information state according to Veltman's semantics; so if the update with *Might* $\phi$ is successful, then we get back the same context that we started with. The facts about modal subordination, however, require us to isolate the set of epistemic possibilities in which $\phi$ holds that further discourse can modify further; e.g., we must isolate those worlds in the context where the wolf walks in as in (2a), in order to further refine those possibilities to those where the hearer gets eaten first. This is simply not possible on the Veltman semantics: we can't isolate the relevant set of epistemic possibilities and we can't modify that set, unless we update with a nonmodal assertion. But the facts about modal subordination show that modification is possible with modals and that this modification is not equivalent to updating with a nonmodal assertion. Veltman's test semantics for *might* alone can't furnish us an appropriate context in which to evaluate subsequent modal claims.

Now, the work by Veltman and Gillies is for a quantifier free fragment only, and so we need to extend their semantics to a quantificational one. Most research in dynamic semantics has adopted the distributive semantics for quantification (e.g., Groenendijk and Stokhof (1991), Kamp and Reyle (1993)), and we will follow suit.[11] The distributive semantic framework of DRT is also the one in which the first accounts of modal subordination were developed. Roberts' (Roberts (1987)) account of modals, for instance, considers them to be two place operators, one argument of which is given by what is in the scope of the modal operator, the other argument (the restrictor) provided by some contextually available proposition. Modal subordination is then a matter of finding an appropriate proposition in antecedent discourse to serve as the restrictor or first argument of the modal. For example, in (2a), the proposition under the scope of the *Might* operator in the first sentence provides the first argument to the operator *Would* in the second sentence, while the second argument is given by the material under the scope of the *would* in the second sentence. Roughly, both Roberts and Frank (1997) give the following semantics for *Would* $(\phi, \psi)$: every element of of some fixed set of modal possibilities associated with that context that satisfies $\phi$ also satisfies $\psi$. So for example in (2a) the formula *it would eat you first* is satisfied in a context just in case every possibility in which a wolf walks in is also an element in which the wolf eats the hearer first. This is a distributive semantics for the modal operators.

Anaphoric accounts of modal subordination are attractive for their simplicity. But we don't think they offer the right approach to modal subordination. First, two place operator accounts like Roberts's (but see also Frank (1997), Geurts (1995)) don't specify the first argument of a modal operator; that's left to pragmatics. When we turn to our compositional account of counterfactuals, we will want the first argument of the modal in the consequent to be grammatically determined by the update in the antecedent.

[11] We cannot simply use the DPL clauses for quantification with the Veltman–Gillies operations for truth functional and modal operators, however. Here's the standard and common sense clause for negation when trying to define operations on sets of world assignment pairs:

- $\sigma + \neg\phi = \sigma - (\sigma + \phi)$.

However, now consider $\sigma + \neg\exists x\phi$. If the existential is to reset values of assignment functions as we expect in dynamic semantics, then $\sigma + \exists x\phi$ may very well be disjoint from $\sigma$ depending on the choice of resetting values. In that case $\sigma + \neg\exists x\phi = \sigma$ and it could very well be that we could have a non-empty update result by updating with $\sigma + \exists x\phi$, which would imply that $\neg\exists x\phi \wedge \exists x\phi$ is satisfiable!

And so we will not consider such an account further here.[12]

The problem of not specifying in any way the antecedents for the modals on the anaphoric approach leads to an appalling lack of logical structure for the modals in natural language. In fact, the anaphoric account verifies *none* of the inferences that we specified earlier as intuitively adequate are valid on any standard notion of validity, dynamic or otherwise. Even simple idempotence inferences like

- *Might* $\phi$. Therefore *Might* $\phi$

fail. On *some* resolutions of the anaphors, the desired inferences follow, but there is nothing in any of the anaphoric accounts that tells us *which* antecedents must or should be selected in a given context. Thus, the anaphoric account of modals yields us no logic for natural language modals. In section 4 we present a constraint on entailments to the effect that ambiguous expressions must be disambiguated the same way both on the left and right of the turnstile. If we extended this constraint to the resolution of anaphors, the logic of modals on the anaphoric view would become much more sensible. But we are dubious that extending entailment this way to underspecification is correct. Ambiguities are a special case of underspecification, and a constraint that is appropriate for the special case does not necessarily carry over to the more general one. The conclusion we think that one must draw from these observations is that modals are not anaphoric expressions.

Our alternative picture is that modals are dynamic operators that take epistemic possibilities as inputs and refine, reset or otherwise modify them.[13] Our view is in many ways closer to that advocated by Kratzer, except that for us the "modal bases" are dynamic and change as the discourse context proceeds. The updated epistemic possibilities serve as inputs to subsequent occurences of modals. If we take the superficial order of sentences to determine the sequence of updates, then we should expect that it is always the most recent set of epistemic possibilities that are relevant to evaluating a modal. If this were right, then modals would behave similarly to tenses in a dynamic semantic theory like DRT (Kamp and Reyle (1993)). But the situation is not so simple, as the following example shows:

(15) a. John may come to the party. He might drink quite a bit. We would all have fun.

b. But then again he might not drink anything. And then we wouldn't have fun.

The first modal in (15b) cannot take as input the last updated set of epistemic possibilites in (15a), because then the updated epistemic possibilities in (15b) should support both that John drinks quite a bit and that he doesn't drink anything. Intuitively no epis-

[12]We reject the anaphoric account for a number of empirical reasons. But we won't repeat them here. For further discussion of the anaphoric approach, see Asher and McCready (forthcoming)

[13]It appears that van van Rooij (2005) takes a similar view. See also Zeevat (1992) for some related discussion. We propose a different approach from Van Rooij's, because his paper is primarily concerned with presupposition, which we feel is a somewhat orthagonal issue to the semantics of modals and modal subordination. While the formalism proposed by Van Rooij is quite elegant, we think that it has problems with simple cases of modal subordination that we will outline once we get to our technical proposal.

temic possibility should do that. This strategy predicts that (15ab) is at least modally inconsistent. But the example is perfectly interpretable and ordinary. What intuitively happens with (15b) is that the input epistemic possibilities are those introduced by the first sentence in (15a). That is, the input epistemic possibilities to the first sentence in (15b) are the output epistemic possibilities from the first sentence of (15a).

The phenomenon observed in (15ab) generalizes to tenses as well. Sometimes the temporal structure of a discourse is more elaborate than what is suggested by the DRT analysis of tenses. There are clearly temporal shifts that show that the treatment of tenses cannot simply rely on the superficial order of the sentences in the text.

(16) a. ($\pi_1$) John had a great evening last night.
b. ($\pi_2$) He had a great meal.
c. ($\pi_3$) He ate salmon.
d. ($\pi_4$) He devoured lots of cheese.
e. ($\pi_5$) He then won a dancing competition.

(16c-d) provides 'more detail' about the event in (16b), which itself elaborates on (16a). (16e) continues the elaboration of John's evening that (16b) started, forming a *narrative* with it (temporal progression). Clearly, the ordering of events does not follow the order of sentences, but rather obeys the constraints imposed by discourse structure, as shown graphically below. Thus the eventualities that are understood as elaborating on others are temporally subordinate to them, and those events that represent narrative continuity are understood as following each other. The relevant parameter for interpreting tenses is *discourse adjacency in the discourse structure*, not superficial adjacency. A theory like SDRT (Asher (1993), Asher and Lascarides (2003)) provides the following discourse structure for (16) and this allows us to get a proper treatment of the tenses therein. Here $\pi_6$ and $\pi_7$ are discourse constituents created by the process of inferring the discourse structure. See Asher and Lascarides (2003) for details.

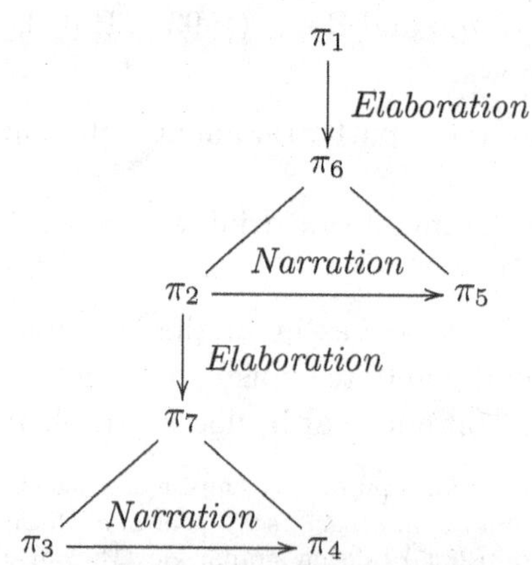


FIGURE 1 SDRT graph for (16)

The same idea is operative with the modals. When we construct an appropriate discourse structure for (15ab), the appropriate attachment site for (15b) is the first sentence of (15a). The rest of the material in (15a) which elaborates on one possibility offers a contrast with the material in (15b), which elaborates a different, in fact disjoint, possibility, something we signal with the discourse relation *Alternation.* Here is an appropriate discourse structure for (15ab). Again, $\pi_6, \pi_7$, and $\pi_8$ are created during the process of inferring the structure.

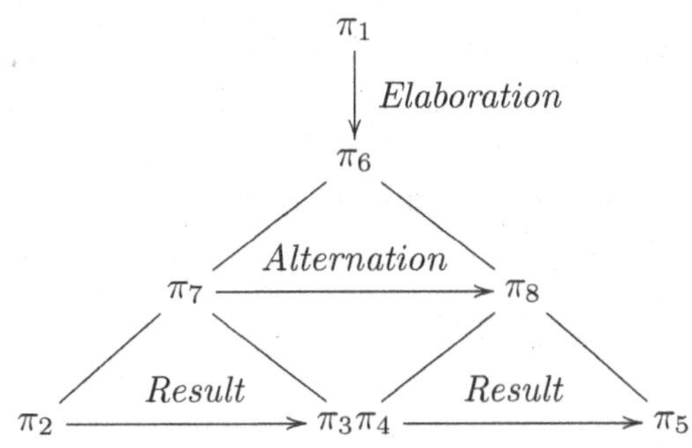


FIGURE 2 SDRT graph for (15ab)

This discourse structure intuitively makes clear that the two contrasting possibilities depend on the possibilities introduced by the discourse constituent that dominates them and that they elaborate. They offer two different ways the possibility of John's coming to the party, which they elaborate on, might proceed. We now turn to providing the semantic details of how to interpret modals, all the while with an eye to using this analysis within a discourse based framework like SDRT and to its applicability to a compositional theory of counterfactuals.

## 8.3 Semantics of Modals

Our account combines a basically distributive dynamic semantics for quantifiers with the non-distributive semantics for the modals. We begin with a standard dynamic semantic formalism like that of DPL with partial assignment functions, which yields a good account of quantification and intersentential anaphora. The elements of the context are world assignment function pairs.[14] To this we add another element for evaluating the modals, a pair consisting of a *basic or global set of epistemic possibilities* and a *focussed set of epistemic possibilities.* Thus each point of dynamic evaluation becomes in effect an information state.

In order to capture Veltman's examples in (1ab), we need to test the current epistemic possibilities when evaluating sentences of the form *Might* $\phi$. Following Fernando (1993) we define a notion of satisfaction at the level of sets that rides piggyback on the underlying distributive interpretation. To handle the modals, we will define certain operations on sets of epistemic possibilities understood collectively.[15]

[14]This semantics is essentially identical to that given for DRT in Fernando (1993) or Asher and Lascarides (2003).

[15]This semantics has in effect the same formal apparatus as an account of plurals which takes seriously both distributive and collective predications. Collective and distributive interpretations of plurals

It appears that epistemic modals can embed, at least in the following way:[16]

(17) It might be the case that it might be the case that $\phi$.

Accordingly, we extend the standard constituents of dynamic meanings in dynamic semantics, world assignment pairs to include two sets of epistemic possibilities, each element of which is set of quadruples consisting of a world, an assignment and two sets of epistemic possibilities. To ensure that our epistemic possibilities can handle arbitrarily deep (though finite) embeddings we proceed inductively. We begin with some choice $\alpha$ of a set of world assignment pairs and use that choice to inductively build up more complicated sets of epistemic possibilities. Let $W$ be the set of possible worlds given in some standard first order modal structure $\mathcal{A}$. Then

- $\epsilon_{\alpha,0} \subseteq W \times \$$, where \$ is the set of all assignment functions.
- $\epsilon_{\alpha,n+1} \subseteq (W \times \$ \times \mathcal{P}(\epsilon_{\alpha,n}) \times \mathcal{P}(\epsilon_{\alpha,n}))$
- $\epsilon_\alpha \subseteq \bigcup_{n\in\omega} \epsilon_{\alpha,n}$[17]

Every set of epistemic possibilities $\epsilon_\alpha$ is thus well-founded. So the basic constituents $\sigma$ of dynamic meanings here are quadruples of the form $\langle w, f, \epsilon, \epsilon' \rangle$ with $\epsilon, \epsilon' \subseteq \epsilon_\alpha$ for some $\alpha$. We will make use of projection functions $1, 2, 3, 4$ on $\sigma$ to pick out the world, assignment function, global set of epistemic possibilities or focussed set of epistemic possibilities of a context element respectively. We adopt the constraint that epistemic possibilities at the outset include the actual world; namely, we stipulate that an intial state for the interpretation of a discourse is: $\epsilon_0 = \{\langle w, \emptyset, \epsilon_1, \epsilon_1 \rangle \ : \ w \in W\}$, where $w \in 1(\epsilon_1)$ and where all assignment functions are undefined. Note that we assume that the focussed set of possibilities is the same as the global set of possibilities in the initial state. As usual it is the task of indefinite noun phrases (*inter alia*) discourse to introduce new discourse referents to which we can refer in subsequent discourse and to narrow down the information present in the initial information state. It is the task of *might* modals and other operators to introduce a focussed set of possibilities distinct from the global epistemic possibilities.

We now state the distributive dynamic DPL style semantics in terms of our new information states. Let $\mathcal{A}$ be a fixed model consisting of a domain, a set of worlds and an interpretation of the non logical constants. The dynamic transitions $[.]^{\mathcal{A}}$ are defined inductively and we let $\|\alpha\|$ be the semantic value of terms. Recall that in dynamic semantics we actually think of an existentially quantified formula $\exists x\phi$ as consisting of two actions, one determined by the quantifier and one determined by $\phi$. Accordingly, we will adopt the convention that $\exists\phi$ is dynamically to be understood as $\exists x \wedge \phi$

- $\sigma[Rt_1, \ldots, t_n]^{\mathcal{A}}\sigma'$ iff $\sigma = \sigma' \wedge \langle \|t_1\|^{\mathcal{A}}_{(1(\sigma),2(\sigma))}, \ldots, \|t_n\|^{\mathcal{A}}_{(1(\sigma),2(\sigma))} \rangle \in R^{\mathcal{A}}_{1(\sigma)}$

are analogous to non-distributive and distributive interpretations of modals: collective interpretations test sets of assignments within a context, while distributive interpretations are determined relative to individual assignments that comprise the individual world assignment pairs in the context.

[16]Some might think that embeddings like these are degenerate if the modal bases are identical. We do not agree completely (though examples like the one in the main text are so uncolloquial that they look rather bad). The following, we think, is perfectly fine.

(i.) It might be that John might come.

Here embedding with identical modalities seems to us perfect.

[17]$\omega$ here denotes, as usual, the set of natural numbers.

- $\sigma[t_1 = t_2]^{\mathcal{A}}\sigma'$ iff $\sigma = \sigma' \wedge \|t_1\|^{\mathcal{A}}_{(1(\sigma),2(\sigma))} = \|t_2\|^{\mathcal{A}}_{(1(\sigma),2(\sigma))}$
- $\sigma[\phi \wedge \psi]^{\mathcal{A}}\sigma'$ iff $\sigma[\phi]^{\mathcal{A}} \circ [\psi]^{\mathcal{A}}\sigma'$
- $\sigma[\neg\phi]^{\mathcal{A}}\sigma'$ iff $\sigma = \sigma' \wedge \neg\exists w'', h \;\; \sigma[\phi]^{\mathcal{A}}\sigma^{\frac{1(\sigma)}{w''}, \frac{2(\sigma)}{h}}$
- $\sigma[\exists x]^{\mathcal{A}}\sigma'$ iff $\exists a \in A \;\; \sigma' = \sigma^{\frac{a}{x}}$, where $\sigma^{\frac{a}{x}}$ is the result of replacing $2(\sigma)$ with $2(\sigma) \cup \{\langle x, a\rangle\}$[18]

We'll speak of $\sigma'$'s being a $\phi$ *descendant* of $\sigma$, just in case $\sigma[\phi]\sigma'$. We will also lift this notion to a set of epistemic possibilities in the spirit of Fernando (1993) and Groenendijk et al. (1994):

- $\epsilon'$ is a $\phi$ descendant of $\epsilon$ iff $\forall\sigma \in \epsilon\exists\sigma' \in \epsilon' \; \sigma[\phi]\sigma'$ and $\forall\sigma' \in \epsilon'\exists\sigma \in \epsilon \; \sigma[\phi] \; \sigma'$.

As discourse proceeds we learn things and so refine and indeed revise our epistemic possibilities in light of what has been learned. The semantics does not yet model this sort of change. Let us call the *discourse context* that set of quadruples that is the result our output of the evaluation of successive sentence-tokens in a discourse. A discourse context is the same sort of animal as an epistemic possibility—a set of world assignment, epistemic possibility quadruples; and it contains the information of what has been said up to this point. Simplifying matters considerably, we will take what has been said in discourse as having been established and accepted as part of the common ground.[19] Thus, whatever is true or supported in such a discourse context should be reflected in the set of epistemic possibilities of those quadruples $\sigma$ that are part of the discourse context.

To define this constraint, we'll introduce a new notion of a *discourse update* and revision. Thanks to the work of Lewis, Spohn and others, it is straightforward to define a revision function $\star$ on worlds that transfers to epistemic possibilities if we assume a partial ordering on worlds. The particular partial ordering we assume is that of Lewis (1973, pp. 13–19). This partial ordering forms a system of spheres centered around each element $\sigma$. A set of such elements $\epsilon$ can also have a system of spheres, where each sphere $S_n$ is such that: $S_n(\epsilon) = \{\cup(S_n(\sigma)) : \sigma \in \epsilon\}$. Note that the global set of epistemic possibilities is just updated with new information, and that given our initial set up, $1(\sigma) \in 3(\sigma)$ for all $\sigma$. It is the focussed epistemic possibilities that may shift to a counterfactual possibility and may need to be revised.

- Let $S^{\phi}_{m}(\epsilon)$ be the smallest sphere around $\epsilon$ such that all elements in $S^{\phi}_{m}(\epsilon)$ have $\phi$ descendants.[20] Then $\epsilon \star \|\phi\| = \{\, \sigma : \exists\sigma' \in S^{\phi}_{m}(\epsilon) \;\; \sigma'[\phi]\sigma \,\}$.
- Suppose $\phi$ is a formula other than $\exists x \wedge \psi$. Then: $\sigma$ is a $\phi$ *discourse update* of $\sigma'$ iff $\exists\sigma_1$ such that $(\sigma'[\phi]^{\mathcal{A}}\sigma_1 \wedge 1(\sigma) = 1(\sigma_1) \wedge 2(\sigma) = 2(\sigma_1)$ and $\langle 3(\sigma_1), 3(\sigma)\rangle \models_d \phi$ and $4(\sigma_1) = 4(\sigma) \star \|\phi\|$

[18] We assume the usual mechanisms to avoid variable clash and the assignment of two objects to the same variable.

[19] Thus, we pass over all the problems of correction, denial and disagreement—but see Asher and Lascarides (2003) or Asher and Gillies (2003) for discussions of these phenomena. In any case, we think that revision involves necessarily some sort of discourse indications that this is taking place, indications that are not present in the simple examples we consider here.

[20] We assume that there is such a smallest sphere in order to simplify the definitions.

- Suppose $\phi := \exists x \wedge \psi$ Then: $\sigma$ is a $\phi$ *discourse update* of $\sigma'$ iff for some $\sigma_3$, $(\sigma'[\exists x]^{\mathcal{A}}\sigma_3$, and each $\sigma_1 \in 3(\sigma)$ and each $\sigma_2 \in 4(\sigma)$ are such that $2(\sigma_1)(x) = 2(\sigma_2)(x) = 2(\sigma_3)(x)$ and $\sigma$ is a $\psi$ discourse update of $\sigma_3$

The notion of discourse update formalizes the idea that information introduced into the discourse must be reflected in the updated epistemic possibilities (hence the need for the revision operator $\star$). The clause for $\exists v\phi$ descendants ensures that the bindings of variables outside of modal contexts carry over into them, when we quantify in. Here's a typical example that our dynamic modal semantics can treat:

(18) A student just walked in. Pat might grant him an interview.

Processing of the first sentence, $\exists x; Sx$, ensures that there is some individual $a$ that verifies $S$; the input context for the second sentence will thus be $\sigma^{\frac{a}{x}}$, where $Sa$. The modal formula will modify this input set in such a way that this assignment is preserved, as we will see momentarily. Discourse update thus helps us to evaluate sequences of formulae that are translations of our examples. For instance in evaluating (1ab), we check whether the translations of those formulae give us a sequence of coherent discourse updates, where a coherent discourse update is one where for some input $\sigma$ there is a non-empty output. Discourse update is also the notion that we need to define logical consequence.

Modal formulas also affect the epistemic possibilities via their basic semantics—that is, in how they affect dynamic transitions over $\sigma$. *Might* $\phi$ updates the value of the focussed set of epistemic possibilities with $\phi$ and then revises the global possibilities so as to ensure that the focussed set remains a subset of the global set, provided that the set of focussed epistemic possibilities does have a $\phi$ descendant. If not, the update fails, as Veltman's observations attest.

- $\sigma[\textit{Might } \phi]_{\mathcal{A}}\langle 1(\sigma), 2(\sigma), \epsilon_1, \epsilon_2, \rangle$, where:
  $\langle \epsilon, \epsilon_2 \rangle \models_d \phi$, $\epsilon$ is the maximal set of elements in $4(\sigma)$ that have $\phi$ descendants, and $\epsilon_1 = (3(\sigma) - \epsilon) \cup \epsilon_2$,
  provided there are $\phi$ descendants in $4(\sigma)$.
  If not, then $\langle \epsilon, \epsilon_2 \rangle \models_d \phi$, $\epsilon$ is the maximal set of elements in $3(\sigma)$ that have $\phi$ descendants, and $\epsilon_1 = (3(\sigma) - \epsilon) \cup \epsilon_2$,
  provided there are $\phi$ descendants in $3(\sigma)$.
  $\sigma[\textit{Might } \phi]_{\mathcal{A}}\emptyset$ otherwise.

*Might* intuitively involves an existential quantification over epistemic possibilities. And like all existentials in dynamic semantics, it involves a special kind of discourse action—that of resetting, in this case, the focussed epistemic possibilities. *Might* resets only the focussed set of epistemic possibilities, because asserting *Might* $\phi$ shouldn't reset all the epistemic possibilities to those in which $\phi$ holds. This semantics incorporates the test idea of Veltman's semantics but involves more than a simple test; it allows information under the scope of the *Might* operator to transform the epistemic possibilities in the input. It also differs from "accommodation" views of *might* like Gillies's (Gillies (2003)), according to which *might* always enlarges the epistemic possibilities under consideration. On our view it rather refines certain epistemic possibilities that must be already in place.

As in Kratzer's original semantics both *might* and *would* depend on an antecedently given set of epistemic possibilities. In our account, however, we specify how these epistemic possibilities evolve as discourse proceeds. The anaphoric accounts of modals allow them to pick up any salient proposition in the context; our account is much more constrained and is closer to Kratzer's original view. However, our semantics for *would* does share a certain feature with anaphoric accounts. *Would* tests and updates the global set of epistemic possibilities *or* the set of focussed epistemic possibilities. *Would* thus semantically underspecifies which set of epistemic possibilities it depends on. Anaphoric accounts, of course, take all modalities to be underspecified and in a much more unrestrained way. In modal subordination cases, the update function of *would* is directed to the focussed set, especially when a failure to do so would leave presuppositions about anaphoric antecedents unsatisfied. However, in order to assess the validity of an argument involving *would* we need to check *both* update possibilities.

- $\sigma[\textit{Would}\ \phi]_{\mathcal{A}}\langle 1(\sigma), 2(\sigma), \epsilon_1, \epsilon_2\rangle$, provided $\epsilon_1$ and $\epsilon_2$ are specified in one of two ways:
  1. $\langle 3(\sigma), \epsilon_1\rangle \models_d \phi$ and $\langle 4(\sigma), \epsilon_2\rangle \models_d \phi$ or,
  2. $\langle 4(\sigma), \epsilon_2\rangle \models_d \phi$ and $\epsilon_1 = (3(\sigma) - 4(\sigma)) \cup \epsilon_2$

  $\sigma[\textit{Would}\ \phi]_{\mathcal{A}}\emptyset$ otherwise.

Notice that if not every element of $3(\sigma)$ has a $\phi$ descendant, then the first possibility of satisfying *Would* $\phi$ will fail; if in addition not every element of $4(\sigma)$ has a $\phi$ descendant, then *Would* $\phi$ will have no output. The specification of the focussed and global epistemic possibilities in the update conditions for *Would* $\phi$ should be understood as two possible interpretations, not one set of update conditions involving a disjunction.

*Might* and *would* are not duals on our semantics, and we think rightly so because of the difference in their discourse behavior—in particular with respect to modal subordination. The standard modal subordination sequence (2a) is not as good when the order of modals is reversed in the same contexts:

(19) A wolf would walk in. It might eat you first.

Our account explains this because in an out of the blue context, both the local and global possibilities are initially set to a very large set of epistemic possibilities, and it seems implausible that all of those possibilities contain a wolf that walks in. But that is what would have to happen in order for the *would* statement in (19) to go through.

Our notions of logical consequence and validity remain like those from DPL with one important change: we replace the basic notion of a dynamic transition with our notion of discourse update. This is needed to ensure that new factual information affects the epistemic possibilities in the relevant way.

- Logical Consequence: Let $\Gamma$ be a sequence of formulae. Then $\Gamma \models \phi$ iff for all models $\mathcal{A}$ and for all information states $\sigma, \sigma'$ such that $\sigma'$ is a $\Gamma$ discourse update of $\sigma$, there is a $\sigma''$ such that $\sigma''$ is a $\phi$ discourse update of $\sigma''$.
- Given an ambiguous expression on the left or right hand side of $\models$, we must test for $\models$ on each disambiguation of the premises and the conclusion modulo a parallelism constraint that tokens of the same ambiguous expressions are all disambiguated in the same way on both sides of the $\models$.
- Validity: $\models \phi$ iff $\emptyset \models \phi$

We will see the effect of the ambiguity condition momentarily. For the present we simply note that it corresponds to the definition of consequence in van Deemter (2003).

We can verify some logical consequences of our definitions.

**Fact 1** *(i) Would $\phi \not\models \phi$; (ii) Might $(\phi) \not\models$ Would $\phi$; (iii) Would $\phi \models$ Might $\phi$; (iv) $\phi \models$ Might $\phi$; (v) $\phi \models$ Would $\phi$; (vi)* Would *obeys the axioms of* $\Box$ *in a K modal system, while* Might *obeys the axioms of* $\Diamond$ *in K.*

(i) follows from the fact that even if an information state $\sigma$ supports *Would* $\phi$ (and hence that either its global or focussed epistemic possibilities support $\phi$), there is no guarantee that $\sigma$ supports $\phi$, which is what our notion of entailment requires. For instance, the focussed epistemic possibilities might have been reset by a *might* claim such that $1(\sigma)$, the world of evaluation, or $2(\sigma)$, the assignment in the context, may not be elements of any of those possibilites.[21]

(ii) is another key non equivalence that holds in our system.[22] This is crucial, because we don't want our existential and universal modalities to collapse. *Might* $\phi$ resets and updates the focussed set of epistemic possibilities, but *Would* $\phi$ will only follow from the output information state, if *both* the global and focussed set of epistemic possibilities support $\phi$. The reason for this is the way we defined $\models$ for potentially ambiguous or underspecified expressions; because *would* in our system has an underspecified meaning, the inference must go through on both readings for the consequence to go through. The fact that the local possibilities support $\phi$ given an update with *Might* $\phi$ does not guarantee that the global possibilities will. Our semantics verifies (iii), regardless of which disambiguation for *would* is chosen.[23]

(iv) and (v) follow from the definition of discourse update. Note that this semantics makes predictions about the cases of stand alone *would*. Consider again (6). When attached to $A$'s assertion it is natural to understand $B$ as saying that in all of his epistemic possibilities, what $A$ says turns out to be true. It marks a form of agreement, which is intuitively what is going on in (6b). The anaphoric account would make $B$'s assertion with stand alone *would* some sort of logical truth on the standard semantics for *would* and so should be ruled out on pragmatic grounds of informativeness.

Like Veltman's original semantics, our semantics verifies $\phi \models$ *Might*$\phi$ by the definition of *Might* and the definition of discourse update. And like Veltman, *Might* $\phi \not\models \phi$. Resetting the epistemic possibilities to reflect $\phi$ doesn't necessarily affect the actual world of evaluation; although the actual world and assignment of evaluation are elements of the

[21]Note, however, that prior to any resetting this claim is true, which makes the inference perhaps defeasibly plausible.

[22]It looks, however, valid for van Rooij (2005) or we are puzzled as to how modal subordination can work in his system. He requires a puzzling clause for the semantics of *would* in order to get standard cases of modal subordination to work in his system (his footnote 19). The requirement is that to evaluate $\Box\phi$ we consider only accessible worlds $u$ such that for any world $v$ accessible to $u$, $u$ and $v$ have exactly the same set of accessible worlds. From this requirement, however, $\Box\phi$ follows from $\Diamond\phi$ on a standard notion of dynamic consequence for van Rooij's system.

[23]In the absence of other information in the discourse that might allow us to distinguish between global and focussed sets of possibilities, we would conclude that *Would* $\phi$ implies $\neg$ *Might* $\neg\phi$. However, this inference is nonmonotonic. If antecedent discourse already forces us to distinguish global and focussed epistemic possibilities, then this implication no longer follows, as *Would* $\phi$ may have been satisfied relative to the focussed epistemic possibilities of some contextual element.

epistemic possibilities associated with them in the initial discourse context. Updating with modal formulas may make our focussed possibilities go counterfactual. Because the epistemic possibilities must always verify what has already been established in the discourse, Veltman's examples (1ab) immediately fall out as predicted. *Might* $\phi$ updates the focussed epistemic possibilities of an element of the discourse context $\sigma$ to those where $\phi$ holds as long as $\phi$ was a global epistemic possibility in $\sigma$. Updating an information state with *it might be sunny* resets the focussed possibilities to those where it's sunny; we can then update with the factual information that it's not sunny which will revise the epistemic possibilites to reflect the fact that we have now learned that it's not sunny. The discourse has a coherent content, assuming that the original input context does have some sunny worlds as possibilities. However, updating first with *it's not sunny* makes a subsequent update with *it might be sunny* fail or return $\emptyset$, because the input information state does not contain it's being sunny as an epistemic possibility; the requirement of discourse update, namely that the facts established in the discourse must be reflected in the set of epistemic possibilities, precludes any such possibility. Our semantics also predicts that examples like (12ab) should not yield any coherent output for any given input state because of the nature of discourse update.

We now turn to our treatment of binding and modal subordination. One of our main goals was to account for the basic facts of this phenomenon. First, note that quantifying in as with (18) works. To see what happens, assume that the first sentence of (18) is of the form $\exists x Wx$. So the existential quantifier will assign a value to $x$ and the input context for $Wx$ will be $\sigma^{\frac{a}{x}}$. Suppose $\sigma^{\frac{a}{x}}$ supports $Wx$. Then the output context's epistemic possibilities will also support $Wx$ with the assignment of $a$ to $x$. The second sentence in (18) resets the epistemic possibilities, but since each one of these is a descendant of one in the input set of epistemic possibilities, this means that subsequent free occurrences of the variable $x$ introduced by pronouns in the second sentence of (18) will carry the same value $a$.

Turning to modal subordination, the classic (2a) works as expected. The set of possibilities introduced by the *might* modality is picked up straight away and modified by a *would* sentence. A *might* sentence can also felicitously follow another *might* sentence; our semantics predicts modal subordination phenomena in that case as well. On the other hand we cannot bind variables outside a modal context with quantifiers introduced inside a *Might* or *Would* operator as in (2b). Suppose that *he* in the second clause of (2b) introduces an occurence of the same variable $x$ that *a wolf* inside the modal *might* binds. Although the *might* clause resets the epistemic possibilities and assigns $x$ a value in all focussed epistemic possibilities, this resetting doesn't affect the actual world of evaluation or the actual assignment function. So the value that the variable is assigned by the existential quantifier cannot be passed onto the occurrence of the variable introduced by the pronoun *he*.

One of the salient features of this approach is that the possible interpretations of modal subordination sentences are quite restricted. For instance, (20) is predicted to be bad, given that the discourse precludes an attachment of the third sentence to the first.

(20) A wolf$_i$ might walk in. Then again one might not. #It$_i$/#The wolf$_i$ would eat you first.

To see why, note that this means that *the wolf would eat your first* must attach to the discourse constituent given by *a wolf might not walk in. would* can either test the global possibilities or the focussed ones; the focussed ones clearly fail to support the anaphoric connection required to interpret the pronoun under the scope of *would* since there are no wolves in the reset, focussed epistemic possibilities. On the other hand, the global epistemic possibilities, though not reset by the *might* claims, must contain possibilities where there are no wolves, in view of the fact that the second *might* claim has been satisfied. So *the wolf would eat you first* also fails to give an output when the global possibilities are used to evaluate the modal. Note also, however, that the first two sentences of (20) are perfectly fine, given that the second *might* claim simply resets the focussed epistemic possibilities to those where there are no wolves. Further, (15ab) is predicted to be good because a discourse attachment of the third to the first is possible, in fact preferred. The difference between these two discourses is that (15a) sets up a contrast with the first possibility elaborated on in (15a) while in (20a), the contrast has already been set up by the first two sentences and the third sentence seeks to elaborate on the first possibility, something not permitted in SDRT (for details see Asher (1993), Asher and Lascarides (2003)).

Discourse structure, in particular the type of discourse relation used to link the new information to the discourse context, plays a role witih other examples too. For instance, it offers us the possibility of accounting for negated examples of modal subordination, which feature prominently in Frank's (Frank (1997)) account of modal subordination.

(21) a. I didn't buy a refrigerator. It would have taken up too much room.
b. I didn't buy a refrigerator. It would have cost too much.

We postulate a special discourse connection here according to which there is a causal link between the possibility described under the negation and the second clause containing the modal, which we gloss as $\neg p$, but if $p$ then the result would have been $q$—or, $p$ would have caused $q$. Furthermore, $q$ in turn is a reason for not doing $p$. The pattern of a negated sentence discourse linked to a sentence with an epistemic modal suggests a type of elliptical explanation involving a conditional, a particular type in other words of discourse relation between two constituents in a discourse. This discourse link differs truth conditionally from the sort of narrative link one gets with the (2) examples. This kind of account is supported by the fact that negated modal subordination is not universally possible, as shown by the examples in (22), which lack the discourse connection we describe.

(22) a. # I didn't buy a refrigerator. I would like it.
b. I didn't buy a refrigerator. I didn't like it. (*de re* OK)

The explanation for the special status of negation in these cases seems not to stem from the meaning of the operator itself but rather from the rhetorical structure that its uses in discourse suggest. Hobbs (2005) has independently told a somewhat similar story about examples like these.

## 8.4 Counterfactuals, Modality and Normality

Now that we have a semantics for modals in place, we are ready to study counterfactuals. We start this project by giving a semantics in our system for the conditional operator itself; this will serve as a foundation for the interpretation of counterfactuals (and, by itself, can interpret indicative conditionals). In the following subsection, 4.2, we turn to the irrealis mood that appears in counterfactuals and give several proposals for its semantics that rely on data about counterfactual semantics. Here we also explore connections with normality conditionals and default reasoning. Sections 4.3 and 4.4 discuss some remaining issues and dynamic effects.

### 8.4.1 The Conditional Operator $\Rightarrow$

Adapting a Veltman-Gillies style semantics for conditionals to our framework, the definition below ensures that all the epistemic possibilities of a given element of the discourse context together with the world of evaluation and assignment support the conditional.

- $\sigma[\phi \Rightarrow \psi]_{\mathcal{A}}\sigma$ iff;
  - every $\phi$ descendant of $\sigma$ has a $\psi$ descendant and,
  - for every $\sigma_1 \in 4(\sigma)$, every $\phi$ descendant of $\sigma_1$ has a $\psi$ descendant.

Because we manage in fact two sets of epistemic possibilities in our discourse contexts, there is a question as to which the conditional is in fact sensitive to. It does appear that conditionals are sensitive to the focussed epistemic possibilities:

(23) a. A: John might come to the party.
b. B: If he's still smoking, he'll annoy everyone else there.

The intended reading of the conditional in (23b) is that If John is still smoking and comes to the party, he'll annoy everyone else there.

Though the interpretation of the conditional is close to Gillies's or Veltman's, our approach has some advantages. First of all, we account for the sensitivity of conditionals to the epistemic modalities that have been introduced in discourse.[24] Second, this account with nested epistemic possibilities allows for the embedding of conditionals within modals and within other conditionals unproblematically. Further, with Gillies's or Veltman's notion of a test, conditionals can't contribute to information growth, not unless we take a more complicated picture of what it is to learn new information (where we might distinguish between different information states and so consider sets of information states as inputs). By separating out elements of discourse contexts from epistemic possibilities we can "learn" (in our simplified sense here) conditionals, eliminating those elements of the discourse context whose epistemic possibilities don't support the conditionals newly introduced into the discourse context. Because of the semantics of conditionals, updating the discourse context with a conditional will automatically be reflected within the epistemic possibilities permitted by the discourse context.

[24] Of course, as we saw with *might* and *would*, discourse structure will determine what the epistemic possibilities are for any sentence to be interpreted in the discourse context.

Some desirable properties for conditionals fall out of this analysis, and in fact we can come close to defining the epistemic conditional in terms of the modals.[25]

**Fact 2** *(i)* $\phi \Rightarrow \psi, \phi \models \psi$; *(ii)* $\phi \Rightarrow (\psi \Rightarrow \chi) \models (\phi \wedge \psi) \Rightarrow \chi$ *and vice-versa; (iii) The deduction theorem holds for* $\Rightarrow$ *(iv) Might* $(\phi \wedge \neg\psi) \models \neg(\phi \Rightarrow \psi)$ *(v)* $\neg(\phi \Rightarrow \psi) \models$ *Might* $(\phi \wedge \neg\psi)$

Discourse structure was important in our analysis of the simple modals *might* and *would*. It is also important in the analysis of some discourse patterns involving conditionals. It helps us explain the important connection between conditionals and disjunction. Zimmerman (2000) argues that disjunctions, at least when read with a falling intonation, present an exhaustive series of epistemic possibilities. Although that seems not be part of the "hard semantics" of disjunction (Asher and Bonevac (2005) present several counterexamples), it does appear to be a robust generalization about the discourse role of disjunctions. That is, disjunctions typically have, and in such contexts as (24) with the proper intonation must have, a role as presenting an exhaustive set of epistemic possibilities that includes the actual context of evaluation (in our sense the given world and assignment of some context element $\sigma$). Thus when (24a) is understood as having that particular discourse function, the inference from (24a) to (24b) is immediate, given the fact that the actual world and assignment are always part of the epistemic possibilities.

(24) a. Either one grounds keeper did it or the driver did.
b. If the grounds keeper didn't do it, the driver did.

### 8.4.2 Irrealis Markers and Counterfactuals

With an account of the conditional marker in place, we can give our compositional semantics of counterfactuals. The semantics of counterfactuals is the result of applying the conditional operator to two arguments, the first given by the antecedent clause and modified by an irrealis operator, the second given by the consequent, which is (in English

[25]To see that $\Rightarrow$ verifies MP, suppose that for an arbitrary $\sigma$, $\sigma[\phi \Rightarrow \psi]_{\mathcal{A}}\sigma$ and $\sigma[\phi]_{\mathcal{A}}\sigma'$. So $\sigma$ has a $\phi$ descendant $\sigma'$; by the semantics of the conditional, every $\phi$ descendant of $\sigma$ has a $\psi$ descendant. So for some $\sigma''$, $\sigma'[\psi]_{\mathcal{A}}\sigma''$, which suffices to validate MP by our definition of logical consequence. This establishes (i).

To show (ii), suppose $\sigma[\phi \Rightarrow (\psi \Rightarrow \chi)]\sigma$ and suppose further that $\sigma[\phi \wedge \psi]\sigma'$, for some $\sigma'$. Now every $\phi$ descendant of $\sigma$ must also have a $\psi \Rightarrow \chi$ descendant. And this implies that every $\psi$ descendant of any $\phi$ descendant of $\sigma$ has a $\chi$ descendant. Now $\sigma'$ is a $\psi$ descendant of a $\phi$ descendant of $\sigma$. So $\sigma'$ has a $\chi$ descendant. Since $\sigma'$ was arbitrary, we've shown that every $\phi \wedge \psi$ descendant of $\sigma$ has a $\chi$ descendant and thus $(\phi \wedge \psi) \Rightarrow \chi$. For the reverse direction, suppose we have $\sigma[(\phi \wedge \psi) \Rightarrow \chi]\sigma$ and suppose we have $\sigma[\phi]\sigma'$. We have to show that every $\psi$ descendant of $\sigma'$ has a $\chi$ descendant. Suppose not for some $\psi$ descendant of $\sigma'$, call it $\sigma*$. But then $\sigma*$ is a $\phi \wedge \psi$ descendant of $\sigma$ and it must have a $\chi$ descendant.

To show (iii), the direction from right to left is just an application of modus ponens, which we've already shown holds for $\Rightarrow$. Now from left to right, assume $\Gamma, \phi \models \psi$, which means that every $\Gamma, \phi$ descendant of some input $\sigma$ has a $\psi$ descendant. Now consider any $\Gamma$ descendant of $\sigma$, call it $\sigma'$ and consider any $\phi$ descendant of $\sigma'$; it also must have a $\psi$ descendant. And since $\sigma$ and $\sigma'$ were arbitrary, we've shown $\Gamma \models \phi \Rightarrow \psi$.

(iv) follows straightforwardly from the semantics of the conditional. To show (v), suppose that $\sigma[\neg(\phi \Rightarrow \psi)]\sigma$. Then either some $\phi$ descendant of $\sigma$ fails to have a $\psi$ descendant or some $\sigma_1 \in 3(\sigma)$ has a $\phi$ descendant but no $\psi$ descendant. In the latter case, $\sigma$ clearly supports *Might*$(\phi \wedge \neg\psi)$. Now suppose $\sigma$ itself has a $\phi$ descendant that has no $\psi$ descendant. So $\sigma$ supports $\phi \wedge \neg\psi$. By Fact 1 (iv), $\sigma$ has a *Might*$(\phi \wedge \neg\psi)$ descendant, which is what we needed to show.

at least) invariably modified by an epistemic modal—either *might* or *would*—or some other modal operator like *should*.[26] (4a), for instance, is analyzed below as (4a'):

(4a) If I were not to sleep tonight, I would topple over tomorrow.

(4a') *Irr*(I not sleep tonight) $\Rightarrow$ *would* (I topple over tomorrow)

Intuitively, such a sentence is satisfied in a structure at an input context or information state just in case revising the input context with my not sleeping tonight makes true that I would topple over tomorrow, and the latter will be true in the adjusted descendant of the input just in case all of the epistemic possibilities of that descendant make my toppling over true. We analyze "past" tense counterfactuals like (4b) in just the same way as we handle present tense counterfactuals, except that the irrealis operator has scope over the past tense operator.[27]

(4b) If I had not slept, I would have toppled over.

(4b') *IrrPast*(I not sleep) $\Rightarrow$ (*would Past* (I topple over))

*Might* counterfactuals receive an entirely similar analysis.

So the only thing we need to do now is to specify a meaning for *irr*. We hypothesize that the antecedent of a counterfactual in Romance and Germanic languages has some sort of "irrealis" operator—either introduced by the subjunctive mood or a special tense morpheme like the imparfait in French, the Konjunktiv II in German and *were* or the pluperfect in English. The exact source of irrealis is rather language-dependent and further depends on the clause itself: it is not difficult to find counterfactual conditionals in English in which irrealis is expressed through past tense alone, without a subjunctive or pluperfect. Since our focus here is not on the morphosyntax of these constructions, we will not go into detail about where exactly irrealis is located.[28] For the purposes of the present paper, we will, however, make the assumption that irrealis is licensed by a feature located on the Mood head that combines with other elements in the clause to yield past tense, pluperfect, or whatever the right morphological realization of irrealis may be for a particular language or construction. While this is rather preliminary, it will suffice for our purposes here.

We will hypothesize that this operator resets or revises at least the focussed epistemic possibilities of each element in the set of epistemic possibilities—i.e., for the purpose of evaluating the consequent of the counterfactual. Indeed such a revision operator is implicit in Lewis's own semantics for counterfactuals. However, our approach will be decidedly more epistemic, based as it is on a semantics for epistemic modalities and and the epistemic conditional.

There are reasons not to be completely happy with Lewis's semantics for counterfactuals. First of all, we can't account for modal subordination cases involving counterfactuals like (3). Such cases show that the Lewis semantics, which exploits a similarity

[26] The same does not hold for some other Germanic languages, according to a reviewer.

[27] The interactions of tense and modality are complex (Condoravdi (2002), Abusch (1997)), and we will not go into them here. Nevertheless, our general analysis applies equally well to past as well as "present" tense counterfactuals. We also note that of course *might* statements can have, as Condoravdi notes, a "counterfactual" reading on which *Past* outscopes *Might*.

[28] See Iatridou (2000) for a discussion of the connection between tense and counterfactuality.

ordering on worlds that is dependent only on the world of evaluation cannot be right. Consider again (3) repeated below:

(3) A wolf might walk in. If it were to eat you first, I'd be unhappy, but not as unhappy as if it ate me first.

If Lewis's semantics were right, then the counterfactual

(25) If it were to eat you first, I would be unhappy.

should be interpretable on its own, but it is not. The anaphoric dependence forces us to interpret the antecedent with respect to those local epistemic possibilities in which the wolf walks in, guaranteed to exist given the update effects of the first sentence of (3). At the very least we need to relativize a Lewis-style semantics to local epistemic possibilities on occasion. This of course already follows for our decompositional analysis of counterfactuals from the way we have treated epistemic conditionals.

Now we have to give a semantics for the irrealis operator. Following Lewis's intuitions, we take it to be an imaging operator. Let's first define this operator in a Lewis-like way–viz:

- First semantics for *Irr*:
  $\sigma[\mathrm{irr}(\phi)]_{\mathcal{A}}\langle w, 2(\sigma), 3(\sigma) \star \|\phi\|, 4(\sigma) \star \|\phi\|\rangle$,
  where $w \in 1(\sigma) \star \|\phi\|$.

The operator works on the world of the discourse context element, but as it shifts that world it must also shift the global and epistemic possibilities to reflect the change in the world of evaluation.

Already with this semantics we can treat some examples that motivate accommodation accounts of *might*. Given that we've argued that accommodation accounts of *might* provide too weak truth conditions to *might* counterfactuals, this would be a good thing. Consider again,

(14) a. If John were to come to the party, it would be fun.
b. But of course if John were to come to the party, he might have a heart attack and that wouldn't be fun.

Our treatment of these examples turns on the systematic underspecification of the epistemic possibilities relevant to *would*—that is, the ability of *would* sentences to be sensitive either to the focussed or global set of epistemic possibilities. By playing on the difference between the sets of global and focussed epistemic possibilities both of which have been revised to take account of the information under the scope of the irrealis operator, we can jointly satisfy the two conditionals. Suppose, for example, that *would* in (14a) is sensitive to the local epistemic possibilities. Then it's possible that in all those possibilities in which John comes the party is fun, even though there are epistemic possibilities in the global set where in fact John gets a heart attack. The *might* in (14b) forces us to reset the local possibilities to those possibilities in which John comes to the party but gets a heart attack. Then when we evaluate the *would* claim with respect to those, it turns out indeed that the party is not fun.[29]

[29] The contrastive particle *but* is a necessary discourse cue, underlining the fact that one is switching from one set of epistemic possibilities to the next.

This change to the Lewis semantics, which seems to be needed in any case, has some important consequences. If the irrealis operator shifts the focussed set of possibilities of those elements relevant to evaluating the conditional and the *would* in the consequent of the counterfactual is sensitive to those possibilities, then it follows that the counterfactual does not obey modus ponens and so does not have a centered semantics.[30] What our counterfacatual validates is the inference $A, A \Box\!\!\rightarrow B \vdash Would\ B$. However, in our semantics *Would B* does not entail $B$. There may be all sorts of facts reflected in the local epistemic possibilities that make $B$ true in those possibilities and make $B$ *expected* to hold in the actual world. But from this it does not follow that $B$ holds in $\sigma$. The failure of modus ponens here follows from the fact that *Would* $\phi$ does not entail $\phi$. Further, if we stipulate that the actual world must be included in the focussed set of epistemic possibilities, we risk destroying the information of the sort that we need, e.g., to make (3) work.

Our semantics takes the epistemic nature of the components of counterfactuals seriously. But is this justified. Suppose we consider pairs like the following well-known examples relating to the the invalidity of Strengthening the Antecedent for counterfactuals:

(26) a. If I were to strike this match it would light.
b. If I were to strike this match and it were wet, it would not light.

These counterfactuals depend for their truth, and their acceptability, on all sorts of facts that we relegate to the background epistemic possibilities. For instance, we would not take either (26a) or (26b) to be true if we accepted as a background epistemic possibility that there was a world just like ours except that when I strike the match it doesn't light or a world just like ours except that when I strike the match and it is wet, it lights. We also think that it can't be the case that counterfactuals like (26ab) are true while the corresponding standard conditionals in (27ab) are also true, if the antecedent of the counterfactual is still epistemically possible.

(27) a. If I strike this match, it won't light.
b. If I strike this match and it's wet, it will light.

In other words, we have the entailment:

- Counterfactuals to conditionals:
  $Might\ (\phi) \rightarrow (\phi \Box\!\!\rightarrow \psi) \rightarrow \neg(\phi \Rightarrow \neg\psi)$

This suggests a close connection between the counterfactual and the epistemic possibilities as well.

We have moved some way away from Lewis's theory of counterfactuals, but we must move, we think, still further. The following axiom, which follows from Lewis's centeredness requirements, seems completely inappropriate for counterfactuals:

(28) $(\phi \wedge \psi) \rightarrow (\phi \Box\!\!\rightarrow \psi)$

[30] The condition for this generally expressed by a selection function for evaluating a conditional is:
- if $w \in p$, then $w \in \star(w,p)$

In Lewis's semantics centeredness is encoded in the similarity relation and the axiom: $\forall w, w' w <_w w'$, where $<_w$ is the similarity ordering with respect to $w$.

This axiom implies that the counterfactual collapses to an extensional connective when its antecedent is true. Since we take seriously the idea that counterfactuals embody laws, we welcome evidence that shows that the counterfactual cannot be an extensional operator even when its antecedent is true. This axiom also has bad empirical consequences. It validates, for instance, the following conditional, since cigarettes are bad for you, and Texas is hot as well. It seems pretty clear that validating conditionals like these is not what we want to do.

(29) If cigarettes were bad for you, then Texas would be hot in the summer.

To solve this problem we need to reinterpret *irr* and replace the semantics we borrowed from Lewis with something more sophisticated. As a preamble to our suggestion, we note that there's a "looseness" to the truth conditions of counterfactuals that Lewis's semantics ignores. Counterfactuals like (26ab) generalize over times and locations. If counterfactuals are supposed to represent laws, then such generalizations must be part of their semantics.[31] Now suppose for instance, that our world unbeknownst to us is one where very occasionally the antecedents of these conditionals hold but their consequents fail to be true, perhaps because of magic, let's say. Or suppose that the worlds closest to ours where these antecedents hold also have, very occasionally, magical events of the sort we've just described. Would these constitute sufficient grounds to claim that (26ab) are false? We doubt it. If counterfactuals are supposed to represent laws, laws themselves have a *ceteris paribus* quality that allows for some exceptions in exceptional circumstances. In fact, we think that for a given match $m$ that is not in some way inherently defective that (26a) is true at the actual world. On the other hand, we also take (26b) to be true of $m$ should it get wet. Now occasionally $m$ might get wet or at least damp, and then dry out again. Do we on those occasions where $m$ gets wet take (26a) to be false while holding it true on all those occasions where $m$ is dry? This would be a strange way to treat a law. However, on Lewis's semantics for counterfactuals, there can be no situation in which the match is struck and wet and (26a,b) are jointly true. Since the counterfactuals collapse in this situation to material conditionals on Lewis's semantics, it cannot be the case that both consequents hold in this situation. But this seems unintuitive. The general laws embodied in (26ab) seem right, even though they have exceptions.

Intuitions, however, differ when we look at more specific laws that are related to those in (26ab)

(30) a. If I were to strike this match here and now, it would light.
b. If I were to strike this match here and now, when it's wet, it would not light.

Our intuition is that in the case outlined above where the match $m$ is wet, (30a) will be false (if $m$ fails to light). Intuitively (30ab) leave no room for exceptions; they've specified everything to the particular case at hand. In particular the "here and now" include all the information about the match and its situation; thus (30a) seems, intuitively, as specific

[31] Though importantly *not* part of their logical form explicitly, since that will generate problems with universal instantiation, given the sort of diverging intuitions we have about super specific counterfactuals. See below.

as (30b). It seems that it is such cases that motivate the thought that counterfactuals do support modus ponens, since it is precisely the rule of modus ponens that would lead us to conclude that (30a) is false in such a circumstance.

This makes it all the more pressing to investigate counterfactuals with respect to normality conditionals. There seems to us to be a tight link. We think that it's inconsistent to hold $\phi$ counterfactually implies $\psi$ but it's not the case that if $\phi$ then normally the case that $\psi$. That is, *if I were to strike a match, it would light* entails, according to our intuitions, *if I strike a match normally it lights.* Counterfactuals imply normality conditionals.

Normality conditionals (Asher and Morreau (1991), Morreau (1997)) have the following update conditions (adapting the basic semantics for $>$ to the dynamic framework here):

- $\sigma[\phi > \psi]_A\sigma$ iff every element in $*(\sigma, ||\phi||)$ has a $\psi$ descendant.

$*$ is a selection function that is understood as picking out all the normal $\phi$ possibilities relative to the element of evaluation $\sigma$.

Suppose that the *irrealis* operator is not just a simple revision operator on context elements but rather uses something like the $*$ function used for normality conditionals to revise epistemic possibilities. Thus, the irrealis operator in formula of the form *Irr* $(\phi) \Rightarrow$ *Would* $(\psi)$ would shift the focussed and the global set of epistemic possibilities to a set of normal $\phi$ epistemic possibilities. On such a view the conflict between (26a-b) would vanish. The set of normal match striking possibilities need not be a superset of the normal wet match striking possibilties; and as we will see below, a semantics that makes use of normal $\phi$ worlds is designed to exploit such pairs of counterfactuals and predicts that it is the second conditional, the one with the logically more specific antecedent, that is operative in our hypothetical situation $w$.

On the other hand, intuitions are quite strong that counterfactuals support modus ponens at least when they are "completely specific" counterfactuals as in (30). In such a case, when their antecedents are satisfied in the circumstance of evaluation there is a strong pressure to exploit a detachment rule and to infer the consequent. This suggests that we do not want the set of focussed epistemic possibilities picked out by *Irr* to be just those set of normal situations picked out by normality conditionals, since even completely specific normality conditionals will fail to validate modus ponens. It appears that this intuition supporting modus ponens with counterfactuals generalizes to those counterfactuals where there are no conflicts with more specific normality conditionals whose antecedents are also satisfied. When there are more specific counterfactuals or normality conditionals as in (26) whose antecedents are satisfied in the circumstance of evaluation there is a strong reluctance to exploit a detachment rule with the counterfactual with the less specific antecedent.

All of these considerations lead to a semantics for *Irr* that differs from a simple revision function that's based on a centered partial ordering over worlds. For one thing we need to link the semantic effects of *Irr* with the semantics of the normality conditional. On the other hand, we have to take account of the intuition that very specific counterfactuals or counterfactuals that have no more specific countering normality conditionals support modus ponens. Rather than try to tinker with the revision function $\star$, we will simply introduce a special selection function $\bullet(\sigma, p)$ to give the semantics of *Irr*. We will place the following constraints on $\bullet$:

1. $*(\sigma, p) \subseteq \bullet(\sigma, p) \subseteq p$
2. $\forall r((\exists\sigma'(\sigma, \sigma') \in r \wedge r \subseteq p) \rightarrow \bullet(\sigma, p) \cap *(\sigma, r) \neq \emptyset) \rightarrow \sigma \in \bullet(\sigma, p)$.
3. for any set of epistemic possibilities $\epsilon$, $*(\epsilon, p) = \bigcup_{\sigma\in\epsilon} *(\sigma, p)$ and $\bullet(\epsilon, p) = \bigcup_{\sigma\in\epsilon} \bullet(\sigma, p)$

The first constraint simply ensures that counterfactual possibilities are supersets of the possibilities used to evaluate normality conditionals. As we've seen the possibilities used to evaluate normality conditionals may be quite narrow; they may fail for instance to include the actual circumstance of evaluation, even when nothing precludes it. Counterfactual possibilities though related are perforce bigger because they do include the actual circumstance of evaluation when certain conditions obtain, viz., those that obtain in constraint 2. The second constraint is the most complicated: it is needed to insure modus ponens works in the cases we have outlined. To understand this constraint though, we need to understand something about normality conditionals, and that is the specificity effect. From the earliest days of research on nonmonotonic reasoning, people noticed that if one had two normality conditionals $A > B$ and $C > \neg B$ where $C$ entailed $A$, then in situations where $C$ obtained one inferred defeasibly $\neg B$ and not $B$. The constraint in the system of Asher and Morreau needed to validate such reasoning patterns is known as the *Penguin Principle*. It has the following form:

- Penguin Principle:
  $(p \subseteq q \wedge *(\sigma, p) \cap *(\sigma, q) = \emptyset) \rightarrow *(\sigma, q) \subseteq (W - p)$[32]

It follows from the Penguin Principle and our observation that counterfactuals entail normality conditionals that any normality conditional whose antecedent is satisfied in the world of evaluation and that is in the sense required "more specific" than the counterfactual whose antecedent expresses the proposition $p$ and that conflicts with a counterfactual involving $p$ will automatically fail to satisfy the antecedent of the second constraint. Thus, in order for a counterfactual to satisfy modus ponens, our second constraint says that it must not conflict with any more specific normality conditional whose antecedent is true at the world of evaluation. Of course, if the counterfactual is "super specific" as is the case in (30) and consistent with the true normality conditionals, this will be guaranteed and so modus ponens will have to work with counterfactuals like those in (30).

To make use of this selection function $\bullet$, we replace our first semantics for the irrealis operator and suppose instead that it makes the following shifts to the epistemic possibilities.

- The right semantics for *Irr*:
  $\sigma[\mathrm{Irr}\phi]_{\mathcal{A}}\langle 1(\sigma), 2(\sigma), \bullet(3(\sigma), \|\phi\|), \bullet(4(\sigma), \|\phi\|)\rangle$,

[32] The rule capturing this frame condition in Asher and Morreau 1991 is:

$$\frac{\vdash \phi \rightarrow \psi}{((\phi > \chi) \wedge (\psi > \neg\chi)) \rightarrow (\psi > \neg\phi)}$$

*Irr* $\phi$ moves the set of focussed epistemic possibilities in an input element to a subset of the set of the normal $\phi$ situations.[33] As before, *Irr* is sensitive to antecedently given focussed possibilities, and so our account for examples of modal subordination like (3) that involve counterfactuals still stands. The revised semantics for *Irr* also gives an improved account of (14). We can imagine that $\bullet(4(\sigma), ||\phi||)$ picks out the paradigmatic party worlds where John comes to the party and where John has fun. On the other hand, the *might* claim in (14b) forces us to reset the focussed epistemic possibilities to another subset in $3(\sigma)$, given our semantics of *might.* When we evaluate the *would* claim against these new focussed epistemic possibilities, in which John gets a heart attack, a different *would* claim naturally follows. These interpretations are preferred, since evaluating the *would* claims against the global set of updated possibilities doesn't tell us much of anything (by assumption the global possibilities countenance both fun and non fun parties).

Our account's interpretation of the unary modals was designed among other things to provide a compositional semantics for counterfactuals, and it certainly does better than the anaphoric approach. The latter must stipulate that the first argument of *would* is in fact "grammatically" specified in a counterfactual. The fact that the semantics for *would* must take the antecedent into account falls out for free on the present account. It follows from the sensitivity of epistemic conditionals to the focussed possibilities as they are determined by previous discourse and to the imaging semantics given for the irrealis operator. Further, our account shows why a *would* or *might* is necessary in a counterfactual construction: the irrealis shifts the epistemic possibilities but not the actual world or assignment, and in order for the proposition under the scope of the irrealis operator in the antecedent of the conditional not to be irrelevant to the evaluation of the consequent, we must use an epistemic modal to test the consequent in the relevant set of possibilities. This story, we think, improves on the Lewis account, which has nothing to say directly about the relationship between the irrealis mood, the modal used, and the type of counterfactual in play, due to the use of the noncompositional operators $\Box\!\!\rightarrow$ and $\Diamond\!\!\rightarrow$.

Most importantly, the revised semantics for *Irr* verifies the entailment from $A \Box\!\!\rightarrow B$ to $A > B$, at least when the focussed epistemic possibilities have not been shifted by *might* claims. That is,[34]

[33]The irrealis operator doesn't have a stand alone use, that is a use outside the scope of some conditional or other non truth functional operator:

(31) # Chris were to come to the party.

While operators like *Might* also reset local epistemic possibilities and have a stand alone use, the irrealis marker also resets the actual point of evaluation as well as the global epistemic possibilities. A stand alone use of the irrealis operator would lead to a *loss* of information.

[34]To see, this suppose that $\sigma$ verifies $\phi \Box\!\!\rightarrow \psi$, This means that all the elements of $4(\sigma)$ as well as $\sigma$ itself that have *Irr* $\phi$ descendants , have *Would* $\psi$ descendants as well. Notice that an *Irr* $\phi$ descendant of $\sigma$ is just like $\sigma$ except that $3(\sigma)$ and $4(\sigma)$ are replaced by $\bullet(3(\sigma), ||\phi||), \bullet(4(\sigma), ||\phi||)$ respectively. By our semantics for *would* and our notion of entailment, this means that we must check the cases when both $\bullet(3(\sigma), ||\phi||)$ has $\psi$ descendants and when $\bullet(4(\sigma), ||\psi||)$ does. But since $\bullet(4(\sigma), ||\phi||) = \bullet(3(\sigma), ||\phi||)$ by hypothesis, we need only check that if $\bullet(3(\sigma), ||\phi||)$ satisfies *psi* then $*(\sigma, ||\phi||)$ does too. This follows immediately, since $*(\sigma, ||\phi||) \subseteq \bullet(\sigma, ||\phi||) \subseteq \bullet(3(\sigma), ||\phi||)$.

**Fact 3** *Suppose* $4(\sigma) = 3(\sigma)$. *Then if* $\sigma$ *has a* $\phi \Box\!\!\rightarrow \psi$ *descendant, then it also has a* $\phi > \psi$ *descendant.*

This entailment doesn't hold necessarily when the focussed epistemic possibilities have been shifted by prior *might* claims. And this makes sense. While both conditionals and counterfactuals are sensitive to shifted epistemic possibilities (cf. example (3)), normality conditionals are not.

(32) John might come to the party. He's normally a lot of fun.

(33) A wolf might walk in. #It's normally very hungry.

The interpretation of the normality conditional could be sensitive to the *might* claim in (32) but it doesn't seem to be. The second clause of (32) is in fact a normality conditional which states a general condition of John's irrespective of whether he's at the party or not. (33) is bad; the anaphoric pronoun in the normality conditional can't access the local epistemic possibilities in which there is a wolf. Normality conditionals can't access information under epistemic modals. They are thus insensitive to the information encoded in epistemic possibilities. They are in this respect quite different from epistemic conditionals or counterfactuals.

Nevertheless, we can strengthen our observation above in view of the following remark. Given the way we have set things up any $4(\sigma)$ that diverges at all from $3(\sigma)$ must do so because it was reset by some sequence of formulas in prior discourse. That is: $4(\sigma) = 3(\sigma) \star \phi_1 \star \ldots \star \phi_n$. So we can generalize the fact above to:

**Fact 4** *Suppose* $4(\sigma) = 3(\sigma) \star \phi_1 \star \ldots \star \phi_n$. *Then if* $\sigma$ *has a* $\phi \Box\!\!\rightarrow \psi$ *descendant, then it also has a* $\phi > \psi$ *descendant or a* $(\phi \wedge \phi_1 \wedge \ldots \phi_n) > \psi$ *descendant.*

Thus, in general we have shown that counterfactuals entail related normality conditionals.

Our compositional account of counterfactuals also validates the following axioms, using the $\Box\!\!\rightarrow$ operator to symbolize *would* counterfactuals (ignoring tense) and $\phi \Diamond\!\!\rightarrow \psi$ to symbolize *might* counterfactuals.

- Idempotence: $\phi \Box\!\!\rightarrow \phi$
- Restricted Modus Ponens: $((\phi \Box\!\!\rightarrow \psi) \wedge \forall \chi(\chi \rightarrow \neg(\phi > \neg\chi))) \rightarrow (\phi \rightarrow \psi)$
- Necessitation:

$$\frac{\vdash \phi}{\vdash \psi \Box\!\!\rightarrow \phi}$$

- Logical Closure on the right:

$$\frac{\vdash \psi \rightarrow \chi}{(\phi \Box\!\!\rightarrow \psi) \vdash (\phi \Box\!\!\rightarrow \chi)}$$

- Logical Equivalence on the Left:

$$\frac{\vdash \psi \leftrightarrow \chi}{(\psi \Box\!\!\rightarrow \phi) \rightarrow (\chi \Box\!\!\rightarrow \phi)}$$

- And: $((\phi \Box\!\!\rightarrow \psi) \wedge (\phi \Box\!\!\rightarrow \chi)) \rightarrow (\phi \Box\!\!\rightarrow (\psi \wedge \chi))$
- $(\neg\phi \Box\!\!\rightarrow \phi) \rightarrow (\psi \Box\!\!\rightarrow \phi)$
- $(\phi \Box\!\!\rightarrow \psi) \rightarrow (\phi \Diamond\!\!\rightarrow \psi)$[35]

[35]This follows from the implication from *Would* $\phi$ to *Might* $\phi$

Missing are Lewis's axioms, $(\phi \wedge \psi) \rightarrow (\phi \Box\!\!\rightarrow \psi)$, and $((\phi \Box\!\!\rightarrow \psi) \wedge \neg(\phi \Box\!\!\rightarrow \neg\chi)) \rightarrow ((\phi \wedge \chi) \Box\!\!\rightarrow \psi)$.

Counterfactuals thus occupy an intermediate position of strength with respect to other modal conditionals. Conditionals that are true at every world, necessary conditionals, clearly entail counterfactuals on our semantics, while counterfactuals, as we've just seen, entail normality conditionals. The normality interpretation of the irrealis operator makes counterfactuals more modally robust than normality conditionals. For the counterfactual $Irr(\phi) \Rightarrow Would\ (\psi)$, to hold at $\sigma$, not only must $\sigma$ support the conditional, in the sense that the epistemic possibilities $\bullet(3(\sigma), \|\phi\|)$ support $\psi$, but further every element $\sigma' \in 3(\sigma)$ must be such that $\bullet(3(\sigma'), \|\phi\|)$ supports $\psi$. This reflects the idea that counterfactuals are lawlike and must hold not only in the actual world but in all other (in our case epistemically close) worlds as well. And finally neither counterfactuals nor normality conditionals entail nor are they entailed by the indicative conditional $\Rightarrow$, though $\Rightarrow$ is a semantic constituent of a counterfactual.

Given the entailment between counterfactuals on the normality interpretation and normality conditionals, we can simply use the nonmonotonic inference system for normality conditionals to deduce defeasible conclusions from counterfactuals. The defeasible inferences from counterfactuals would be exactly those that follow from the associated normality conditionals. In particular following Morreau (1995) or Asher and Morreau (1991), we predict the following sorts of reasoning patterns to be defeasibly valid for counterfactuals.[36]

**Fact 5** *Letting $\approx\!\!\!\!\!\mid$ stand for the defeasible, nonmonotonic inference relation based on normality conditionals,*

- *Defeasible Strengthening of the Antecent:* $\phi \Box\!\!\rightarrow \psi \mid\!\approx (\phi \wedge \chi) \Box\!\!\rightarrow \psi$
- *Defeasible Modus Ponens:* $\phi \Box\!\!\rightarrow \psi, \phi \mid\!\approx \psi,$
- *Defeasible Transitivity:* $\phi \Box\!\!\rightarrow \psi, \psi \Box\!\!\rightarrow \chi \mid\!\approx \phi \Box\!\!\rightarrow \chi$
- *Defeasible Modus Tollens:* $\phi \Box\!\!\rightarrow \psi, \neg\psi \mid\!\approx \neg\phi$

[36]Nonmonotonic inference using $>$ essentially relies on a transformation of $>$ statements into $\rightarrow$ statements provided this operation is consistent with all the information given in the premises for the inference. The proceedure developed in Morreau (1995) and refined in Asher and Mao (2001) works on the outermost $>$ in the sentences of a set of premises and attempts to convert to a material implication $\rightarrow$ all the $>$ with the widest scope not under the scope of negation in the premises, and then checks the result for consistency or satisfiability. All $>$ statements with logically equivalent antecedents have to be considered together: either they can all be consistently turned into $\rightarrow$ statements or none of them can. Roughly, a set of sentences $\Gamma$ nonmonotonically implies a conclusion $\phi$ just in case all acceptable ways of turning $>$ statements in $\Gamma$ into $\rightarrow$ statements, call these $\Gamma^{\rightarrow}$, are such that $\Gamma^{\rightarrow} \models \phi$. To give a very simple example in the propositional $>$ logic, suppose that the premises $\Gamma$ we have for our inference are $A > D, A > B, A$. To reason nonmonotonically with $\Gamma$, we have to add to $\Gamma$ the pair $(A > D) \rightarrow (A \rightarrow D)$ and $(A > B) \rightarrow (A \rightarrow B)$ and check whether the result is consistent. It is, and since there are no other $>$ to turn into $\rightarrow$, we see that we can nonmonotonically infer $B$ and $D$. A slightly more complex example is one where we suppose that the premises $\Gamma = \{A > D, A > B, B > C, A, \neg C\}$. There are three $>$ statements all of which have a $>$ with maximal scope. Now we could either consider whether adding $(B > C) \rightarrow (B \rightarrow C)$ to $\Gamma$ preserves consistency or whether the pair $(A > D) \rightarrow (A \rightarrow D)$ and $(A > B) \rightarrow (A \rightarrow B)$ does. We can add either the $A$ transformations or the $B$ transformations and preserve consistency but not both. So from $\Gamma$ nothing nonmonotically follows that doesn't follow from $\Gamma$ in the underlying monotonic logic for our $>$ language.

- *Penguin Principle:*

$$\frac{\vdash \phi \rightarrow \psi}{\phi \Box\!\!\rightarrow \chi, \psi \Box\!\!\rightarrow \neg\chi, \phi \mathrel{|\!\!\approx} \chi}$$

These defeasible inferences are intuitively compelling with counterfactuals. For example,

(34) If the match were struck it would light, then I can defeasibly infer that if the match were struck and I wanted to light a cigarette, then the match would light.

(35) If the match were struck it would light, then supposing that the match is struck, I can at least defeasibly infer that the match lights .

(36) If the match were struck it would light, and if the match lighted, it would burn, then if the match were struck it would burn.

(37) If the match were struck it would light, but if the match were struck and it were wet, it would not light, then supposing that the match is struck and that it is wet, I can at least defeasibly infer that the match does not light.

(34) is an instance of a defeasibly strengthening of the antecedent; (35) is an instance of defeasible modus ponens; (36) is an instance of a defeasible transitivity; and (37) is an instance of the Penguin Principle. All of these seem compelling at least as defeasible inferences, which can be defeated when more detailed information is available but in the absence of such, they seem acceptable. Our account explains these intuitions as well as the intuition that counterfactuals pattern with the predictions of normality conditionals.

### 8.4.3 Discourse effects with conditionals

Our account of counterfactuals makes conditionals and counterfactuals change the discourse context. This gives us a simple way of treating discourse effects of conditionals like the following one discussed by various authors (including Frank (1997) and von Fintel (2002)).

(38) a. If the USA threw its weapons into the sea tomorrow, there would be war; but if all the nuclear powers threw their weapons into the sea tomorrow, there would be peace.

b. ??If all the nuclear powers threw their weapons into the sea tomorrow, there would be peace, but if the USA threw its weapons into the sea tomorrow, there would be war.

Similar asymmetries also feature in many different sorts of constructions.

(39) a. If the USA throws its weapons into the sea tomorrow, there will be war; but if all the nuclear powers throw their weapons into the sea tomorrow, there will be peace.

b. ?If all the nuclear powers throw their weapons into the sea tomorrow, there will be peace, but if the USA throws its weapons into the sea tomorrow, there will be war.

(40) a. The USA's throwing its weapons into the sea tomorrow will normally lead to war be war; but all the nuclear powers throwing their weapons into the sea tomorrow will normally lead to peace.

b. ?All the nuclear powers throwing their weapons into the sea tomorrow will normally lead to peace, but the USA's throwing its weapons into the sea tomorrow will normally lead to war.

(41) a. When the USA threw its weapons into the sea, there was war. But when all the nuclear powers threw their weapons into the sea, there was peace.

b. ?When all the nuclear powers threw their weapons into the sea, there was peace. But when the USA threw its weapons into the sea, there was war.

(42) a. John is a pain to have at a party. But John and Mary are fine.

b. ?John and Mary are fun to have at a party. But John is a pain.

The data discussed by von Fintel and Frank (among many others) is one instance of a general feature of contrasting constituents in discourse. Take for example (42). It is a natural implicature to read (42b) as a distributive predication over John and Mary. Once this update has taken place, to make sense of the claim in (42b), a revision of the discourse context has to take place. On the other hand, when interpreting (42a), no revision has to take place, except that a different collective interpretation of the predication of John and Mary is forced in the second sentence and a bit of extra content is accommodated with the first constituent—namely that John *on his own* is a pain.[37] For the conditionals there is a similar story; once we update with the general claim, we are updating with each one of its entailed instances in effect as well. So a revision is forced in order to understand the second claim, something which is dispreferred in a contrast. However, when we take the specific claim first, it's easy to give a collective interpretation to *all the nuclear powers* in the second claim, and we also add the implicature that the antecedent of the first conditional applies only to its explicitly mentioned subject.[38] Our analysis therefore directly yields an explanation of these discourse effects.

## 8.5 Conclusions

This paper has made two main contributions. The first was giving a new semantics for epistemic modals that validates both the Veltman 'eliminative' intuitions and Roberts/Frank-style 'distributive' intuitions; this is something that existing accounts have not been able to do, and we see the step we have taken as an important one in giving a universally valid theory of modality. The second contribution crucially builds on the first: an account of counterfactuals that takes seriously the notion that they can be compositionally built up from their semantic constituents: the conditional itself, the modals that appear in the consequent, and irrealis mood. The particular implementation of this idea we presented also brought out the parallels that exist between counterfactual and default reasoning, a connection that we think is important.

---

[37]For a more thorough discussion of the semantics of Contrast, see Asher (1993).

[38]Note that this explanation is needed in the case of normality conditionals, as well as counterfactuals. This is because of the inherently distributive interpretation of the universally quantified normality sentences.

The research project described here is just a part of a much larger project: a full semantics of English modals and conditionals. The semantic proposal in this paper provides a way to analyze many other complex conditionals that we did not discuss here—viz., those involving *must*, *ought*, and *should* for instance. We've presented in effect a family of semantic theories for complex conditionals that use the basic epistemic conditional together with various modals. We've also produced an account of the basic epistemic modals that answers to intuitions about modal subordination as well as Veltman's observations about the non distributive semantics of epistemic modals. These basic positions can be extended to a host of other modalities, if the facts warrant.

## References

Abusch, D. 1997. Sequence of Tense and Temporal *De Re*. *Linguistics and Philosophy* 20 (1):1–50.

Asher, N. 1993. *Reference to Abstract Objects in Discourse*. Dordrecht: Kluwer Academic Publishers.

Asher, N. and D. Bonevac. 2005. Free Choice Permission is Strong Permission. *Synthese* 145-3:303–323.

Asher, N. and A. Gillies. 2003. Common Ground, Corrections et Coordination. *Argumentation* 17:481–512.

Asher, N. and A. Lascarides. 2003. *Logics of Conversation*. Cambridge: Cambridge University Press.

Asher, N. and Y. Mao. 2001. Negated Defaults in Commonsense Entailment. *Bulletin of the Section of Logic* 30:41–60. Also in *Proceedings of Logic Colloquium 2000*.

Asher, N. and E. McCready. forthcoming. Were, Would, Might, and a Compositional Account of Counterfactuals. *Journal of Semantics* .

Asher, N. and M. Morreau. 1991. Commonsense Entailment: A Modal Theory of Non-Monotonic Reasoning. In *IJCAI*, pages 387–392.

Condoravdi, C. 2002. Temporal interpretation of modals. In B. C. D. Beaver, S. Kaufmann and L. Casillas, eds., *The construction of meaning*, pages 59–88. Stanford: CSLI Publications.

Fernando, T. 1993. Generalized quantifiers as second order programs—'dynamically' speaking, naturally. In *Proceedings, Ninth Amsterdam Colloquium*. University of Amsterdam.

Frank, A. 1997. *Context Dependence in Modal Constructions*. Ph.D. thesis, University of Stuttgart.

Geurts, B. 1995. *Presupposing*. Ph.D. thesis, University of Stuttgart.

Gillies, A. 2003. Modal scorekeeping and 'might' counterfactuals. In P. Dekker, ed., *Proceedings of Fourteenth Amsterdam Colloquium*. Amsterdam: ILLC Publications.

Gillies, A. 2004. Epistemic Conditionals and Conditional Epistemics. (Forthcoming).

Groenendijk, J. and M. Stokhof. 1991. Dynamic Predicate Logic. *Linguistics and Philosophy* 14:39–100.

Groenendijk, J., M. Stokhof, and F. Veltman. 1994. This might be it. Manuscript.

Hobbs, J. 2005. Toward a Useful Concept of Causality for Lexical Semantics. *Journal of Semantics* 22:181–209.

Iatridou, S. 2000. The grammatical ingredients of counterfactuality. *Linguistic Inquiry* 31 (2):231–270.

Kamp, H. and U. Reyle. 1993. *From Discourse to Logic*. Dordrecht; Boston: Kluwer Academic.

Kaufmann, S. 2005. Conditional Truth and Future Reference. *Journal of Semantics* 22:231–280.

Kratzer, A. 1977. What 'must' and 'can' must and can mean. *Linguistics and Philosophy* 1 (3):337–355.

Kratzer, A. 1981. Partition and Revision: The Semantics of Counterfactuals. *Journal of Philosophical Logic* 10:201–216.

Kratzer, A. 1986. Conditionals. *Chicago Linguistics Society* 22:1–15.

Kratzer, A. 1991. Modality. In A. von Stechow and D. Wunderlich, eds., *Semantik: Ein internationales Handbuch der zeitgenössischen Forschung*, pages 639–650. Berlin: Walter de Gruyter.

Lewis, D. 1973. *Counterfactuals*. Oxford: Basil Blackwell.

McCawley, J. 1996. Conversational scorekeeping and the interpretation of conditional sentences. In M. Shibatani and S. Thompson, eds., *Grammatical Constructions: their Form and Meaning*, pages 77–101. Oxford: Clarendon Press.

Morreau, M. 1995. Allowed Arguments. In *IJCAI*, pages 1466–1473.

Morreau, M. 1997. Fainthearted Conditionals. *Journal of Philosophy* 94:187–211.

Roberts, C. 1987. *Modal Subordination, Anaphora, and Distributivity*. Ph.D. thesis, Department of Linguistics, University of Massachussetts at Amherst.

Roberts, C. 1989. Modal Subordination and Pronominal Anaphora in Discourse. *Linguistics and Philosophy* 12 (6):683–721.

Stalnaker, R. 1975. Indicative conditionals. *Philosophia* 5:269–286.

van Deemter, K. 2003. Towards a logic of ambiguous expressions. manuscript.

van Rooij, R. 2005. A modal analysis of presupposition and modal subordination. *Journal of Semantics* 22:281–306.

Veltman, F. 1985. *Logics for Conditionals*. Ph.D. thesis, Department of Philosophy, University of Amsterdam.

Veltman, F. 1996. Defaults in update semantics. *Journal of Philosophical Logic* 25:225–261.

von Fintel, K. 2002. Counterfactuals in a dynamic context. In M. Kenstowicz, ed., *Ken Hale: A Life in Language*, pages 123–152. Cambridge, MA: MIT Press.

Zeevat, H. 1992. Presupposition and Accommodation in Update Semantics. *Journal of Semantics* 9:379–412.

Zimmerman, T. E. 2000. Free Choice Disjunction and Epistemic Possibility. *Natural Language Semantics* 8:255–290.

# 9

# The rhetorical attachment of questions and answers

PHILIPPE MULLER AND LAURENT PRÉVOT

## 9.1 Introduction

Placing ourselves in the tradition of dynamic semantic approaches to discourse in natural language (Kamp and Reyle (1993), Groenendjik and Stokhof (1991)), we investigate here how some of the principles underlying these approaches can be extended to the study of human dialogue, taking over some hypotheses of Asher and Lascarides (1998). In this perspective, a dialogue is made of segments just like any discourse; the semantics of each one of these segments is represented in a logical framework and linked to other segments by rhetorical relations that also carry semantic or intentional content, in the spirit of Segmented Discourse Representation Theory (Asher (1993)). Thus can be integrated linguistic phenomena tackled by formal semantics and more dialogue-specific characteristics such as turn-taking conventions or common ground establishment.

We will concentrate in this paper on the issue of multiple question/answer pairs and the way they structure some of the established conversational content. More specifically, we have focused on Yes/No questions (questions for which the expected answer can be Yes or No, possibly with some additional material). In order to do so, we have collected a corpus of dialogues from phone conversations in a specific, constructed setting.[1] Each dialogue relates a "giver" and a "receiver": the giver explains to the receiver how to go from one place to another in the same city. The global subject or topic of this kind of discussion is the explained route.

After a brief introduction to SDRT (section 9.2.1), we will look in section 9.2.2 at the classical proposals of this theory for attaching yes/no questions in the rhetorical structure of a dialogue, and pursue with a critical analysis of these solutions. Section 9.3 will focus on the link between question/answer pairs and the other rhetorical relations.

[1] This corpus collecting is an ongoing effort, from which we have transcribed 21 usable elements so far. Phone conversations eliminate deictics and gestures as well as facial expressions or other aspects difficult to transcribe or model.

*Meaning, Intentions, and Argumentation.*
Kepa Korta and Joana Garmendia (eds.).

In the process we will introduce and stress the need for a set of additional relations, especially for treating interrogative narration or correction and request for confirmation. We will then propose a new solution (section 9.4) for attaching questions and answers.

## 9.2 SDRT and Dialogue

### 9.2.1 SDRT: the basics

We will give here a very rough outline of Segmented Discourse Representation Theory (Asher (1993)). Asher's theory assumes that a dialogue is a kind of discourse involving two participants. SDRT also assumes, as the RST of Mann and Thompson (1987), that a discourse can be seen as a set of segments linked with (rhetorical or intentional) relations. These relations can be hierarchical or not. Hierarchical relations between segments induce a tree structure which imposes constraints on the interpretation of current utterances (e.g. anaphora resolution can be limited to certain segments of the current interpretation).[2] More generally, constraints based on the structure induced by the segmentation determine what is a coherent dialogue. New utterances will be attached to some segment incrementally within an already existing dialogue structure as they come, by taking into account lexical semantics, world knowledge and semantic-pragmatic rules selecting an appropriate relation in context, (Asher and Lascarides (1998)). These aspects, which are often taken for granted in theories taking as primitives propositions and speech acts related to these propositions, makes SDRT perspective more fine-grained than game-based or intentional analysis. SDRT still remains somewhat unpolished with respect to some aspects related to dialogue and we will question in this paper some of its current choices on the attachment of questions. We will therefore keep the following principles, while leaving aside the presently less stable aspects of the still-in-progress theory:

- the global representation of a dialogue is composed of a set of labelled speech acts (SAs) and rhetorical relations between these occurrences of SAs. A speech act will be of the form ⟨Speaker,Mood,Content⟩, where the mood can be interrogative(?), declarative(.) or imperative(!). A basic semantic content will be a DRS, cf. Kamp and Reyle (1993), that is a set of linguistic referents and of conditions (predicates) on those referents. Speech acts, seen in other frameworks as having an intentional content, take on an intentional dimension only when linked together by relations bearing an intentional content.
- We have divided them into the following categories :
  —**monologic relations**: The set of these relations is given in the work of Asher (1993) updated in Busquets et al. (2001); it is composed of subordinating relations (*elaboration, explanation,...*) and coordinating ones (*narration,...*).
  —**dialogic relations**: The set of these relations coming from Asher and Lascarides (1998) has been updated in the most recent paper on this subject, Asher et al. (2001); it is composed of *Plan-elaboration, Question-elaboration, Question-Answer-*

[2] Rhetorical relations are thus either *subordinating* in the tree structure, or *coordinating*, i.e. linking two daughters of a same mother node.

*Pair,*[3] *Not-Enough-Information, Acknowledgement, Correction.* In Asher and Lascarides (2003) a systematic account of mood is added to the relations. Each indicative relation of monologue can now be uttered with interrogative (e.g $narration_q$, $elaboration_q$,[4]...) or imperative mood. There are also some additional relations (e.g *Plan-correction, ...*).

### 9.2.2 Attachment of questions

Example (1) shows how questions and answers can be related by different relations, $A_{3a}$ $A_{3b}$, $A_{3c}$ and $A_{3d}$ being possible continuations of $A_1$-$B_2$. Here $\pi_i$ is the label of the speech act made in turn $i$ (each turn being here only one segment). Graphically, we will represent a subordinating relation with a vertical segment between two labels, and a coordinating relation with an horizontal one.

(1) $A_1$. You take the Pomme street.
$B_2$. Is it the street leading to the Salengro square?
$A_{3a}$. Yes.
$A_{3b}$. No.
$A_{3c}$. I don't know.
$A_{3d}$. Is there a fountain on this square?

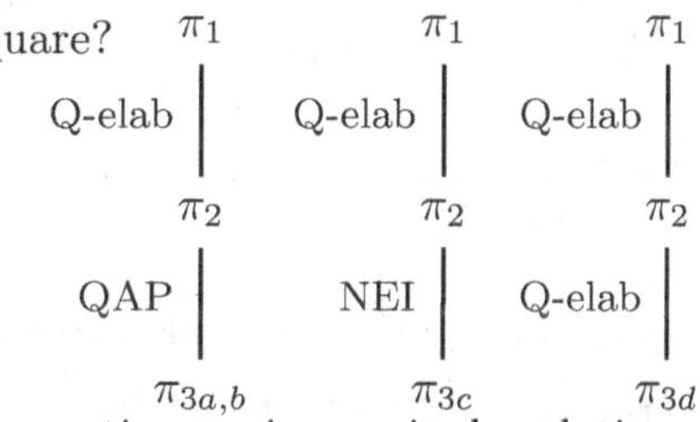


Initially, SDRT's proposal was to attach questions using a single relation, namely *Q-elab*. This relation is the interrogative version of *plan-elab*.

**Plan-elab($\alpha, \beta$):** It holds just in case $\beta$'s content provides information which elaborates a plan for achieving $\alpha$'s SARG (Speech Act Related Goal).

**Q-elab($\alpha, \beta$):** It holds if all correct answers to $\beta$ elaborate a plan for achieving $\alpha$'s SARG.

As we can see, these relations pertains to the cognitive modelling module of SDRT. They attempt to model Intentions and Beliefs of the dialogue participants. They are similar to *discourse plans* presented in Litman and Allen (1990) and to the *intentional structure* proposed by Grosz and Sidner (1986).

In Asher and Lascarides (2003), another level is introduced for the attachment of questions: the **content level** (the level used for monologue). At this level relations link utterances by way of inferences on events and individuals. Those relations are $elaboration_q$, $narration_q$... which are interrogative versions of classical indicative ones (e .g $elab_q$).

[3]Noted QAP, with a distinction as proposed in Karttunen (1977) between QAP, Indirect QAP (IQAP) and Partial QAP (PQAP).

[4]The interrogative nature of these relations makes them subordinating.

**elab**$_q(\alpha, \beta)$**:** It holds if all correct answers $\gamma$ to $\beta$ satisfy $elab(\alpha, \gamma)$.

The attachment of an answer is done by "Question Answer Pair" ($QAP$) introduced in Asher and Lascarides (1998).

$QAP(\alpha, \beta)$**:** It holds if $\alpha$ is a question and $\beta$ is a (true direct) answer to that question, as determined by compositional semantics.

Roughly, this amounts to considering that semantics of questions and answer are unsatured, and have to be combined.[5] In SDRT, the combination result is put in the SDRS of the answer itself and attached to the question. However we will see another way of doing it because of a structural problem. $IQAP$ is the indirect version of $QAP$ in which the participant have to infer a direct answer to his question from his partner's utterance. Finally there is also *NEI*$(\alpha, \beta)$ a relation which appears when $\beta$ does (N)ot supply (E)nough (I)nformation to satisfy the associated goal of $\alpha$.

To recapitulate, *Q-elab* captures the very common fact that when a speaker utters a question he does so for obtaining a satisfying answer (it is the Question Related Goal). *Relation*$_q$ (where *relation* is narration, etc) makes this attachment precise by capturing the relation between events and individuals. However, the hierarchical nature of these relations (subordinating or coordinating) is unclear since there may be a conflict between the subordinating nature of a question and the possible coordinating nature of the *Relation*.

## 9.3 Questions and other rhetorical relations

In this section we will look at the different rhetorical roles that a question could play in dialogue structure. We have seen that from the classical point of view the only way for attaching a question at the cognitive level in SDRT is the relation *Q-elab*. In the following, we will present a set of examples (inspired from our corpus of route explanation dialogues) illustrating this case. However, we will also have a look at some other cases where different cognitive-level relations are involved.

### 9.3.1 Elaboration

First, let's consider the case of a question elaborating the previous utterance. *Elaboration* is the canonical case, in discourse, of the subordination relation. In the figure, $QAP_+$ and $QAP_-$ are employed to represent positive and negative answers.

[5] The semantics of interrogatives is discussed in Hamblin (1973) Karttunen (1977) Ginzburg (1995).

(2) $A_1$. Tu tournes à gauche juste avant Monoprix.
*You turn on the left before Monoprix.*
$B_2$. La rue à sens unique?
*The one way street?*
$A_{3a}$. Oui, celle-là.
*Yes, this one.*
$A_{3b}$. Non, celle d' après.
*No, the next one.*

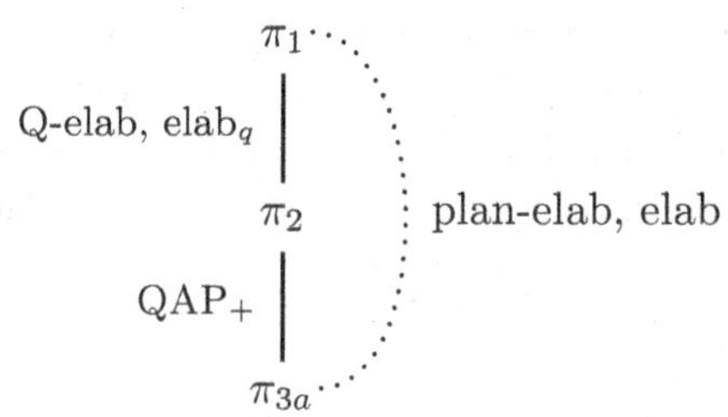


$B_2$ elaborates the SARG of $A_1$ (B asks a question in order to be able to follow A's prescription). Consequently $B_2$ is related to $A_1$ by *Q-elab.* But the description in $B_2$ also elaborates the event of turning in a street. It leads to a relation of content level: *elaboration*$_q$.

**elab**$(\alpha, \beta)$**:** "The content of the elaborated segment depends on the content of the elaborating material. So if $\beta$ elaborates $\alpha$, then the eventuality or eventualities that $\beta$ describes are part of, or a sub-event of the eventuality described by $\alpha$" (Asher et al. (2001)).

Now we will consider two answers to B's question: a positive $B_{3a}$ and the negative one $B_{3b}$. If the answer is "Yes," it just resolves the question and allows us to infer *plan-elab* and *elaboration* between $A_1$ and $A_{3a}$.[6] The SDRS for this dialogue are given below.

| | $K_1$: | $y_1, y_2, d_1, u, t_1, e_1$ | |
|---|---|---|---|
| ⟨A, ., | | speaker(B,u)<br>name($y_1$,"Monoprix")<br>turn($e_1$,u,$t_1$)<br>on_the_left($e_1$,u,$y_2$,$t_1$)<br>segment($y_2$)<br>direction($d_1$)<br>segment($t_1$)<br>before($e_1$,$y_1$,$d_1$,$t_1$) | ⟩ |

[6]A reformulation could be: *"You turn on the left before Monoprix. It's a one way street."*

$K_2$: ⟨B,?, [box] ⟩

| $e_2\ y_3$ |
|---|
| street($y_3$) <br> one_way($y_3$) <br> $y_3$ =? |

$K_{2+3}$:

| $e_2\ y_3$ |
|---|
| street($y_3$) <br> one_way($y_3$) <br> $y_3$=$t_1$ |

$B_2$ asks for a precision on an element of $A_1$: there is an object (the street) related to the event of $A_1$ (the turning), since the lexical representation[7] of the verb *"tourner"* implies a segment of a path where the turning ends up,[8] and this is all the more obvious as B's answer is a phrasal fragment and not a sentence or a question (thus implying that some of the previous utterance has to be associated with the answer, Ginzburg (1995)).

The negative case could not be a single "No" because of the cooperative nature of our dialogue. A is supposed to add some material to his negative answer. We will look at two different scenarii in the next section about narration.

### 9.3.2 Narration

Now we consider a question introducing the next step of the itinerary which is in monologue the narration case. *Narration* is the canonical case of the coordination relation in discourse.

(3) $A_1$. Tu tournes à gauche juste avant Monoprix.
*You turn on the left before Monoprix.*
$B_{2a}$. Et après, Dois-je aller jusqu'à la place du Capitole?
*And after that, do I have to go to the Capitole square?*
$B_{2b}$. Dois-je aller jusqu'à la place du Capitole?
*Do I have to go to the Capitole square ?*
$A_{3a}$. Oui, exactement.
*Yes, exactly.*
$A_{3b}$. Non, jusqu'au prochain carrefour seulement.
*No, just to the the next crossroad.*
$A_{3c}$. Non, cette rue ne mène pas à la place du Capitole.
*No, this street doesn't lead to the Capitole square.*

In this example, question ($B_{2a}$) asks for the following step of the prescription of the route. The temporal preposition "après" indicates this, but it is not necessary ($B_{2b}$ is correct too). Indeed the question is clearly about a segment of the explained route (part of the global topic) and by default we can assume this segment is the next step.[9]

[7]For a more precise account on this point see Krause et al. (2001).

[8]The complete semantic representations of the dialogue turns are here just for completeness. What matters is just the information that allows the bridging inference.

[9]In contrast, if the preposition used was "before", it would be necessary because it is harder to backtrack on the route in an explanation: *"And before that, was it the Augustin's Museum that I had on my right?"*. In the light of theses examples it seems reasonable to consider a temporal structure in the route explanation dialogue, and more generally in prescription dialogues, as in narrative monologue.

At the cognitive level, things are slightly different from *elaboration*. The *plan-elaboration* involved previously corresponds in the intentional structure of Grosz and Sidner (1986) to the *dominance relation*. Here, it is the *satisfaction-precedence* one which is involved. We suggest a new coordinating relation named *plan-sequence*. This relation is a cognitive one: $A_1$ and $B_{3a}$ elaborate the same higher SARG (Prescription of the Path) in the dialogue. In order to perform this higher SARG, participants have to perform $A_1$'s SARG and then $B_{3a}$'s SARG which are prescriptions of two steps of this path.

**Plan-sequence($\alpha, \beta$):** It holds just in case where contents of $\alpha$ and $\beta$ provides information which elaborates a plan for achieving a higher SARG. Thus $\alpha$'s SARG has to be satisfied before $\beta$'s resolution.

**Q-sequence($\alpha, \beta$):** It holds if the SARG of all correct answers to $\beta$ elaborates a higher SARG which is elaborated by $\alpha$'SARG too.

Now we will consider two possible answers to B's question: the positive one $B_{3a}$ and the negative one $B_{3b,c}$. If the answer is "Yes," it just solves the question and allows us to infer *Plan-sequence* and *Narration* between $A_1$ and $A_{3a}$.[10] Indeed, $B_2$ is about the next step of the route and so the topical relevance common to elements of a same narration is respected: it elaborates the global topic "How to go from ... to ...?"

$$\langle \text{A},. \quad K_1: \begin{array}{|l|} \hline y_1\ y_2\ d_1\ \text{u}\ t_1\ e_1 \\ \hline \text{speaker(B,u)} \\ \text{name}(y_1,\text{"Monoprix"}) \\ \text{turn}(e_1,\text{u},t_1) \\ \text{on\_the\_left}(e_1,\text{u},y_2,t_1) \\ \text{segment}(y_2) \\ \text{direction}(d_1) \\ \text{segment}(t_1) \\ \text{avant}(e_1,y_1,d_1,t_1) \\ \hline \end{array} \rangle \ \langle \text{B},?, \quad K_2: \begin{array}{|l|} \hline \text{v}\ e_2\ e_3\ y_3\ d_2\ t_2 \\ \hline \text{speaker(B,v)} \\ \text{name}(y_3,\text{"Place du Capitole"}) \\ \text{go\_to}(e_2,\text{v}) \\ \text{until}(e_2,y_3,d_2,t_2) \\ \text{segment}(t_2) \\ \text{direction}(d_2) \\ e_3 < e_2 \\ e_3 = ? \\ d_2 = ? \\ t_2 = ? \\ \hline \end{array} \rangle$$

After $A_3a$ ("Yes"), the resolved question is of the following form (after anaphora resolution):

[10] A reformulation could be: *"You turn on the left before Monoprix. And after that you have to go to the Capitole square."*

$K_{2+3}$:

| v $e_2$ $e_3$ $y_3$ $d_2$ $t_2$ |
|---|
| speaker(B,v)<br>name($y_3$, "Place du Capitole")<br>go_to($e_2$,v)<br>until($e_2$,$y_3$,$d_2$,$t_2$)<br>segment($t_2$)<br>direction($d_2$)<br>$e_3 < e_2$<br>$e_3 = e_1$<br>$d_2 = d_1$<br>$t_2 = t_1$ |

Again, there are two kinds of "No" answer. In the first case $A_{3b}$ the extra-information gives an answer to the question. Thus, we again consider $A_{3b}$ as a narration of $A_1$.[11] This is a negative narration but content gives us clues about the next step in the path.

But in terms of dialogue structure this case raises a difficult question. On the one hand $B_2$ is a question and if we follow the general proposition of SDRT it must be subordinated to the previous segment. On the other hand $B_2$ is a kind of "prescriptive narration" which should be a coordination relation. So do we attach $B_2$ by a subordination or a coordination? If the two relations were of the same type it wouldn't be a problem, because we can attach a constituent by more than one relation, provided that their semantics are compatible, but this is not the case here.

In a more general perspective, this analysis still seems valid if we consider less specific kinds of dialogue: there is always a global topic and a part-whole relation between topics and subtopics, along with an order between subtopics of a same level; this more or less corresponds to the notion of "topic chain" of Polanyi (1988); in the case of task-oriented dialogue, the task to be accomplished can be seen as the global topic, which can be divided into sub-goals. Sub-goals of a same goal can sometimes be ordered and this is reflected for instance in the satisfaction-precedence relation of Grosz and Sidner (1986). The bottom line is that a question can be coordinating elements.

In the second negative answer, $A_{3c}$ only corrects the question and doesn't give an answer. And following moves must resolve this "dispute". We focus here on questions and answers, and will not go any further on this correction problem.[12]

---

[11] We can reformulate it as *"Turn on the left just before Monoprix. Go on to the next crossroad."*

[12] For more details see Asher et al. (2001).

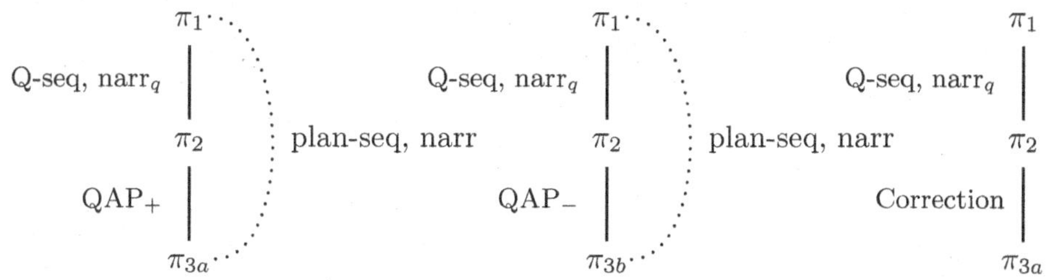


### 9.3.3 Acknowledgment (Request for confirmation)

(4) $A_1$. Tu tournes à gauche juste avant Monoprix.
*You turn on the left before Monoprix.*
$B_{2a}$. Avant Monoprix?
*Before Monoprix?*
$A_{3a}$. Oui, avant Monoprix.
*Yes, before Monoprix.*
$B_{2b}$. Après Monoprix?
*After Monoprix?*
$A_{3b}$. Non, avant.
*No, before.*

In this kind of question, there is no new material introduced in the question. It corresponds to what is usually called a request for confirmation[13] (Bilange (1991)), and appears when one of the participants has not well understood some part of the previous utterance, or wants a strong acknowledgement on a crucial information. *Acknowledgement* is a relation of the cognitive level. $B_2$ doesn't bring any elaboration on the SARG of $A_1$, but an interrogative realization of the *Acknowledgement* relation. This relation has a twin: *Plan-correction.*

**Acknowledgement**($\alpha$,$\beta$)**:** holds just in case $\beta$ entails that his producer has accepted or achieved the SARG of $\alpha$.

**Q-Acknowledgement**($\alpha$,$\beta$)**:** holds if all correct answers to $\beta$ makes accepted or achieved $\alpha$'s SARG.

**Plan-correction**($\alpha$,$\beta$)**:** holds just in case $\beta$ entails that his producer doesn't accept or is unable to achieve the SARG of $\alpha$.

[13]Echo questions as in our example may have other lectures in addition to the request for confirmation. Here, we consider only clausal lectures of Ginzburg (2001) reformulated as *"Do you say before Monoprix?"* instead of *"What do you mean by before Monoprix?"* which is a kind of clarification request (treated as an elaboration in our framework).

When a confirmation request is positevely answered,[14] the confirmation takes effect and the material enters into the common ground. Moreover we can infer a classical acknowledgement between $A_1$ and $A_{3a}$.

(5) $B_{2b}$. Après Monoprix?
*After Monoprix?*
$A_{3b}$. Non, avant.
*No, before.*
$A_{4a}$. Puis, tu continues dans cette rue.
*Then, you continue on this street.*
$B_{4b}$. D'accord.
*OK.*
$B_{4c}$. Je ne vois pas cette rue!
*I can't see this street.*

The negative answer is, as usual, more complicated than the positive one. Cooperativity forces the responder to re-utter the good information in addition to the negative answer. $A_{3b}$ can be followed by the next step of explanation $A_{4a}$. In this case there is an implicit acknowledgment of this subdialogue. But B can make an explicit acknowledge before the explanation goes on ($B_{4b}$). B can also dispute the prescription given by A ($B_{4c}$). These three scenarii are equally acceptable.

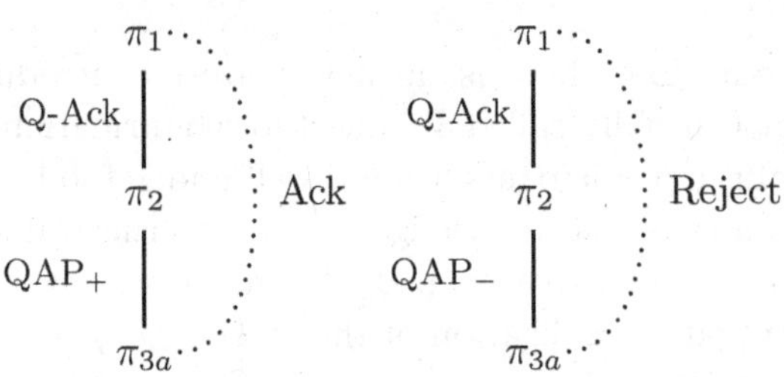


### 9.3.4 Correction

When corrections come up in disputes, a relation of *plan-correction* is assumed, and should modify a SARG of the agent. *Correction* otherwise only concerns the semantics of utterances. More precisely this relation presupposes some inconsistence between the contents of the two utterances that it relates.

[14] Very often, information during a request for confirmation is repeated.

(6) $A_1$. Tu tournes à gauche juste avant Monoprix.
*You turn on the left before Monoprix.*
$B_2$. N'est-ce pas juste après Monoprix plutôt?
*Isn't it before Monoprix instead?*
$A_{3a}$. Oui, tu as raison.
*Yes, you're right.*
$A_{3b}$. Non.
*No.*

The presence of a negation in the question introduces a correction of the prescription. Some elements of the correction $B_2$ are correcting the target $A_1$. The proper treatment of the classical case of a correction is the matching between the correction and the target except for the corrected parts.[15]

When the answer is positive ($A_{3a}$) we can rephrase the resolved question with *"No, it is after Monoprix"* and it constitutes a *correction* of the previous utterance. It also leads us to infer a *plan-correction* between $A_1$ and $A_{3a}$.

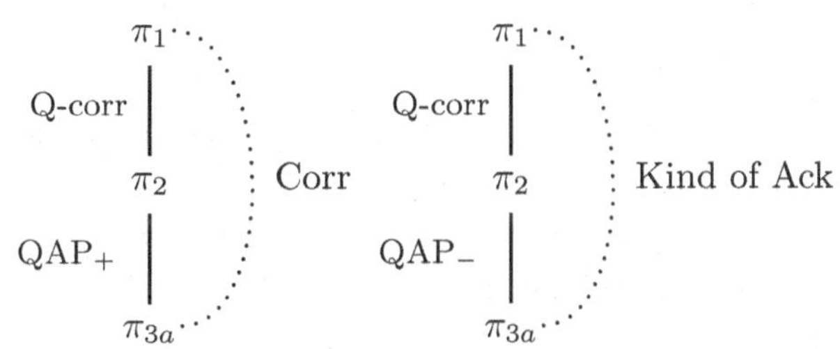


Notice here that A can answer by a single "No" without violating the cooperativity constraint. The results of this negative answer are comparable to those of an *acknowledgement.*

(7) $A_{3b}$. Non.
*No.*
$A_{4a}$. Maintenant, continues dans cette rue.
*Now you continue on this street.*
$B_{4b}$. D'accord.
*OK.*
$B_{4c}$. Es-tu vraiment sûr?
*Are you really sure?*

[15]The correction is thus usually closely linked to the information structure, Gardent et al. (1996), Txurruka (1997).

## 9.4 Defining new types of question/answer pairs relations

The previous section has shown difficulties with the current SDRT proposal for attaching questions. First there is an incompatibility in the structure itself. Remember the case of the interrogative narration: $Narration_q$ and $QAP$ are subordination relations and *Narration* is a coordination relation. Thus, it would seem impossible to keep the tree-like hierarchical structure induced by the subordination relations, something few authors would consider satisfying for a rhetorical approach.

The problem of the nature of the dialogic relations still remains open, especially when the corresponding monologic relation is a coordinating one. If we put the resolved question in the answer then it seems problematic to keep the structure of a narration (since the answer is below the question in the structure). A first step towards the solution is to keep the structural nature of the monologic relation.We could go one step further and consider the attachment on the right-hand side of the following figure for interrogatives[16] instead of the left-hand side one:

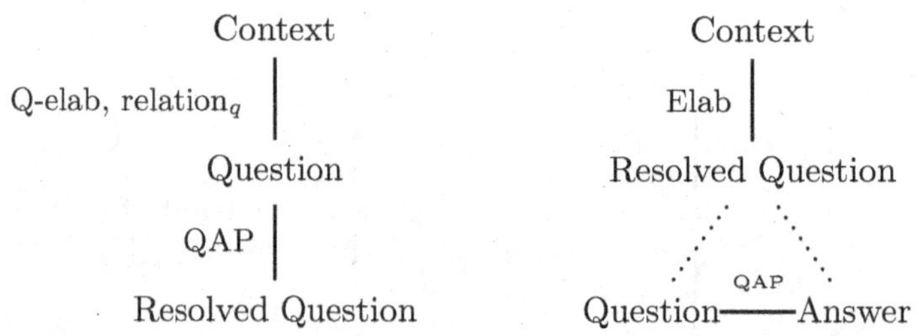


What this means is a question-answer pair is regarded as a single rhetorical unit in the global dialogue structure (whether there are embedded questions elaborating further the point under discussion or not). Thus we keep track of the different levels of resolution of questions (if there are embedded questions) and we can still represent the rhetorical functions of resolved question-answer sequences in the general dialogue.

Incidentally, this raises another point: if a question can take any rhetorical role, does "questioning" really add something to the rhetorical dimension? We could instead consider that the resolved question/answer pair plays that role. In a task oriented setting this means for instance we can represent successful question-answer pairs as partial accomplishments towards the task under discussion. If we adopt this view, the resulting structures are then the following for the previous examples:

[16]Dashed lines used in place of solid lines mark that lower constituents are only parts of the higher node. These links are not rhetorical relations.

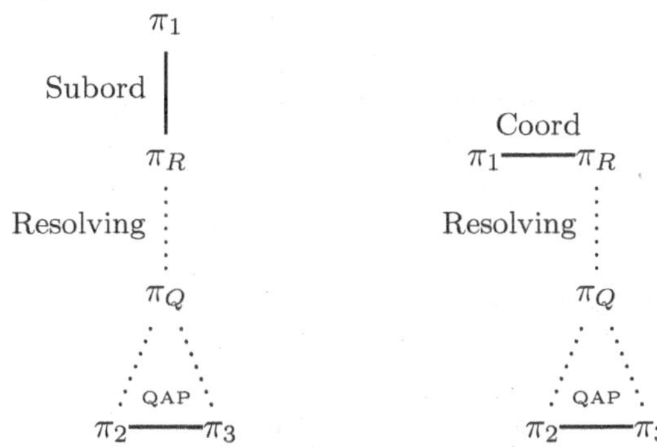


This will also change the constraints on anaphoric resolution, once we have defined availibility of referents between the context, a resolved Q/A pair and the content of questions and answers.

We have just looked at the two canonical relations and leave others for future work. It will be necessary now to look more precisely into the semantics of these relations, especially in the light of other types of questions, such as wh-questions and alternative questions.

## 9.5 Conclusion

In this paper, we address an important aspect of questioning in dialogue: the rhetoric role of questions. We defend the position that a question can have different rhetoric roles. Up to now, SDRT has only explored the question at the cognitive level, leaving aside the semantic relations of the content level.[17] Yet, approaches using dialog acts already distinguish between requests for information and requests for a confirmation (Bilange (1991), Poesio and Traum (1997)). We claim in addition that any monologue relation can be realized by a question and its answer considered as a single unit. We have therefore investigated the different cases of question/answer sequences and tried to show how they are related to more discursive rhetorical functions. Our proposal have some consequences on question attachment in SDRT or any rhetorical theory of dialogue.

First, we have seen that some $relation_q$ can be coordinations. However, the main issue from our point of view is really the following: is the interrogative nature of a segment of a discourse relevant to the rhetorical structure? Indeed, could we not consider attaching questions to the context with equivalent monologic relations (e.g. what we have called so far $narration_q$ would boil down to *narration*)? This solution need some sort of combining of the question and its answer in a higher node (composed by the semantically unsatured question and answer) instead of in the answer node itself. This higher node could be seen as the discourse topic of the question/answer sequence. Then a question is only a part of this unit. This could moreover prove useful in the study of how participants establish a common ground through a series of questions and answers, but we leave this discussion for future work.

[17] In Asher and Lascarides (2003) a more complete account on dialogue issues is proposed.

## References

Asher, N. 1993. *Reference to Abstract Objects in Discourse*. Kluwer Academic Publisher.

Asher, Nicholas. 2004. Discourse topic. *Theoretical Linguitics* (30):161–201.

Asher, N., J. Busquets, and A. Le Draoulec. 2001. Cooperativity in dialogue. In M. Bras and L. Vieu, eds., *Experimenting with current Dynamic Theories*. Elsevier, Oxford.

Asher, N. and A. Gillies. 2003. Common ground, corrections and coordination. *Argumentation* 17(4).

Asher, N. and A. Lascarides. 1998. Questions in dialogue. *Linguistics and Philosophy* 21:237–309.

Asher, N. and A. Lascarides. 2003. *Logics of conversation*. Cambridge University Press.

Asher, Nicholas and Laure Vieu. 2005. Subordinating and coordinating discourse relations. *Lingua* 115(4):591–610.

Bilange, Eric. 1991. *Modélisation du dialogue oral finalisé personne-machine par une approche structurelle.* Ph.D. thesis, Université de Rennes I.

Busquets, Joan, Laure Vieu, and Nicholas Asher. 2001. La SDRT : une approche de la cohérence du discours dans la tradition de la sémantique dynamique. *Verbum* 22(1):73–102.

Gardent, C., M. Kohlhase, and N. van Leusen. 1996. Corrections and higher-order unification. In *Proceedings of KONVENS*. Bielefeld, Germany.

Ginzburg, Jonathan. 1995. Resolving questions I. *Linguistics and Philosophy* 5(18):359–423.

Ginzburg, Jonathan. 2001. Fragmenting meaning: Clarification ellipsis and nominal anaphora. In *Computing Meaning, Vol 2.*. Kluwer.

Groenendjik, J. and M. Stokhof. 1991. Dynamic predicate logic. *Linguistics and Philosophy* 14:39–100.

Grosz, Barbara and Candace L. Sidner. 1986. Attention, intentions, and the structure of discourse. *Computational Linguistics* 12(3):175–204.

Hamblin, C.L. 1973. Questions in Montague English. *Foundations of language* 10:41–53.

Hobbs, J. R. 1985. On the coherence and structure of discourse. Tech. Rep. CSLI-85-37, Center for the the study of language and information, Stanford University.

Kamp, H. and U. Reyle. 1993. *From Discourse to Logic*. Kluwer Academic Publishers.

Karttunen, L. 1977. Syntax and semantics of questions. *Linguistics and Philosophy* 1(1):3–44.

Krause, Peter, Uwe Reyle, and Michael Schiehlen. 2001. Spatial inferences in a localization dialogue. In M. Bras and L. Vieu, eds., *Semantic and Pragmatic Issues in Discourse and Dialogue: Experimenting with Current Dynamic Theories*, vol. 9 of *Current Research in the Semantics/Pragmatics Interface*, chap. 7, pages 183–216. Elsevier, Oxford.

Litman, D.J. and J.F Allen. 1990. *Discourse Processing and Commonsense Plans*, pages 365–388. MIT Press.

Mann, W. and S. Thompson. 1987. Rhetorical structure theory : a theory of text organization. Tech. rep., Information Science Institute.

Poesio, Massimo and David R. Traum. 1997. Conversational actions and discourse situations. *Computational Intelligence* 13(3):309–347.

Polanyi, L. 1988. A formal model of the structure of discourse. *Journal of Pragmatics* 12.

Prévot, Laurent. 2004. *Structures sémantiques et pragmatiques pour la modélisation de la cohérence dans des dialogues finalisés*. Ph.D. thesis, Université Paul Sabatier.

Prévot, Laurent and Laure Vieu. 2005. The moving right frontier. In *Workshop on Constraints in Discourse*. Dortmund.

Txurruka, Isabel Gómez. 1997. *Particion Informacional en el discurso*. Ph.D. thesis, University of the Basque Country.

# 10

# Epideictic Rhetoric and the Representation of Human Decision and Choice

MARC DOMINICY

> Hay tres clases de hombres: los que primero piensan y obran luego,
> o sea los prudentes; los que obran antes de pensarlo, los arrojadizos;
> y los que obran y piensan a la vez, pensando lo que hacen a
> la vez misma que hacen lo que piensan. Éstos son los fuertes.
> Miguel de Unamuno (2002: 293)

## 10.1 Introduction

According to Aristotle (*Rhetoric*, 1358a-b),

> Rhetoric falls into three divisions, determined by the three classes of listeners [ἀκροαταί] to speeches. For of the three elements in speech-making—speaker, subject and person addressed—it is the late one, the hearer [ἀκροατής], that determines the speech's end and object. The hearer must be either a judge [κριτής], with a decision to make about things past or future, or an observer [θεωρός]. A member of the assembly [ἐκκλησιαστής] decides about future events, a juryman [δικαστής] about past events, while those who merely decide on the orator's skill [δύναμις] are observers. From this it follows that there are three divisions of oratory—deliberative [συμβουλευτικός], forensic [δικανικός], and epideictic [ἐπιδεικτικός].

This characterization of the three oratorical genres is rather puzzling. Indeed, one may wonder why Aristotle starts from a two-term classification of hearers, instead of relying on his subsequent trichotomy of rhetorical acts (*Rhetoric*, 1358b): advise to do something, or warning against doing something (deliberative); accuse or defend (forensic); praise or blame (epideictic) (Eggs 1994: 13-16). The usual explanation runs as follows (see, e.g., Danblon 2001a). Rhetoric and dialectic, as 'counterparts' [ἀντίστροφος] of each other (*Rhetoric*, 1354a), are 'the only arts that draw opposite conclusions impartially', in that they deal with 'problems' or 'questions' to which opposite answers can be given (*Rhetoric*, 1355a). Deliberative and forensic speeches clearly aim at providing answers to such problems or questions: 'Should we bomb Afghanistan?', 'Is the defendant

*Meaning, Intentions, and Argumentation.*
Kepa Korta and Joana Garmendia (eds.).

guilty?', etc. But the actions for which the epideictic orator praises or blames some agent(s) are neither disputable nor subjected to any ethical debate. So, what is the problem or question one should make a decision about? Aristotle's way out consists in assuming that the epideictic hearer has to decide on the orator's skill — which entails, in fact, that not all rhetorical problems or questions have a dialectical counterpart.

I have argued elsewhere (Dominicy 1995, 1996) that the counterparts of rhetoric should be sought both in dialectic (for the deliberative and forensic genres) and in poetics (for the epideictic genre). Yet, one might attempt to restore the conceptual unity of Aristotelian rhetoric by concentrating on rhetorical acts, and on the effects they are supposed to cause on the hearer's mind. While the deliberative or forensic speaker aims at convincing or persuading, the epideictic speaker would aim at triggering the emotions associated with praise or blame: pride or shame, admiration or contempt. Although this reconstruction seems to blur Aristotle's otherwise rigid distinction between 'logos' and 'pathos' (*Rhetoric*, 1356a, 1378a), it would allow us to reconstruct the whole rhetorical domain without doing too much violence to our intuitions concerning the peculiar status of epideictic speeches (Perelman & Olbrechts-Tyteca 1969: 47-51; Dominicy 2006).

In the following, I will try to show that this naïve approach is doomed to failure. I will first define the notion of an 'Aristotelian Rhetorical Act' (in short, *ARA*). This will lead me to the conclusion that an *ARA*, when satisfied and thus successfully performed, Intentionally causes a mental act of the hearer's. It will appear that, by contrast to the *ARA*s of advising or warning, of accusing or defending, praise and blame do not need to Intentionally cause a mental act of the hearer's in order to be satisfied. Finally, I will argue that Aristotle's attempt, and failure, to rationalize praise and blame in terms of deliberative advice or warning stem from the very nature, and internal inconsistency, of his ethical theory.

## 10.2 On the notion of an *ARA*

### 10.2.1 *IA*s, *PA*s, and *DA*s

If I address to Peter the utterance *It is raining*, it may be the case that, in producing this utterance, I tell Peter that it is raining, and that, by producing this utterance, I also convince Peter of the fact that Mary's garden party will not take place. According to Austin (1962), my 'illocutionary act' (in short, *IA*) of telling should be distinguished from my 'perlocutionary act' (in short, *PA*) of convincing. In such a perspective, *PA*s differ from *IA*s in terms of both complexity and action planning; see, for instance, the clear acceptability contrasts in examples (1-4):

(1) I told Peter that it was raining because I wanted / intended to convince him of the fact that Mary's garden party would not take place.

(2) ??? I convinced Peter of the fact that Mary's garden party would not take place because I wanted / intended to tell him that it was raining.

(3) ??? It is only when I said 'It is raining' that I managed to tell Peter that it was raining.

(4) It is only when I said 'It is raining' that I managed to convince Peter of the fact that Mary's garden party would not take place.

The contrast between (1) and (2) shows that the desire or intention to perform a *PA* can cause the performance of an *IA*, but not conversely (Bach & Harnish 1979: 16-18, 81-83; Gaines 1979: 211-213). As for the oddity of (3), it stems from the fact that, if Peter is a competent hearer (who understands English, for instance), any competent speaker who wants to tell Peter that it is raining will make use of linguistic means that are, at least, as communicatively efficacious as the production of the utterance *It is raining*; whereas addressing such an utterance to Peter as in example (4) is but one of the variously efficacious means available to the same speaker if s/he wants to convince Peter of the fact that Mary's garden party will not take place.

In the typology of 'situations' put forth by Kenny (1963: 171-186) and Mourelatos (1981), both *IA*s and *PA*s are 'performances.'[1] But while illocutionary performances are 'punctual', in that *IA*s cannot be said to be successfully performed in a certain amount of time (examples 5-6), perlocutionary performances are 'culminative'; indeed, *PA*s can be said to be successfully performed in a certain amount of time (examples 9-10). This distinction also holds for non-linguistic performances; compare the 'punctual' seing or hearing of examples (7-8) with the 'culminative' finding or recognizing of examples (11-12):

(5) [Context: the speaker addresses to Peter the utterance *Mary is very angry with you*]
??? I told him in a few seconds that Mary was very angry with him.

(6) [Context: the lieutenant addresses to the speaker the utterance *Attention!*]
??? The lieutenant ordered me in one second to stand to attention.

(7) ??? I saw him in three seconds cross the street.

(8) ??? I heard Beethoven's Ninth in one-and-a-half hours.

(9) I convinced Peter in a few seconds of the fact that Mary was wrong.

(10) Mary persuaded me in a few seconds to go to the station.

(11) I found the paper in a few seconds.

(12) Peter recognized Mary in a few seconds.

According to Mourelatos (1981: 202 footnote 21), what gives rise to the oddity of (7) and (8)

> is the implication that seeing or hearing, which are PASSIVE developments [Vendlerian accomplishments—see my footnote 1] that necessarily must reflect the duration of the

[1] Vendler (1967, 1972: 14-15) and Mourelatos (1981) distinguish between two kinds of performances, viz. 'accomplishments' (Vendler) or 'developments' (Mourelatos) on the one hand, and 'achievements' (Vendler) or 'punctual occurrences' (Mourelatos) on the other hand. In contrast to achievements, accomplishments can be said to be complete or incomplete by means of the 'finish *V*-ing' construction (see also Dowty 1979: 56-60): compare *I have not yet finished painting the picture* (accomplishment) with ??? *I have not yet finished finding the car* (achievement). Unfortunately, this aspectual test does not always lead to clear-cut results. According to Mourelatos (1981: 193), the oddity of *I have not yet finished convincing Mary* shows that convincing is an achievement. But the reason why such an utterance sounds strange may be the fact that, in normal circumstances, we are uncertain about the success or failure of an attempt of ours to convince, and thus unable to evaluate the time we still have to spend before we finally manage to convince.

object occurrence they capture, could somehow be sped up or slowed down.

Although *IA*s like telling and ordering are active performances, they exhibit a similar temporal dependency upon the duration of some active performances, viz. Austinian 'phonetic acts.'[2] In other words, the speaker may speed up or slow down his/her production of such utterances as *Mary is very angry with you* or *Attention!*; but once s/he controls the duration of his/her phonetic act, s/he has no additional control left on the duration of his/her illocutionary act. Compare with a similar example like (13), slightly adapted from Mourelatos:

(13) ??? I tape-recorded my own lecture in one-and-a-half hours.

Again, once the speaker controls the duration of his/her lecture, s/he obviously cannot exert any additional control on the duration of his/her tape-recording.[3] By contrast, 'culminative' performances like finding and recognizing, convincing or persuading, have a duration of their own; so that it is sometimes possible for an agent to adapt his/her action planning to the time s/he is willing to spend in trying to arrive at a successful culmination of his/her *PA*, independently of the duration of such-and-such phonetic act.

This aspectual parameter also helps us to establish that not all linguistic acts whose performance requires the performance of some subordinate *IA*(s) are *PA*s. Consider, for instance, examples (14) and (15):

(14) I told him in a few seconds that Mary was angry with him.

(15) I encouraged / incited her in a few seconds to apply for this job.

In such sentences, the use of tell or *encourage / incite* implies that I have done something more than simply uttering *Mary is very angry with you* or *Personally, I would apply for this job.* In other words, any illocutionary performance of telling or encouraging / inciting is 'punctual', while non-illocutionary performances of telling or encouraging / inciting are 'culminative'. This does not mean, however, that non-illocutionary performances of telling or encouraging / inciting are perlocutionary. Indeed, examples (16-19) show a striking contrast between telling or encouraging / inciting, and convincing or persuading:[4]

(16) I almost told him that Mary was very angry with him, but I changed my mind, and I did not make the slightest attempt to tell him that Mary was very angry with him.

(17) I almost encouraged / incited her to apply for this job, but I changed my mind, and I did not make the slightest attempt to encourage / incite her to apply for

[2] In the Austinian paradigm (Austin 1962), the duration of the 'phonetic act' constrains the duration both of the *IA*, and of the whole 'locutionary act' that includes, along with the 'phonetic act', a 'phatic act' and a 'rhetic act'. Searle (1973) dispenses with both notions of a 'rhetic act' and a 'locutionary act', but his 'phatic' and 'propositional' acts obviously exhibit the temporal dependency I am commenting here.

[3] Notice that the sentence *I tape-recorded my lecture in one-and-a-half hours* can be used to mean *I read, and therefore tape-recorded, my lecture in one-and-a-half hours.*

[4] On this test, see Dowty (1979: 56-60). Leech's (1983: 204-205) test, based on the 'try to *V*' construction, fails to make a clear-cut distinction between *IA*s and *PA*s (see Van Hecke 2001: 139-141).

this job.

(18) ??? I almost convinced him of the fact that Mary was very angry with him, but I changed my mind, and I did not make the slightest attempt to convince him of the fact that Mary was very angry with him.

(19) ??? I almost persuaded her to apply for this job, but I changed my mind, and I did not make the slightest attempt to persuade her to apply for this job.

Any quasi-performance of a *PA* requires the agent to make at least some attempt to successfully perform the *PA* at hand. Consequently, even though my quasi-performance of telling or encouraging / inciting can be interpreted, in (16-17), as an illocutionary or non-illocutionary quasi-performance, in neither case does it pertain to the perlocutionary level. In the following, I will call 'discourse acts' (in short, *DA*s) those non-perlocutionary linguistic acts, such as non-illocutionary telling or encouraging / inciting, whose performance requires the performance of some subordinate *IA*s.[5]

### 10.2.2 Vanderveken on *DA*s

In a series of papers devoted to the 'Logic of Discourse', Vanderveken (1997, 1999, 2001) argues that any sound theory of *DA*s should be modelled on 'Illocutionary Logic' (see Searle 1983; Searle & Vanderveken 1985; Vanderveken 1990, 1991, 1994). More specifically, he claims that 'discursive goals' can be fully characterized by means of five parameters: direction-of-fit (in short, *DOF*), mode of achievement, thematic conditions, background conditions, and sincerity conditions.

The first parameter—*DOF*—allows him to distinguish between four 'discourse types': descriptive (words-to-things *DOF*), deliberative (things-to-words *DOF*), declaratory (words-to-things and things-to-words *DOF*), expressive (empty *DOF*). Thus, the inventory of 'discourse goals' corresponds almost exactly to the Searlean inventory of 'illocutionary forces' and 'illocutionary points': assertive (words-to-things *DOF*), directive-commissive (things-to-words *DOF*), declarative (words-to-things and things-to-words *DOF*), expressive (empty *DOF*). The main difference lies in the fact that Speech Act Theory separates commissives from directives, on the ground that, in successfully performing a directive *IA*, the speaker is supposed to express a desire, while s/he is supposed to express an intention in successfully performing a commissive *IA* (for a discussion of this issue, see Franken & Dominicy 2001).

The second parameter—mode of achievement—is common to both illocutionary forces and discourse goals. It can be used, for instance, to capture Aristotle's idea that the performance of certain rhetorical acts requires the speaker to resort to some particular form of argument. Thus, deliberative advices or warnings must be 'paradigmatically' grounded, in that they must rely on at least one rhetorical 'example' (or 'paradigm'; παράδειγμα), while forensic accusation or defence must be 'enthymematically' grounded, in that it must rely on at least one rhetorical 'enthymeme' (*Rhetoric*, 1368a, 1391b, 1417b-1418a).

[5]Kurzon (1998) convincingly argues (against Leech 1983: 202-203) that incitement is no *PA*; however, since he does not take *DA*s in consideration, he has to classify all incitements (whatever their complexity) among *IA*s.

The third parameter—thematic conditions—corresponds to the 'propositional content conditions' of illocutionary forces. It can be used, for instance, to capture Aristotle's idea that the performance of certain rhetorical acts requires the speaker to deal with some particular kind of data. Thus, a deliberative advice or warning must deal with some possible (future) action of the hearer's, while a forensic accusation or defence must deal with some (real or counterfactual) past action of the defendant's (*Rhetoric*, 1358b, 1418a).

The fourth parameter—background conditions—corresponds to the 'preparatory conditions' of illocutionary forces. It can be used, for instance, to capture Aristotle's idea that the performance of certain rhetorical acts requires their propositional content to be qualified in specific terms. Thus, in deliberative advices or warnings, the action described by the propositional content should be either expedient [συμφέρον] or harmful [βλαβερός] to the hearer; in forensic defence or accusation, it should be either just [δίκαιος] or unjust [ἄδικος] (*Rhetoric*, 1358b).

Like the mode of achievement, the fifth parameter—sincerity conditions—is common to both illocutionary forces and discourse goals. In sum, among the six components of an illocutionary force (illocutionary point, mode of achievement, propositional content conditions, preparatory conditions, sincerity conditions, degree of strength), only one—the degree of strength—does not have any counterpart in a 'discourse goal'; but, in fact, it does not seem unreasonable to think that, in some cases at least, booing differs from protesting in function of their respective degree of strength. Consequently, one may wonder why 'discourse goals' should not be reduced to 'discursive forces'.

According to Searle and Vanderveken, $IA$s have the logical form '$F(p)$', where '$F$' is an illocutionary force and '$p$' a propositional content. This logical form determines both the conditions of success and the conditions of satisfaction of each $IA$. The 'discursive goal' determines the conditions of success of each $DA$ in a similar way. But, in Vanderveken's view, the satisfaction of a $DA$ only depends on the satisfaction of certain subordinate 'master' $IA$s, which have the same $DOF$ (hence, conditions of satisfaction of the same kind) as the whole $DA$. Another option, favoured by text linguistics (see, e.g., Kintsch & van Dijk 1978; van Dijk & Kintsch 1983), consists in attributing to each $DA$ a (macro)-propositional content that encapsulates its theme or topic: e.g. the propositional content which describes the possible (future) expedient or harmful action the hearer is advised to perform, or warned not to perform (in the deliberative genre); the propositional content which describes the past (real or counterfactual) action that is claimed to have been unjustly performed by the defendant, or not to have been (unjustly) performed by the defendant (in the forensic genre).

In the following, I will assume that $IA$s, $DA$s, and $PA$s have similar logical forms, viz. '$F(p)$', '$f(p)$' and '$\Phi(p)$', where '$F$', '$f$' and '$\Phi$' are an illocutionary force, a discursive force, and a perlocutionary force, respectively.[6] This will allow me to compare the conditions of success and conditions of satisfaction of these three types of linguistic acts.

[6] According to Cerf (1969: 354),

[Austin] disallows that 'he performed a perlocutionary act' and 'his utterance had a perlocutionary force' are mutually substitutable. In fact, I do not remember him ever using 'perlocutionary force'. Austin reserves the term 'force' rather arbitrarily, it would seem, for illocutionary acts.

### 10.2.3 On the success of *IA*s, *PA*s, and *DA*s

When successfully performed by the speaker (in short, $S$) in the presence of the hearer (in short, $H$),[7] both *IA*s and *PA*s cause $H$ to entertain a certain mental state (a belief, an intention, some emotive state, etc.). More precisely, successful *IA*s cause $H$ to recognize $S$'s illocutionary intention. According to a commonly held view (Bach & Harnish 1979: 12-16; Grice 1989; Searle 1983; Sperber & Wilson 1995; Strawson 1969), this entails that a higher-order (communicative) intention of $S$'s is satisfied — or, in other words, that this higher-order intention Intentionally causes its own realization; thus, $S$'s illocutionary intention is necessarily 'overt.'[8] For the sake of simplicity, we can reduce $H$'s recognition of $S$'s illocutionary intention to a second-order belief, entertained by $H$, which bears on the existence and Intentional content of $S$'s illocutionary intention. For instance, if $S$ successfully performs an order '$F(p)$', and thus entertains the corresponding illocutionary intention '$I_S$ ($S$ attempts to get $H$ to perform the action described by $p$)', $H$ will entertain a belief of the form '$B_H(I_S$ ($S$ attempts to get $H$ to perform the action described by $p$))'.

By contrast, not all successful *PA*s cause $H$ to recognize $S$'s perlocutionary intention. No higher-order (communicative) intention of $S$'s has to be satisfied; thus, $S$'s perlocutionary intention may be 'covert' (Bach & Harnish 1979: 81-83; Crosby 1990: 70). This difference between *IA*s and *PA*s is shown by the following data (see Van Hecke 2001: 144-145):[9]

(20) ??? I told him that Peter was wrong, but I did not intend him to realize that I / someone had told him that Peter was wrong.

(21) ??? I ordered him to go to the station, but I did not intend him to realize that I / someone had ordered him to go to the station.

(22) I convinced him of the fact that Peter was wrong, but I did not intend him to realize that I / someone had convinced him of the fact that Peter was wrong.

(23) I persuaded him to go to the station, but I did not intend him to realize that I / someone had persuaded him to go to the station.

On the other hand, the successful performance of an *IA* '$F(p)$' does not entail the existence of any first-order mental state of $H$'s which would bear on the state of affairs described by $p$: not all successful assertions cause $H$ to entertain the first-order belief '$B_H(p)$'; not all successful orders cause $H$ to entertain the first-order intention '$I_H(p)$',

[7] Some expressive *IA*s do not need an audience in order to be successfully performed (Dominicy & Franken 2001). Such intentionally audienceless performances should be distinguished from the cases where $S$ either fails to successfully perform the *IA* at hand (because, e.g., s/he does not speak loud enough; see Alston 1991: 59; Searle 1991: 99-100) or simply pretends to perform it (as in Bennett's Andy Capp example; see Bennett 1991: 6-7; Searle 1979).

[8] In such a perspective, insinuation can be viewed either as a self-defeating *IA* (Vendler 1972: 207-209) or as a non-illocutionary act (Strawson 1969: 394).

[9] I have introduced the *I / someone* alternation in order to exclude the readings where the speaker only wants to conceal his/her identity. I guess some readers, at least, will have misgivings about example (22). Personally, I do not quite know if I accept or reject its French counterpart. I suspect that, on this point, everyday use may conflict with the normative distinction between 'conviction' and 'persuasion' (see Perelman & Olbrechts-Tyteca 1969: 26-31). Jackendoff (1985) and Wierzbicka (1987: 65-66) disagree on the acceptability of the 'convince to $V$' construction.

etc. (see my footnote 12). But the successful performance of a $PA$ '$\Phi(p)$' entails the existence of a first-order mental state of $H$'s which bears on the state of affairs described by $p$: all successful acts of convincing $H$ of $p$ cause $H$ to entertain the first-order belief '$B_H(p)$'; all successful acts of persuading $H$ to perform the action described by $p$ cause $H$ to entertain the first-order intention '$I_H(p)$', etc.[10] This difference between $IA$s and $PA$s is shown by the following data:

(24) Even after I told him that Peter was wrong, he did not believe that Peter was wrong.

(25) Even after I ordered him to go to the station, he did not intend to go to the station.

(26) ??? Even after I convinced him of the fact that Peter was wrong, he did not believe that Peter was wrong.

(27) ??? Even after I persuaded him to go to the station, he did not intend to go to the station.

$DA$s behave like $IA$s at this level:

(28) ??? I encouraged / incited her (in a few seconds) to apply for this job, but I did not intend her to realize that I / someone had encouraged / incited her to apply for this job.

(29) ??? I warned him (in a few seconds) against publishing this paper, but I did not intend him to realize that I / someone had warned him against publishing this paper.

(30) Even after I encouraged / incited her (in a few seconds) to apply for this job, she did not intend to apply for this job.

(31) Even after I warned him (in a few seconds) against publishing this paper, he intended to publish this paper.

### 10.2.4 On the satisfaction of $IA$s, $PA$s, and $DA$s

In Speech Act Theory, the conditions of satisfaction of an $IA$ are determined by the $DOF$ associated with its illocutionary point. An assertive $IA$ '$F(p)$' is satisfied iff $p$ is true; a directive or commissive $IA$ '$F(p)$' is satisfied iff it Intentionally causes the hearer to perform the action described by $p$. Consequently, a directive or commissive $IA$ is successfully performed if it is satisfied, while for assertive $IA$s, satisfaction does not entail successful performance. Given their two-way $DOF$, declarative $IA$s are satisfied iff they are successfully performed. Finally, Searle and Vanderveken claim, somewhat hesitantly, that expressive $IA$s do not have any conditions of satisfaction (see Franken & Dominicy 2001; Van Hecke 2001).

Contrary to $IA$s, $PA$s cannot be true or false, obeyed or disobeyed, kept or broken, etc. Indeed, as shown by examples (26-27), the successful performance of a $PA$ entails its satisfaction, and conversely. At this level, $PA$s prove comparable to declaratives, i.e. to $IA$s that create states of affairs by virtue of their successful performance only. So

[10] Obviously, $H$ may change his/her mind afterwards, or fail to realize his/her intention (Kurzon 1998: 578; *pace* Gaines 1979: 210).

the question is what kind of states of affairs *PA*s produce when successfully performed. Examples (26-27) suggest that any *PA* Intentionally causes a first-order mental state of *H*'s, i.e. triggers a mental state change in *H*'s mind. This change may be either an event which simply happens to *H*—like, e.g., an event of coming to believe (caused by a *PA* of making believe) or an event of becoming frightened (caused by a *PA* of frigthening)—, or a mental act performed by *H* — like, e.g., an act of assenting (caused by a *PA* of convincing of something) or an act of deciding to do something (caused by a *PA* of persuading to do something).[11]

Although the notion of a mental act raises intricate problems (see Proust 2001), examples (32-34) clearly show that the first-order belief or intention Intentionally caused by a successful *PA* of convincing or persuading should result from a mental act of *H*'s:

(32) Mary has a weak character. She let herself be ordered to go to the station. (But she did not intend to go to the station.)

(33) Mary has a weak character. She let herself be convinced of the fact that Peter was wrong. (???But she did not believe that Peter was wrong.)

(34) Mary has a weak character. She let herself be persuaded to apply for this job. (???But she did not intend to apply for this job.)

In (32), Mary's weakness of character shows itself through the fact that she accepted to be ordered — which is, at least, a mental act. But in (33-34), what reveals her weakness is a mental act of assenting or deciding.[12]

For the sake of the argument, I will define the act of assenting as a 'move' to believing (in short, '$MOVE(B(p))$'), and the act of deciding to do something as a 'move' to intending (in short, '$MOVE(I(p))$'). So, any successful *PA* of convincing or persuading Intentionally causes a mental act of 'moving' (see Jackendoff 1985). Schematically:

(35) $CONVINCE(p)$ is successful iff $CONVINCE(p)$ is satisfied iff ($CONVINCE(p)$ causes $MOVE(B(p))$)

(36) $PERSUADE(p)$ is successful iff $PERSUADE(p)$ is satisfied iff ($PERSUADE(p)$ causes $MOVE(I(p))$)

Furthermore, I will assume that the mental active operator '$MOVE(...)$' has the same logical properties as declarative or perlocutionary forces; that is, a mental act of 'moving'

[11] According to Gu (1993, 1994), who appears to be reasoning as if all mental state changes were mental acts,

> perlocution is in fact a transaction involving at least one speech act performed by *S* and one response-act performed by *H*. The relation between the two acts is not causal, but rhetorical in the sense that *S* influences *H* in adopting *S*'s goals. Successful perlocution therefore presupposes rhetorical cooperation between *S* and *H*. (Gu 1994: 189)

I do not understand why cooperation should prove incompatible with causation: common sense allows us to say that, by calling for help from John, Peter caused John to (decide to) help him.

[12] On assent, see De Sousa (1971) and Dennett (1978/81). It is important to recall here that, in classical Speech Act Theory, assertives have a words-to-things *DOF*, so that they cannot cause belief Intentionally. Therefore, if by performing an assertive *IA* '$F(p)$', *S* intentionally causes *H* to entertain the belief '$B(p)$', *S* must have performed a *PA* of the form '$\Phi(p)$'. Moreover, the mental state change by virtue of which *H* comes to believe does not need to take the form of an assent; in Searlean terms, we could say that the cognitive event that underlies this change may occur in the Background (Searle 1983, 1992, 1995).

is successfully performed iff it Intentionally causes the state of affairs described by its propositional content.[13] Schematically:

(37) $MOVE(B(p))$ is successful iff $MOVE(B(p))$ is satisfied iff ($MOVE(B(p))$ causes $B(p)$)

(38) $MOVE(I(p))$ is successful iff $MOVE(I(p))$ is satisfied iff ($MOVE(I(p))$ causes $I(p)$)

From this it follows that any successful *PA* of convincing or persuading Intentionally causes a first-order belief or intention with the same propositional content.

Now, what are the conditions of satisfaction of a *DA*? If *DA*s have a logical form '$f(p)$', similar to that of *IA*s and *PA*s, we expect them to behave, to a certain extent, like *IA*s. For instance, in order for a deliberative advice or warning to be satisfied, successful performance does not suffice: like illocutionary advices or warnings, such *DA*s should Intentionally cause *H* either to perform the action *S* advises him/her to perform, or to perform the action that consists in not performing the action *S* warns him/her not to perform (Eggs 1994: 13-16; Danblon 2001a: 34-35, 2002a: 99-116). If we stop at this point, the conditions of satisfaction of deliberative advices or warnings do not differ from the conditions of satisfaction of their illocutionary counterparts. But the analysis of *PA*s we have just provided allows us to make a clear distinction here, by stating that a deliberative advice or warning of the form '$f(p)$' is satisfied iff it Intentionally causes *H* to perform the action described by *p* through the following causal chain:

(39) $ADVICE/WARNING(p)$ is satisfied iff:
a. $ADVICE/WARNING(p)$ causes $PERSUADE(p)$,

[13]Thus, I claim, with De Sousa (1971: 63-64), that assent entails belief, but not conversely. Dennett's (1978/81: 307-309) opposite view that assent does not entail belief seems to rest on a confusion between assenting, i.e. $MOVE(B(p))$, and deciding to believe, i.e. $MOVE(I(B(p)))$. If we follow Dennett (see also Baier 1985: 70-71), 'akratic' belief consists in the fact that an agent both assents and does not believe, whereas self-deception consists in the fact that an agent both believes and fails to assent. But it is more appropriate to define 'akratic' (dis)belief as the fact, for an agent, to assent (respectively, to refrain from believing) while deciding not to believe (respectively, to believe); schematically:

$$MOVE(B(p)) \text{ and } MOVE(I(not\text{-}B(p)))$$
$$MOVE(not\text{-}B(p)) \text{ and } MOVE(I(B(p)))$$

As for self-deception, I would define it as the fact that an agent both decides to believe and fails to assent:

$$MOVE(I(B(p)) \text{ and } not\text{-}MOVE(B(p))$$

(In my view, 'wishful thinking' does not involve a failure to rationalize a belief (or assent)—as claimed by Davidson (1982: 298, 1985: 142; see Pears 1982: 266-267)—but a failure to rationalize a decision to believe.) Since an agent who indulges in either 'akratic' (dis)belief or self-deception necessarily intends (not) to believe, s/he may try to assent (or to refrain from believing) and/or try (not) to believe, i.e. act in such a way as to 'produce' or 'promote' the belief (or lack of belief) at hand (see Davidson 1985: 145; and his reply to Marcia Cavell, in Hahn 1999: 423). Notice, by the way, that, even if any trying is an action (which some authors doubt; see Hornsby 1980: 33-45; Antoniol 1998: 63-65), we should not conclude, from the fact that an action can be described by means of a 'try (not) to *V*' construction, that the verb '(not-) *V*' itself describes a (potential) action: both trying to assent and assenting are conceivable mental acts; trying to believe is a conceivable mental act, but believing is not (Searle 1991: 298). So that, *pace* Proust (2001), the 'try to' test does not help us very much in identifying mental acts.

thus $PERSUADE(p)$ is satisfied,
thus $PERSUADE(p)$ causes $MOVE(I(p))$,
thus $MOVE(I(p))$ is satisfied,
thus $MOVE(I(p))$ causes $I(p)$; and

b. $I(p)$ is satisfied, thus $I(p)$ causes $p$.

In other words, the satisfaction of a deliberative advice or warning entails the satisfaction (hence, the successful performance) of a *PA* of persuading.

When applying this analytical scheme to forensic accusations or defences, we run into additional difficulties. Aristotle conceived of such *DA*s as 'descriptive' in Vanderveken's sense, i.e. as discursive counterparts of assertive *IA*s (Eggs 1994: 13-16; Danblon 2001a: 34-35, 2002a: 72-99). However, whereas an assertive *IA* is satisfied as soon as its propositional content is true, it seems necessary, for a *DA* of accusing or defending to be satisfied, that *H* perform some assertive *IA* with the same propositional content.[14] Therefore, I propose the following clause:

(40) $ACCUSE/DEFEND(p)$ is satisfied iff:

a. $ACCUSE/DEFEND(p)$ causes $CONVINCE(p)$,
thus $CONVINCE(p)$ is satisfied,
thus $CONVINCE(p)$ causes $MOVE(B(p))$,
thus $MOVE(B(p))$ is satisfied,
thus $MOVE(B(p))$ causes $B(p)$; and

b. $B(p)$ causes $I(ASSERT(p))$; and

c. $I(ASSERT(p))$ is satisfied, thus $I(ASSERT(p))$ causes $ASSERT(p)$.

In such a perspective, forensic interactions are intrinsically more complex than deliberative interactions, in that they involve a causal link between a belief of *H*'s and *H*'s successful performance of the corresponding assertive *IA*.

One could object to my approach that *IA*s and *DA*s, while being 'perlocutionary causes', cannot bring about *PA*s, but only 'perlocutionary effects': 'my telling you that there is a spider on your lap does not cause my frightening you, rather it causes you to be frightened' (Davis 1980: 39-40). This point has been made in more general terms by Stoutland (1968: 471-472):

> since the intrinsic result of turning the switch is different from the intrinsic result of opening the safe, it is possible that [the agent] may have turned the switch without opening the safe. But they are not factually or temporally distinct, and they cannot, therefore, by related by causality.

In fact, we should distinguish here between events and their description in actional terms (Davidson 1980; Dominicy 2005). Suppose a burglar opens the safe by turning the switch (see Figure 1).

[14] As shown by Danblon (2002a: 87-92, 2002b, 2004a), the Aristotelian approach to forensic *DA*s does not capture the fact that their satisfaction requires the jury and/or the judge to perform a declarative *IA*, by which a new social fact comes into existence (Searle 1995).

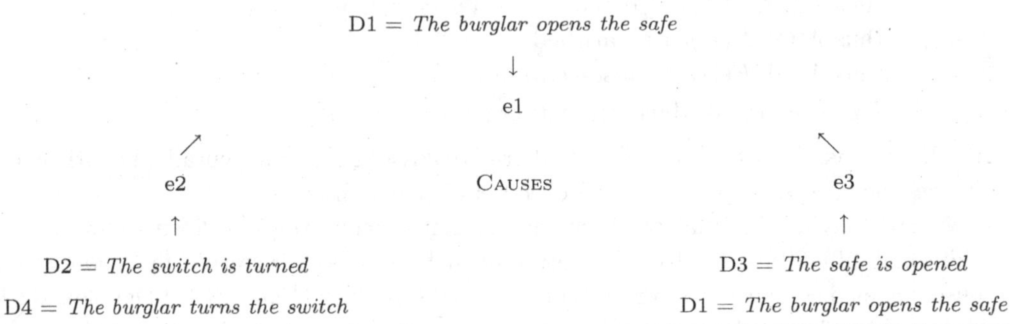


FIGURE 1

The sentence *The burglar opens the safe* provides an actional description D1 of the complex event e1 consisting of the whole causal chain going from the switch being turned to the safe being opened. The sentence *The switch is turned* provides a (static) description D2 of the event e2 (intrinsically) resulting from the act of turning the switch, while the sentence *The safe is opened* provides a (static) description D3 of the event e3 (intrinsically) resulting from the act of opening the safe. Given that the relation between an act and its 'result' is internal (von Wright 1963: 39-41; Garver 1984), the sentence *The burglar turns the switch* provides an alternative (actional) description D4 of e2, while D1 = *The burglar opens the safe* is an alternative (actional) description of e3. Indeed, the act of turning the switch (resp. of opening the safe) is successfully performed iff it is satisfied, i.e. iff the turn is switched (resp. the safe is opened). By contrast, the (intrinsic) result of the act of opening the safe is but a 'consequence' of the act of turning the switch (see von Wright 1963: 39-41; Stoutland 1968: 471-472; Garver 1984; Neuberg 1993: 37). In other words, the relation between an act, and an intended or unintended consequence of it, is external: it is possible for the act of turning the switch to be both successful and satisfied while the safe remains unopened. In short, the sentence *The burglar opens the safe* may be used to describe (actionally) either e1 or e3; but when it is connected in causal terms to an actional description of e2, it should receive the 'narrow' interpretation where it describes e3 only. This approach accounts for examples like:

(41) The burglar opened the safe because s/he turned the switch and not because s/he dialled Peter's secret code.

Suppose, now, that Peter persuades Mary to apply for a job by telling her that Jane will apply (see Figure 2). Again, the sentence *Peter persuades Mary to apply for the job* may be used to describe (actionally) either e1 or e3; but when it is connected in causal terms to an actional description of e2, it should receive the 'narrow' interpretation where it describes e3 only, as shown by example (42):

(42) Peter persuaded Mary to apply for this job because he told her that Jane would apply, and not because he told her that she would get a good wage.

D1 = *Peter persuades Mary to...*

↓

e1

↗ ↖

e2 CAUSES e3

↑ ↑

D2 = *Mary is told that...* D3 = *Mary is persuaded to...*

D4 = *Peter tells Mary that...* D1 = *Peter persuades Mary to...*

FIGURE 2

### 10.2.5 A tentative definition of an *ARA*

Our description of deliberative and forensic *DA*s allows us to formulate a tentative definition of an *ARA*: an *ARA* is a *DA* of the form '$f(p)$' whose satisfaction entails the satisfaction (hence, the successful performance) of a *PA* of the form '$\Phi(p)$' such that the perlocutionary intention of the form '$I_S(\Phi(p))$' is 'overt', which means that $S$ entertains a second-order communicative intention of the form '$I_S(B_H(I_S(\Phi(p))))$'.

The 'overtness' of the perlocutionary intention results from the fact, mentioned above, that the conditions of success of *ARA*s include a mode of achievement which constrains the speaker to ground, in some definite way, the *DA* s/he is performing.

Deliberative *ARA*s should be 'paradigmatically' grounded; i.e., the advice or warning performed should occur as the conclusion of at least one 'example' or 'paradigm' that has one of the following two forms:

(43) $ASSERT(q)$, where $q$ describes some past action of some agent, and
$ASSERT(q$ was expedient to its agent), and
$ASSERT(q$ is analogous to $p)$, where $p$ describes a possible (future) action of $H$'s

---

Therefore, $ASSERT(p$ would be expedient to $H)$

---

Therefore, $ADVICE(p)$

(44) $ASSERT(q)$, where $q$ describes some past action of some agent, and
$ASSERT(q$ was harmful to its agent)
thus, $ASSERT($*not*-$q$ would have been expedient to its agent), and
$ASSERT(q$ is analogous to $p)$, where $p$ describes a possible (future) action of $H$'s
thus, $ASSERT($*not*-$q$ is analogous to *not*-$p)$

---

Therefore, $ASSERT(p$ would be harmful to $H)$
thus, $ASSERT($*not*-$p$ would be expedient to $H)$

---

Therefore, $WARNING(p)$, i.e. $ADVICE($*not*-$p)$

Forensic *ARAs* should be 'enthymematically' grounded; i.e., the accusation or defence performed should occur as the conclusion of at least one enthymeme that has one of the following two forms:[15]

(45) $ASSERT(q)$, and
$ASSERT(W)$, where $W$ is some warrant of the form 'If $q$, then ($p$ and $p$ is unjust)', where $p$ describes some (real or counterfactual) past action of the defendant's

---

Therefore, $ASSERT$($p$ and $p$ is unjust) unless $r$, where $r$ is some rebuttal such that there is a warrant $W'$ = 'If $q$ and $r$, then (either *not-p* or $p$ is just)'

---

Therefore, $ACCUSE(p')$, where $p' = p$, or $p'$ provides an alternative description of the same (real) past action of the defendant

(46) $ASSERT(q)$
$ASSERT(W)$, where $W$ is some warrant of the form 'If $q$, then (either *not-p* or $p$ is just)', where $p$ describes some (real or counterfactual) past action of the defendant's

---

Therefore, $ASSERT$ (either *not-p* or $p$ is just) unless $r$, where $r$ is some rebuttal such that there is a warrant $W'$ = 'If $q$ and $r$, then ($p$ and $p$ is unjust)'

---

Therefore, $DEFEND(p')$, where $p'$ = *not-p*, or $p'$ provides an alternative description of the same (real) past action of the defendant

Again, forensic arguments prove more complex than deliberative arguments, in that their conclusion frequently involves a re-description of the (real) past action for which the defendant may have to answer (see Danblon 2002a: 72-99, 2002b, 2004a).

Anyway, the speaker who successfully performs an *ARA* gives at least one of the reasons s/he has for performing this very *ARA*, and by doing so, s/he provides the hearer with at least one reason for assenting or for deciding to act.[16] Consequently, if an *ARA* is successful, the corresponding *PA* must be Intentionally caused by an 'overt' perlocutionary intention.

## 10.3 Is praise or blame an *ARA*?

### 10.3.1 Amplification as an 'argument'

Let us suppose, as a first step, that praise and blame are *ARAs*. As epideictic speeches typically deal with some (real) past action of some agent,[17] we may include this feature among the thematic conditions of the corresponding discursive forces. We can also

[15] Technically speaking, enthymemes exhibit a Toulminian deductive structure with two premises ('data' and 'warrant') and a 'claim'. The 'force' or 'strength' of the claim is inversely proportional to the number of 'rebuttals' whose negation cannot be asserted; it follows that 'enthymematic' reasoning is non-monotonic (see Toulmin 1958; Hempel 1965; Danblon 2002a: 36-37; Dominicy 1993, 2002a, 2006; Dominicy, Michaux & Kreutz 2004).

[16] In this sense, the satisfaction of an *ARA* involves some form of rhetorical cooperation, as argued by Gu (1993, 1994).

[17] According to Aristotle (*Rhetoric*, 1358b),

express the fact that the ethical valuation of the action at hand is undebatable by introducing the preparatory condition that this action is good (ethically right) or bad (ethically wrong). Furthermore, we will try to encapsulate, under the mode of achievement of both praise and blame, the Aristotelian requirement that epideictic *DA*s should be grounded on 'amplification' [αὔξησις] (*Rhetoric*, 1368a, 1391b, 1417b). Amplification allows the praising speaker to 'show' how some good action is noble (i.e. beautiful; καλός); it allows the blaming speaker to 'show' how some bad action is base (i.e. ugly; αἰσχρός) (*Rhetoric*, 1358b, 1366a).

Strangely enough, Aristotle never made the slightest attempt to define amplification in general terms. I have argued elsewhere (Dominicy 1995, 1996, 2002a) that he was simply unable to provide such a definition. Indeed, whereas examples and enthymemes have dialectical counterparts—viz. induction and the dialectical syllogism (*Rhetoric*, 1356b, 1357b, 1394a)[18]—, amplification seems to rely on discursive and cognitive strategies that commonly operate in poetic diction (see Dominicy 1994; Michaux & Dominicy 2001). Sure, I will look at the examples Aristotle gives us to illustrate the different ways of 'amplifying' good actions of some agent $A$ (see *Rhetoric*, 1368a), we can identify three possible schemes:

(47) a. 'The agent is the only one (among the few ones) who performed the action'

b. $ASSERT(p)$, where $p$ describes some (real) good action of $A$'s
$ASSERT(n$ agents performed the action described by $p)$

---

$p$ is beautiful in the degree $n$, where 1 is the upper bound of the scale

(48) a. 'The agent is the first one (or among the first ones) who performed the action'

b. $ASSERT(p)$, where $p$ describes some (real) good action of $A$'s
$ASSERT(n$ agents performed the action described by $p$ before $A$ did)

---

$p$ is beautiful in the degree $n{+}1$, where 1 is the upper bound of the scale

(49) a. 'The agent contributed to the performance of the action in a more significant way than anyone else (than most other agents)'

b. $ASSERT(p)$, where $p$ describes some (real) good action of $A$'s

> the epideictic orator is, properly speaking, concerned with the present, since all men praise or blame in view of the state ot things existing at the time, though they often find it useful also to recall the past and to make guesses at the future.

For a tentative interpretation of this puzzling statement, see Dominicy (1995).

[18] In fact, while rhetorical enthymemes and dialectical syllogisms have the same underlying Toulminian form, rhetorical examples differ from dialectical induction on a crucial aspect (see Danblon 2002a: 99-118, 194-230, 2004b; Dominicy 2002a), which can be captured by von Wright's (1951: 14, 83) distinction between 'induction of the first order' and 'induction of the second order'. Examples lead to 'predictions':

> from the propositions that something has been the case under certain conditions and that the conditions are repeated we infer, as we say, the proposition that the same thing will be the case again. (von Wright 1951: 14)

Induction leads to 'theories (laws)':

> from the information that something has been the case under certain conditions we anticipate that, *if* the same conditions are repeated, *then* the same thing will be the case again. (von Wright 1951: 14)

In Carnap's logic of first-order induction, the degree of confirmation of a law always equals 0 (see Carnap 1950; Popper 1963).

$ASSERT$(*A* contributed to the performance of the action described by *p* in a degree *n*), where 1 is the upper bound of the scale

---

*p* is beautiful in the degree *n*, where 1 is the upper bound of the scale

But, in contradistinction to 'paradigmatic' or 'enthymematic' arguments, such semi-formal reconstructions do not to fit in with any (classical or non-classical) inferential structure. If arguments of the forms (47-49) could be integrated within the formal system of the *Topics*, we should apply to them the inferential rule which says that 'if two things create a certain quality, then that which creates it in a greater degree, possesses it in a greater degree' (*Topics*, 119a). So, if the action is nobler / more beautiful when *A* was the first one to perform it than when *A* was the fifth one to perform it, then the circumstance consisting in the fact that *A* was the first one to perform the action should be—*simpliciter*—nobler / more beaufiful than the circumstance consisting in the fact that *A* was the fifth one to perform it. This conclusion is obviously wrong: the circumstance consisting in the fact that Hitler was the first one to plan a holocaust of Jewish people cannot reasonably be said to have the highest degree of nobleness or beauty (see Dominicy 2002a).

### 10.3.2 The satisfaction of praise and blame

In an earlier paper (Franken & Dominicy 2001), it was suggested that epideictic *DA*s have the same *DOF* as expressive *IA*s. As pointed out above, this would entail, for Vanderveken, that such *DA*s have no conditions of satisfaction. However, we have just seen that the conditions of satisfaction of a deliberative or descriptive *DA* differ from those of the corresponding (directive-commissive or assertive) *IA*s. So, it is at least conceivable that expressive *DA*s have non-empty conditions of satisfaction, which would involve the successful performance and satisfaction of a *PA*.

Suppose, for instance, that any successful performance of an expressive *DA* of praise or blame causes *H* to entertain some emotive mental state: pride or shame, admiration or contempt (see Kreutz 2001). The occurrence of this mental state could result from the successful performance (and the satisfaction) of a *PA* of making *H* feel pride or shame, admiration or contempt. On the other hand, we could assume that, in order to be satisfied, an expressive *DA* of praise or blame should cause some disposition to act in *H*'s mind; this disposition to act would be caused, in turn, by the mental state caused by the successful performance (and the satisfaction) of the *PA*: pride and admiration, shame and contempt, induce *H* to act in certain ways, provided certain conditions are met.

Does this mean that praise and blame are plausible *ARA*s? I have defined an *ARA* as a *DA* whose satisfaction entails the satisfaction (hence, the successful performance) of a *PA* such that the corresponding perlocutionary intention is 'overt'. This 'overtness' depends both on the mode of achievement of the *DA*, and on the conditions of satisfaction of the *PA* (which should Intentionally cause a mental act of *H*'s): *H* has a reason for assenting or for deciding to act, because *S* has given a reason for performing his/her own *DA*. In the case of praise or blame, the 'overtness' of the *PA* does not seem to be ensured, nor even imperative: first, amplification cannot be characterized in (classical or non-classical) inferential terms; second, and more significantly, we need no reason for entertaining emotive mental states. In sum, the fact that the epideictic speaker gives no true reason for performing his/her expressive $DA$ could be linked to the fact that the epideictic hearer does not perform any mental act.

### 10.3.3 Causes and reasons

Suppose, now, I am the hearer $H$ of an expressive $DA$ of blame that deals with the actions performed by Nazis during World War II. The epideictic speaker $S$ successfully performs his/her $DA$, and thus succeeds in 'amplifying', i.e. in 'showing' the baseness or ugliness of those actions. Due to his/her successful performance of the corresponding $PA$, I feel both shame and contempt—which induces me to act in a determined way when I am facing some supporter of Hitler's regime. If my disposition to act were caused by the epideictic $DA$ only, would I act without no reason at all? Would I, under this hypothesis, be an irrational agent whose actions, while being caused, could not be rationalized?

Aristotle (*Rhetoric*, 1368a, 1414a) tried to escape this disturbing conclusion by assuming that any action caused by the efficaciousness of an epideictic $DA$ can be Intentionally caused by a deliberative $ARA$.[19] That is: if you want to rationalize an action induced by the disposition to act which is Intentionally caused by an expressive $DA$ of praise or blame, reconstruct a deliberative advice or warning that will provide you with a reason for acting. But this way out does not help us to bridge the gap between the two 'arguments' used, viz. an amplification and an example, respectively. Even if some circumstance—e.g. the fact that the fireman was the first and only one to enter the building on fire—does 'add' nobleness or beauty to the action, this does not mean that the action was particularly expedient; on the contrary, it may happen (and it frequently happens) that the fireman would have been better advised to wait for some help.

In fact, the discrepancy between Aristotle's rationalizing programme and his empirical description of praise and blame goes even farther. When praising,

> we must assert coincidences [συμπτώματα] and accidents [τύχη] to have been chosen. Produce a number of good actions, all of the same kind, and people will think that they are signs of excellence [virtue] and choice. (*Rhetoric*, 1367b)

Thus, 'if a man has often achieved the same success, we must mention this; that is a strong point; he himself, and not luck [τύχη], will be given the credit' (*Rhetoric*, 1368a). I have argued in my earlier papers (Dominicy 1995, 1996, 2001, 2002a) that this rhetorical strategy blurs the boundary between intentional and non-intentional descriptions of human actions: unintended and even uncontrollable consequences will be integrated, along truly intentional features, in descriptions that trigger the appropriate emotions and disposition to act.[20] Interestingly enough, researchers in social psychology (see e.g. Lerner 1980; Walster 1966) have observed that the risk, for an agent, of incurring blame increases in proportion to the harm done by his/her action, independently of the

---

[19] As recalled by Pernot (1993: 710-724), Greek rhetoric sometimes distinguished between 'symbouleutic' (deliberative) advices or warnings, and 'parenetic' (epideictic) advices or warnings. Perhaps we may reduce the latter to those $PA$s that cause the hearer to entertain a specific disposition to act (on this technical point, see Danblon 1999, 2001a: 35-40; Franken & Dominicy 2001: 103-106).

[20] See also *Physics*, 195b; *Poetics*, 52a (Dominicy 2001: 68-71; Sorabji 1980).

intentions s/he may have entertained and the control s/he may have been able to exert on the results or consequences at hand.[21] A more disturbing example, which fascinated Jean Paulhan (see Dominicy 1995, 1996, 2001, 2002a), appears in headings frequently used by French-speaking popular tabloids when reporting a foul crime: 'Assassin pour cinq Euros', literally 'Murderer for five Euros'. Generally, what happened in reality is that someone unintentionally committed a murder when attempting to steal some important amount of money, or something valuable. But the heading integrates under one and the same description not only the unintentional murder, but also the unintentionally derisory result of the robbery. In other words, the fact that the robbery (committed with unintentional lethal violence) only produced a derisory gain appears as a circumstance that 'adds' baseness or ugliness to a bad action: as pointed out by Paulhan, the event is described as if the delinquent knew beforehand that s/he would make a derisory gain and decided nonetheless to murder and rob.[22] Obviously, this does not mean that a murder and robbery that would produce a significant gain would have to be evaluated as less harmful—or, even worse, as more expedient—in a reconstructed warning or advice which would, in itself, rationalize actions of this sort. Furthermore, in forensic contexts, the counsel for the defence might emphasize the fact that the delinquent made a derisory gain only, in order to suggest that s/he did not plan his/her murder, and thus in order to water down the unjust action performed; and the jury or the judge might prove sensitive to this argument.[23] In sum, deliberative and forensic *ARA*s, which provide the hearer with reasons to assent or to decide, seem to have nothing in common with such apparently irrational varieties of blame.

## 10.4 The asymmetry of praise and blame

### 10.4.1 Prudence, deliberation, and the ethical virtues

From an ethical point of view, each agent can be defined as the conjunction of a series of (ethical) virtues or vices (Dominicy 2001). Each (ethical) virtue or vice is a disposition to choose [ἕξις προαιρετική] that involves a disposition to act accordingly [ὄρεξις προαιρετική] which, in turn, causes the agent to act in a certain way as soon as certain conditions are met, unless 'akrasia' (or 'weakness of the will') impedes that causation from taking place (see, on this question, Davidson 1980, 1982, 1985; Ogien 1993).

While each virtue is unique, an agent may lack it either because s/he dispositionally tends to indulge in an 'excess' or because s/he dispositionally tends to indulge in a 'defect' or 'deficiency'. Thus, each virtue is a 'middle', a 'mean' or an 'intermedi-

[21] This tendency accounts for the most common use of the verbe *blame* in English:

> in accusing, the speaker is concerned with somebody's bad action as such (not necessarily because of this action's bad results); whereas in blaming, the speaker is concerned with somebody's bad action only in so far as this action is responsible for further 'bad effects'. Thus, one can accuse somebody of lying (because lying is generally regarded as bad), but one cannot blame somebody for lying; one can, on the other hand, blame someone's (inept) lying as a cause of public discontent, failure to win the elections, etc. (Wierzbicka 1987: 153)

[22] The same kind of retrospection is at work in those evaluations that involve what has been called (good or bad) 'moral luck' (Nagel 1979; Williams 1981; Robinson 2002).

[23] The prosecution will counter this argument by sticking to the delinquent's wishes and intentions: among 'the states of mind in which men do wrong to others', Aristotle mentions the feeling 'that the gain to be got by wrong-doing is great' (*Rhetoric*, 1372).

ate' between two 'extremes': for instance, courage is the middle, rashness the excess, and cowardice the defect or deficiency; liberality the middle, prodigality the excess, and meanness the defect or deficiency; temperance (or moderation) the middle, self-indulgence (or intemperance) the excess, and insensibility the defect or deficiency; and so on (see the ethical treatises; Dominicy 2002b). Such triadic clusters allow us to define ethical 'characters' [ἦθος]: the Brave, the Rash, the Coward; the Liberal, the Prodigal, the Mean; the Moderate, the Intemperate, the Insensible; and so on.

Since an ethical virtue or vice is a disposition to choose (and a disposition to act) in a specific set of situations, agents cannot be said to be virtuous or vicious *simpliciter*, unless some superordinate virtue or vice rules out certain conjunctions of subordinate (ethical) virtues or vices. In the Aristotelian system, the (intellectual) virtue of 'prudence' or pratical wisdom [φρόνησις] ensures that, whenever dealing with a given situation, the (wo)man who may be called 'virtuous' *simpliciter* makes the choice (and thus entertains the disposition to act) which conforms to the ethical virtue applying to the situation at hand. Therefore, Aristotle defines the notion of an ethical virtue by referring to an intellectual 'character'—the Prudent [φρόνιμος] (see Aubenque 1997):

> Excellence [i.e. ethical virtue] is a state concerned with choice [i.e. a disposition to choose], lying in a mean relative to us, this being determined by reason and in the way in which the man of practical wisdom [i.e. the Prudent] would determine it. (*Nicomachean Ethics*, 1106b)

In short, if a (wo)man is prudent, s/he is brave, liberal, moderate, etc. 'Men are good in one way, but bad in many' (*Nicomachean Ethics*, 1106b) not only because vice can consist in an excess or a defect (a deficiency), but also because being vicious *simpliciter* amounts to satisfying a disjunction of the different possible lacks of an ethical virtue, while being virtuous *simpliciter* amounts to being prudent, i.e. to satisfying the unique conjunction of ethical virtues.

The intellectual virtue of prudence can be described as a disposition to deliberate reasonably on ethical issues, which makes the prudent (wo)man able to act, whenever necessary, in conformity with the requirements of ethical virtues. So, this disposition to deliberate involves a disposition to choose that involves, in turn, a disposition to act. Aristotle clearly modelled inner deliberation on deliberative oratory, so that the same terms of 'prudence' [φρόνησις] and 'prudent' [φρόνιμος] apply both to the intellectual component of virtuous action and to the rhetorical 'ethos' — i.e. the social and public image — of the speaker (*Rhetoric*, 1356a, 1366a-b, 1378a; see Amossy 1999). In other words, he was inclined to consider prudence as the disposition to advise or warn oneself on a 'paradigmatic' ground, i.e. to provide oneself with ethical reasons for acting (Dominicy 2001: 59 footnote 10). This parallel between ethical deliberation and political deliberation in the assembly explains why he claimed prudence to be a privilege of experienced men, to which young people cannot access (*Nicomachean Ethics*, 1142a; *Rhetoric*, 1388b-1390b; *Topics*, 117a). It also explains why he considered virtuous and vicious actions to be (respectively) expedient and harmful to their agent, i.e. to his/her ethical happiness [εὐδαιμονία].[24]

[24]On εὐδαιμονία, see *Rhetoric*, 1360b, and the ethical treatises (Austin 1970; Dominicy 2001). As

### 10.4.2 Can we praise Prudence or the Prudent?

When he attempts to rationalize epideictic *DA*s, Aristotle equates 'the noble (or beauty) and the base (or ugliness)' with virtue and vice, respectively (*Rhetoric*, 1366a). If an agent acts virtuously or viciously, s/he deserves praise or blame, respectively; and the disposition to act introduced, into the hearer's mind, by the *DA* of praise or blame determines, in specific contexts, actions of the hearer's which a deliberative speaker could Intentionally cause by a *DA* of advice or warning, and thus by providing the hearer with reasons for acting formulated in terms of expediency or harmfulness — that is, in terms of prudence. One would expect, in such a perspective, prudent agents to deserve praise. But, surprisingly enough, Aristotle's wavers on this issue (see Dominicy 2001). In the *Magna Moralia* (1185b),[25] it is claimed that, while

> temperance, justice, courage, and such other states [i.e. dispositions] of character as are held to be praiseworthy ... no one is praised for being (theoretically) wise [σοφός] or for being prudent [practically wise; φρόνιμος].

Yet, in a later development of the same work (1197a), we are told that 'prudent men are praiseworthy'.

One could solve this literal contradiction by assuming that prudence deserves praise insofar as it gives rise to ethical virtues; so that it would be impossible to praise somebody for being prudent only, i.e. abstracting away from any ethical virtue. However, this interpretive move cannot account for what Aristotle has to say on 'ethical narration' in epideictic oratory, i.e. on that kind of narration that depicts the 'ethos' of the praised or blamed agent: when narrating in an epideictic *DA* of praise, he says,

> do not let the agent's words seem inspired so much by intelligence [διανοία] as by (ethical) choice: e.g. 'I willed this; aye, it was my (ethical) choice; true, I gained nothing by it, still it is better thus'. For the other way shows prudence [are words of a Prudent; φρόνιμος], but this shows good character [are words of a Good Man; ἀγαθός]; prudence making us go after what is useful, and good character after what is noble [beautiful]. (*Rhetoric*, 1417a)

If prudence does not aim at nobleness or beauty, while praise 'shows' the nobleness or beauty of some good action, then prudence is not praiseworthy—even though the actions inspired by it cannot be distinguished, in rational terms, from those actions

---

pointed out by Danblon (2002a: 200-202, 2004a), every deliberative orator is a member of the political assembly s/he is trying to persuade, so that one can describe the successive turn-takings of the debate as functional dissociations between two aspects of each member of the assembly, considered either as a speaker or as a hearer belonging to the audience. If inner deliberation is modelled on political deliberation, the ultimate end of ethics—ethical happiness—plays the same role as the public good. The deliberative speaker $S$ evaluates some possible (future) action of the audience, including $S$, as (un)desirable to $S$ because s/he thinks it to be (un)desirable for (expedient / harmful to) the audience, including $S$. The ethical agent $A$ evaluates some possible (future) action of $A$'s as (un)desirable to $A$ because s/he thinks it to be (un)desirable for (expedient / harmful to) $A$. Altruism is ensured by the fact that the Prudent advises or warns rightly in both public and inner deliberation. For an analysis of altruistic acts in terms of 'desirability to' versus 'desirability for', see Danblon (2001b); Dominicy & Franken (2001).

[25] I am aware of the fact that the authenticity of the *Magna Moralia* is doubted by most specialists. But, due to its very clumsiness and naïveté, this treatise sometimes sheds a crude light on the internal inconsistencies of Aristotle's ethical doctrine.

that really deserve praise.

We are thus coming back to our dilemma concerning reasons and causes. Any *DA* of praise (or blame) must deal with a good (or bad) action, thus with an action the agent had a reason (or had no reason) for performing.[26] But praise and blame also require, for the action at hand to be noble or base, that it be caused by a spontaneous (ethical) disposition to act, i.e. a disposition to act whose realization in a certain context did not result from a prudent deliberation. Consequently, a potential conflict appears, in the case of praise, between deliberative goodness and spontaneous nobleness. This is surely the reason why some circumstances 'add' nobleness or beauty to a good action, in spite of the fact that this very aspect of the agent's behaviour escapes any rationalizing strategy. We consider it noble and beautiful for a fireman to be the first and only one to enter a building on fire; but we think it possible, at the same time, that a prudent man would not have acted that way—so that we have no more reasons for admiring (or for being proud of) the fireman than the fireman had to enter the building the way he did.[27]

The Aristotelian analysis of courage provides us with a striking illustration of this dilemma (Dominicy 2001: 64-66; see also Garver 1984: 481-482). While defining the true virtue of courage, Aristotle endeavours to distinguish it from different kinds of dispositions to act that look like it while failing to meet one crucial requirement. Among this inventory, he lists 'political' or 'civic' courage (*Nichomachean Ethics*, 1116a; see also *Magna Moralia*, 1191a; *Eudemian Ethics*, 1229a):

> Citizens seem to face dangers because of the penalties imposed by the laws and the reproaches they would otherwise incur, and because of the honours they win by such action ... This kind of courage ... is due to excellence [virtue?]; for it is due to (the sense of) shame [αἰδώς] and to desire of a noble effect (i.e. honour) and avoidance of disgrace [blame], which is ignoble [base, shameful].

From a rhetorical point of view, there is no doubt that 'political' or 'civic' courage deserves praise (*Rhetoric*, 1366b-1368a; see also 1361a):

> those actions are noble for which the reward is simply honour ... Noble also are those actions whose advantage [i.e. honour] may be enjoyed after death ... And the opposites of those things of which men feel ashamed, for men are ashamed of saying, doing, or

[26] The vicious agent had no reason either for performing or for not performing the action s/he performed. The 'akratic' agent had a reason for not performing it, and — if s/he is supposed to act according to his/her 'all-things-considered' judgment — s/he had no reason for performing it (Davidson 1982). For a criticism of this approach to 'akrasia', see Lazar (1999) and Searle (2001: 219-237).

[27] In order to justify his distinction between epideictic and deliberative oratory, Aristotle (*Rhetoric*, 1358b-1359a; see also *Rhetoric*, 1366b-1367a) points out that

> those who praise or blame a man do not consider whether his acts have been expedient [συμφέρον] or harmful [βλαβερός], but often make it a ground of actual praise that he has neglected his own interest to do what was honourable [beautiful; καλός]. Thus they praise Achilles because he championed his fallen friend Patroclus, though he knew that this meant death, and that otherwise he need not die: yet while to die thus was the nobler [i.e. more beautiful] thing for him to do, the expedient thing was to live on.

In ethical deliberation, however, actions have to be evaluated as expedient or harmful with respect to the ultimate end: ethical happiness; the expedient [συμφέρον] does not differ, at this level, from the good [ἀγαθόν] (*Rhetoric*, 1362a-1363a). Thus, we may wonder how Aristotle would eventually describe Achilles' heroic action: as ethically (altruistically) expedient but harmful from a selfish perspective, or as noble (beautiful) but 'imprudent' (i.e. devoid of any deliberative ground)?

> intending to do shameful things ... Those things also are noble for which men strive anxiously, without feeling fear; for they feel thus about the good things which lead to fame ... Victory, too, and honour belong to the class of noble things ... So are the things that continue even after death; those which are always attended by honour.

Similarly, if we want to praise a man, we must mention the fact that 'it is on his account that observances have been devised and instituted to encourage or honour such achievements as his own'. When dealing with the question whether (the sense of) shame [αἰδώς] is an ethical virtue, Aristotle first seems hesitant; but he eventually claims that, although (the sense of) shame deserves praise, as a 'middle', 'mean' or 'intermediate' passion between bashfulness (the 'excess') and shamelessness (the 'defect' or 'deficiency'), it 'is not an ethical virtue' because it 'is not characteristic of a good man' (*Nicomachean Ethics*, 1108a, 1128b; *Rhetoric*, 1383b-1385b). Consequently, 'political' or 'civic' courage, while being both praiseworthy and a prototypical topic of epideictic speeches (see Loraux 1981), should not be confused with the (deliberatively grounded) virtue of courage. So far so good. But in Aristotle's conception, the reason why a prudent (wo)man may choose to die heroically is that s/he realizes that his/her braveness or cowardice would be, respectively, expedient or harmful to his/her ethical happiness [εὐδαιμονία]; and the only happiness an agent is liable to enjoy after death boils down to the emotive or 'pathic' feelings of pride and admiration, or shame and contempt, that his/her actions may trigger in other minds (*Nicomachean Ethics*, 1100a). So, either the agent, when imagining the emotive or 'pathic' impact of his/her actions on other minds, contagiously entertains these feelings (and, then, s/he is 'politically' courageous) or s/he has no motive at all for acting.

### 10.4.3 What is the cause of a noble action?

In spite of its shortcomings, Aristotle's analysis accounts for the fact that, *ceteris paribus*, we are definitely more inclined to blame than to praise (see French 1985: 78). Since a vicious (wo)man cannot be prudent (in Aristotle's sense), no action of his/hers that turns out to be bad can give rise to any conflict between a putative 'deliberative badness' and a spontaneous baseness: s/he has no reason for acting, anyway. We find it easy to blame agents for the unintended (and even uncontrollable) consequences of their bad actions because, in any case, their vicious 'ethos' is the ultimate cause of whatever happened. But when faced with a good action, we are always free to look for reasons, and thus to attribute to the agent a prudent deliberation that may weaken the nobleness or beauty of his/her action. For instance, a frequent negative reaction to praise consists in recalling that, after all, the agent was a professional who only did his/her job, or that s/he only complied with his/her duty. This is the reason why the epideictic speaker will systematically emphasize the exceptional (and even inappropriate) nature of the action performed (*Rhetoric*, 1368a). In short, blamable actions differ from praiseworthy ones in that the former are necessarily caused by a vicious ethical character (or 'ethos'), while the latter, when not proceeding from any reasons, cannot be caused by the virtuous 'ethos' of the Prudent.

What, then, may be the cause of such noble actions? Aristotle has three different words—εὐφυΐα 'good nature', εὐγένεια 'good birth', and εὐτυχία 'good luck'—to describe those (biological or social) qualities which cause an agent to spontaneously act in a virtuous way without needing to be prudent (see *Nicomachean Ethics*, 1114b, 1143b; *Eudemian Ethics*, 1248a; Dominicy 2001). Although this part of his work has a definitely aristocratic flavour, I think it possible to reinterpret it in more general terms (see Dominicy 2002b). Recall that each virtue—e.g. courage, liberality, temperance (or moderation)—is a 'middle', a 'mean' or an 'intermediate' between two 'extremes'. Aristotle notices that one of these 'extremes'—viz. cowardice, meanness, or intemperance (self-indulgence)—differs from the true virtue in such a manner that no confusion between them remains possible; while the other 'extreme'—viz. rashness, prodigality, or insensibility—shows itself by actions which may be indiscriminable from truly virtuous acts (*Nicomachean Ethics*, 1109a-b, 1116a-1119a, 1121b; *Magna Moralia*, 1186b, 1190b-1191a; *Eudemian Ethics*, 1222a-b, 1229a-1230a, 1234b). We ordinarily tend to believe that 'if a man runs in danger needlessly, much more will he do so in a noble cause; and [that] if a man is open-handed to anyone and everyone, he will be so to his friends also' (*Rhetoric*, 1367b). Consider, in the same perspective, the acceptability contrasts within the following example pairs:

(50) a. Peter is not a coward, but a brave man and even a rash man.
b. ??? Peter is not a rash man, but a brave man and even a coward.

(51) a. Peter is not mean, but liberal and even prodigal.
b. ??? Peter is not prodigal, but liberal and even mean.

(52) a. Peter is not intemperate, but moderate and even insensible.
b. ??? Peter is not insensible, but moderate and even intemperate.

(53) a. Rashness is a sort of spontaneous courage.
b. ??? Cowardice is a sort of spontaneous courage.

(54) a. Prodigality is a sort of spontaneous liberality.
b. ??? Meanness is a sort of spontaneous liberality.

(55) a. Insensibility is a sort of spontaneous moderation.
b. ??? Intemperance is a sort of spontaneous moderation.

While the Platonistic tradition contented itself with denouncing this commonsensical confusion between apparent and true virtues, Aristotle frequently reasons as if the 'extreme' that looks closer to the true virtue could be transformed into it by way of social education and experience. For instance, when listing the vices that make us choose 'harmful and wicked acts contrary to law' (*Rhetoric*, 1368b), he mentions cowardice (but not rashness), meanness (but not prodigality), and intemperance (but not insensibility). In such a perspective, the cause of 'unreasonable' noble actions would be a spontaneous disposition to act, such as, e.g., the rashness of young (hence, 'imprudent') people—that is, a (biological or social) quality for which agents of certain good actions are praised, even if their behaviour does not lend itself to any rationalization.

## 10.5 Conclusion

Rhetoric deals with the different ways language may cause human action. Whereas deliberative and forensic speeches aim at triggering a decision to act grounded on reasons, epideictic oratory relies on an apparently irrational faith in spontaneous ethical choices. However incomplete or naïve we may judge Aristotle's approach, it would be inconsiderate to think that modern discourse theory does not run against the same problems. Why is it so?

In order to shed some light on this question, we should examine systematically those cases where praise or blame do not conform to our common criteria of ethical value or rationality, and question ourselves on the possible accounts of such data. We may wonder, for instance, why victims not only cannot be praised as such, but also prove liable to incur blame (see Danblon 2002a: 85-86, 2004c: 57-60; Danblon & Delvenne 2005; Delvenne & Dominicy 2001; Delvenne, Michaux & Dominicy 2005: 113-114, 138-144; Michaux & Dominicy 2001: 157-165). Lerner's (1980) experimental evidence suggests that, although we pity (innocent) victims and even admire noble victims, we are inconsciously prone to blame them for their own fate; which sometimes induces us to rationalize this mental disposition by claiming that 'people get what they deserve'.

To take another example, why can we praise, but not blame, inanimate objects (see Dominicy 2001: 49-50)? It would indeed be strange to blame anthrax (even when certain agents spread it intentionally), while nothing impedes us from praising penicillin. Except for metaphorical projections into the domain of human beings, praising inanimate objects requires that 'they reflect somehow on people', in that they should result from a praiseworthy action and/or contribute to ensuring our happiness: praising penicillin may be a way to praise its discoverer, praising water may be a way to celebrate the wonderful world we happen to live in; but we may also praise penicillin as a component of this wonderful world, or praise water in order to praise Nature or God (Wierzbicka 1987: 198). One would expect blame to be possible in comparable conditions. Perhaps this surprising asymmetry relates to the fact that, *ceteris paribus*, we feel all the more anxious to look for responsibility that some harm has been done. Praising an inanimate object suggests, in some way, that good luck helps us to live through happy days; blaming it would imply the comparable suggestion that only bad luck is at work, and thus conflict with our wish to associate every harmful event with an agent who can be held responsible for it.

Such irrational inclinations as our 'Belief in a Just World' (Lerner 1980), and our (equally irrational) need of laying the responsibility of each harmful event on an agent, presumably originate in the teleological activity of our mind and brain. Similarly, our representation of human decision and choice might derive from our confused awareness of those mental and neural mechanisms that lead us to act. According to Damasio (1994), emotions drastically restrict the number of our possible actions, and therefore allow us to deliberate on our decisions and choices in an efficacious way. Libet (1999) claims that the volitional process is initiated before free will comes to control (and possibly veto) the performance of the voluntary act. In such conceptions, mental acts like assenting or deciding can be seen as opportunistic Intentional moves (Proust 2001), whose dependency upon pre-existing non-Intentional processes or states would explain our incapacity to reduce ethical choice to the simple product of rational deliberation.

## References


Amossy, R., ed. 1999. *Images de soi dans le discours. La construction de l'ethos*. Lausanne / Paris: Delachaux et Niestlé.

Amossy, R., R. Koren, and G.-E. Sarfati, eds. 2002. *Après Perelman: quelles politiques pour les nouvelles rhétoriques? L'argumentation dans les sciences du langage*. Paris / Montreal: L'Harmattan.

Antoniol, L. 1998. *Things People Do*. Doctoral dissertation, University of Stirling.

Aristotle. 1985. *Complete Works*. No. 71 in Bollingen Series. Princeton (N.J.): Princeton University Press. (J. Barnes (ed.)).

Aubenque, P. 1997. *La prudence chez Aristote*. Paris: Presses Universitaires de France, 2nd edn.

Austin, J.L. 1962. *How to Do Things with Words*. Oxford: Clarendon Press. (J.O. Urmson (ed.)).

Austin, J.L. 1970. αγαθόν and εὐδαιμονία in the *Ethics* of aristotle. In J. Urmson and G. Warnock, eds., *Philosophical Papers*. Oxford: Oxford University Press, 2nd edn.

Bach, K. and R.M. Harnish. 1979. *Linguistic Communication and Speech Acts*. Cambridge (Mass.) / London: The MIT Press.

Baier, A. 1985. Mind and change of mind. In *Postures of the Mind. Essays on mind and morals*. London: Methuen.

Bennett, J. 1991. How do gestures succeed? In Lepore and Van Gulick (1991), pages 3–15.

Carnap, R. 1950. *Logical Foundations of Probability*. Chicago: University of Chicago Press.

Cerf, W. 1969. Review of *How to Do Things with Words*. In Fann (1969), pages 351–379.

Crosby, J.F. 1990. Speech act theory and phenomenology. In A. Burkhardt, ed., *Speech Acts, Meaning and Intentions. Critical approaches to the philosophy of John R. Searle*, pages 62–88. Berlin / New York: Walter de Gruyter.

Damasio, A.R. 1994. *Descartes' Error. Emotion, reason, and the human brain*. New York: A. Grosset / Putnam Books.

Danblon, E. 1999. Is praise a kind of advice? In F. Eemeren et al., eds., *Proceedings of the Fourth International Conference of the International Society for the Study of Argumentation*, pages 109–111. Amsterdam: SIC SAT.

Danblon, E. 2001a. La rationalité du discours épidictique. In Dominicy and Frédéric (2001), pages 19–47.

Danblon, E. 2001b. Le conseil dans la théorie de la politesse: réflexion autour de la notion de désir altruiste. In M. Wauthion and A. Simon, eds., *Politesse et idéologie. Rencontres de pragmatique et de rhétorique conversationnelles*, pages 45–51. Louvain: Peeters (Bibliothèque des Cahiers de l'Institut de Linguistique de Louvain, 107.

Danblon, E. 2002a. *Rhétorique et rationalité. Essai sur l'émergence de la critique et de la persuasion*. Brussels: Éditions de l'Université de Bruxelles.

Danblon, E. 2002b. Éthique et rhétorique: entre les faits et les normes. In Amossy et al. (2002), pages 89–120.

Danblon, E. 2004a. Rhétorique de la chose jugée. In R. Amossy and R. Koren, eds., *Argumentation et prise de position dans le discours*, pages 99–109. Besançon: Presses Universitaires de Franche-Comté. (= *Semen* 17).

Danblon, E. 2004b. Un discours rapporté dans une argumentation délibérative: le 'paradeigma' d'aristote. In L. Rosier et al., eds., *Le discours rapporté dans tous ses états. Question de frontières*, pages 437–444. Paris / Montreal: L'Harmattan.

Danblon, E. 2004c. Le témoignage: vérité ou évidence? In J. Schreiber et al., eds., *Oralités. Les usages de la parole des gens en sciences humaines. Actes du séminaire Prosopopée 1*, pages 53–66. Brussels: Université Libre de Bruxelles (Unité de Recherches 'Sources audiovisuelles en histoire contemporaine').

Danblon, E. and S. Delvenne. 2005. Rationalité discursive et construction de l'identité discursive. analyse de témoignages de rescapés de la shoah. *Journal de Sémantique et de Pragmatique* .

Davidson, D. 1980. *Essays on Actions and Events*. Oxford: Clarendon Press.

Davidson, D. 1982. Paradoxes of irrationality. In Wollheim and Hopkins (1982), pages 289–305.

Davidson, D. 1985. Deception and division. In Lepore and McLaughlin (1985), pages 138–148.

Davis, S. 1980. Perlocutions. In F. K. J.R. Searle and M. Bierwisch, eds., *Speech Act Theory and Pragmatics*, pages 37–55. Dordrecht / Boston / London: Reidel.

De Sousa, R.B. 1971. How to give a piece of your mind: or, the logic of belief and assent. *The Review of Metaphysics* 25:52–79.

Delvenne, S. and M. Dominicy. 2001. La construction 'éthique' dans les témoignages de déportés. In V. N. H. Paugam-Moisy and J. Caron-Pargue, eds., *La cognition entre individu et société. Modèles et méthodes. Actes d'ARCo'2001*, pages 241–253. Paris: Hermès Sciences.

Delvenne, S., C. Michaux, and M. Dominicy. 2005. *Catégoriser l'impensable. La figure du 'musulman' dans les témoignages de rescapés des camps nazis. Prosopopée 2*. Brussels: Université Libre de Bruxelles (Unité de Recherches 'Sources audiovisuelles en histoire contemporaine').

Dennett, D.C. 1978/81. How to change your mind. In *Brainstorms. Philosophical essays on mind and psychology*. Cambridge (Mass.) / Brighton: MIT Press (Bradford Books) / The Harvester Press.

Dominicy, M. 1993. De toulmin à perelman: analyse d'un réseau argumentatif. *Verbum* 1-2-3:241–250.

Dominicy, M. 1994. Du 'style' en poésie. In G. Molinié and P. Cahné, eds., *Qu'est-ce que le style?*, pages 115–137. Paris: Presses Universitaires de France.

Dominicy, M. 1995. Rhétorique et cognition: vers une théorie du genre épidictique. *Logique et Analyse* 150-151-152:159–177.

Dominicy, M. 1996. Le genre épidictique: une argumentation sans questionnement? In C. Hoogaert, ed., *Argumentation et questionnement*, pages 1–12. Paris: Presses Universitaires de France.

Dominicy, M. 2001. L'épidictique et la théorie de la décision. In Dominicy and Frédéric (2001), pages 49–77.

Dominicy, M. 2002a. Les 'topoï' du genre épidictique: du modèle au critère, et vice-versa. In E. Eggs, ed., *Topoï, discours, arguments (= Zeitschrift für französische Sprache und Literatur, Beiheft 32*, pages 49–65. Stuttgart: Franz Steiner Verlag.

Dominicy, M. 2002b. La dimension sémantique du discours argumentatif: le travail sur les notions. In Amossy et al. (2002), pages 121–150.

Dominicy, M. 2005. La 'dissociation des notions' et le problème du 'réalisme'. In D. Bouget and S. Karsenty, eds., *Regards croisés sur le lien social*, pages 87–99. Paris: L'Harmattan.

Dominicy, M. 2006. Perelman und die brüsseles schule. In J. Kopperschmidt, ed., *Die neue Rhetorik. Studien zu Chaim Perelman*. Munich: Wilhelm Fink Verlag.

Dominicy, M. and N. Franken. 2001. Speech acts and relevance theory. In D. Vanderveken and S. Kubo, eds., *Essays in Speech Act Theory*, pages 263–283. Amsterdam / Philadelphia: John Benjamins. Pragmatics and Beyond Series, NS 77.

Dominicy, M. and M. Frédéric, eds. 2001. *La mise en scène des valeurs. La rhétorique de l'éloge et du blâme*. Lausanne / Paris: Delachaux et Niestlé.

Dominicy, M., C. Michaux, and P. Kreutz. 2004. Les stéréotypes: du lieu spécifique à la (re)qualification. In E. Danblon, ed., *Les stéréotypes féminins. Une étude rhétorique et discursive (= Degrés 117)*, pages a1–a28.

Dowty, D.R. 1979. *Word Meaning and Montague Grammar. The semantics of verbs and times in Generative Semantics and in Montague's PTQ*. Dordrecht / Boston / London: Reidel.

Eggs, E. 1994. *Grammaire du discours argumentatif. Le topique, le générique, le figuré*. Paris: Kimé.

Fann, K.T., ed. 1969. *Symposium on J.L. Austin*. London / New York: Routledge & Kegan Paul / The Humanities Press.

Franken, N. and M. Dominicy. 2001. Épidictique et discours expressif. In Dominicy and Frédéric (2001), pages 79–106.

French, P.A. 1985. Fishing the red herrings out of the sea of moral responsibility. In Lepore and McLaughlin (1985), pages 73–87.

Gaines, R.N. 1979. Doing by saying: toward a theory of perlocution. *The Quarterly Journal of Speech* 65:207–217.

Gu, Y. 1993. The impasse of perlocution. *Journal of Pragmatics* 20:405–432.

Gu, Y. 1994. Pragmatics and rhetoric: a collaborative approach to conversation. In H. Parret, ed., *Pretending to Communicate*, pages 173–195. Berlin / New York: Walter de Gruyter.

Hahn, L.E., ed. 1999. *The Philosophy of Donald Davidson*. Chicago / La Salle (Ill.): Open Court.

Hempel, C.G. 1965. *Inductive Inconsistencies. Aspects of Scientific Explanation*. London / New York: Collier-Macmillan / The Free Press.

Hornsby, J. 1980. *Actions*. London: Routledge and Kegan Paul.

Jackendoff, R.S. 1985. Believing and intending: two sides of the same coin. *Linguistic Inquiry* 16:445–460.

Kenny, A. 1963. *Action, Emotion and Will*. London / New York: Routledge & Kegan Paul / The Humanities Press.

Kintsch, W. and T.A. van Dijk. 1978. Toward a model of text comprehension and production. *Psychological Review* 85:363–394.

Kreutz, P. 2001. L'épidictique et les émotions. In Dominicy and Frédéric (2001), pages 107–134.

Kurzon, D. 1998. The speech act of incitement: perlocutionary acts revisited. *Journal of Pragmatics* 29:571–596.

Lazar, A. 1999. Akrasia and the principle of continence or what the tortoise would say to achilles. In Hahn (1999), pages 381–405.

Leech, G.N. 1983. *Principles of Pragmatics*. London / New York: Longman.

Lepore, E. and B. McLaughlin, eds. 1985. *Action and Events. Perspectives on the philosophy of Donald Davidson*. Oxford: Blackwell.

Lepore, E. and R. Van Gulick, eds. 1991. *John Searle and His Critics*. Oxford: Basil Blackwell.

Lerner, M.J. 1980. *The Belief in a Just World. A fundamental delusion*. New York / London: Plenum Press.

Libet, B. 1999. Do we have free will? In B. Libet, A. Freeman, and K. Sutherland, eds., *The Volitional Brain. Towards a neuroscience of free will (= Journal of Consciousness Studies, 6/8-9)*, pages 47–57. Thoverton: Imprint Academic.

Loraux, N. 1981. *L'invention d'Athènes. Histoire de l'oraison funèbre dans la 'cité classique'*. Paris / The Hague / New York: Mouton / Éditions de l'École des Hautes Études en Sciences Sociales.

Michaux, C. and M. Dominicy. 2001. Le jeu réciproque du cognitif et de l'émotif dans le genre épidictique. In Dominicy and Frédéric (2001), pages 135–165.

Mourelatos, A.P.D. 1981. Events, processes, and states. In P. Tedeschi and A. Zaenen, eds., *Syntax and Semantics. Volume 14: Tense and Aspect*, pages 191–212. New York: Academic Press.

Nagel, T. 1979. Moral luck. In *Mortal Questions*. Cambridge: Cambridge University Press.

Neuberg, M. 1993. *Philosophie de l'action. Contribution critique à la théorie analytique de l'action*. Brussels: Académie Royale de Belgique (Classe des Lettres).

Ogien, R. 1993. *La faiblesse de la volonté*. Paris: Presses Universitaires de France.

Pears, D. 1982. Motivated irrationality, freudian theory and cognitive dissonance. In Wollheim and Hopkins (1982), pages 264–288.

Perelman, C. and L. Olbrechts-Tyteca. 1969. *The New Rhetoric. A Treatise on Argumentation*. Notre Dame (Ind.) / London: University of Notre Dame Press.

Pernot, L. 1993. *La rhétorique de l'éloge dans le monde gréco-romain*. Paris: Institut d'Études Augustiniennes.

Popper, K.R. 1963. The demarcation between science and metaphysics. In *Conjectures and Refutations. The growth of scientific knowledge*. London / New York: Routledge & Kegan Paul / Basic Books.

Proust, J. 2001. A plea for mental act. *Synthese* 129:105–128.

Robinson, D.N. 2002. *Praise and Blame. Moral realism and its application*. Princeton / Oxford: Princeton University Press.

Searle, J.R. 1973. Austin on locutionary and illocutionary acts. In S. Berlin et al., eds., *Essays on J.L. Austin*, pages 141–159. Oxford: Clarendon Press.

Searle, J.R. 1979. The logical status of fictional discourse. In *Expression and Meaning. Studies in the theory of speech acts*. Cambridge: Cambridge University Press.

Searle, J.R. 1983. *Intentionality. An essay in the philosophy of mind*. Cambridge: Cambridge University Press.

Searle, J.R. 1991. Responses. In Lepore and Van Gulick (1991).

Searle, J.R. 1992. *The Rediscovery of the Mind*. Cambridge (Mass.): The MIT Press.

Searle, J.R. 1995. *The Construction of Social Reality*. New York / London: Simon & Schuster (The Free Press) / Allen Lane (The Penguin Press).

Searle, J.R. 2001. *Rationality in Action*. Cambridge (Mass.) / London: The MIT Press.

Searle, J.R. and D. Vanderveken. 1985. *Foundations of Illocutionary Logic*. Cambridge: Cambridge University Press.

Sorabji, R. 1980. *Necessity, Cause and Blame. Perspectives on Aristotle's theory*. London: Duckworth.

Sperber, D. and D. Wilson. 1995. *Relevance. Communication and cognition*. Oxford: Blackwell, 2nd edn.

Stoutland, F. 1968. Basic actions and causality. *The Journal of Philosophy* 65:467–475.

Strawson, P.F. 1969. Intention and convention in speech acts. In Fann (1969), pages 380–400.

Toulmin, S.E. 1958. *The Uses of Argument*. Cambridge: Cambridge University Press.

Unamuno, M. de. 2002. *Amor y pedagogía. Epistolario Miguel de Unamuno / Santiago Valentí Camp*. Madrid: Biblioteca Nueva. (B. Vauthier (ed.)).

van Dijk, T.A. and W. Kintsch. 1983. *Strategies of Discourse Comprehension*. New York: Academic Press.

Van Hecke, T. 2001. *Contribution à la théorie des actes de langage. Le remerciement*. Doctoral dissertation, Universiteit Antwerpen.

Vanderveken, D. 1990. *Meaning and Speech Acts. Volume I: Principles of Language Use*. Cambridge: Cambridge University Press.

Vanderveken, D. 1991. *Meaning and Speech Acts. Volume II: Formal Semantics of Success and Satisfaction*. Cambridge: Cambridge University Press.

Vanderveken, D. 1994. *Principles of Speech Act Theory = Cahiers d'Épistémologie 188*. Université du Québec à Montréal.

Vanderveken, D. 1997. La logique illocutoire et l'analyse du discours. In D. Luzzati et al., eds., *Le Dialogique*, pages 59–94. Bern: Peter Lang.

Vanderveken, D. 1999. La structure des dialogues intelligents. In B. Moulin, S. Delisle, and B. Chaib-draa, eds., *Analyse et simulation des conversations. De la théorie des actes de discours aux systèmes multiagents*, pages 61–100. Limonest: L'Interdisciplinaire.

Vanderveken, D. 2001. Illocutionary logic and discourse typology. *Revue Internationale de Philosophie* 55(216):243–255.

Vendler, Z. 1967. Verbs and times. In *Linguistics in Philosophy*. Ithaca (N.Y.): Cornell University Press.

Vendler, Z. 1972. *Res Cogitans. An essay in rational psychology*. Ithaca (N.Y.) / London: Cornell University Press.

von Wright, G.H. 1951. *A Treatise on Induction and Probability*. London: Routledge & Kegan Paul.

von Wright, G.H. 1963. *Norm and Action. A logical enquiry*. London / New York: Routledge & Kegan Paul / The Humanities Press.

Walster, E. 1966. Assignment of responsibility for an accident. *Journal of Personality and Social Psychology* 3:73–79.

Wierzbicka, A. 1987. *English Speech Act Verbs. A semantic dictionary*. Sydney: Academic Press.

Williams, B. 1981. Moral luck. In *Moral Luck. Philosophical Papers 1973-1980*. Cambridge: Cambridge University Press.

Wollheim, R. and J. Hopkins, eds. 1982. *Philosophical Essays on Freud*. Cambridge: Cambridge University Press.

11

# Within the bounds of reason: Strategic maneuvering in argumentative discourse

FRANS H. VAN EEMEREN AND PETER HOUTLOSSER

## 11.1 Some metatheoretical starting-points

"Quirites!" This is the infamous one-word speech by which Julius Caesar won his rebellious legions over to fight the republican army in North Africa, in 46 BC. After having fought a great many battles under Caesar's command, the soldiers had refused to follow him again. Caesar's use of the word *quirites* as form of address had a devastating effect. According to the classical scholar Anton Leeman (1992), 'quirites' was the dignified word a Roman magistrate used to address an assembly. Caesar's use of this word to his soldiers made it clear to them that they had not only lost their privilege of being addressed as *commilitones*, or 'comrades,' but were even no longer entitled to a Roman general's normal form of address for his soldiers: *milites*. "We are *milites!*" they reportedly shouted when they all volunteered to follow Caesar once more into battle. In our view, this is an excellent illustration of how the communicative and interactional meaning of argumentative discourse can only be really grasped if it is put in the functional perspective of the speech event in which it plays a part.

Not only in formal, but also in informal logical approaches, in studying argumentation, 'structural elements' of reasoning such 'major premise,' 'minor premise,' and 'conclusion' are often abstracted from the functional process of communication in which they occur. However much such structural descriptions may have to recommend them, they tend to ignore the rationale of argumentative discourse. Argumentation arises in response to—or in anticipation of—a difference of opinion, and the specific lines of verbal justification are contrived to serve the management of disagreement and are reflected in the functional design of the discourse. As a consequence, the study of argumentation requires *functionalization*, which can be achieved by taking account of the fact that argumentative discourse occurs through—and over—speech acts and by concentrating on their identity and correctness conditions.

In approaches only concerned with argumentation as a product, argumentation is

*Meaning, Intentions, and Argumentation.*
Kepa Korta and Joana Garmendia (eds.).

typically viewed as a manifestation or representation of an individual thought process. Argumentative discourse, however, does not consist in a single person privately drawing a conclusion: it involves two or more people having a difference of opinion and making an attempt to arrive at a resolution. Argumentation presupposes two different interactional roles: that of a defender of a standpoint, and that of doubting or oppositional interlocutors or readers who are to be convinced. As a consequence, *socialization* of the study of argumentation is required, which can be achieved by concentrating on the ways in which—real or projected—doubts or objections are responded to in the context of a fundamentally dialogical interaction. By extending the speech act perspective from the communicative level of functional meaning to the social level of verbal interaction, it can be shown how argumentative 'cases' are developed through co-operative verbal exchanges.

The beliefs and inferences underlying argumentation (or any other discourse activity) are channeled by a system of public accountability that is expressed or projected in the discourse. While people's motives for holding a position might be different from the grounds they offer and accept in its defense, what they can be held committed to is the position they have expressed in the discourse, whether directly or indirectly. The study of argumentative discourse should therefore concentrate on the participants' externalizable commitments. This *externalization* can be achieved by focusing on the obligations created by the performance of speech acts, varying from the obligation to be capable of doing what one has promised to the obligation to take an interest in the answer to one's question—or to accept the responsibility for those premises one has left unexpressed or unarticulated. Notions which are basically psychological, such as 'accepting' and 'disagreeing,' can then be defined externally as 'giving a positive type of response to an arguable act' and 'expressing an opposition between speech acts pertaining to the same proposition.'

Argumentation theorists are not just interested in the effectiveness of argumentation in convincing people of a certain viewpoint, but also in the standards argumentative discourse should comply with in order to be sound. For many, the *raison d'être* of the study of argumentation is the critical analysis of argumentative discourse—i.e., the interpretation and evaluation of actual cases in the light of normative standards for argumentative conduct (van Eemeren et al. (1993, p. 37)). Argumentative discourse is therefore a subject for research with an empirical dimension as well as a critical dimension, and the study of argumentation can best be seen as part of the broader enterprise that van Eemeren (1990) dubbed 'normative pragmatics.' In taking this approach, his view was that argumentative discourse is to be judged not only in terms of its success in gaining the audience's assent, but also in terms of its problem-solving capacity, i.e., its appropriateness for resolving a difference of opinion. In judging argumentative discourse, the pragma-dialectical ideal is to make use of a procedure for testing standpoints against critical reactions which is 'problem-valid,' i.e., capable of doing the job well, as well as 'intersubjectively valid,' i.e., acceptable to the arguers.

The 'dialectical' procedure we have in mind is a procedure for testing standpoints critically in the light of commitments assumed in empirical reality. The primary theoretical device to accomplish the required integration of pragmatic insight in the empirical dimension and critical insight in the dialectical dimension of argumentative discourse is, again, the speech act. The speech act conditions are codifications of what speakers and writers may be held responsible for when engaged in argumentative discourse and the performance of speech acts is embedded in a set of principles similar to the Gricean maxims that account for what the participants in the discourse are obliged to defend. As a consequence, the desired *dialectification* of the study of argumentative discourse can best be achieved by constructing a model of critical discussion that specifies the nature and the distribution of the speech acts playing a part in resolving a difference of opinion and defining the rules applying to the performance and exchange of speech acts in this endeavor.

Functionalization, socialization, externalization, and dialectification are the metatheoretical principles of our approach to argumentative discourse. They serve as the methodological starting-points of our theorizing (van Eemeren and Grootendorst (1984)).

## 11.2 Dialectical approaches to argumentation

### 11.2.1 Dialogue logic and formal dialectics

In 1982, in *From axiom to dialogue*, an inspiring contribution to the dialectification of the study of argumentation was made by the logicians Else Barth and Erik Krabbe. Building upon the dialogue logic developed earlier by Paul Lorenzen and other members of the Erlangen School (see Kamlah and Lorenzen (1984)), they described formally regimented procedures to check whether a given statement can be logically maintained in the light of certain assumptions. This dialectical interpretation of formal logic is known as *formal dialectics*.

In formal dialectics, the smallest complete unit of argumentative discourse is an exchange between language users A and B, who are parties in a dispute that have interactional roles that are each other's opposite. One party is the *proponent* of a certain thesis and the other party is the *opponent*. Together they attempt to find out whether the thesis can be successfully defended against critical attacks. In the defense of the thesis, the proponent can make use of 'concessions' made by the opponent: statements for which the opponent is prepared to take responsibility. The proponent must parry any attack on one of its own statements, either by providing a 'direct defense' or by undertaking a 'counterattack' on a concession of the opponent. The opponent is obliged to defend any concession that comes under attack. If this results in the opponent being unable to do anything other than assert something he had attacked earlier in the dialogue, the proponent has successfully defended his position; since the proponent's success is dependent on the opponent's concessions, it is a defense *ex concessis*.

In formal dialectics these dialogue games are formalized in *dialogue tableaus* (see Figure 1):

| | Opponent | Proponent |
|---|---|---|
| | B | A |
| Dispute | 1. | $\sim X$ |
| | 2. $(\sim X)$ | |
| | 3. | $(Z \supset \sim X).Z$ |
| | 4. $Z$? | |
| | 5. | $Z$ |
| | 6. $\sim X$ | |

| | Opponent | Proponent |
|---|---|---|
| | B | A |
| Dispute | 1. | $\sim X$ |
| | 2. $(\sim X)$ | |
| | 3. | $(Z \supset \sim X).Z$ |
| | 4. $(\sim Z)$ | |
| | 5. | $(Y \supset Z).Y$ |
| | 6. $(\sim X)$ | |

FIGURE 1. ARGUMENTATIVE DIALOGUE TABLEAUS

In these dialogues, A defends a negative thesis ($\sim X$), while B expresses his doubts in respect of the acceptability of $\sim X$. In the third move, A gives arguments for $\sim X$. In the first tableau, language user B then expresses in move 4 doubt as to the acceptability of one of the statements ($Z$) which go to make up A's argumentation. In the second tableau, B makes in move 4 an objection by asserting the opposite of that statement, viz. $\sim Z$. A justifies in the fifth move the attacked statement by means of argumentation: $(Y \rightarrow Z)$ & $Y$. In the first tableau, A uses a different method to render the statement acceptable: asserting $Z$. Both maneuvers evidently force B to withdraw the earlier doubts and accept the thesis.

The descriptions embodied in Figure 1 make it clear that the statements of one language user are not merely a reaction to statements made by the other language user, but are directly associated with the commitments the other language user has accepted in advancing certain statements. Thus statement $Z$? made by B in the fourth move of the first tableau is only relevant because it relates to the commitment taken on by A in the third move, when A advances $(Z \rightarrow\sim X)$ & $Z$.

On closer inspection, dialogue logic amounts to a translation of the well-known rules of logical deduction (such as *modus ponens*) into 'dialogue' rules, with the 'thesis' taking the place of the 'conclusion' and the 'premises' becoming 'concessions' of the opponent—also called 'hypotheses.' This observation explains why a discussion as envisioned in formal dialectics differs fundamentally from a discussion in ordinary argumentative practice: in formal dialectics, a procedure to check if the thesis can be logically concluded from the premises that constitute the argumentation can only be started *after* these premises have been presented and accepted by the party that is prepared to take on the role of opponent. This party must add the proponent's premises as a set of concessions to its own commitments and be prepared to defend these concessions. In case of a real dispute between a protagonist of a standpoint, A, and an antagonist, B, it is unlikely that B will automatically accept the set of statements that constitute the premises of A's argumentation, let alone assume an obligation to defend them. In argumentative practice, such concessions are usually not made in advance. And as soon as B does *not* accept A's premises, A's point of departure requires further argumentation itself.

### 11.2.2 The pragma-dialectical model of critical discussion

In formal approaches to argumentative discourse, even when they are dialectical, argumentation is usually viewed as part of a logical deduction that happens to be difficult to analyze because it is couched in a vernacular liable to imperfections inherent in ordinary language use. At the other extreme, there are the conversation analysts and other empirically-minded students of argumentative discourse who concentrate on argumentation as it really occurs in argumentative practice and reject any form of formalization beforehand. Adherents of both approaches often start from the false assumption that certain subjects lend themselves, for practical purposes or even *sui generis*, either only to a formal or only to an informal treatment. They ignore that there can be different *sorts* and *degrees* of formalization—ranging from the use of abstract formulas and symbols with meanings that are defined *a priori* to distinguishing fixed patterns and referring to more or less established conventions. Ultimately, it depends on the stage of development a theoretical approach has reached what the possibilities for formalization are: in some instances formalization is premature and would spoil the view of the phenomena concerned while in other cases refraining from formalization prevents a theory from developing any further. In practice, it may be the case that the state of theorizing is such that only certain parts or aspects of the subject-matter are ready for formal treatment while others can only be formalized at the expense of harmful reductions.

Pragma-dialectics is a theory of argumentative discourse, not primarily a theory of logical deduction or artificial dialogue. This, however, does not automatically mean that formalization is right away excluded. Unlike so-called informal logicians, we do not think that the informal status of the subject of investigation automatically means that the theorizing should also remain informal. Because pragma-dialectics involves the development of a model of regimented ways of resolving a difference of opinion, this approach to argumentation is at least formal in a procedural sense. Unlike formal dialectics, pragma-dialectics is a discourse dialectic closely aligned with a pragmatic approach to communication and interaction and is concerned with the problems of assessing the adequacy of ordinary argumentative cases, the conditions of informal argument, and the verbal means by which argumentation is conducted.

A pivotal concept in the pragma-dialectical theory is the model of critical discussion that defines the procedures for establishing methodically whether a standpoint can be defended against doubt or criticism (van Eemeren and Grootendorst (1984)). The model provides a description of what argumentative discourse would be like if it were optimally and solely aimed at resolving a difference of opinion. It specifies the resolution process, the stages that can analytically be distinguished in this process, and the types of speech act that are instrumental in resolving the difference in each particular stage. In the *confrontation* stage, the difference of opinion is defined; in the *opening* stage, the various kinds of commitment are established that are the starting point of the discussion and serve as a frame of reference during the discussion; in the *argumentation* stage, arguments and critical reactions are exchanged; in the *concluding* stage, the result of the discussion is determined.

In real argumentative discourse , at every stage of the critical discussion projected in the discourse, specific obstacles may arise that can be an impediment to the resolution of the difference of opinion. These impediments are traditionally known as *fallacies.* The pragma-dialectical rules for critical discussion, which provide a definition of the general principles of constructive argumentative discourse, are designed to prevent such obstacles from interfering and to enable the analyst to identify them as interfering with the resolution process. Unlike the rules of formal dialectics, which are rules for generating rational arguments, the pragma-dialectical rules do not only pertain to argumentation proper; they aspire to cover all speech acts performed in all stages of a critical discussion. They are supposed to reflect all necessary conditions for resolving a difference by means of argumentative discourse.

The pragma-dialectical rules are procedural rules intended to enable a systematic evaluation and sustained criticism of argumentative practice. The quality of the rules depends first and foremost on their problem-solving validity. The additional requirement of intersubjective validity creates a pressure to ascertain that people who aim to resolve their differences by means of argumentative discourse will maintain norms that are, at least for the most part, equivalent with the pragma-dialectical rules. To determine precisely to what extent the rules agree with the norms favored by ordinary language users, we test their intersubjective validity by carrying out a prolonged series of empirical tests. In these experimental investigations fragments of argumentative discourse that contain fallacious moves because they violate a particular rule of critical discussion are assessed for their acceptability by people who have not had any special training in argumentation theory, let alone pragma-dialectics. The results provide a general insight into ordinary arguers' reasonableness conceptions (see, e.g., van Eemeren et al. (2000)).

The model of critical discussion can also serve as a point of departure for identifying the verbal means that are used in argumentative discourse to indicate the communicative and interactional functions of the various moves. At the University of Amsterdam, we are carrying out a research project aimed at making an inventory of verbal and other indicators of moves that are relevant to resolving a difference of opinion—and to identify the conditions for attributing a specific function in the resolution process to expressions that point to a certain pattern of argumentation, such as the expression 'for because,' which points to so-called 'subordinative' argumentation. The scope of the inventory is not limited to the well-known relational indicators, such as 'therefore,' and explicit references to argumentation, such as 'my reasons for this are,' but extends to indicators of counterarguments, 'argument schemes,' and structural relations between arguments, and also to indicators of moves in other stages of the resolution process, such as expressing antagonism, granting a concession, and adding a rebuttal (see, e.g., Snoeck Henkemans (1995)).

## 11.3 Combining dialectical and rhetorical insight

### 11.3.1 Strategic maneuvering in resolving a difference of opinion

In a pragma-dialectical analysis, argumentative discourse is 'reconstructed' as an attempt to resolve a difference of opinion. This reconstruction results in an *analytic overview* of the resolution process—a representation of the discourse in terms of a critical discussion (van Eemeren and Grootendorst (1992, pp. 93–94)). The analytic overview constitutes the basis for a critical evaluation. It clarifies the difference of opinion at issue and the positions of the participants, identifies the procedural and substantive premises that serve as the starting point of the discussion, surveys the arguments and criticisms that are—explicitly or implicitly—advanced, the argument schemes that are used, the argumentation structures that are developed, and the conclusion that is reached. Because the model of critical discussion provides a survey of all speech acts and combinations of speech acts that operate in the various stages of the resolution process, it serves as a heuristic and analytic tool for the reconstruction of the speech acts that are relevant to resolving a difference of opinion, but may remain implicit or opaque in the actual discourse (van Eemeren et al. (1993)).

People engaged in argumentative discourse are characteristically oriented toward resolving a difference of opinion and may be regarded as committed to norms instrumental in achieving this purpose—maintaining certain standards of reasonableness and expecting others to comply with the same critical standards.[1] This does not mean, however, that these people are not interested in resolving the difference *in their own favor*. Their argumentative speech acts may, in fact, even be assumed to be designed to achieve precisely this effect. There is, in other words, not only a 'dialectical,' but also a 'rhetorical' aspect to argumentative discourse. Initially, the pragma-dialectical method of analysis concentrated solely on the dialectical aspect. Meanwhile we have shown that the reconstruction of argumentative discourse can be strengthened considerably by incorporating rhetorical considerations in the analysis, and particularly in its justification (van Eemeren and Houtlosser (1998, 1999, 2000a,b)).

The balancing of a resolution-minded dialectical objective with the rhetorical objective of having one's own position accepted is occasion for 'strategic maneuvering' by the parties. By means of this strategic maneuvering they attempt to reconcile their

[1] See for some empirical confirmation of this claim van Eemeren et al. (2000).

rhetorical aims with their resolution-minded dialectical obligations. In this endeavor, the parties attempt to exploit the opportunities afforded by the dialectical situation for steering the discourse rhetorically into the direction that serves their own interests best. An analysis of argumentative discourse can only provide a sound basis for a critical evaluation if it makes clear for each move in the discourse what purpose it is designed to achieve. This means that the analysis of the discourse should not only take account of its dialectical dimension, but also of the rhetorical dimension.

Making use of rhetorical insight leads to a clearer understanding of the strategic rationale behind the various moves that are made in the discourse. Because we view the strategic maneuvering that takes place in the discourse as a means of realizing the rhetorical aims of the disputants while complying at the same time with the requirements of reasonable dispute resolution, we put the strategic maneuvering in a dialectical framework of analysis—more precisely, in the theoretical framework of pragma-dialectics. In developing this perspective, it is important to realize that the rhetorical pervasion of argumentative discourse does not mean that the parties involved in the discourse are only interested in having things their way. However hard they may try to have their point of view accepted, they generally have to maintain the image of people who play the resolution game by the rules. This means that they may be held committed to what they have said, assumed or implicated. If a certain move proves fallacious, they cannot escape from their dialectical responsibility by simply saying "Never mind, I was only being rhetorical." As a rule, the participants in argumentative discourse will at least have to pretend to be primarily interested in having the difference of opinion resolved.

### 11.3.2 The traditional conceptions of dialectic and rhetoric

How does our position relate to the traditional conceptions of dialectic and rhetoric? Already since Aristotle there has been a distinct division between rhetoric and dialectic, in spite of their initial close connection. Plato viewed dialectic as a means of finding the truth. Aristotle developed it in the *Topics* into a system of regulated dialogues for refuting a claim, starting from concessions of the other party. In the *Rhetoric* Aristotle provided the conceptual framework for the study of rhetoric by his 'argumentative' definition of rhetoric as an ability or capacity (*dynamis*) in each case to see the available means of persuasion. Beside the Aristotelian perspective, an Isocratian tradition developed that concentrated more on style and literary aspects. In Cicero's *De oratore* (Ed. 1942) these aspects are integrated in the Aristotelian framework and until the seventeenth century western history of the theory of rhetoric remained foremost Ciceronian, although after its rediscovery in the fifteenth century, in education Quintilian's *Institutio oratoria* became the major classical authority on rhetoric (Kennedy (1994, pp. 158, 181)).[2]

In medieval times dialectic achieved an importance at the expense of rhetoric, which—

[2]In later years, a distinction can be made between philosophically-oriented persuasion rhetoric, inspired by Aristotle and Whately, and elocutionary, decorative, belletristic rhetoric. As Gaonkar (1990) explains, in the United States there is also a tradition stemming from Burke that expands the frontiers of rhetoric from 'persuasion' to 'identification'-as-an-explanation-for-social-cohesion. According to van Eemeren et al. (1993, p. 213), modern-day persuasion theories are 'heavily oriented to analysis of attitude formation and change' and bear little resemblance to Aristotle's rhetoric.

after the study of *inventio* and *dispositio* was moved from rhetoric to dialectic—was reduced to a doctrine of *elocutio* and *actio*. With Ramus this development culminated in a strict separation between dialectic and rhetoric, rhetoric being devoted exclusively to style, and dialectic being incorporated into logic (Meerhoff (1988)).[3]Although there were these precursory symptoms of a widening gap between rhetoric and dialectic, according to Toulmin (2001), the division did not become 'ideologized' before the Peace of Westphalia (1648). Then the division resulted in the separate existence of two mutually isolated paradigms, each conforming to a different conception of argumentation, which were considered incompatible. Rhetoric has within the humanities become a field for scholars in communication, language and literature. With the further formalization of logic in the nineteenth century, dialectic has almost disappeared from sight. Although in the twentieth century the dialectical approach to argumentation has been taken up again, there is still a yawning gap among argumentation theorists between the theorists who opt for a dialectical approach and the protagonists of a rhetorical approach.[4]

On closer inspection there have always been authors who saw a connection between rhetoric and dialectic (see van Eemeren and Houtlosser (1998)). For Aristotle, rhetoric is the mirror image or counterpart (*antistrophos*) of dialectic;[5] in the *Rhetoric*, he assimilates the opposing views of Plato and the sophists (Murphy and Katula (1994, Ch. 2)). According to Reboul, Aristotle wrote 'que la rhétorique est le "rejeton" de la dialectique, c'est à dire son application, un peu comme la médicine est une application de la biologie. Mais ensuite, il la qualifie comme une "partie" de la dialectique' Reboul (1991, p. 46). For Cicero rhetoric is also *disputatio in utramque partem*, speaking on both sides of an issue. In late antiquity, Boethius subsumes rhetoric in *De topicis differentiis* under dialectic (Kennedy (1994, p. 283)). According to Mack, dialectic is for Boethius more important, 'providing rhetoric with its basis' (Mack (1993, p. 8, n. 19)). The development of humanism 'provoked a reconsideration of the object of dialectic and a reform of the relationship between rhetoric and dialectic' (Mack (1993, p. 15)). In *De inventione dialectica libri tres* (1479/1967), a major contribution to humanist argumentation theory, the humanist scholar Agricola builds on Cicero's view that dialectic and rhetoric cannot be separated and incorporates the two into one theory. Unlike Perelman and Olbrechts-Tyteca (1969), who much later bring elements from dialectic into rhetoric, Agricola merges elements from rhetoric into dialectic.[6]

[3]According to Mack, with the foundation of the universities, from the thirteenth century onward dialectic became the 'intellectually dominant part of the *trivium*, while rhetoric was left with the important practical task of teaching official letter-writing' (Mack (1993, p. 8)).

[4]Among the dialectical theories of argumentation with a formal character are, apart from Barth and Krabbe (1982), Hamblin (1970), Rescher (1977) and the Woods and Walton's studies of the fallacies (Woods and Walton (1989)). Influential rhetorical approaches are Perelman and Olbrechts-Tyteca (1969) 'new rhetoric' and some traditions in American speech communication (see van Eemeren et al. (1996, Ch. 7)).

[5]Reboul (1991, p. 46) observes that for *antistrophos* the translators 'donnent [...] tantôt "analogue", tantôt "contrepartie".' He adds: '*Antistrophos*: il est gênant qu'un livre commence avec un terme aussi obscur!'

[6]Mack explains that Agricola's work is unlike any previous rhetoric or dialectic: '[He] has selected materials from the traditional contents of both subjects' (Mack (1993, p. 122)). In Meerhoff's (Meerhoff (1988, p. 273)) view, 'pour Agricola, [...] loin de réduire la dialectique à la seule recherche de la vérité rationelle, il entend parler de celle-ci en termes de *communication*.'

To overcome the sharp and infertile ideological division between dialectic and rhetoric, dialectics is in pragma-dialectics—more or less in line with Agricola—viewed as a theory of argumentation in natural discourse and rhetorical insight is fitted in with a dialectical approach. Van Eemeren, Grootendorst, Jackson, and Jacobs define dialectic as 'a method of regimented opposition' in verbal communication and interaction 'that amounts to the pragmatic application of logic, a collaborative method of putting logic into use so as to move from conjecture and opinion to more secure belief' (van Eemeren et al. (1993, p. 214)). By conceiving dialectic pragmatically as discourse dialectic, a conception of dialectic is promoted that differs in various ways from the conceptions favored in Aristotelian dialectic or formal dialectics. Rhetoric is in pragma-dialectics viewed as the theoretical study of practical persuasion techniques.[7] There is no reason to assume that the rhetorical norm of successful persuasion is necessarily in contradiction with the ideal of reasonableness that lies at the heart of pragma-dialectics. Why would it be impossible to comply with critical standards for argumentative discourse when one attempts to shape one's case to one's own advantage? Argumentative moves that are considered rhetorically strong by a critical audience will in practice almost certainly be in accordance with the dialectical norms applying to the discussion stage concerned.[8] Viewed from this perspective, there is a sound basis for overcoming the traditional division between dialectic and rhetoric by integrating the rhetorical dimension into the pragma-dialectical method of analysis.[9]

### 11.3.3 Strategic maneuvering within the bounds of reason

An understanding of the role of strategic maneuvering in resolving differences of opinion can be provided by examining how the opportunities available in a certain dialectical situation are used to handle that situation most favorably for a certain party. Each of the four stages in the resolution process is characterized by a specific dialectical aim. Because the parties involved want to realize this aim to their best advantage, they can be expected to make the strategic moves that serve their interest best. In this way, the dialectical objective of a particular discussion stage always has a rhetorical analogue and the presumed rhetorical objectives of the participants must be specified according to stage: it depends on the dialectical stage one is in what kind of advantages can be gained.

In the view we developed, strategic maneuvering can take place in making an expedient choice from the options constituting the 'topical potential' associated with a particular discussion stage, in selecting a responsive adaptation to 'audience demand,' and in exploiting the appropriate 'presentational devices.' Both parties may be expected

[7] According to Simons (1990), rhetoric is, most neutrally, the study and the practice of persuasion. Kienpointner (1995, p. 453) points out that many scholars see rhetoric as 'a rather narrow subject dealing with the techniques of persuasion and/or stylistic devices,' but others conceive of rhetoric as 'a general theory of argumentation and communication' (while still others deny that it is a discipline at all).

[8] Other theoreticians, such as Reboul, also recognize that rhetorically strong argumentation should comply with dialectical criteria: 'On doit tout faire pour gagner, mais non par n'importe quels moyens: il faut jouer [le jeu] respectant les règles' Reboul (1991, p. 42). See also Wenzel (1990).

[9] For earlier proposals to subordinate rhetoric to dialectic, see, for example, Natanson (1955). See also Weaver (1953).

to select the material they can handle well, or that suits them best, develop the perspective most agreeable to their audience, and present their contributions in the most effective way. With respect to each of these three aspects of strategic maneuvering, they have an opportunity to influence the result of the discourse in their own favor.

The *topical potential* associated with a particular dialectical stage can be regarded as the set of relevant alternatives available in that stage of the resolution process.[10] As Simons (1990) observes, the ancient Greeks and Romans were already aware that on any issue there is a range of 'stratagems' that can be called upon when discussing a case. Perelman and Olbrechts-Tyteca rightly emphasize that from the very fact that certain elements are selected, 'their importance and pertinence to the discussion are implied' Perelman and Olbrechts-Tyteca (1969, p. 119). Apart from endowing elements with a 'presence,' deliberate suppression of presence is also a noteworthy phenomenon of choice (Perelman and Olbrechts-Tyteca (1969, p. 116)).[11]

As regards choosing from the topical potential, strategic maneuvering in the confrontation stage aims for the most effective choice among the potential issues for discussion—restricting the 'disagreement space' in such a way that the confrontation is defined in accordance with the party's preferences.[12] In the opening stage, strategic maneuvering attempts to create the most advantageous starting point, for instance by calling to mind, or eliciting, helpful 'concessions' from the other party. In the argumentation stage, starting from the list of 'status topes' associated with the type of standpoint at issue, a strategic line of defense is chosen that involves a selection from the available *loci* that best suits the speaker or writer. In the concluding stage, all efforts will be directed towards achieving the conclusion of the discourse desired by the party concerned, by pointing out, for instance, the consequences of accepting a certain complex of arguments.

For optimal rhetorical result, the moves that are made must in each stage of the discourse also in such a way be adapted to *audience demand* that they comply with the listeners' or readership's good sense and preferences. Argumentative moves that are entirely appropriate to some may be inappropriate to others. In general, adaptation to audience demand will consist in an attempt to create in each stage the required empathy or 'communion.' In the confrontation stage, this may, for example, be manifested by the avoidance of unnecessary or unsolvable contradictions. According to Perelman and Olbrechts-Tyteca, disagreement with respect to values is sometimes communicated as disagreement over facts, because that disagreement is easier to accommodate. As a rule, a speaker's or writer's effort is directed to 'assigning [...] the status enjoying the widest agreement to the elements on which he is basing his argument' (Perelman and Olbrechts-Tyteca (1969, p. 179)). This explains why, in the opening stage, the status of a widely shared value judgement may be conferred on personal feelings and impressions, and the status of a fact on subjective values. In the argumentation stage, strategic adaptation to

[10] In the way we use the term, there are *aggretates of topical potential* or 'topical systems' for all discussion stages, not just for the argumentation stage.

[11] How suppression of presence can be used strategically, is clearly illustrated in Edward Kennedy's 'Chappaquidick speech.' See van Eemeren et al. (1993, pp. vii-xi), and van Eemeren and Houtlosser (1998).

[12] For the notion of 'disagreement space,' see van Eemeren et al. (1993, p. 95).

audience demand may be achieved by quoting arguments the listeners or readers agree with or by referring to argumentative principles they adhere to.

For optimally conveying rhetorical moves, the available *presentational devices* must be strategically put to good use. This means that discursively effective means should be sought to convey the various moves in the discourse. The phrasing and stylistic framing of the moves should be systematically attuned to their discursive effectiveness—exploiting the Gricean maxims of Manner in a specific and deliberate way. In *De oratore*, Cicero (Ed. 1942) observes an unbreakable unity between expression and content—*verbum* and *res*. Anscombre and Ducrot identify expression with orientation: 'Signifier, pour un énoncé, c'est orienter' (Anscombre and Ducrot (1983, p. i)), or, as Anscombre puts it, 'diriger le discours dans une certaine direction' (Anscombre (1994, p. 30)). According to Perelman and Olbrechts-Tyteca, all argumentative discourse presupposes 'a choice consisting not only of the selection of elements to be used, but also of the technique for their presentation' (Perelman and Olbrechts-Tyteca (1969, p. 119)).

Rhetorical figures are specific modes of expression that can be used as presentational devices; they are ways of presenting that make things present to the mind.[13] Perelman and Olbrechts-Tyteca regard a figure as argumentative if it brings about a change of perspective (Perelman and Olbrechts-Tyteca (1969, p. 169)).[14] Among the rhetorical figures that can serve argumentative purposes are, of course, classical ones such as rhetorical questions and *praeteritio*—drawing attention to something by saying that you will refrain from dealing with it. The success of a figure depends on the stage of the discourse in which it is employed. Figures such as *conciliatio*—in one interpretation, adopting the opponent's premises to support one's own position—can, for instance, be brought to bear in the opening stage to prepare the way for convincing the opponent in the argumentation stage.

We shall say that a fully-fledged 'argumentative strategy' is being followed only if the speaker's or writer's strategic maneuverings in the discourse converge with respect to choosing from the topical potential, adapting to the audience demand, and the exploitation of presentational devices. Argumentative strategies in our sense are methodical designs of moves for influencing the result of a particular dialectical stage, or the discussion as a whole, to one's own advantage, which manifest themselves in a systematic, coordinated and simultaneous exploitation of the opportunities afforded by that stage. There are specific confrontation strategies, opening strategies, argumentation strategies and concluding strategies. Among the confrontation strategies used in defining the difference of opinion when choosing the issues that define the 'disagreement space' are evasion and 'humptydumptying.' There are also specific opening strategies, such as creating a broad zone of agreement or, the opposite, a 'smokescreen.' The argumentation strategies include spelling out undesirable consequences that are supposed to intimi-

[13] Perelman and Olbrechts-Tyteca regard a rhetorical figure as 'a discernible structure, independent of the content, [...] a form (which may [...] be syntactic, semantic or pragmatic) and a use that is different from the normal manner of expression, and, consequently, attracts attention' (Perelman and Olbrechts-Tyteca (1969, p. 168)).

[14] 'If the argumentative role of figures is disregarded, their study will,' in Perelman and Olbrechts-Tyteca's opinion, 'soon seem to be a useless [or literary] pastime' (Perelman and Olbrechts-Tyteca (1969, p. 167)).

date the opponent. A notorious concluding strategy is forcing the audience to 'bite the bullet.' The various rhetorical styles of argumentative discourse can be characterized in terms of a particular combination of such strategies. Clearly, the one strategy or style is more acceptable than the other is.

### 11.3.4 Fallacies as derailments of strategic maneuvering

In pragma-dialectics, argumentative moves are only considered sound if they are in agreement with the rules for critical discussion. Any violation of any of these rules obstructs the aim of dispute resolution and the move concerned is then considered fallacious. Clear criteria are required to determine methodically for all the stages of the resolution process whether or not certain argumentative moves are fallacious. Our concept of strategic maneuvering as an attempt to alleviate the potential tension between arguing perfectly reasonably and having things one's own way can be of help in clarifying the problems involved in identifying such criteria.

In argumentative practice, the two objectives involved in strategic maneuvering are not always in perfect balance. On the one hand, arguers may neglect their persuasive interests for fear of being perceived as unreasonable; on the other hand, in their assiduity to win the other party over to their side, they may neglect their commitment to the critical ideal. Neglect of persuasiveness comes down to bad strategy—or even to a blunder (Walton and Krabbe (1995)). It harms the arguer but not the adversary and is therefore not 'condemnable' in the sense of being fallacious. A party, however, whose strategic proceedings allow its commitment to a reasonable exchange of argumentative moves to be overruled by the aim of persuading the opponent, may victimize the other party. Then the strategic maneuvering has got "derailed," and is condemnable for being fallacious. All derailments of strategic maneuvering are fallacious and all fallacies can be regarded as derailments of strategic maneuvering.

This view of the fallacies as derailments of strategic maneuvering explains why it is so difficult to establish general, clear-cut and fixed criteria that apply to all cases of fallacious argumentative behavior. Each form of strategic maneuvering has, as it were, its own continuum of sound and fallacious acting and no *a priori* touchstones can be established to predict precisely when a particular way of strategic maneuvering will go astray. This predicament, however, neither means that fallacy judgements are ultimately always merely contextual, and *ad hoc*, nor that there must, of necessity, always remain a gray, or even dark, zone. Specific 'types' or 'categories' of strategic maneuvering can certainly be pinned down as fallacious for their correspondence with a particular type of rule violation in a specific discussion stage. Also there are types of strategic maneuvering that can definitely be recognized as sound. A careful analysis of the maneuvering in relation to the rules for critical discussion generally results in a better understanding of the conditions leading to a 'derailment' that can be characterized as an occurrence of a particular fallacy.[15]

[15]This approach explains that fallacies are often not immediately *apparent* or *manifest*: a party that commits a fallacy will normally pretend to uphold a commitment to obey the rules of a critical discussion.

## 11.4 Argumentation *in vivo: Clear thinking in troubled times*

We shall illustrate how integrating rhetorical considerations into a pragma-dialectical theoretical framework can be of help in achieving a satisfactory analysis and evaluation of argumentative discourse by giving a reconstruction of an 'advertorial' by Shell published in the *Observer* of November 19, 1995. Although the argument remains partly hidden, this advertorial is a good example of argumentation *in vivo* because Shell maneuvers strategically to defend its economic and political involvement in Nigeria. Having only just recovered from the damage suffered from the Brent Spar case, the company responds to the massive, worldwide protests inflamed by the conviction and execution by the Nigerian regime of the writer, dissident critic and environmental activist Ken Saro-Wiwa.

At first sight, the text appears to be pretty straightforward: Shell informs the public about the exact nature of its involvement in Nigeria. As soon as it is taken into account, however, that the advertisement was published at a time when Shell was accused of lending support to the dictatorial Nigerian regime, and it is assumed that Shell responds relevantly to the accusations, it becomes clear that the advertorial is a sophisticated defense of Shell's actions and an attempt to convince the public of the superiority of its policies in Nigeria.

Clear thinking in troubled times

In the great wave of understandable emotion over the death of Ken Saro-Wiwa, it's very easy for the facts to be swamped by anger and recriminations. But people have the right to the truth. Unvarnished. Even uncomfortable. But never subjugated to a cause, however noble or well-meaning. They have the right to clear thinking.

The situation in Nigeria has no easy solutions. Slogans, protests and boycotts don't offer answers. There are difficult issues to consider.

First, did discreet diplomacy fail? Perhaps we should ask instead why the worldwide protests failed. Our experience suggests that quiet diplomacy offered the very best hope for Ken Saro-Wiwa. But as worldwide threats and protests increased, the Government position appeared to harden. As Wura Abiola, daughter of the imprisoned unofficial winner of the last Nigerian presidential election said on Newsnight "The regime does not react well to threats. I believe that this is the way of showing that they will not listen to threats." Did the protesters understand the risk they were taking? Did the campaign become more important than the cause?

There have also been charges of environmental devastation. But the facts of the situation have often been distorted or ignored. The public—who rightly care deeply about these issues—have too often been manipulated and misled.

There are certainly environmental problems in the area, but as the World Bank Survey has confirmed, in addition to the oil industry, population growth, deforestation, soil erosion and over-farming are also major environmental problems there.

In fact, Shell and its partners are spending US$100 million this year alone on environment-related projects, and US$20 million on roads, health clinics, schools, scholarships, water schemes and agricultural support projects to help the people of the region. And, recognising that solutions need to be based on facts, they are sponsoring a $4.5 million independent environmental survey of the Niger Delta.

But another problem is sabotage. In the Ogoni area—where Shell has not operated since January 1993—over 60% of oil spills were caused by sabotage, usually linked to claims for compensation. And when contractors have tried to deal with these problems, they have been forcibly denied access.

It has also been suggested that Shell should pull out of Nigeria's Liquefied Natural Gas project. But if we do so now, the project will collapse. Maybe for ever. So let's be clear who gets hurt if the project is cancelled. A cancellation would certainly hurt the thousands of Nigerians who will be working on the project, and the tens of thousands more benefiting in the local economy. The environment, too, would suffer, with the plant expected to cut greatly the need for gas flaring in the oil industry. The plant will take four years to build. Revenues won't start flowing until early next century. It's only the people and the Nigerian Government of that time who will pay the price.

And what would happen if Shell pulled out of Nigeria altogether? The oil would certainly continue flowing. The business would continue operating. The vast majority of employees would remain in place. But the sound and ethical business practices synonymous with Shell, the environmental investment, and the tens of millions of dollars spent on community programmes would all be lost. Again, it's the people of Nigeria that you would hurt.

It's easy enough to sit in our comfortable homes in the West, calling for sanctions and boycotts against a developing country. But you have to be sure that knee-jerk reactions won't do more harm than good.

Some campaigning groups say we should intervene in the political process in Nigeria. But even if we could, we must never do so. Politics is the business of governments and politicians. The world where companies use their economic influence to prop up or bring down governments would be a frightening and bleak one indeed.

**Shell.** We'll keep you in touch with the facts.

### 11.4.1 An integrated pragma-dialectical analysis

In our analysis we shall show for each discussion stage how Shell strategically uses the topical potential of the discussion situation, adapts its message strategically to the beliefs and preferences of the audience, and strategically exploits certain presentational devices.

*Confrontation stage*

Shell's advertorial constitutes a response to accusations leveled against its involvement in Nigeria as well as a justification of its policies. Viewed rhetorically, the advertorial is therefore both an apologia and a policy statement.[16] Shell's claim in the apologetic part (lines 4-22) is that its involvement in Nigeria is not blameworthy. The main claim defended in the political part (lines 23-37) is that it should continue its involvement in Nigeria. Both claims are subsumed under the general position that Shell's presence in Nigeria is justified.

The object of the apologetic defense is 'juridical.' Shell addresses two issues: its involvement in the death of Ken Saro-Wiwa and the part it plays in environmental devastation. When dealing with the first issue (lines 6-11), Shell opts for the status of *qualitas*: the company has made serious attempts to help Saro-Wiwa, but these attempts were frustrated by the protesters, sloganeers and would-be boycotters. In addressing the second issue (lines 12-22), Shell assumes the status *coniecturalis*, shifting the issue to other causes of environmental devastation and thereby suggesting that its share in the devastation is negligible.

In its discussion of the main policy claim, Shell selects three issues to deal with: its participation in Nigeria's Liquified Natural Gas (NLNG) project (lines 23-28), its overall involvement in Nigeria (lines 29-34), and its non-intervention policy (lines 35-37). All three issues relate to the fundamental ('stock') issue of advantages and disadvantages: pulling out of the project and withdrawing from Nigeria altogether would have undesirable consequences for the people of Nigeria, and intervention would be disastrous for the political morals. Making use of the pragma-dialectical tools for reproducing the structure of argumentation, this analysis can be represented as follows:

*Juridical: (1) Shell is not to be blamed*

**1.1a Shell is not to be blamed for the death of Ken Saro-Wiwa**
- 1.1a.1a Shell has made efforts to help Saro-Wiwa
- 1.1a.1b These efforts were frustrated by the campaigners

**1.1b Shell is not to be blamed for any environmental devastation**
- 1.1b.1a There are other problems in the area
  - 1.1b.1a.1 The World Bank confirms this
- 1.1b.1b Shell is in fact contributing to saving the environment
  - 1.1b.1b.1a They are substantially subsidizing environment-related projects
  - 1.1b.1b.1b They are substantially subsidizing other 'good' projects
  - 1.1b.1b.1c They are substantially subsidizing an environment survey
- 1.1b.1c A substantial component of environmental devastation is not caused by Shell
  - 1.1b.1c.1a In the Ogoni-area 60 % of the environmental devastation is caused by sabotage
  - 1.1b.1c.1b The contractors have been denied access when they tried to deal with these problems
  - 1.1b.1c.2 Shell has not been operative in the Ogoni-area since 1993

[16] See for the *apologia* as a text genre, e.g., Ware and Linkugel (1973) and Benoit and Lindsey (1987). For a characterization of policy statements, see Freeley (1993).

*Policy: (2) Shell's involvement in Nigeria is justified*

**2.1a Shell should not pull out of the NLG-project**
- 2.1a.1a The people would suffer
- 2.1a.1b The environment would suffer
- 2.1a.1c The future Nigerian government would suffer
  - 2.1a.1a-c.1 If Shell would pull out of the NLG-project, the project would collapse

**2.1b Shell should not pull out of Nigeria**
- 2.1b.1 The people of Nigeria would get hurt
  - 2.1b.1.1 All kinds of advantages for the Nigerian people would be lost

**2.1c Shell should not intervene in Nigerian politics**
- 2.1c.1a Politics is the business of politicians
- 2.1c.1b A world in which oil companies use their influence to prop up or bring down governments would be a frightening and bleak world

FIGURE 1. DIALECTICAL ANALYSIS OF THE ARGUMENTATION STRUCTURE OF SHELL'S ADVERTORIAL

In this structural analysis Shell's strategic maneuvering is not yet fully taken into account. By leaving the main claims addressed in the confrontation stage implicit in its presentation, Shell is able to select from the available 'disagreement space' the issues that are easiest to cope with. One of the main accusations directed at Shell at the time was that it indirectly supported the regime. Shell was, of course, expected to address this difficult issue, but refrains from doing so. At least explicitly, for at the very end of the text Shell declares that the company will not intervene in Nigerian politics (lines 35-37) and adds (in line 37) that it rejects *propping up* a government as much as bringing it down—thus implicating that, in addition to not intervening, it also does not support the regime. In this way, Shell accommodates to audience demand by addressing the issue of support without explicitly answering the accusation involved. It can do so by exploiting the fact that the text, at this stage, has changed from an apologia into a policy statement. This change makes it only natural that the last paragraph of the text reads as another justification of Shell's policy. Nevertheless, Shell is back to its apologetic endeavor: the issue is no longer whether Shell should adopt a certain policy, but whether the company is, politically and morally, *to blame* for its policy. This disclosure of Shell's manipulation of the 'intervention' issue calls for a slightly different structural analysis:

*Juridical: (1) Shell is not to be blamed*

**1.1a Shell is not to be blamed for the death of Ken Saro-Wiwa**
- 1.1a.1a Shell has made efforts to help Saro-Wiwa
- 1.1a.1b These efforts were frustrated by the campaigners

**1.1b Shell is not to be blamed for any environmental devastation**
- 1.1b.1a There are other problems in the area
  - 1.1b.1a.1 The World Bank confirms this
- 1.1b.1b Shell is in fact contributing to saving the environment
  - 1.1b.1b.1a They are substantially subsidizing environment-related projects
  - 1.1b.1b.1b They are substantially subsidizing other 'good' projects
  - 1.1b.1b.1c They are substantially subsidizing an environment survey
- 1.1b.1c A substantial component of environmental devastation is not caused by Shell
  - 1.1b.1c.1a In the Ogoni-area 60 % of the environmental devastation is caused by sabotage
  - 1.1b.1c.1b The contractors have been denied access when they tried to deal with these problems
    - 1.1b.1c.2 Shell has not been operative in the Ogoni-area since 1993

**[1.1c' Shell is not propping up the Nigerian regime]**
- 1.1c'.1 Shell should not intervene in Nigerian politics
  - 1.1c'.1.1a Politics is the business of politicians

1.1c'.1.1b A world in which oil companies use their influence to prop up or bring down governments would be a frightening and bleak world

*Policy: (2) Shell's involvement in Nigeria is justified*

**2.1a Shell should not pull out of the NLG-project**

2.1a.1a The people would suffer

2.1a.1b The environment would suffer

2.1a.1c The future Nigerian government would suffer

2.1a.1a-c.1 If Shell would pull out of the NLG-project, the project would collapse

**2.1b Shell should not pull out of Nigeria**

2.1b.1 The people of Nigeria would get hurt

2.1b.1.1 All kinds of advantages for the Nigerian people would be lost

FIGURE 2. INTEGRATED PRAGMA-DIALECTICAL ANALYSIS OF THE ARGUMENTATION STRUCTURE OF SHELL'S ADVERTORIAL

This amendment to the structural representation of the argumentation clearly illustrates that taking rhetorical considerations into account can have real consequences for the analysis.

*Opening stage*

Taking account of Shell's strategic maneuvering in the opening stage of the projected discussion makes it clear that the company creates a solid starting point for its case. It does so in the first place by contrasting the factual basis of its views with the emotional basis of the opinions of its opponents. The company makes it clear that its position is only based on objective facts. Some facts are known due to the company's own experience (lines 6-7), some other facts are provided by authorities such as Wura Abiola—the daughter of the then imprisoned winner of the last election (lines 8-10)—or by the World Bank (lines 14-15). Shell even makes a few concessions to strengthen its image of objectivity. One of these is the undeniable fact that there are indeed environmental problems in the Nigeria region (line 14).

Shell further enhances its credibility as an objective, disinterested and rational protagonist by emphasizing its knowledge of Nigerian affairs (lines 6-7, 16-19, 25-28, 29-32), its reliance on genuine data and respect for the truth (lines 2-5, 12-15, 18-19, 33-34, 39). In its presentation, Shell sustains this image by labeling the issues as 'difficult' (line 4), eluding 'easy solutions' (line 4), and having to do with 'unvarnished truth' (line 2) rather than being 'subjugated to a cause' (line 3). To enhance its humanitarian ethos, Shell shifts the focus of attention from its own problems to a concern with the problems of Nigeria: SHELL HELPS! (lines 6-7, 16-19, 25-27, 30-32). This is the perspective it is going to exploit thoroughly in its argumentation, elaborating extensively on its "development aid."

In contradistinction to Shell, the public is portrayed as allowing its judgements to be clouded by emotions (lines 1-2) and being easily manipulated and misled (lines 12-13). The campaigners are even worse: they are people whose perceptions are suffused with anger and recriminations (line 2), who utter nothing but 'slogans, protests and boycotts' (line 4) and for whom the campaign has become more important than the cause (lines 10-11).

Shell also maneuvers strategically with the positions of the parties in the discussion. Dialectically speaking, we have here two opposing parties—Shell and the campaigners—

and a third party—the public—that is supposedly neutral.[17] At the time, however, public opinion was against rather than in favor of Shell, and Shell was fully aware of this. Therefore, the rhetorical situation was so that Shell was not only required to resolve a mixed dispute with the campaigners, but also with the public. Nevertheless, the company initially acts as if there was only a standard 'non-mixed' dispute, thus adjusting this situation to its own objectives. Shell even treats the public as a possible ally, ready to close ranks with Shell against the campaigners (lines 1-32). This definition of the positions in the dispute is reinforced by the way in which Shell adapts to its audience: it attempts to create a degree of communion that makes its starting point more easily acceptable. Goodwill is invoked by flattering the public at this stage: they are sensible people who are concerned about the same problems as Shell; they are entitled to clear thinking and can cope with the unvarnished truth (lines 2-3). Thus the public is dissociated from Shell's opponents in the conflict. In addition, Shell appeals to the public's responsibility: because rights imply duties, it is the public's duty to think clearly and accept only what is objectively true, however unsettling the truth may be (lines 2-3, 33-34, 39). One of the presentational means used to strengthen Shell's communion with the public consists in addressing them in the way a father speaks to his children: although the emotions they feel are 'understandable' (line 1), they should learn the truth; and although they 'rightly care deeply' (line 13), they are easily 'manipulated and misled' (line 13), especially when a cause seems 'noble and well-meaning' (line 3). But if they take sides with Shell, all will end well. On the other hand, if they don't, chances are that they end up in the same bad position as the campaigners: cloaked in a warning, the public is put on a par with those it was initially, together with Shell, supposed to ridicule (lines 33-34). Among the presentational devices Shell employs to widen the dissociation between the campaigners and the public, is the passive voice: 'there have [...] been charges' (line 12), 'the facts [have] been distorted' (line 12), 'it has been suggested' (line 23), et cetera. In this way, the campaigners are portrayed as anonymous accusers. Shell's repeated use of antithesis serves to put more emphasis on the contrast between its own clear thinking and rational attitude and the irrational attitude and muddled thinking of the campaigners (and sometimes the public): it is 'facts' versus 'emotions' (lines 1-3), 'discreet diplomacy' versus 'threats and protests' (lines 6-10), 'clear thinking' versus 'troubled times' (title), et cetera.

*Argumentation stage*

In the case of the juridical not-to-blame claim (1.1), Shell selects for its defense primarily factual arguments from authority; in the case of the policy claim (1.2), the arguments are causal and pragmatic. The first issue associated with the 'Shell is not to blame' claim, Ken Saro-Wiwa's death (1.1.1a), invokes Shell's own authority (lines 6-7) and that of Wura Abiola (lines 8-10). The second blame-issue, environmental devastation (1.1.1b), calls in the authority of the World Bank (line 14-15) as well as Shell's own authority (lines 16-19). The policy issues, Shell's withdrawal from the NLNG project (1.2.1a) and from Nigeria in general (1.2.1b) as well as Shell's intervention in Nigerian

[17] When two parties have contradictory standpoints, the dispute is *mixed*. When one party has a standpoint and the other party is neutral in the sense that it questions the standpoint but has no standpoint of its own, the dispute is *non-mixed* (van Eemeren and Grootendorst (1992, pp. 16–22)).

politics (which we reconstructed as a disguised argument for the not-to-blame claim), are all dealt with by pointing at the supposedly catastrophic consequences (lines 23-28, 29-32, 35-37).

Shell's preference for factual arguments from authority and causal arguments is entirely in line with its recurrent emphasis on the factual status of its position. Factual and causal arguments are often regarded more conclusive kinds of support: facts cannot be doubted and a causal chain suggests, unlike an analogical relation, a tight and unbreakable connection. There is one exception to the factual and causal treatment: Shell's refutation of the accusation that it supports the Nigerian regime (lines 35-37). Although the advertorial appears to provide causal argumentation, it is clear that in this case a causal argument will not do. Because the inference from Shell's non-intervention statement to the implied claim that it does not support the Nigerian regime cannot be causally warranted, from necessity, a weaker—symptomatic—inference has to do the job.

When we look at the way in which Shell's argumentation is adapted to its audience, two types of maneuvering stand out. The first pertains to the issue of blame. In refuting any suggestion of guilt with regard to both Ken Saro-Wiwa's death and environmental devastation, Shell exploits the SHELL HELPS-perspective earlier invoked. Shell has helped Saro-Wiwa by means of discreet diplomacy (lines 6-7); and Shell has helped to get environmental devastation under control by providing financial and material aid (lines 16-19, 25-27, 30-32). In both cases, Shell claims, the effects of its help were frustrated by the actions of others (lines 10-11, 20-22).

In the justification of Shell's policy standpoint, adaptation to the audience takes place by evoking a frightening perspective of catastrophe and collapse: if Shell pulls out, calamity awaits the people of Nigeria (lines 24, 28, 32). By referring to 'the people [...] that *you* would hurt' (our italics), the public is once more reminded of its responsibility (line 32). By also emphasizing that 'the environment, too, would suffer' (line 26), Shell employs an argument based on the figure of *conciliatio*: Shell's opponents' supposed concern about the Nigerian people and the environment is turned against them. The perspective of calamity is contrasted with that of Shell's prolonged activities in Nigeria, when the 'sound and ethical business practices' synonymous with Shell will continue to bear their blessed fruit (lines 30-32).

As can be expected, in refuting the 'blame'-issues a businesslike style prevails. The facts are (in lines 6-10 and 14-22) supposed to speak for themselves. In its presentation of the arguments for the policy standpoint, Shell hammers in the picture of calamity by asking suggestive rhetorical questions—'What would happen if Shell pulled out of Nigeria altogether?' (line 29)—and by issuing warnings—'So let's be clear who gets hurt if the project is cancelled' (line 24) and 'Again, it's the people of Nigeria you would hurt' (line 32). At a certain stage (in lines 29-32), some concessions are presented in a staccato of short and unconnected sentences that suggest lack of coherent thinking. They are then followed by a long and carefully constructed sentence that suggests that Shell has the situation under control. There is again no lack of suggestive wording: 'the oil would certainly continue *flowing*' (with connotations of 'uncontrolled' and 'idle'), 'the business would continue *operating*' (*cui bono*?), and 'the vast majority of employees would *remain in place*' (but will they work?) (lines 29-30).

*Concluding stage*

By leaving the general conclusion of the discussion of its involvement in Nigeria implicit, Shell suggests that it has said all there is to say and that the conclusion is obvious. What else can the readers conclude than that Shell is neither to blame for the killing of Ken Saro-Wiwa nor for any environmental disaster? On the contrary, Shell is a great help to the people of Nigeria and should stay there to prolong its generous "development aid." To ensure that the public reaches this favorable view, Shell again makes an appeal to the public's responsibility. Having paved the way by the repeated warnings that the fate of the Nigerian people is in their hands, Shell strikes the final blow at the end of the text, when it starts to lecture the people about their attitude. The public acts irresponsibly: their opinions of the Nigerian problems amount to empty slogans, and their response is nothing but a knee-jerk reaction that can only harm this poor developing country (lines 33-34). They do indeed need Shell to put them straight.

Shell's last move in the argumentation stage of the discussion was to invoke a straightforward image of doom and horror. This exploitation of the presentational device of a metaphor is aimed at eradicating any idea that the company could be doing a thing so evil as supporting the Nigerian regime (lines 36-37). The implication of this move for the concluding stage of the discussion is clear: if it is evident to all what horrific consequences supporting the Nigerian regime will have, Shell can only be accused of such misbehavior by those extreme malevolents whose sole aim is to destroy Shell's political and moral ethos. The final words, 'We'll keep you in touch with the facts' (line 39), are not just a slogan, but should reassure the public that Shell will prevent the menacing perspective of a frightening and bleak world from becoming a reality—clear thinking will prevail. These words, however, also convey a veiled counter-accusation: 'You, the public, are not capable of keeping in touch with the facts. This is why Shell will do it for you.'

### 11.4.2 An evaluation of Shell's strategic maneuvering

*The use of* conciliatio

We would like to elucidate the pragma-dialectical approach to evaluating argumentative discourse by first discussing a specific instance of strategic maneuvering: Shell's use of the figure of *conciliatio*. In a *conciliatio*, the proponent uses an argument of the opponent to support his own standpoint. In terms of strategic maneuvering, making use of a *conciliatio* amounts to making a selection from the available argumentative potential that is evidently expedient and clearly optimally adapted to the opponent's starting point. Certain presentational devices, such as the use of a rhetorical question, are well-suited to make it obvious that the argument the proponent is going to use is in fact already part of the opponent's commitments.

Because the opponent's adherence is secured in advance, this form of strategic maneuvering is rhetorically strong. Because the proponent proceeds by arguing *ex concessis*, it is also pre-eminently dialectical. The danger of derailment stems from the fact that the opponent may be assumed to agree with the *content* of the argument, but may *not* be assumed to agree with the way in which the argument is used to support precisely the opposite standpoint. According to the correctness conditions applying to the speech act of advancing argumentation, an argument only counts as a felicitous attempt to convince the opponent if both parties not only accept the propositional content of the argument but also accept this proposition as a potential justification of the standpoint at issue (see van Eemeren and Grootendorst (1992)). In the case of a *conciliatio*, the former is—typically—granted, but the latter is most unlikely—at any rate in the first instance.

This speech act analysis points to a condition that can be of help in evaluating actual manifestations of *conciliatio*: such manifestations can only be 'sound' if the proponent offers sufficient support for his view that the argument taken over from his opponent has an unquestioning and overriding justificatory potential with regard to his standpoint and leaves it eventually to the opponent to decide whether this is indeed the case.[18] The use of *conciliatio* can be said to be a 'derailment' if the proponent just presupposes that the adopted argument has an unquestioning justificatory potential for his standpoint and leaves the opponent no room to question this presupposition. If a *conciliatio* is in this way derailed, the proponent relies on a starting point that is not yet accepted by the opponent and commits the fallacy of *begging the question.*

In 'Clear thinking in troubled times,' Shell makes use of a *conciliatio* when the company justifies its not pulling out of Nigeria's Liquified Natural Gas project by pointing out that not Shell but the Nigerian people and the environment would suffer if Shell pulled out (lines 25-26). These arguments are clearly derived from the opponents' professed concerns for the people and the environment: given their political preferences, Shell's opponents may be assumed to be in favor of a prospering native population and a non-polluted environment. At the propositional level, Shell can therefore be sure of acceptance. But how does the oil company proceed to ensure the opponents' acceptance of the justificatory potential of these two points for its standpoint that Shell should not pull out of the project? Shell does so by claiming that there is a causal relation between its pulling out of the project and a deterioration of the human and environmental circumstances. In this way, Shell lends at least some support to the view that its opponents' arguments have an unquestioning justificatory potential for its standpoint. Although the insertion of 'certainly' conveys a suggestion of obviousness, Shell does not actually deter the reader from questioning the supposed causal link. Therefore, no actual derailment of strategic maneuvering with *conciliatio* has taken place and it is not appropriate to accuse Shell of question begging.

We shall now have a closer look at Shell's strategic maneuvering in the various stages of the discourse and point out some fallacies that are committed.

*Confrontation stage*

Our first evaluative observation is that Shell slyly manipulates the issues of the discussion: the company addresses the crucial issue of its involvement in Nigeria only in an implicit way. As transpired in the analysis, Shell emphasizes that it is undesirable that companies use their economic influence to prop up or bring down governments to support its standpoint that the company should not intervene in Nigeria. In order to

[18]Additional conditions are that the proposition concerned is really part of the opponent's commiments and that the proponent himself is prepared to live up to the commitments involved.

defend this standpoint, however, it suffices to argue that it is wrong for companies to use their economic influence *to bring down* governments. Adding that the company's influence may also never be used *to prop up* governments is only relevant if Shell implicitly also attempts to convey the idea that *it does not support the Nigerian regime.* This is, in fact, precisely the point Shell should get across, because when the advertorial was published the primary accusation was that Shell kept the Nigerian regime going.[19] Shell is apparently unwilling to confront this accusation outright, but needs to deny it all the same. The company does this implicitly by providing an argument from which the denial can be deduced.

Shell thus engages in a confrontation strategy of circumvention. The company employs this strategy to evade the crucial issue in the difference of opinion. According to the dialectical standards, one of the rules of critical discussion is that arguments should be relevant to the standpoint at issue. This rule is violated in Shell's argument for the reconstructed standpoint that Shell does not support the Nigerian regime: it is undesirable for companies to use their economic influence to prop up or bring down governments. Although this argument is analytically relevant to the standpoint—it is precisely because of this analytic relevance that the standpoint could be reconstructed —, it lacks any evaluative relevance:[20] that it is undesirable to use economic influence to prop up or bring down governments may lend support to the political standpoint that Shell should not intervene in Nigeria's political situation, but could never support the *factual* standpoint that Shell does not support the Nigerian regime.[21] In the process, Shell not only violates the relevance rule for critical discussion, but also the *language use rule*: given that what now only becomes apparent after a radical reconstruction would have been immediately clear if Shell had advanced the standpoint explicitly, Shell is guilty of being misleadingly vague.

By using a distorted arrow for the fallacious maneuver in the defense of Shell's standpoint that it does not support the Nigerian regime, we can give the following evaluative overview of the formal representation the structure of Shell's argumentation:

*Juridical: (1) Shell is not to be blamed*

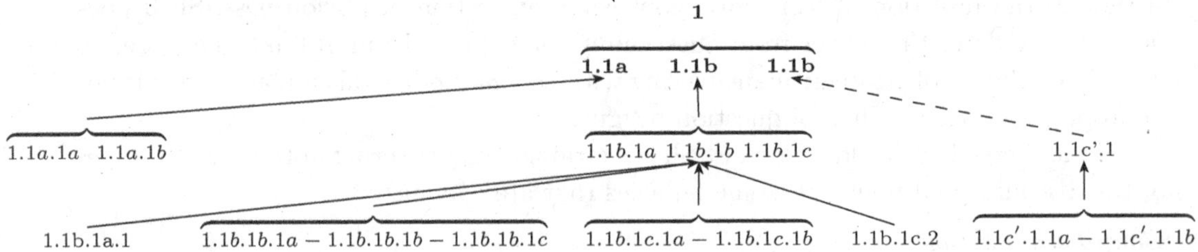


[19] There were cries for intervention after Ken Saro-Wiwa had been sentenced to death and had not yet been executed, but no such cries were heard *after* the execution, i.e., at the time when Shell published its advertorial. By then, the only demand was that Shell should get out of Nigeria.

[20] See for the distinction between analytic and evaluative relevance van Eemeren and Grootendorst (1992).

[21] Even for the standpoint that Shell should not intervene, this argument offers only very weak support, but because this explicit standpoint is much less controversial than the implicit standpoint, this support might suffice.

FIGURE 3. PARTIAL PRAGMA-DIALECTICAL EVALUATION OF SHELL'S ADVERTORIAL AS ANALYZED IN FIGURE 2

*Opening stage*

The dominant opening strategy is involving the readers as closely as possible in Shell's view. In the first instance, this is achieved by acting as if the public is not really in opposition to Shell, but has merely some doubts—resulting from ignorance rather than careful reflection. Shell thus presents the public as a possible ally rather than a potential opponent. In leading on the readers in this way, Shell chooses an opening strategy of inclusion. Near the end of the advertorial, when the public's comfortable position is suddenly made questionable, the final consequence of this strategy becomes apparent: a public that does not take sides with Shell should distance itself from this reasonable position and join the campaigners—which has by then become a highly unattractive perspective. How is the use of this strategy to be evaluated? First, we should notice that at the end of the text Shell offers the public an unrealistic alternative when it confronts the public with the need of a choice. In times when the need of support is overwhelmingly urgent, forcing the public in a you-are-with-or-against-us situation could be acceptable in a policy speech. In an apology aimed at proving someone's innocence, however, this strategy is clearly inadmissible: establishing the facts is not a matter of making choices, let alone the choices presented by Shell. In this case, Shell is guilty of fallacious maneuvering: the company creates a *false dilemma*. Second, it should be noticed that the dilemma presented here can only have persuasive force because it is based on Shell's perpetual *ad hominem* attacks on the campaigners. Most of these attacks are abusive (the campaigners are unrealistic idealists, sloganeers who distort or ignore facts, irresponsible egocentrists who do not understand the risk they are taking), some are just circumstantial (the campaign became more important than the cause). Had the campaigners been portrayed as sensible people, the dilemma would not have existed. These *ad hominem* fallacies are thus a constitutive part of the fallacious maneuvering.

*Argumentation stage*

The strategic maneuvering favored by Shell in the argumentation stage consists in founding its arguments on facts and authority and in suggesting that its actions are motivated by charity. This points to a combination of the argumentation strategies of certification and humanization. It is not so hard to see what could go dialectically wrong: derailments of the *ad verecundiam* type and ethical fallacies may occur. But do they occur? In the *ad verecundiam* case, the issue is whether making an appeal to authority is acceptable to the adversary and, if so, whether the authority appealed to is a genuine and relevant authority. The first question cannot really be answered in this monologal situation, but the last two questions can. The authorities Shell appeals to are Wura Abiola, the World Bank and Shell itself. Wura Abiola's authority is invoked to sustain a view concerning how the Nigerian regime tends to react when threatened. Her authority is supposedly based on the fact that she is the daughter of a former presidential candidate. The question is now: can she, just because of that background, indeed be regarded as an expert on the psychology of Nigerian politics? The fact that, apart from Shell, Newsnight too values her opinion on this issue may be seen as evidence that she can. This argument from authority is therefore probably not fallacious. This is also the case with the appeal to the authority of the World Bank to sustain certain data concerning environmental devastation. Although we have only Shell's word for it that the data that are mentioned are correct, the World Bank may indeed be expected to provide authoritative information that is also relevant. A remaining reservation can still be that Shell does not say whether the World Bank Survey puts the other environmental problems indeed on a par with the problems caused by Shell. It could well be the case that the latter problems outweigh the former by far.

A more definitive judgement can be given when we consider Shell's emphasis on its own authority as an expert on Nigerian affairs. This emphasis, which is present throughout the text but pre-eminently in Shell's reference in line 6 to its own experience in dealing with the issue of Ken Saro-Wiwa's pending execution, exemplifies how strategic maneuvering cannot only derail but also be weak. The maneuvering derails because whether Shell knows best how to handle the situation in Nigeria is precisely the issue. It is also weak because neither Shell's opponents nor the public can be expected to accept Shell's authority at face value.

Shell's strategy of bestowing a pre-eminent status on factual reasoning connects well with its appeals to authority. It is, again, not too difficult to see what kind of fallacious maneuvering could take place. Are the "facts" presented by Shell indeed facts? And if so, are they relevant to the case? It is noticeable that Shell, in presenting its arguments against the accusation of environmental devastation, states the facts of the case in an unclear way. Who are the claimants in the sabotage cases? Who are the saboteurs? It is the elusive phrasing that prevents these questions from being answered. Again, Shell commits the fallacy of using misleadingly vague language. A similar fallacious strategy can be detected in Shell's argumentation against the accusations that it did nothing to prevent Ken Saro-Wiwa's execution. Shell suggests that the facts speak for themselves, but whether they do is another matter. A host of presuppositions is smuggled in that take an agreement for granted which probably not exists. Asking whether 'discreet diplomacy' failed, for instance, presupposes that Shell has indeed made diplomatic efforts to save Ken Saro-Wiwa, that these efforts were rightly made in secret, et cetera. In all these instances, Shell can be accused of violating the *starting point rule* that allows arguments to be advanced only on the basis of a commonly accepted starting point. Apart from the dubious status of the facts, it is not transparent what relevance the facts are supposed to have. This maneuver connects in fact closely with Shell's recurrent reference to its charitable motives. It is, for instance, unclear how exactly combating environmental devastation relates to Shell's financing of roads and health clinics. Apparently the company does a lot of good, but should this automatically mean that it cannot be guilty of environmental devastation? Shell violates, again, the *relevance rule* of critical discussion.

*Concluding stage*

Shell's concluding move is to use a strategy of termination. After having first implied that the public might end up on a par with the campaigners, the company concludes by invoking a catastrophic scenario that would become reality should the campaigners' wishes be fulfilled. The aim of this move clearly is to discourage the public to maintain any doubts concerning Shell's dealings in Nigeria. Instead of concluding that its standpoints are adequately defended by its own arguments, Shell thus suggests that its standpoints are acceptable because no doubts can be raised against them. In this way, Shell makes a fallacious attempt to end the discussion.

## 11.5 Conclusion

The analysis of Shell's advertorial shows how in argumentative discourse the rhetorical opportunities offered by the dialectical situation can be used strategically in making a self-serving choice from the available topical potential, responding expediently to audience demand, and making a crafty use of presentational devices. The strategy of circumvention used by Shell in the confrontation stage consists in manipulating the difference of opinion, and changing its focus, by highlighting and addressing selectively only those issues that Shell can cope with and dealing only indirectly with the main issue it is expected to address. The strategy of inclusion, which is dominant in the opening stage, amounts to involving the public as closely as possible in Shell's view of the case by presenting them as a possible ally rather than an opponent and leading them in this way up the garden path. In the argumentation stage, Shell's strategic maneuvering combines the strategies of certification and humanization: while demeaning its opponents as not knowledgeable and irresponsible, Shell lends the prerogative to causal reasoning based on "authorized" facts (restricted to those facts that can be put in a perspective that is attractive to the public) and establishes at the same time its own image as a social conscience company. Shell's concluding strategy of termination appeals to the public's common sense by impregnating them with responsibilities at variance with their present unrealistic attitude through rubbing in the facts. All told, Shell's defense cannot be evaluated so positively as its clever use of *conciliatio* may have suggested. Several of Shell's moves are derailments of strategic maneuvering that are fallacious because they violate a rule for critical discussion. Shell's advertorial is, in fact, a good illustration of how supposedly clever strategic maneuvering can become rhetorically inappropriate when it is dialectically not acceptable.

In this paper we have shown that the analysis and evaluation of argumentative discourse benefits in several ways from using rhetorical insight in a pragma-dialectical reconstruction. It may also have become apparent that a satisfactory rhetorical reconstruction cannot be carried out either if dialectical considerations are not taken into account: the rhetorical function of a speech act can only be determined systematically if it is first put in a well-defined perspective of what is at stake in a certain stage of the discourse. Because the methodical enrichment we have obtained allows us to get a firmer grasp on the various aspects of strategic maneuvering, we achieve a deeper and more comprehensive view of what may be called 'argumentative reality.' Gaining a thorough understanding of the strategic rationale behind specific discussion moves made in argumentative discourse strengthens the analysis by making it not only more profound and more informed but also better-justified. Achieving a clear view of the strategic design of the discourse also results in a more refined sense of when and why certain types of strategic maneuvering are to be considered fallacious in actual argumentative practice.

**Acknowledgments**

This paper is based on a lecture presented by van Eemeren on November 24, 2001 at the First International Workshop on Semantics, Pragmatics, and Rhetoric, Donostia-San Sebastian. Earlier versions were published by van Eemeren and Houtlosser in the journals *Discourse Studies* (1999), *Argumentation* (2000a), and Informal Logic (2002).

## References

Agricola, R. 1479/1967. *De inventione libri tres.* A translation of selected chapters by J.R. McNally. *Speech Monographs* 34:393–422.

Anscombre, J. C. 1994. La nature des topoï. In J. C. Anscombre, ed., *La théorie des topoï*, pages 49–84. Paris: Editions Kimé.

Anscombre, J. C. and O. Ducrot. 1983. *L'Argumentation dans la langue.* LiŔge: Pierre Mardaga.

Barth, E. M. and E. C. W. Krabbe. 1982. *From Axiom to Dialogue: A Philosophical Study of Logics and Argumentation.* Berlin/New York: Walter de Gruyter.

Benoit, W. L. and J. J. Lindsey. 1987. Argument strategies: Antidote to tylenol's poisoned image. *Journal of the American Forensic Association* 23:136–146.

Cicero. 1942. *De oratore*. London: Heinemann. E. W. Sutton and H. Rackham (eds.).

Freeley, A. J. 1993. *Argumentation and Debate. Critical Thinking for Reasoned Decision Making*. Belmont, CA: Wadsworth. 8th ed.

Gaonkar, D. P. 1990. Rhetoric and its double: Reflections on the rhetorical turn in the human sciences. In H. W. Simons, ed., *The Rhetorical Turn. Invention and Persuasion in the Conduct of Inquiry*, pages 341–366. Chicago: The University of Chicago Press.

Hamblin, C. L. 1970. *Fallacies*. London: Methuen. Reprinted at Newport News: Vale Press.

Kamlah, W. and P. Lorenzen. 1984. *Logical Propaedeutic: Pre-School of Reasonable Discourse.* Lanham, MD: University Press of America. Transl. by Hoke Robinson of Logische Propädeutik; Vorschule des vernünftigen Redens. Mannheim: Hochschultaschenbücher-Verlag, 1967.

Kennedy, G. A. 1994. *A New History of Classical Rhetoric*. Princeton, NJ: Princeton University Press.

Kienpointner, M. 1995. Rhetoric. In J. O. Ě. J. Verschueren and J. Blommaert, eds., *Handbook of Pragmatics. Manual*, pages 453–461. Amsterdam/Philadelphia: John Benjamins.

Mack, P. 1993. *Renaissance Argument. Valla and Agricola in the Traditions of Rhetoric and Dialectic*. Leiden: Brill.

Meerhoff, C. G. 1988. Agricola et ramus: dialectique et rhétorique. In F. Akkerman and A. J. Vanderjagt, eds., *Rodolphus Agricola Phrisius 1444-1485*, pages 270–280. Leiden: Brill.

Murphy, J. J. and R. A. Katula. 1994. *A Synoptic History of Classical Rhetoric.* Davis, CA: Hermagoras Press. Originally published 1972.

Natanson, M. 1955. The limits of rhetoric. *Quarterly Journal of Speech* 41:133–139.

Perelman, Ch. and L. Olbrechts-Tyteca. 1969. *The New Rhetoric. A Treatise on Argumentation.* Notre Dame/London: University of Notre Dame Press. Translation of *La nouvelle rhétorique. Traité de l'argumentation.* Paris: Presses Universitaires de France, 1958.

Reboul, O. 1991. *Introduction Ĺ la rhétorique. Théorie et pratique [Introduction to rhetoric. Theory and practice]*. Paris: Presses Universitaires de France.

Rescher, N. 1977. *Dialectics: A Controversy-Oriented Approach to the Theory of Knowledge.* Albany, NY: SUNY Press.

Simons, H. W. 1990. The rhetoric of inquiry as an intellectual movement. In H. W. Simons, ed., *The Rhetorical Turn: Invention and Persuasion in the Conduct of Inquiry*, pages 1–31. Chicago: The University of Chicago Press.

Snoeck Henkemans, F. 1995. 'But' as an indicator of counter-arguments and concessions. *Leuven Contributions in Linguistics and Philology* 84:281–294.

Toulmin, S. E. 2001. *Return to Reason*. Cambridge, Mass: Harvard University Press.

van Eemeren, F. H. 1990. The study of argumentation as normative pragmatics. *Text* 10:37–44.

van Eemeren, F. H. and R. Grootendorst. 1984. *Speech Acts in Argumentative Discussions: A Theoretical Model for the Analysis of Discussions Directed towards Solving Conflicts of Opinion*. Dordrecht/Berlin: Foris/Mouton de Gruyter.

van Eemeren, F. H. and R. Grootendorst. 1992. *Argumentation, Communication, and Fallacies: A Pragma-Dialectical Perspective*. Hillsdale, NJ: Lawrence Erlbaum.

van Eemeren, F. H., R. Grootendorst, A. F. Snoeck Henkemans, J. A. Blair, R. H. Johnson, E. C. W. Krabbe, Chr. Plantin, D. N. Walton, C. A. Willard, J. Woods, and D. Zarefsky. 1996. *Fundamentals of Argumentation Theory: A Handbook of Historical Backgrounds and Contemporary Developments*. Mahwah, NJ: Lawrence Erlbaum.

van Eemeren, F. H., R. Grootendorst, S. Jackson, and S. Jacobs. 1993. *Reconstructing Argumentative Discourse*. Tuscaloosa and London: The University of Alabama Press.

van Eemeren, F. H. and P. Houtlosser. 1998. Rhetorical rationales for dialectical moves: Justifying pragma-dialectical reconstructions. In J. F. Klumpp, ed., *Argument in a Time of Change: Definitions, Frameworks, and Critiques*, pages 51–56. Annandale, VA: National Communication Association. Proceedings of the tenth NCA/AFA Conference on Argumentation.

van Eemeren, F. H. and P. Houtlosser. 1999. Strategic manoeuvring in argumentative discourse. *Discourse Studies* 1:479–497.

van Eemeren, F. H. and P. Houtlosser. 2000a. Rhetorical analysis within a pragma-dialectical framework. *Argumentation* 14:293–305.

van Eemeren, F. H. and P. Houtlosser. 2000b. Managing disagreement: Rhetorical analysis within a dialectical framework. *Argumentation and Advocay* 37:150–157.

van Eemeren, F. H., B. Meuffels, and M. Verburg. 2000. The (un)reasonableness of the argumentum ad hominem. *Language and Social Psychology* 19, 4:416–435.

Walton, D. N. and E. C. W. Krabbe. 1995. *Commitment in Dialogue: Basic Concepts of Interpersonal Reasoning*. Albany, NY: State University of New York Press.

Ware, B. L. and W. A. Linkugel. 1973. They spoke in defense of themselves: On the generic criticism of apologia. *Quarterly Journal of Speech* 59:273–283.

Weaver, R. 1953. The *Phaedrus* and the nature of rhetoric. In R. Weaver, ed., *The Ethics of Rhetoric*, pages 3–26. Chicago: Henry Regnery.

Wenzel, J. W. 1990. Three perspectives on argument: Rhetoric, dialectic, logic. In R. Trapp and J. Schuetz, eds., *Perspectives on Argumentation. Essays in the Honor of Wayne Brockriede*, pages 9–26. Prospect Heights, Ill.: Waveland Press.

Woods, J. and D. N. Walton. 1989. *Fallacies: Selected Papers, 1972–1982*. Dordrecht/Berlin: Foris/Mouton de Gruyter.

# Index